The View from Afar

THE VIEW FROM AFAR

Claude Lévi-Strauss

TRANSLATED BY

JOACHIM NEUGROSCHEL

AND

PHOEBE HOSS

The University of Chicago Press

The University of Chicago Press, Chicago 60637
English translation copyright © 1985 by Basic Books, Inc.
Originally published in French as *Le Regard Eloigné*,
© 1983 Librairie Plon
Published by arrangement with Basic Books, a division of
HarperCollins Publishers Inc.

99 98 97 96 95 94 93 92   6 5 4 3 2 1

ISBN 0-226-47474-7

Library of Congress Cataloging-in-Publication Data

Lévi-Strauss, Claude.
   [Regard éloigné. English]
   The view from afar / Claude Lévi-Strauss ; translated by Joachim
Neugroschel and Phoebe Hoss. — University of Chicago Press ed.
      p. cm.
   Includes bibliographical references and index.
   1. Structural anthropology. 2. Ethnology.
GN362.L47413   1992
306 — dc20   92-22905
                                                                CIP

⊗ The paper used in this publication meets the minimum
requirements of the American National Standard for
Information Sciences — Permanence of Paper for
Printed Library Materials, ANSI Z39.48-1984

In memory of Roman Jakobson

Le grand défaut des Européens est de philosopher toujours sur les origines des choses d'après ce qui se passe autour d'eux.

JEAN-JACQUES ROUSSEAU

Essai sur l'origine des langues

Contents

Contents

Preface

THIS BOOK logically follows two earlier volumes that appeared in France in 1958 and 1973, and could have been entitled *Structural Anthropology*, volume III.* But there were several reasons why I did not choose to do this. The title of the 1958 book was meant as a manifesto. Fifteen years later, when structuralism was no longer in fashion, it was expedient for me to declare my loyalty to the principles and methods that have never ceased to guide me. Repeating the same title a third time could have given the impression that, during the past decade when my research has led me along paths new to me, I had been content to mark time, and that the results submitted to the reader today were merely a repetition of the past.

Furthermore, it seemed to me, rightly or wrongly, that if each of the first two books was self-contained, then this volume might be even more so. The decade that has passed since volume II of *Structural Anthropology* has brought me to the end—if not, I hope, of an active life —then, in any case, of an academic career of fifty years. Realizing that I would soon stop teaching, I wanted to deal with problems that I had been forced to put aside, and without being overly concerned whether they were connected. Imitating a stretto, I devoted the little time available to touching rapidly on the major themes that have been the focus of my research—kinship, social organization, mythology, ritual, art—at the slower pace than was now permissible.

The result is that the present book—a gathering of scattered and hard-to-find writings like the two preceding books—has the pace of a short treatise on anthropology or of an introduction to this discipline, whose main aspects are largely represented. This character could be emphasized by a special title expressing what I consider the essence and originality of the anthropological approach, as illustrated by field

*The two volumes of *Structural Anthropology* were published in the United States in 1963 and 1976, respectively (see bibliography).

work and laboratory experiments (part IV) bearing on a wide range of subjects.

The desire for thoroughness persuaded me, not without some reluctance, to include an older piece on the family, especially since it had been requested by many people. This article was originally written in English for what is known in that language as a "textbook," made up of the writings of various authors, and was published in a French translation, in 1971, in the *Annales de l'Université d'Abidjan*. I do not disavow this scrupulous translation, which I reread; but, since it was a verbatim rendering, I felt I ought to prepare a new French version that was not so literal (chapter 3). Despite my revisions, I cannot pretend that this text is anything but baldly didactic, and the data it is based on, although traditional at the time I was writing, are out of date.

Let me add two more excuses for republishing this article. So far as I can recall, this is the only text where I attempted an overview of the problems I dealt with, though from another angle, in *Elementary Structures of Kinship* (1969). Thus, the reader who is unfamiliar with this book will have the advantages (and also disadvantages) of finding a digest of it here. Also, for the benefit of novice readers, I wanted to explain the "Copernican revolution" that the structural linguists had brought to the human sciences: that is, if one wishes to understand the nature of social ties, one should not first take a few objects and try immediately to establish connections between them. Reversing the traditional approach, one should first perceive the relations as terms and, then, the terms themselves as relations. In other words, in the network of social bonds, the knots have logical priority over the lines, even though, empirically, the lines form knots by crisscrossing one another.

Chapter 7 of this volume was also originally written in English; when rendering it into French, however, I did not venture to view it from afar as I did chapter 3. Thus, a brief explanation is in order. The author who undertakes to translate into French a text he has written in a language he poorly commands is at a disadvantage. What he has to say in a foreign language he would say differently in French. Above all, he would say it more economically, freed from the anxiety of having to express his ideas in modes whose inadequacy too often obliges him to be heavy-handed, lest he fail to be understood the first time.

Was it, then, necessary to rewrite the entire text, ignoring the English original, and thus be more succinct? But the text in question has been quoted, commented on, discussed, and even been the object of a polemical exchange. To take liberties with the text would expose the author to the suspicion of having altered it in order to avoid criticism. I therefore felt obliged to stick to the original and—in light of the circumstances and the language in which it was written—to ask the reader's indulgence for a discussion that, rendered into French, strikes me as basically valid, but often imprecise, and always diffuse.

I come belatedly to the text entitled "Race and Culture," which starts off this collection, since it requires a longer and very different explanation. In 1971, the United Nations Educational, Scientific, and Cultural Organization asked me to deliver a public lecture to open the International Year of Action to Combat Racism and Racial Discrimination. I was chosen probably because, twenty years earlier, I had written "Race and History" for UNESCO (reprinted in Lévi-Strauss 1973, chapter 18), which had excited some interest. Using a possibly new approach, I had stated a few basic truths; and, in 1971, I soon realized that UNESCO expected me to repeat them. But twenty years earlier, in order to serve the international institutions, which I felt I had to support more than I do today, I had somewhat overstated my point in the conclusion to "Race and History." Because of my age perhaps, and certainly because of reflections inspired by the present state of the world, I was now disgusted by this obligingness and was convinced that, if I was to be useful to UNESCO and fulfill my commitment honestly, I should have to speak in complete frankness.

The result was a lively scandal. I submitted the text of my speech forty-eight hours ahead of time. The day came; and, without warning me, René Maheu, then director general of UNESCO, took the floor to speak. The purpose of his speech was not only to exorcise my blasphemies by anticipating them, but also—and above all—to upset the timetable and thereby force me to make a few cuts that, from UNESCO's point of view, would be a gain. I succeeded, nevertheless, in reading my entire text and finished it in the time allotted. But afterward, in the corridors, I ran into members of the UNESCO staff, who were dismayed that I had challenged a catechism that was for them all the more an article of faith because their acceptance of it—achieved at the price of laudable efforts that flew in the face of their local traditions and social milieus—had allowed them to move from modest jobs in developing countries to sanctified positions as executives in an international institution.*

---

*I must admit that, all things considered, my 1971 lecture was apparently not so indecent, since the full text was published several months later in *Revue internationale des Sciences sociales* under the auspices of UNESCO.

Of what sins, then, did I make myself guilty? In retrospect, I can discern five. First of all, I wanted to make the audience aware of the fact that, since UNESCO's early campaigns against racism, something had occurred in scientific research. And also that, in order to get rid of racial prejudices, it no longer sufficed to reiterate the same arguments against the old physical anthropology—its measurements of skeletons; its calibrations of eye, hair, and skin colors; and so on. Today the struggle against racism requires a broad dialogue with population genetics, if only because geneticists are in a better position than we to demonstrate any incapacity of fact or of law to determine, in man, the role of nature and nurture. However, since the question is now asked in scientific rather than in philosophical terms, even the negative answers have lost their dogmatic character. Cultural anthropologists and physical anthropologists used to debate racism in a vacuum. When I pointed out that geneticists have blown a blast of fresh air into the discussion, I was accused of putting the fox in the sheepfold.

Secondly, I rebelled against the abuse of language by which people tend more and more to confuse racism in the strict sense of the term with attitudes that are normal, even legitimate, and in any case unavoidable. Racism is a doctrine that claims to see the mental and moral characteristics of a group of individuals (however the group may be defined) as the necessary effect of a common genetic heritage. One cannot put in the same category, or impute automatically to the same prejudice, the attitude held by individuals or groups that their loyalty to certain values makes them partially or totally insensitive to other values. It is not at all invidious to place one way of life or thought above all others or to feel little drawn to other people or groups whose ways of life, respectable in themselves, are quite remote from the system to which one is traditionally attached. Such relative incommunicability certainly does not authorize anyone to oppress or destroy the values one has rejected, or their representatives; but within these limitations, it is not at all repugnant. It may even be the price to be paid so that the systems of values of each spiritual family or each community are preserved and find within themselves the resources necessary for their renewal. If, as I have written in "Race and History," human societies exhibit a certain optimal diversity beyond which they cannot go, but below which they can no longer descend without danger, we must recognize that, to a large extent, this diversity results from the desire of each culture to resist the cultures surrounding it, to distinguish itself from them—in short, to be itself. Cultures are not unaware of one another, they even borrow from one another on occasion; but, in order not to perish, they must, in other connections, remain somewhat impermeable toward one another.

All these matters had to be recalled in my lecture—and must be again today, when nothing so much compromises the struggle against racism, or weakens it from the inside, or vitiates it, as the undiscriminating use of the word *racism*, by confusing a false, but explicit theory with common inclinations and attitudes from which it would be illusory to imagine that humanity can one day free itself or even that it will care to do so. This verbal bombast is comparable to the one that, at the time of the Falkland conflict, led many politicians and journalists to speak in terms of a struggle against a vestige of colonialism, about what was, in fact, simply a squabble like those which occur about the regrouping of land among peasants.

However, since these inclinations and attitudes are in some degree consubstantial with our species, we have no right to deny that they play a part in our history: always inevitable, often fruitful, and even dangerous when exacerbated. I therefore asked my audience to question carefully, even sadly if they wished, the future of a world whose cultures, all passionately fond of one another, would aspire only to celebrate one another in such confusion that each would lose any attraction it could have for the others and its own reasons for existing.

Fourth, since it seemed necessary, I warned that it was not enough to revel in high-flown words year after year if they wished to change humanity. Finally, I emphasized that, to avoid facing reality, the UNESCO ideology all too readily hid behind contradictory assertions. It did so, for example—a point better illustrated by the program of the World Conference of Cultural Policies, held in Mexico in 1982—by imagining that one can use well-meaning words to surmount contradictory statements such as one endorsing "the reconciliation of loyalty to oneself and openness toward others" or one favoring simultaneously "the creative affirmation of each identity and the rapprochement of all cultures." It therefore seems to me that, although written twelve years ago, my text is still timely. In any event, it shows that I did not wait for the vogue of sociobiology, or even for the appearance of the term, to state certain problems. I was not, however, prevented eight years later (see chapter 2 of the present collection) from expressing my opinion of this would-be science or from criticizing its vagueness, its reckless extrapolations, its internal contradictions.

Aside from the chapters I have already mentioned, there is little to say about those that follow, except that several, written for *Festschrifts*, in honor or in memory of colleagues, suffered from the flaws inherent in occasional pieces. One makes a promise out of friendship, admiration, or esteem, and then immediately turns back to tasks that one has neither the wish nor the freedom to interrupt. Then, when the deadline is up, one hurries over a text on which more care should have been spent, while excusing oneself by saying that the dedicatee will care more about the thought than the article, and that, in any event, such miscellaneous collections usually draw few readers. I have therefore closely reviewed these texts, to make my words more precise, to rectify omissions, and to fill in occasional gaps in the reasoning.

Finally, in the last part, I have gathered diverse writings with no immediately apparent link: thoughts on painting, memories of my life in New York some forty years ago, statements on education and on human rights. A single thread passes through all of these pieces, however, tying them to the first chapter of the book: as a whole, they offer reflections on the relationship between constraint and freedom. For if anthropological research can teach something to modern man, it is mostly that societies often described as being ruled by tradition—and having no other ambition, even in their minor customs, than to remain as their gods or ancestors created them at the dawn of time—nevertheless offer the researcher an abundance of customs, beliefs, and art forms that bear witness to the inexhaustible creativity of the human mind.

The fact is that there is no opposition between constraint and liberty, and that, on the contrary, they support each other—since all liberty attempts to overturn or overcome a constraint and every constraint has cracks or points of least resistance that invite liberty to pass through. Nothing better than the awareness of these two facts may better dissipate the contemporary illusion that liberty brooks no restraint and that education, social life, and art require for their expansion an act of faith in the omnipotence of spontaneity. This illusion, although certainly not the cause, can nevertheless be seen as a significant aspect of the crisis that afflicts Western civilization today.

PART I

THE INNATE

AND THE ACQUIRED

La coustume est une seconde nature qui destruit la première. Mais qu'est-ce que nature, pourquoy la coustume n'est-elle pas naturelle? J'ai grand peur que cette nature ne soit elle-mesme qu'une première coustume, comme la coustume est une seconde nature.

PASCAL

Pensées

Chapter I

Race and Culture

IT does not behoove an anthropologist to try and define what is or is not a race, because the specialists in physical anthropology, who have been discussing this question for almost two centuries, have never agreed on a definition, and nothing indicates that they are any closer to agreement today. Recently, they informed us that hominidae, indeed highly dissimilar ones, first appeared some three or four million years ago, or even earlier: that is, in a past so remote that we will never know enough to determine whether the different types whose bones we unearth were simply one another's victims or actually interbred. According to certain anthropologists, the human species must have given birth very early to differentiated subspecies, which, in the course of prehistorical times, produced all kinds of exchanges and crossbreedings: the persistence of a few ancient traits and the convergence of recent traits would combine to explain the diversity that can be noted today among human beings. Then again, other anthropologists feel that the genetic isolation of human groups occurred at a far more recent date, which they place toward the end of the Pleistocene. In this case, the observable differences could not have resulted from accidental deviations among traits having no adaptive value and able to be maintained indefinitely in isolated groups: rather, these differences would have come from local differences in selection factors. The term *race*, or any other term used in its stead, would therefore designate a population or a set of populations that differ from others by the more or less frequent presence of certain genes.

In the first hypothesis, the reality of race is lost in eras so distant that we cannot possibly learn anything about them. It is a question not of a scientific hypothesis—that is, verifiable, even indirectly, by remote consequences—but of a categorical statement, tantamount to an axiom in absolute terms, without which it is deemed impossible to explain present-day differences. This was the doctrine formulated by Gobineau,* who is styled the father of racism, even though he was perfectly aware that races are not observable phenomena; he merely postulated them as *a priori* conditions for the diversity of historical cultures, which he felt could not be otherwise accounted for. At the same time, however, he did acknowledge that the populations that had given birth to cultures were the hybrids of crossbreeding between human groups that were themselves the products of earlier crossbreedings. Thus, if we attempt to trace racial differences back to their origins, we condemn ourselves to ignorance; and the subject of our debate becomes the diversity not of races but of cultures.

The second hypothesis raises other problems. First, the variable genetic blends, to which the man in the street refers in speaking of races, all involve highly visible characteristics: size, skin color, shape of skull, hair type, et cetera. Even assuming that these genetic variations correspond to one another (as is far from certain), nothing proves that they do not also correspond to other variations, involving characteristics that are not immediately perceptible to the senses. Nevertheless, the invisible features are no less real than the visible ones; and it is conceivable that the former are geographically distributed in one or more ways that are totally different from the latter ones, and also differ among themselves; so that, depending on the repressed qualities, "invisible races" could be revealed within the traditional races or else could cut across the already vague boundaries they have been assigned. In the second place, the limits drawn are arbitrary, since we are dealing in every case with a genetic blend. In fact, these genetic blends increase or diminish by imperceptible gradations, and any thresholds established are contingent on the types of phenomena that the investigator chooses to retain for classification. Hence, in the one case, the notion of race becomes so abstract as to go beyond experience and becomes a kind of logical presupposition to justify a certain line of reasoning. In the other case, the notion of race sticks so close to experi-

*Count Joseph Arthur de Gobineau (1816–82) was a French diplomat, Orientalist, and writer who promoted the theory that while pure races vanished ages ago, the still ongoing process of racial mixture dooms mankind to an inescapable degradation. His followers developed the theory of the racial superiority of the blond Aryan.

ence as to fuse into it, so that one no longer has any idea what one is talking about. No wonder so many anthropologists simply refuse to employ this notion.

Actually, the history of the concept of race overlaps with the investigation of traits lacking adaptive value. For how else could they have survived as such for millennia? And since they have no function, good or bad, because their presence would be wholly arbitrary, how could they testify now to a very distant past? Still, the history of the notion of race is also the history of the uninterrupted setbacks suffered in the course of this research. All the traits successively cited to define racial differences have turned out to be linked to adaptation phenomena, even if the reasons for their selective value occasionally elude us. This linkage holds for the shape of the skull, which, as we know, tends to be round everywhere; it also holds for the color of the human skin, which, among tribes settling in temperate climates, grew lighter by way of selection to compensate for inadequate sunlight and to allow the organism to defend itself against rachitis. Anthropologists then swooped down on the blood groups. However, it is now suspected that these, too, might have adaptive value: as a function perhaps of nutritional factors or as a consequence of (the bearer's) differing sensitivities to diseases such as smallpox or bubonic plague. And a similar function is likely true of the blood-serum proteins.

If this descent into the innermost depths of the human body proves disappointing, will one have better luck in trying to go all the way back to the earliest beginnings of individual lives? Some anthropologists have tried to understand the differences that can manifest themselves, from the moment of birth, among Asiatic, African, and white or black North American babies. Such differences seem to exist, and they concern both motor behavior and temperament. (*Current Directions in Anthropology* 1970, p. 106; Kilbride, Robbins, and Kilbride 1970). Yet even in a case that seems so favorable for proving racial differences, researchers admit their helplessness, for two reasons. First of all, if these differences are innate, they appear too complex to be tied to a single gene; and, at present, geneticists have no sure methods for studying the transmission of characteristics produced by the combined action of several factors. In the best theories, they have to content themselves with establishing statistical averages, which add nothing to those theories that seem, moreover, inadequate for defining a race with any precision. Second, and more important, nothing proves that these differences are innate and that they do not result from intrauterine conditions accepted by a culture, since pregnant women eat and behave in different ways according to the society they live in. In addition, the motor activities of infants evince differences that are likewise cultural; they may result from a baby's lying in a cradle for long hours or being continually held against the mother's body and feeling her movements, or also from the diverse ways a baby is picked up, held, and fed. That these reasons alone may be operative arises from the fact that the differences observed between African and North American babies are incomparably greater than those observed between black and white North American babies. Indeed, whatever their racial background, American babies are brought up more or less in the same way.

The problem of the relationship between race and culture would thus be poorly stated were one content to express it in this way. We know what a culture is, but not what a race is; and we probably do not need to know in order to attempt to answer the question raised by the title of this chapter. In fact, it would be profitable to formulate this question in a way that is perhaps more complicated and yet simpler. There are differences between cultures; and certain cultures, which differ from others more than they seem to differ among themselves (at least to the eye of the inexperienced outsider), are characteristic of populations whose physical appearance distinguishes them from other groups. These latter groups feel that the differences among their particular cultures are not as great as those between their cultures and the cultures of the other groups. Is there a conceivable tie between these physical and cultural differences? Can one explain and justify the cultural differences without citing the physical ones? This, in sum, is the question that I am expected to try and answer.

Yet answering it is impossible for the reasons that I have already given, chief of which is that geneticists declare themselves incapable of plausibly connecting highly complex modes of behavior—such as those that can give distinctive traits to a culture—to determined and specific hereditary factors that scientific research can grasp now or in the foreseeable future. It is therefore necessary to restrict the question even further, and I will formulate it as follows: Does anthropology feel that it can on its own explain the diversity of cultures? Can it succeed in doing so without citing factors that elude its own rationality—without, moreover, making too hasty a judgment about their ultimate nature, which is beyond anthropology's province to declare biological?

Indeed, all we can say about the problem of the possible relationship between culture and the "other thing" that is, supposedly, not in the same category as culture would be (to reformulate a famous phrase) that we have no need of such a hypothesis.*

Nevertheless, even on this basis, we might be making things too easy for ourselves by oversimplification. By itself, the diversity of cultures would pose no problem beyond the objective fact of its existence. Nothing really prevents different cultures from coexisting and maintaining comparatively peaceful relations, which, as proved by historical experience, can have different foundations. Sometimes each culture calls itself the only genuine and worthwhile culture; it ignores the others and even denies that they are cultures. Most of the peoples that we term "primitive" give themselves a name that signifies "The True Ones," "The Good Ones," "The Excellent Ones," or even, quite simply, "The Human Beings," and apply to other peoples a name that denies their humanity—for example, "earth monkeys" or "louse eggs." Hostility and sometimes even warfare may have prevailed between cultures, but the aims were chiefly to avenge wrongs, to capture victims for sacrifices, and to steal women or property—customs that may be morally repugnant to us, but that seldom or never went so far as to wipe out or subjugate a whole culture as such because one did not accept the other's existence. When the great German anthropologist Curt Unkel—better known by the name Nimuendaju, given him by the Indians of Brazil to whom he devoted his life—returned to the native villages after a lengthy stay in a civilized center, his hosts would burst into tears at the thought of the suffering he must have endured so far from the only place in which, so they felt, life was worth living. Such profound indifference to other cultures was, in its way, a guarantee that they could exist in their own manner and on their own terms.

There is, however, another attitude, which complements rather than contradicts the preceding assumption, and according to which the foreigner enjoys the prestige of exoticism and, by his presence, embodies the opportunity of widening social ties. During a visit with a family, the outsider is asked to name a newborn child; and marital alliances are all the more valuable when concluded with a faraway group. On a different level, we know that, long before encountering white men, the Flathead Indians in the Rocky Mountains were so fascinated by what they heard about the whites and their beliefs that they did not hesitate to send successive expeditions through territories

*The French astronomer Pierre Simon Laplace (1799–1827), asked by Emperor Napoleon what place God had in his system, answered: "I did not need that hypothesis."

occupied by hostile tribes in order to make contact with the Christian missionaries in St. Louis, Missouri. So long as cultures regard themselves simply as diverse, they can readily either ignore each other or consider one another partners for a mutually desirable dialogue. In either case, they may threaten and even attack one another, but they will never really imperil their respective existences. The situation is altogether different when the notion of mutually acknowledged diversity is replaced by one culture's feeling of superiority based on force, and when positive or negative recognition of the diversity of cultures gives way to affirmation of their inequality.

Thus, the true problem is not the one posed scientifically by the possible link between the genotypes of certain groups and their practical success, which they cite to claim their superiority. For even if physical anthropologists and cultural anthropologists agree that the problem is insoluble and can sign a declaration of insolvency, as it were, affirming that they have nothing more to say to one another as they make their fond farewells and go their separate ways (Benoist 1966), it remains no less true that the Spaniards of the sixteenth century regarded themselves as, and proved, superior to the Mexicans and the Peruvians, because they, the Spaniards, had boats that could carry soldiers, horses, armor, and firearms across the sea. Also, following the same logic, the Europeans of the nineteenth century proclaimed themselves superior to the rest of the world because of the steam engine and a few other technological achievements. That Europeans were actually superior in all these respects and in the more general respect of scientific knowledge, which was born and bred in the Western world, seems even less debatable when we see that, aside from rare and precious exceptions, all the peoples subjugated by the West or forced to follow it have recognized its superiority; and, having wrested or gained their independence, they pursue the goal of overcoming what they themselves consider their backwardness in the line of common development.

Because of the existence of this relative superiority, which affirmed itself in a remarkably short period of time, we cannot infer that it reveals distinct basic attitudes or, above all, that it is definitive. The history of civilizations shows that one or another has been able to shine with extraordinary magnificence for several centuries—but that development was not necessarily unique or always in the same direction. For several years, the West has recognized the evidence that its immense triumphs in certain domains have brought serious drawbacks —to the point that it has come to wonder whether the values it was obliged to give up, in order to enjoy other values, may not have been more deserving of respect. The idea, prevalent until recently, of continuous progress along a road on which the West alone forged ahead without stopping, while other societies lagged behind, has yielded to the concept of choices in different directions, so that each society or culture risks losing on one or more scenarios what it had hoped to win on others. Agriculture and the establishment of fixed communities have vastly developed our food resources and have, in consequence, allowed the human population to increase. One result of this development has been the spread of infectious diseases, which tend to disappear when a population is too small to support pathogenic germs. We can therefore say—albeit not with full certainty—that the peoples who became agricultural chose certain advantages, and risked certain disadvantages against which the peoples who remained hunters and gatherers were better protected: the latter's way of life prevents the spread of contagious diseases from one person to the next and from domestic animals to humans—but, naturally, at the price of other drawbacks.

Faith in the unilinear evolution of living forms appeared in social philosophy long before it appeared in biology. But it was biology that, in the nineteenth century, reinforced this faith, allowing it to claim a scientific status; while at the same time, the bearers of this faith hoped to reconcile the diversity of cultures with the affirmation of their inequality. In viewing the different observable states of human society as if they illustrated the successive phases of a unique development, and for lack of a causal tie between biological heredity and cultural achievements, these scientists even claimed that there was at least an analogy between the two domains. This relationship was supposed to promote the same moral evaluations that biologists used to describe the world of living things, a world forever growing toward greater differentiation and complexity.

However, a remarkable reversal took place among the biologists themselves—the first in a series of reversals that I shall discuss in the course of this chapter. At the same time that sociologists were invoking biology to disclose a more rigid and intelligible pattern of an evolution behind the uncertain flukes of history, biologists were realizing that what they had seen as an evolution subject to a few simple laws was actually a highly complicated history. In biology, the notion of a "journey" that the various living forms always had to take, one after another, in the same direction, was replaced, first, by that of a "tree," which allowed scientists to establish between the species collateral relations rather than ones of direct descent; for the latter was revealing itself to be ever less warranted as evolutionary forms proved to be sometimes divergent, but sometimes also convergent. Next, the tree was changed into a "trellis," a figure whose lines intersect as frequently as they move away from one another, so that the historical description of these entangled meanderings came to replace the overly simplistic diagrams into which it had once seemed possible to impose an evolution whose numerous modalities differ in pace, direction, and effects.

Anthropology, however, urges an analogous view if, ever so little, direct knowledge of the societies most different from ours permits an appreciation of the reasons for existence that they have provided for themselves, rather than their being judged and condemned for reasons that are not theirs. To an observer who has been trained by his own society to recognize its values, a civilization intent on developing its own very different values appears to possess no values at all. It seems to the observer as if something is happening only in his culture, as if only his culture is privileged to have a history that keeps adding events to one another. For him, only this history offers meaning and purpose (in the twofold thrust of the French word *sens*—that is, *sense* and *direction*). In all other societies, so he believes, history does not exist: at best, it marks time.

But this illusion is comparable to the one afflicting old people within their own society and even, moreover, the adversaries of a new regime. Excluded from the mainstream by age or political choice, they feel as stagnant the history of an era in which they are no longer actively involved—in contrast to the young people or the militants in power who are fervently engaged in this period, whose events leave others more or less immobilized. The wealth of a culture or of the unfolding of one of its phases does not exist as an intrinsic feature; it is a function of the observer's situation in regard to that wealth, of the number or diversity of the interests he has invested in it. To employ another image, one could say that cultures are like trains moving each on its own track, at its own speed, and in its own direction. The trains rolling alongside ours are permanently present for us; through the windows of our compartments, we can observe at our leisure the various kinds of car, the faces and gestures of the passengers. But if, on an oblique or a parallel track, a train passes in the other direction, we perceive only a vague, fleeting, barely identifiable image, usually just a momentary blur in our visual field, supplying no information about the event itself and merely irritating us because it interrupts our placid contemplation of the landscape which serves as the backdrop to our daydreaming.

Race and Culture

Every member of a culture is as tightly bound up with it as this ideal traveler is with his own train. From birth and, as I have said, probably even before, the things and beings in our environment establish in each one of us an array of complex references forming a system—conduct, motivations, implicit judgments, which education then confirms by means of its reflexive view of the historical development of our civilization. We literally move along with this reference system, and the cultural systems established outside it are perceptible to us only through the distortions imprinted upon them by our system. Indeed, it may even make us incapable of seeing those other systems.

The preceding comments can be proved by the remarkable change in attitude that has recently occurred among geneticists toward so-called primitive peoples, and by those of their customs that bear directly or indirectly upon their demography. For centuries, these customs—which consist of bizarre marriage rules, arbitrary prohibitions such as those against sexual relations between husband and wife while the wife is nursing the last-born child (sometimes until the latter reaches the age of three or four), polygamic privileges for chiefs or elders, or even practices that revolt us, such as infanticide—seemed devoid of meaning or value. They were fit only to be described and listed as instances of the caprices and singularities of which human nature is capable if not (as observers went so far as to say) guilty. It took a new science—population genetics—emerging around 1950, to give meaning to, and reveal the reasons for, all those practices that had been previously put down as absurd or criminal.

In 1970, the review *Science* informed a wide audience about the results of the research pursued for several years by J. V. Neel and his collaborators. Their investigations among some of the best preserved groups in tropical America have been confirmed by other studies done independently in South America and New Guinea (Neel 1970).

We tend to consider the alleged "races" most distant from ours as being the most homogeneous; to a white man, all yellow people look alike, and the reverse is no doubt equally true. The real situation seems far more complex, for if the Australian aborigines, for example, appear morphologically homogeneous throughout their continent (Abbie 1951; 1961), considerable differences in the genetic outfit have been noted among several South American tribes living within one geographic area; and these differences are almost as great between villages of one tribe as between tribes distinct in language and culture. Contrary to what one might have thought, the tribe itself does not constitute a biological unity. How can this phenomenon be explained? By the fact, no doubt, that new villages take shape by way of a twofold process of fission and fusion: first, a family separates from its genealogical lineage and establishes itself elsewhere; later, blocks of related individuals join those people and share the new habitat. A genetic stock that crystallizes in this way is much more internally differentiated than if it has resulted from random interbreeding.

There is one consequence of this process: if the villages of the same tribe consist of genetic makeups that were originally differentiated—with each tribe living in relative isolation, and all tribes objectively competing with one another because of their unequal reproduction rates—they provide a set of conditions well known to biologists as being favorable to an incomparably swifter evolution than that generally observed in animal species. Now we know that the evolution leading from the last fossil Hominidae to present-day man took place very rapidly (comparatively speaking). So far as we grant that observable conditions in some backward groups approximately reflect, at least in certain respects, the conditions that humanity experienced long, long ago, we must recognize that these conditions, which strike us as miserable, were exactly right for making us what we have become, and moreover, that they remain the most capable of keeping human evolution in the same direction and of preserving its rhythm; while our vast contemporary societies, in which genetic exchanges occur in a different manner, tend to slow down evolution or push it in other directions.

These researches have also demonstrated that, among the supposed savages, infant mortality and the death rate from infectious diseases (considering only, of course, tribes free of outside contamination) are far from being as high as one might think. Hence, these two factors cannot explain the slowness of the population growth, which is actually due to other factors: the practice of abortion and infanticide, and voluntary spacing of births because of sexual prohibitions and lengthy breast-feeding periods. As a result, during its fertile period, a couple produces a child on the average of every four or five years. However odious we may find infanticide, it does not differ fundamentally as a birth control method, either from the high rate of infant mortality that once prevailed in the "big" societies and that still prevails in certain present-day societies, or from the contraceptive methods that we consider necessary today to spare millions and even billions of people, likely to be born on an overpopulated planet, a fate no less lamentable than the one forestalled by their early elimination.

Like so many other cultures around the world, the ones that were the subject of these investigations reward social success and longevity with several wives. As a result, if all women tend to bear the same number of children for the reasons I have indicated, a man's rate of reproduction will vary considerably, depending on how many wives he has. These rates will vary even more if—as I observed long ago among the Tupi-Kawahib Indians, who live in the basin of the Madeira River in western Brazil—unusual sexual potency is one of the attributes of a chief, who, in this small society of about fifty people, has a kind of sexual monopoly on all the women who are or will soon become nubile.

Now in such groups, the position of chief is not always hereditary; and when it is, then there is a wide latitude of choice. In 1938 when staying among the Nambikwara, whose small, semi-nomadic bands each had a chief designated by collective assent, I was struck by the fact that aside from the privilege of polygamy, his position brought him more burdens and responsibilities than advantages. If a man wanted to be chief or, more often, gave in to the group's wishes, he had to have an unusual character and not only the necessary physical skills but a spirit of initiative, the habit of command, and a taste for public affairs. Whatever one may think of such talents, however much we like or dislike them, it is nonetheless true that if they have, directly or indirectly, any genetic basis, polygamy will favor their perpetuation. And, indeed, investigations of similar populations have demonstrated that a polygamous man has more children than other men, thus supplying his sons with half-sisters to exchange with other families in order to obtain wives, so that it is possible to say that polygyny engenders polygyny. Thus certain forms of natural selection are encouraged and strengthened.

Aside from the infectious diseases introduced by colonizers or conquerors, which wreaked untold havoc, sometimes wiping out entire ethnic groups within a few weeks or even days, so-called primitive peoples seem to enjoy a remarkable immunity to their own endemic illnesses. This resistance is explained by the infant's great intimacy with his mother's body and the surrounding milieu. Early exposure to all sorts of pathogenic germs evidently assures smoother transition from passive immunity, acquired from the mother during gestation, to active immunity developed by each person after birth.

So far I have focused on factors of inner demographic and sociological equilibrium. However, I ought to mention those vast systems of rites and beliefs that may strike us as ridiculous superstitions but help to keep a human group in harmony with the natural environment. A plant may be viewed as a respectable being, which one does not pick without a legitimate motive and without first appeasing its spirit with offerings; animals hunted as food may, depending on their species, be under the protection of their respective supernatural masters, who punish any abusive hunters guilty of bagging too many kills or of not sparing the females and the young. Indigenous philosophy may even contain the idea that human beings, animals, and plants share a common stock of life, so that any human abuse of any species is tantamount to lowering the life expectancies of human beings themselves. All these beliefs may be naïve, yet they are highly effective testimonies to a wisely conceived humanism, which does not center on man but gives him a reasonable place within nature, rather then letting him make himself its master and plunderer, without regard for even the most obvious needs and interests of later generations.

Our knowledge had to evolve, and we had to become aware of new problems, in order to recognize an objective value and a moral significance in ways of life, in customs and beliefs, that had once aroused our ridicule or, at best, our condescending curiosity. But with the appearance of population genetics on the anthropological scene, another turn occurred—one with perhaps even greater theoretical implications. All the facts that I have just cited are cultural. They concern the way in which certain human groups divide and reshape themselves, the ways in which custom imposes on both sexes to mate and reproduce, and the prescribed manner of avoiding childbirth or of begetting and raising children, as well as law, magic, religion, and cosmology. Now we have seen that, directly or indirectly, these factors shape and steer natural selection. Hence, the assumptions about the problem of the relationship between the concept of race and the concept of culture are completely overturned. Throughout the nineteenth and in the first half of the twentieth century, scholars wondered whether and in what way race influences culture. After establishing that the problem stated in this way cannot be solved, we now realize that the reverse situation exists: the cultural forms adopted in various places by human beings, their ways of life in the past or in the present, determine to a very great extent the rhythm of their biological evolution and its direction. Far from having to ask whether culture is or is not a function of race, we are discovering that race—or what is generally meant by this term—is one function among others of culture.

And how could it be otherwise? The culture of a group determines the geographic limits it assigns itself or submits to, its friendly or hostile relations with neighboring peoples, and, consequently, the relative importance of genetic exchanges that can result from intermarriages that are permitted, encouraged, or prohibited. Even in our societies, we know that marriages do not come about purely by chance: conscious or unconscious factors—such as the distance between the homes of future spouses, their ethnic origin, their religious and educational background—can each play a determining role. If we extrapolate from the practices and customs that until recently were extremely common among illiterate peoples and may therefore be viewed as quite old, we will admit that, from the very start of societal life, our ancestors must have known and applied very strict rules of marriage. For example, those that equate parallel cousins—the offspring of two brothers or two sisters—with actual brothers or sisters and outlaw marriage between them as incestuous; while on the other hand, a union between so-called cross-cousins—the offspring of brother and sister—is authorized if not prescribed, contrary to other societies where any kinship link, no matter how distant, is an impediment invalidating marriage. Another and even more subtle rule concerning cross-relatives divides female cousins into two categories—the daughter of the father's sister, and the daughter of the mother's brother: one category is permitted; the other, absolutely forbidden, though it is not always and everywhere the same category. How would such rules, applied for generations, fail to modify the transmission of the genotypes?

Furthermore, the health and hygiene rules observed by every society, the relative importance and efficacy of the treatment for each kind of illness or deficiency, allow or prevent in varying degrees the survival of certain individuals and the dissemination of genetic material that would otherwise have disappeared sooner. The same holds true for cultural attitudes toward certain hereditary anomalies and, as we have seen, for such practices as infanticide, which affect both sexes alike in specific situations—births considered abnormal, twins, and so on—or, more particularly, girls. Finally, the relative age of husband and wife, and the variation in fertility and fecundity according to standard of living and social functions, are, at least in part, directly or indirectly subject to rules whose ultimate origin is social and not biological.

This reversal of the problem of the relationship between race and culture—a reversal we have been witnessing for several years—is strikingly illustrated by the disease known as drepanocythemia or sickle-cell anemia, a congenital anomaly of the red-blood cells, which is often fatal when inherited from both parents, but which, when inherited from only one parent—as it has been known for the past twenty years —offers some protection against malaria. Hence, it is one of those traits that were once thought to have no adaptive value—a kind of biological fossil whose frequency gradients enable us to track down the ancient links that existed among populations. Hopes of having finally unearthed a stable criterion of racial identification were dashed when scientists discovered that individuals heterozygotic for the sickle-cell gene could have a biological advantage and could therefore reproduce at a relatively higher rate than both the biologically doomed individuals who are homozygotic for the same gene, and the non-carriers who risk early death because of their greater vulnerability to a certain form of malaria.

F. B. Livingstone, in a memorable article (1958), pointed out the theoretical—one might almost say philosophical—implications of this discovery by geneticists. A comparative study of the malaria rate, the sickle-cell anemia rate, and the distribution of languages and cultures throughout western Africa allowed the author to spell out the first coherent set of biological, archeological, linguistic, and ethnographic data. He also convincingly showed that the appearance of malaria and the subsequent diffusion of sickle-cell anemia must have followed the introduction of agriculture: while pushing back or destroying the fauna, the intense clearing of the land led to the formation of swampy areas and pools of stagnant water, thus encouraging the reproduction of contaminating mosquitoes, and forced these insects to adapt to *Homo sapiens*, the most abundant of the mammals on which they could become parasites. Along with other factors, the sickle-cell anemia rates, varying from group to group, suggest plausible hypotheses about the period in which a people settled in the places they occupy today, and about the movements of tribes and the relative dates of their acquisition of agrarian techniques.

Thus, one can state both that a genetic irregularity cannot bear witness to a very distant past (since it spreads, at least in part, because of the protection against the biological consequence of cultural changes); and, on the other hand, that a genetic irregularity sheds great light on a more recent past, since the introduction of agriculture in Africa cannot go back more than a few thousand years. What is lost on one side is gained on the other. We no longer use racial characteristics to explain great differences we thought we could discern among cultures when viewing them on too broad a basis; but these very same racial traits (which we can no longer view as such when using a finer scale of observation), combined with cultural phenomena of which they are less the cause than the result, supply precise information on comparatively recent periods. Furthermore, contrary to the other history, this information can be confirmed by archeological, linguistic, and ethnographic data. So long as we replace the point of view of "cultural macro-evolution" with that of "genetic micro-evolution," collaboration becomes possible once again between the study of races and the study of cultures.

Indeed, these new perspectives, partly analogous and partly complementary, enable us to compare these two fields, which are both analogous and complementary. They are analogous because, in several senses, cultures are comparable to irregular dosages of the genetic traits that are generally designated as "races." A culture consists of a multiplicity of traits, some of which it shares, in varying degrees, with nearby or distant cultures, and some of which distinguish it more or less sharply from the others. These traits are balanced within a system that, in either case, must be viable if the culture is not to be gradually eliminated by other systems more capable of propagating or reproducing themselves. In order to develop differences, so that the boundaries enabling us to distinguish one culture from its neighbors may become sufficiently clear-cut, the conditions are roughly the same as those promoting biological differentiation between human groups: relative isolation for a long period; limited cultural and genetic exchange. Cultural barriers are almost of the same nature as biological barriers; the cultural barriers prefigure the biological barriers all the more as all cultures leave their mark on the human body: through styles of costume, hair, and ornament, through physical mutilation, and through gestures, they mimic differences comparable to those that can exist between races, and by favoring certain physical types, they stabilize and perhaps even spread them.

Over thirty years ago, in a booklet written at the request of the United Nations Educational, Scientific and Cultural Organization (1952), I used the notion of coalition to explain that isolated cultures cannot hope to create by themselves the conditions for a truly cumulative history. For such conditions, I said, diverse cultures must voluntarily or involuntarily combine their respective stakes, thereby giving themselves a better chance to realize, in the great game of history, the long winning series that allows history to progress. Geneticists now express similar views on biological evolution when they show that a genome actually constitutes a system in which certain genes play a regulatory part and others operate concertedly on a single characteristic, or—vice versa—a single gene determines several characteristics. What is true of an individual genome is also true of a population, which must always be such that, through the combined action within it of several genetic inheritances that were mistaken for a racial type, an optimal equilibrium is established and improves the group's chances of survival. In this sense, we may say that, in the history of populations, genetic recombination plays a part comparable to that of cultural recombination in the evolution of the ways of life, the techniques, the bodies of knowledge, and the beliefs whose distribution distinguishes the various societies.

These analogies can, no doubt, be proposed only with some reservation. On the one hand, indeed, cultural legacies evolve far more swiftly than genetic legacies: there is a world of difference between the culture of our great-grandparents and our culture; and yet we perpetuate their genotype. On the other hand, the number of cultures that exist on the face of the earth, or that still existed several centuries ago, is far greater than the number of races that even the most meticulous observers care to enumerate: several thousand as opposed to a few dozen. These enormous disparities provide a decisive argument against the theoreticians who claim that ultimately it is heredity that determines the course of history; for the latter changes much more quickly and in infinitely more diversified ways than does heredity. What heredity determines in human beings is the general aptitude to acquire any culture whatever; the specific culture, however, will depend on random factors of birth and on the society in which one is raised. Individuals predestined by their genetic makeup to acquire only a particular culture would have singularly disadvantaged descendants, since the cultural variations to which the latter are exposed will come more quickly than their genotype can possibly evolve and diversify in response to these new situations.

For one fact cannot be overemphasized: while selection enables living species to adapt to a natural environment or to resist its transformation more effectively, for humans this environment is no longer primarily natural but draws its distinctive features from technological, economic, social, and mental conditions, which, through the workings of the culture, create a particular environment for each human group. We can then take a further step and see that organic evolution and cultural evolution are not only analogous but also complementary. I have stated and shown that cultural traits, which are not genetically determined, may affect organic evolution—but in directions that trigger counteraction. Not all cultures demand exactly the same abilities from their members; and if, as is probable, certain abilities have a genetic basis, then the individuals who possess them to the highest degree will be favored within their culture. If their number grows as a result, they are bound to act upon the culture itself in such a way as to push it even farther in the same direction or in new directions that are indirectly linked to it.

At the origin of humanity, biological evolution may have selected pre-cultural traits, such as the erect position, manual dexterity, sociability, symbolic thought, and the ability to vocalize and communicate. In contrast, since its genesis, culture has been consolidating and spreading these traits. When cultures specialize, they strengthen and favor other traits, such as resistance to cold or heat, among societies that have adapted, willy-nilly, to climatic extremes; or aggressive or contemplative dispositions; or technological ingenuity. On a cultural level, none of these traits can be clearly shown to have a genetic basis; yet we cannot exclude the possibility of partial, remote, and intermediate connections. In this case, it would be correct to say that each culture selects genetic aptitudes, which have a reciprocal influence on the very culture that originally contributed to reinforcing them.

By looking to an ever more distant past, now calculated in millions of years, at the very dawn of humanity, physical anthropology has pulled out one of the linchpins of racist theories, since the unknowable thereby increases far more rapidly than the number of available signposts for mapping the routes taken by our earliest ancestors in the course of their evolution.

Geneticists struck even more decisive blows against racist theories when they replaced the notion of *type* with that of *population*, the notion of *race* with that of *genetic stock*. Furthermore, they have shown that a wide gulf separates hereditary differences that can be attributed to the operation of a single gene (these differences being of little racial significance, since they probably have adaptive value) from those that can be attributed to the combined action of several genes, which makes the genes practically indeterminable.

However, once we have driven out the old demons of racist ideology or at least proved that it cannot claim any scientific basis whatsoever, the road is clear for a positive collaboration between geneticists and anthropologists to investigate how and in what way the distribution maps of biological and cultural phenomena shed light on one another and can also inform us about a past that—while not stretching back to the earliest origins of racial differences, whose vestiges are forever out of reach—can, by way of the present, link up with the future and allow us to examine its physiognomy. What not long ago was called the problem of the races eludes the domain of philosophical speculation and moral homilies, with which we were too frequently satisfied. This problem escapes even the domain of the first clumsy attempts with which the anthropologists tried to bring it down to earth, in order to supply provisional answers, which were inspired by practical knowledge of the different races and by the observed data. In a word, the problem leaves the domains of the old physical anthropology and general anthropology and becomes a subject for specialists, who, within limited contexts, ask technical questions and offer answers unsuitable for arranging nations in different places in a hierarchy.

Only for the past ten years or so have we begun to understand that we are discussing the problem of the relationship between organic and cultural evolution in terms that Auguste Comte would have labeled metaphysical. Human evolution is not a byproduct of biological evolution; nor is it entirely distinct from the latter. A synthesis of these two traditional attitudes is now possible on the condition that biologists and anthropologists refuse to be satisfied with *a priori* answers and dogmatic solutions and become aware of the help they can give one another and of their respective limits.

This inadequacy of the traditional answers may explain why the ideological struggle against racism has proved ineffective in practice. Nothing indicates that racial prejudices are declining; and after brief periods of local calm, everything points to their resurfacing elsewhere with greater intensity. Hence the need felt by UNESCO periodically to resume a struggle whose outcome appears uncertain at best. Furthermore, are we so sure that the racist form of intolerance results chiefly from the wrong ideas of this or that group of people about the dependence of cultural evolution on organic evolution? Might not these ideas be simply ideological camouflage for more concrete oppositions based on a desire to subjugate other groups and maintain a position of power? Such was certainly the case in the past. But, even granting that these relationships of force are diminishing, might not racial differences continue to serve as a pretext for the increasing difficulty of living together, as unconsciously felt by a humanity in the grips of the population explosion? And of a humanity that—like those flour worms that, with the toxins they secrete, poison one another at a distance long before their density exceeds the available food supply in their sack—is beginning to despise itself because of its secret prescience that it is growing too large for each of its members freely to enjoy the essential goods—free space, pure water, unpolluted air? Racial prejudices have reached their greatest intensity when directed toward human groups that have been limited by other groups to inadequate territory and to an insufficient allowance of natural goods so as to reduce their dignity in their own eyes and in those of their powerful neighbors. Yet is not humanity as a whole tending to dispossess itself and, on a planet that has become too small, to inflict upon itself a situation comparable to the one that certain of its representatives have inflicted upon unfortunate tribes of Oceania or the Americas? And what, finally, would become of the ideological struggle against racial prejudices if, as suggested by certain psychological experiments, we had only to divide several subjects of any background into teams and place these teams in a competitive situation; so that there would develop in each team a sense of partiality for its own members and of injustice toward its rivals. Minority communities that we have seen emerging in various parts of the world—for instance, hippies—have been distinguished from the mainstream of the population not by race but only in life style, morals, hair length, and clothing. Are the feelings of repulsion and even hostility that they have inspired in most people substantially different from racial hatred? And would we achieve any real progress if we were satisfied with dispelling the special prejudices on which these hatreds alone, taken in the strict sense, may be said to be based? In all these hypotheses, the anthropologist's possible contribution to solving the racial problem would be insignificant. And it is not certain that hypotheses offered by psychologists and educators would prove any more fruitful, while it is true, as the example of so-called primitive peoples teaches us, mutual tolerance presupposes two conditions that contemporary societies are farther than ever from experiencing: relative equality and sufficient physical distance from one another.

Today geneticists are anxiously wondering about the way that demographic conditions are imperiling the positive feedback between organic evolution and cultural evolution—a process of which I have given several examples and that has enabled humanity to ensure itself first place among living species. Populations are growing in size but shrinking in number. However, the development of mutual assistance within each population group, the progress of medicine, the lengthening of human life, and the growing capacity of each member of the group to reproduce as he or she sees fit, are all increasing the number of harmful mutations and giving them the means to perpetuate themselves. At the same time, the removal of barriers between small groups is eliminating the possibility of evolutionary experiments that might assure the species a chance of new beginnings.

Naturally, the implication is not that humanity is ceasing or will cease to evolve. Its evolution on a cultural level is obvious; and even despite the lack of direct proof of the persistence of biological evolution (demonstrable only in the long haul), its close relationship to man's cultural evolution guarantees that if the latter exists, then the former must necessarily continue. However, natural selection cannot be judged solely by the great advantage of self-reproduction that it offers a species; for, if this multiplication destroys the indispensable balance with what is now called the ecosystem, and which must always be seen in its totality, then population growth may prove disastrous for the particular species that once viewed it as evidence of its own success. Even assuming that humanity will perceive the dangers threatening it, manage to ward them off, and become master of its biological future, one fails to see how the systematic practice of eugenics will escape the dilemma that undermines it: either its practitioners may be inept and ultimately produce something entirely different from what they set out to do; or they may succeed, and the products, being superior to their creators, will inevitably discover that the latter should have produced something entirely different.

The foregoing considerations add further fuel to the doubts that an anthropologist may feel about his ability to solve, on his own and purely with the resources of his discipline, the problems posed by the struggle against racial prejudices. For some twenty-five years, he has become increasingly aware that these problems reflect, on a human scale, a far vaster problem, whose solution is even more urgent—that is, the problem of the relationship between man and the other living species—and that it is useless to try and solve this problem on the lower level if we do not tackle it on a higher scale. Also, the respect we want man to feel for his fellow man is but one specific case of the general respect that he ought to feel for all forms of life. By isolating man from the rest of creation and defining too narrowly the boundaries separating him from other living beings, the Western humanism inherited from antiquity and the Renaissance has deprived him of a bulwark; and, as the experiences of the nineteenth and twentieth centuries have proved, has allowed him to be exposed and defenseless to attacks stirred up within the stronghold itself. This humanism has allowed ever closer segments of humanity to be cast outside arbitrary frontiers to which it was all the easier to deny the same dignity as the rest of humanity, since man had forgotten that he is worthy of respect more as a living being than as the lord and master of creation—a primary insight that should have induced him to show his respect for all living beings. Far Eastern Buddhism has wonderful teachings along these lines, and one could only wish that the whole of humanity might continue, or learn, to be inspired by them.

There is, finally, one last reason why the anthropologist hesitates—not, of course, to fight against racial prejudices, for his science has greatly contributed to this struggle and will keep on doing so—but to believe, as he has been incited to do too often, that the spread of knowledge and the development of communication among human beings will some day let them live in harmony, accepting and respecting one another's diversity. Throughout this chapter, I have repeatedly emphasized that the gradual fusion of groups previously separated by geographic distance as well as by linguistic and cultural barriers has marked the end of a world: the world of human beings who, for hundreds of thousands of years, lived in small and durably separated groups, each evolving differently on both a biological and a cultural level. The upheavals unleashed by an expanding industrial civilization, and the rising speed of transportation and communication, have knocked down these barriers. At the same time, we have lost the possibilities offered by these barriers for developing and testing new genetic combinations and cultural experiences. Now we cannot close our eyes to the fact that, despite its urgent practical necessity and the high moral goals it has set itself, the struggle against all forms of discrimination is part of the same movement that is carrying humanity toward a global civilization—a civilization that is the destroyer of those old particularisms, which had the honor of creating the aesthetic and spiritual values that make life worthwhile and that we carefully safeguard in libraries and museums because we feel ever less capable of producing them ourselves.

We are doubtless deluding ourselves with a dream when we think that equality and fraternity will some day reign among human beings without compromising their diversity. Humanity, however, if not resigned to becoming the sterile consumer of the values that it managed to create in the past, is capable only of giving birth to bastard works, to gross and puerile inventions, and must learn once again that all true creation implies a certain deafness to the appeal of other values, even going so far as to reject them if not denying them altogether. For one cannot fully enjoy the other, identify with him, and yet at the same time remain different. When integral communication with the other is achieved completely, it sooner or later spells doom for both his and my creativity. The great creative eras were those in which communication had become adequate for mutual stimulation by remote partners, yet was not so frequent or so rapid as to endanger the indispensable obstacles between individuals and groups or to reduce them to the point where overly facile exchanges might equalize and nullify their diversity.

Thus, humanity is exposed to a double peril, whose threat both the anthropologist and the biologist are measuring. Convinced that cultural evolution and organic evolution are linked, these scientists know that we cannot return to the past, but also that the road we are taking today is so fraught with tension that racial hatreds offer but a meager image of the regime of exacerbated intolerance that might be established tomorrow, without even having to use ethnic differences as a pretext. To circumvent these perils—the ones facing us today and the even more ominous ones looming in the near future—we must understand that their causes are far deeper than those rooted simply in ignorance and prejudice. We can pin our hopes only on a change in the course of history—even harder to achieve than progress in the development of ideas.

Chapter 2

The Anthropologist and the Human Condition

ETHNOLOGY—or anthropology, to use the more current term—takes man as its object of study but differs from the other sciences of man in striving to understand that object in its most diverse manifestations. Hence, for anthropology, the idea of the human condition still has a certain ambiguity: by its generality, this term seems to ignore—or, at least, to reduce to a unit the differences that anthropology's essential goal has been to point out and isolate in order to underscore special characteristics; but, in so doing, anthropology postulates an implicit criterion—the human condition itself—which is the only thing that enables this science to circumscribe the outer limits of its subject matter.

All intellectual traditions, including ours, have been faced with this difficulty. The population groups studied by anthropologists grant the dignity of a truly human condition only to their own members and place outsiders on an animal level. This practice occurs not only among so-called primitive people but also in ancient Greece as well as ancient China and Japan; and, by a curious parallel, which requires closer study, all three of these cultures called other groups barbarians and likened their languages to the chirping of birds. And it should not be forgotten that for classical humanism, the goal of culture (whose original meaning, and for a long time its only meaning, was "farming, *cultivation* of the soil") was to perfect a savage nature—either of the soil or of the individual who was still "fallow." This perfectability would ultimately free the individual from the mental servitude inherent in his past and in his group, and enable him to reach a civilized state.

Even early anthropology did not hesitate to place the peoples it was studying into categories separate from ours. It put them closer to nature, as implied by the etymology of the term *savage** and, more explicitly, by the German term *Naturvolkern;*† or else it put them outside history by calling them "primitive" or "archaic," which was simply another way of denying them a name that would make them part of the human condition.

From its beginnings in the early nineteenth century until the first half of the twentieth, anthropological thinking focused largely on trying to find a way of reconciling the assumed unity of its subject matter with its diverse, and often incomparable, particular manifestations. For this purpose, the concept of civilization—connoting a set of general, universal, and transmissible abilities—had to give way to the concept of culture in its new meaning: it now signified particular life styles that are not transmissible, that can be grasped only as concrete products—skills, customs, folkways, institutions, beliefs—rather than as virtual capacities, and that correspond to observable *values* instead of to *truths* or presumed *truths*.

It would take too long to retrace the philosophical background of this development. Its origins are obviously twofold. First is the German historical school, which—from Goethe to Fichte, and from Fichte to Herder—gradually shifted from setting up generalizations to presenting differences instead of resemblances and defended, in opposition to the history of philosophy, the rights and virtues of the monograph. From this perspective, we should not forget that the great twentieth-century advocates of the thesis of cultural relativism—Franz Boas, Alfred Louis Kroeber, and, in part, Bronislaw Malinowski —had had a German training. A second trend goes back to British empiricism as formulated by John Locke and then Edmund Burke. Imported into France by Louis de Bonald, it blended with the ideas of Vico (that anti-Cartesian whose role as a forerunner of anthropological thinking is being discovered today) and turned into positivism, a school that was overly anxious to systematize the diverse modes of human thought and action on a still summary experimental foundation.

*From Latin *silva*, "woods, forest." (Trans.)
†"People in the natural state." (Trans.)

The Anthropologist and the Human Condition

As it has developed through the twentieth century, anthropology has primarily sought to find, in the notion of culture, a criterion for recognizing and defining the human condition; these efforts parallel the way in which Emile Durkheim and his school resorted to the concept of society during the same era and with a comparable goal. Now the concept of culture immediately raises two issues, which, if I may say so, derive from its use in both singular and plural. If *culture* in the singular—and even, perhaps, with a capital *C*—is the distinctive attribute of the human condition, what universal traits does it cover and how are we to define its nature? If, on the other hand, culture is manifest only in the prodigiously diverse forms illustrated, each in its own way, by the four or five thousand societies that exist or have existed on the earth and about which we possess useful information, are these forms wholly equivalent despite appearances, or are they subject to value judgments, which, in the affirmative, are bound to re-echo the very meaning of the notion of culture?

In 1917, in a famous article entitled "The Superorganic," the great American anthropologist Alfred Kroeber attempted to answer the first question. In his eyes, culture is a specific category, as distinct from life itself as life is distinct from inanimate matter. Each category implies the preceding one, but the passage from the one to the other is marked by significant discontinuity. Somewhat in the way that a coral reef is continuously made up of secretions from the individual beings it shelters—although it existed before its present occupants, which will in turn be replaced by others—so culture must be thought of as a concretion of skills, customs, ideas, and beliefs, no doubt engendered by individuals but always outlasting them.

As for the question of the equivalency of the various cultures, anthropology has traditionally replied with the theory of cultural relativism. Anthropologists do not deny the reality of progress or the possibility of comparing certain cultures with others—in terms not of overall structure but of isolated aspects. Still, it is felt that this possibility, even when restricted, remains subject to three limitations:

1. Incontestable when human evolution is viewed in a cursory fashion, progress nevertheless manifests itself only in particular sectors, and discontinuously at that, without affecting local stagnation and regression.
2. When examining and comparing in detail the pre-industrial societies which are its special province, anthropology has yet to come up with a method for arranging them all on a common scale.
3. Finally, anthropology admits itself to be incapable of making an intellectual or a moral judgment about the specific values of this or that system of beliefs or this or that social organization, since one of its basic assump-

tions is that the criteria of morality are always a function of the particular society in which they are articulated.

For almost fifty years now, cultural relativism, and the assumed separation it implies between nature and culture, have had the force almost of dogma. But this dogma has been gradually challenged on several fronts. First of all from within, because of oversimplifications attributable to the so-called functional school, which, chiefly with Malinowski, underestimates the differences between cultures, even reducing the diversity of customs, beliefs, and institutions to so many equivalent methods of satisfying the most elementary needs of the species, so that ultimately, according to this viewpoint, one could say that culture is nothing but an immense metaphor for reproduction and digestion.

On the other hand, out of a deep respect for the peoples they were studying, anthropologists were refusing to make comparative values of their cultures and ours at the very time when these peoples were achieving independence and seemed to have no doubts whatsoever, at least according to their leaders, about the superiority of Western culture. Their leaders, indeed, sometimes accused European anthropologists of insidiously prolonging colonial rule by focusing exclusively on, and thereby helping to perpetuate, antiquated practices, which were felt to be an obstacle to development. Thus, the dogma of cultural relativism was challenged by the very people for whose moral benefit the anthropologists had established it in the first place.

For the past quarter of a century or so, however, the notion of culture, the discontinuity of the superorganic, and the fundamental distinction between the domains of nature and culture have been enduring concerted attacks by specialists in adjacent disciplines, whose objections boil down to three categories of facts.

First of all, the discovery of the remains of tool-making hominidae in Eastern Africa seems to prove that culture anticipated *Homo sapiens* by several million years. Even a stone industry as complex as the Acheulean, hundreds of thousands of years ago, is now attributed to *Homo erectus*, who was already human, but whose skull shape was clearly different from ours.

More serious still is the discovery that chimpanzees living in the wild make and use primitive tools, and that captive chimpanzees and gorillas can be taught a sign language like that of deaf mutes or one based on manipulating tokens of different shapes and colors. In the eyes of some observers, these facts nullify the previously undisputed belief that tools and articulate speech are the two distinctive attributes of the human condition.

Finally, especially during the last fifteen or twenty years, a new discipline has been officially established in the United States—sociobiology, which challenges the very notion of the human condition. According to its founder, Edward O. Wilson, "Sociology and the other social sciences, as well as the humanities, are the last branches of biology waiting to be included in the modern synthesis" (1975, p. 4). An eminent specialist on the social life of insects, Wilson wrote a book on this topic in 1971. Next, he applied his conclusions to vertebrates and then—in the last part of his 1975 book and in his recent *On Human Nature* (1978)—to humanity itself.

This whole undertaking sets itself within the framework of neo-Darwinism—that is, Darwinism as illuminated and refined by genetics. Yet it would never have come about without a theory, advanced in 1964, that helped the British mathematician W. D. Hamilton feel able to resolve a difficulty in the Darwinian hypotheses. At the approach of a predator, the first jay to notice it utters a special cry to alert fellow jays, and a rabbit alerts other rabbits by thumping on the ground. One could cite other examples. Now how can we explain such altruistic behavior on the part of an individual animal, which exposes itself by signaling its presence and thereby risks becoming the first victim? The answer proposed is twofold: it has been assumed, first, that natural selection operates on the level of the individual rather than of the species; and, then, that an individual's biological interest is always and everywhere to assure the perpetuation and, if possible, the expansion of his genetic heritage. Now an individual that sacrifices itself for the good of close or even distant relatives, which carry all or some of the same genes, can—as often complicated calculations demonstrate—better assure the survival of its genetic heritage than if it alone escaped the destruction of all its kin. An individual shares half of its genes with its brothers and sisters, one fourth with its nephews and nieces, one eighth with its cousins. Its genetic heritage will therefore benefit if the individual sacrifices itself for at least three siblings, five nephews or nieces, or nine cousins. By coining the term *inclusive fitness*, American and British sociobiologists wanted to say that the *adaptation* of the individual in the most egoistic sense is defined in terms of the individual's genes and, as such, also *includes* the vectors of the same biological heritage.

On such a basis, everything becomes possible for the theoretician. A bee has half its genes in common with its mother, but three quarters with its sisters (owing to the haplodiploidy of the species: the males hatch from unfertilized eggs; the females, from eggs fertilized during the nuptial flight). Thus, each worker perpetuates its genotype more effectively by remaining sterile—a condition that allows it to rear its sisters instead of producing daughters.

Nothing could be more tempting than to extend this line of reasoning to human societies, in which much institutionalized behavior seems like an aberration from the point of view of classical Darwinism. One has only to reduce to inclusive fitness the whole complex of laws, customs, mores, and institutions so that they amount to so many devices at the individual's disposal to better perpetuate his or her genetic heritage. And if they do not, at least they will allow the individual to perpetuate more effectively the genetic heritage of his or her relatives. And if no relative appears on the horizon, as in the case of the soldier who sacrifices himself for his comrades—who have different genetic heritages—one will introduce, along with the hypothesis of "soft altruism," that of "hard altruism": that is, the sacrifice of a hero with the goal of maintaining and reinforcing a moral climate in which, in an undetermined future, the carriers of his genetic heritage will benefit from a similar sacrifice by a fellow citizen.

It is true that Wilson repeatedly claims that he is trying to explain only a part of culture, something like ten percent. Yet surprising assertions keep belying this show of modesty: for example, that the ideology of the rights of man stems directly from our mammal nature; that the sole function of morality is to keep genetic material intact; that art and religion can be systematically analyzed and explained as products of the evolution of the brain; and so on. Indeed, Wilson writes that "no species, ours included, possesses a purpose beyond the imperatives created by its genetic history" (1978, p. 2).

Homosexuality, however, poses a problem. How can genes predisposing their carriers to homosexuality be handed down if, by definition, homosexuals have no children? Imperturbable as ever, the sociobiologist replies that, in ancient societies, homosexuals, having no family responsibilities of their own, could all the more easily help their close relatives raise a larger number of children, who, in turn, contributed to spreading the family's genetic heritage. Colleagues of Wilson find a biological justification even for the infanticide of girls, as practiced in several societies: the girls who are spared have a biological advantage in that the oldest child in the family is a son, who will protect his younger sisters, make sure they get married, and obtain wives for his younger brothers (Alexander 1974, p. 370).

Young anthropologists are following suit by discovering biological reasons for the diverse—and not very natural—ways in which the populations they are studying think of kinship relations. Patrilineal societies do not recognize uterine kinship, while matrilineal societies have the reverse discrimination. Yet the recognized kin share the same genotype as the unrecognized ones. Be that as it may, we are told that unilineal descent offers such great advantages of simplicity and clarity that it allows millions of individuals to assure more effectively an adaptation that is always claimed to be inclusive, even though it actually excludes half their kin. On a matter closer to us, according to these authors, the meaning of revolutions is chiefly biological: as manifestations of competition between groups trying to control scarce or depleted resources, possession of which ultimately determines a group's reproductive capacity.

Clearly, such all-encompassing hypotheses can be used to explain anything—any situation and its opposite. This is both the advantage and the drawback of reductive theories. Psychoanalysis had already accustomed us to these balancing stunts in which, at the price of a certain dialectical agility, one is always assured of landing on one's feet.

But the arguments of the sociobiologists are not only simplistic; their very wording is self-contradictory. How could the ideology of the rights of man derive from our mammal nature (long gestation period, small broods helping to give each individual a special value) if —as Wilson himself remarks (1978, p. 198)—the idea of the rights of man is not universal but appeared as a recent invention of Euro-American civilization? Furthermore, to explain the persistence of the genes that he feels are responsible for homosexuality (and whose existence seems extremely hypothetical), Wilson is forced to postulate that "most of the pleasures of human sex constitute primary reinforcers to facilitate bonding," and that they are only secondarily a means of assuring procreation (p. 141). He then concludes that Judaism and Christianity, especially the Catholic Church, have understood nothing of "the biological significance of sex" (p. 141). Yet what success Christianity has had from a sociobiological point of view!

Sociobiological thinking has an even more serious and apparently fundamental contradiction. It asserts, on the one hand, that all forms of the mind's activity are determined by inclusive fitness; and, on the other hand, that we can alter the fate of our species by deliberately choosing among the instinctive orientations that our biological past has transmitted to us. Yet the two things boil down to one: either the choices are themselves dictated by the demands of all-powerful inclusive fitness, and we are actually obeying it when we think we are choosing; or this possibility of choice is real, and nothing allows us to say that human destiny is ruled purely by our genetic heritage.

It is such lax thinking that is particularly disturbing in the sociobiologists. For, if their naïve and simplistic reflections did not push them to extremes—from their consideration of language in general, or from the general aptitude for culture, to the exorbitant claim for their being a genetic source for the particular characteristics of a given culture—then we could readily agree with them that research into the innate and the acquired in the human condition is of cardinal importance; and that it is possible to tackle this problem seriously now that the old physical anthropology and its racial hypotheses have given way to population genetics.

Regrettably, the debate on sociobiology instantly took a passionate turn, whose largely artificial character certainly sprang from the fact that, in France, leftist authors were the first to be captivated by sociobiology, which they saw as virtually a neo-Rousseauian way of integrating man into nature. At the same time, liberal factions in the United States were denouncing sociobiology as a neo-fascist doctrine and all but prohibited any research that aimed at finding hereditary and distinctive characteristics in man. Needless to say, these political positions were aligned on both sides of the Atlantic, but nothing would be more deplorable for the progress of knowledge than to decree any subject taboo in this or any other domain.

Today, advances in neurology give hope of resolving very old philosophical problems, such as the origin of geometric notions. But if first the eye and then the lateral geniculate bodies* do not photograph objects but react selectively to abstract relationships—a horizontal, a vertical, or an oblique direction; the contrast between a figure and its background; and other such primary data from which the cortex

*The lateral geniculate bodies are areas in the thalamus with nerve cells that receive impulses from the retina and, from there, transmit them to the occipital cortex. (Ed.)

reconstructs objects—it therefore no longer makes sense to ask whether geometric notions belong to a world of Platonic ideas or are drawn from experience: these notions are inscribed in the body. Likewise, if the universality of articulate speech in man is due to the existence of certain cerebral structures peculiar to our species, then, like these structures themselves, the aptitude for articulate speech must have a genetic basis.

One has no right to place limits on research of this type, provided that one always understands that the problems raised by the diversity of human groups require a prudence that researchers have all too often lacked. Even in cases where certain observable phenomena depend directly or indirectly on genetic factors, one must realize that these factors consist of infinitely complex dosages that the biologist confesses himself incapable of defining or analyzing.

Above all, we must never forget that while at the beginning of human life, biological evolution may have selected pre-cultural traits —for example, erect posture, manual skill, sociability, symbolic thinking, the ability to vocalize and communicate—determinism very quickly began to work in the opposite direction. Unlike most sociobiologists, geneticists fully realize that every culture—with its physiological and technological constraints, its marriage rules, its moral and esthetic values, its greater or lesser openness to immigrants—exercises upon its members a selection pressure that is much more lively, and whose effects are felt much sooner, than the slow motion of biological evolution. To take an overly simple example: it is not the gene for resistance to polar temperatures (assuming the gene exists) that gave the Inuit Eskimos their culture; rather, it was their culture that favored individuals with the greatest resistance to cold and handicapped the others. The cultural forms adopted in various places by human beings, their past or present ways of life, determine the rhythm and the direction of their biological evolution, rather than vice versa. Thus, far from having to wonder whether culture is or is not a function of genetic factors, it is the selection of these factors, their relative dosage, and their reciprocal arrangements that are one effect among others of culture.

Sociobiologists reason as if the human condition obeyed only two kinds of motivation: one kind unconscious and determined by genetic heritage; the other deriving from rational thought. However, even in sociobiological terms, it is hard to understand why the second type cannot be reduced to the first. Indeed, we are told, the man who does not know what he is doing has a genetic advantage over the one who does know; for the former benefits if his selfish motive is viewed by both others and himself as altruism (Alexander 1974, p. 337). Along with this selfish calculation, to which all unconscious human behavior is reduced, and which oddly conjures up the specter of the old *Homo oeconomicus*, transformed today into *Homo geneticus*—the one adding up his gains; the other, his genes—is the misunderstanding that the essence of the human condition is to be found entirely within a third category—that of culture, to which we return after a long detour.

Culture is neither natural nor artificial. It stems from neither genetics nor rational thought, for it is made up of rules of conduct, which were not invented and whose function is generally not understood by the people who obey them. Some of these rules are residues of traditions acquired in the different types of social structure through which, in the course of a very long history, each human group has passed. Other rules have been consciously accepted or modified for the sake of a specific goal. Yet there is no doubt that, between the instincts inherited from our genotype and the rules inspired by reason, the mass of unconscious rules remains more important and more effective; because reason itself, as Durkheim and Mauss understood, is a product rather than a cause of cultural evolution.

This is true even if the demarcation line between nature and culture seems more tenuous and sinuous today than we once fancied. Elements of what we view as culture appear here and there, though disjointed and dispersed, in various animal families. Chamfort has stated, "Society is not, as is usually believed, the development of nature, but its decomposition. It is a second edifice, built with the rubble of the first" (1982, p. 23).* What characterizes man is thus not so much specific elements as their synthesis in an organized whole. Man and the chimpanzee share the same chromosomes in a 9-to-10 ratio, and one must consider the arrangement of their respective chromosomes in any attempt to explain the differences in skills that separate the two species.

It is not enough, however, to define culture in terms of formal properties. If we are to see it as the essential attribute of the human condition, in all eras and among all peoples, then culture should, as a rule, have roughly the same content. In other words, are there *universals* in culture? Vico, who seems to have been the first to ask this question, discerned three universals: religion; marriage, together with

*Nicolas de Chamfort (1741–94) was a French writer noted for his wit and is best known for his *Maximes*, which were published after his death during the French Revolution. (Ed.)

an incest taboo; and burial of the dead. While these traits may be universal in the human condition, they do not teach us much: all nations in the world have religious beliefs and marriage rules. It is not enough to establish this fact; we must also understand why these beliefs and rules differ from one society to the next, why they are sometimes contradictory. Concern for the dead—whether fear or respect—is universal. It sometimes manifests itself, however, in practices aimed at removing the dead, who are considered dangerous, once and for all from the world of the living; and sometimes, on the contrary, by actions aimed at holding onto the dead, at constantly involving them in the struggles of the living.

By scrutinizing hundreds of population groups, anthropologists—especially Americans—have greatly enriched our inventory and drawn up a list of universal traits: age rankings, sports, dress, calendar, standard of bodily cleanliness, collective organization, cooking, cooperative work, cosmology, politeness, dance, decorative art, and so on. In addition to the oddity of being put, by the analysts, in alphabetical order, these widely heterogeneous traits are vague and meaningless. As posed by anthropologists today, the problem of culture—hence, the problem of the human condition—is to discover the consistent laws underlying the observable diversity of beliefs and institutions.

The languages of the world differ to varying degrees in phonetics and grammar; yet, however remote they may be, they obey restraints that are themselves universal. In any language, the presence of certain phonemes involves or excludes other phonemes: no language has nasal vowels if it does not also have oral ones; the presence of two opposing nasal vowels in a language implies that two oral vowels can be defined by the same opposition; and the presence of nasal vowels implies that of nasal consonants. No language distinguishes the phonemes *u* and *i* if it does not also possess a phoneme *a* to which the other two are opposed.

Many languages form the plural by adding a morpheme to a noun; no language does the opposite. A language having one word for *red* is bound to have a pair of words for *white* and *black*, or *light* and *dark*; if there is a word for *yellow*, there will be one for *red*; and so on. Investigations seem to show that, in any language, the presence of a word for *square* presupposes a word for *circle*.

Early in my career, I studied the rules of marriage. I endeavored to show that rules that seem to be the most contradictory actually illustrate various modalities of exchange of women between human groups —whether the process be direct, reciprocal, or otherwise—following long or short cycles of reciprocity, which can be determined, despite the apparent diversity of beliefs and customs.

Subsequent chapters will illustrate this process. We will also see how contemporary anthropology endeavors to discover and formulate such systematic laws in several aspects of human thought and activity. Unvarying throughout eras and cultures, these laws alone will enable us to surmount the apparent antinomy between the uniqueness of the human condition and the apparently inexhaustible quantity of forms it offers us.

PART II

FAMILY, MARRIAGE,

KINSHIP

Il est peu d'occupations aussi intéressantes, aussi attachantes, aussi pleines de surprises et de révélations pour un critique, pour un rêveur dont l'esprit est tourné à la généralisation, aussi bien qu'à l'étude des détails, et, pour mieux dire encore, à l'idée d'ordre et de hiérarchie universelle, que la comparaison des nations et de leurs produits respectifs.

BAUDELAIRE

Exposition universelle de 1855

Chapter 3

The Family

SO PLAIN seems the word *family*, and so close to daily experience is the reality to which it refers, that one may expect to be confronted in this chapter with a simple situation. Anthropologists, however, discover complications even in "familiar" things. As a matter of fact, the comparative study of the family has given rise to bitter arguments among anthropologists and has resulted in a spectacular reversal of anthropological thought.

During the second half of the nineteenth century and the beginning of the twentieth, anthropologists, influenced by biological evolutionism, were trying to organize in a unilineal sequence the institutions that they observed throughout the world. Departing from the assumption that our own institutions are the most complex and evolved, they saw, in the modern institutions of so-called primitive people, the image of institutions that could have existed in prehistoric periods. And since the modern family is founded essentially on monogamous marriage, these anthropologists immediately inferred that savage societies—equated, for the purpose of their argument, with the societies of man at the beginning of his existence—could only have institutions of an exactly opposite type.

It was thus necessary to gather and distort facts to fit the hypotheses. Fanciful "early" stages of evolution were invented—such as "group marriage" and "promiscuity"—to account for the period when man was still so barbarous that he could not possibly conceive of the niceties of the social life it is the privilege of civilized man to enjoy.

Assigned its predetermined place and properly labeled, every custom different from our own could illustrate one of the stages encountered by humanity from its origin to our own day.

This position became ever less tenable in proportion to anthropology's accumulation of new findings. These demonstrated that the style of family characterized, in contemporary society, by monogamous marriage, by independent establishment of the young couple, by warm relationships between parents and offspring, and so on (traits that we sometimes have difficulty disentangling from the intricate skein that the customs of savage peoples present to our eyes) exists clearly also among those societies that remained on, or returned to, a cultural level that we judge rudimentary. To cite a few examples, the insular Andamanese of the Indian Ocean, the Fuegians of the southernmost tip of South America, the Nambikwara of central Brazil, and the Bushmen of South Africa lived in small, semi-nomadic bands; they had little or no political organization; and their technological level was very low: some of these people had no knowledge of weaving or did not practice pot making or construct permanent dwellings. Among them, however, the only social structure worthy of the name was the family, often even the monogamous family. The fieldworker had no trouble identifying married couples, who were closely united by sentimental bonds, by economic cooperation in every case, and by a common interest in their children.

The conjugal family thus predominates at the two ends of the scale on which one can arrange human societies according to their degree of technical and economic development. This fact has been interpreted in two ways. In societies that they place at the bottom of the scale, some writers have seen the ultimate evidence of a sort of golden age, which would have prevailed before men suffered the hardships and were exposed to the perversions of a more civilized life. At this archaic stage, it is claimed, humanity knew the benefits of the monogamous family, only to forget it later until Christianity rediscovered it. But if we except the Vienna school (whose position I have just stated), the general trend is rather to acknowledge that family life is present everywhere in human societies, even in those whose sexual and educational customs seem the most remote from our own. Thus, after having claimed for nearly a century that the family, as modern societies know it, is a relatively recent development, the outcome of a slow and lengthy evolution, anthropologists now lean toward the opposite conviction: the family—based on a union, more or less durable, but socially approved, of two individuals of opposite sexes who establish a household and bear and raise children—appears to be a practically universal phenomenon, present in every type of society.

These extreme positions suffer from simplicity. We know cases—rare, it is true—where family bonds as we conceive of them seem not to exist. Among the Nayar, an important large group living on the Malabar coast of India, the men, engrossed in war, could not establish a family. A purely symbolical ceremony, marriage did not create permanent ties between spouses: the married woman had as many lovers as she wished; and the children belonged to the maternal line. Family authority and property rights were exercised not by the ephemeral husband—a negligible person—but by the wife's brothers. Since land was cultivated by an inferior caste, subservient to the Nayar, a woman's brothers were as completely free as her insignificant husband to devote themselves to military activities.

Bizarre institutions have frequently been misunderstood by being viewed as the vestige of an archaic social organization, once common in most societies. Highly specialized, the Nayar are the product of a long historical evolution and can teach us nothing about the early stages of humanity. On the other hand, there is little doubt that the Nayar represent an extreme form of a tendency that is far more frequent in human societies than is generally believed.

Without going as far as the Nayar, some human societies restrict the role of the conjugal family: they recognize it, but only as one pattern among others. Such is the case in Africa, among the Masai and the Chagga, whose youngest class of adult men were dedicated to warlike activities, lived in military settings, and established very free emotional and sexual relations with the corresponding class of adult girls. It was only after this active period that the men could marry and start a family. In such a system, the conjugal family existed side by side with institutional promiscuity.

For different reasons, the same dual pattern prevailed among the Boróro and other tribes of central Brazil, and among the Muria and other tribes of India and Assam. All the known instances could be arranged in such a way as to make the Nayar represent the most consistent, systematic, and logically extreme case. But the tendency that it illustrates is manifested elsewhere, and one sees it reappear in embryonic form even in modern societies.

Such was the case of Nazi Germany, where the family unit was beginning to split: on the one hand, the men dedicated to political and military work and enjoying a special prestige that allowed them a wide latitude of behavior; on the other hand, the women, whose vocation consisted of the three *K*'s—*Küche, Kirche, Kinder* (that is "kitchen," "church," and "children"). Had this separation of masculine and feminine functions been maintained for several centuries, along with the increasing inequality of their respective states, it could very well have led to a social organization without a recognized family unit, as among the Nayar.

Anthropologists have taken great pains to show that, even among people who practice wife lending (during religious festivals or, on a more regular basis, between bereaved couples and including such reciprocal rights), these customs do not constitute survivals of "group marriage": they coexist with the family and involve it. It is true that, in order to be able to lend a wife, a man must first have one. However, several Australian tribes, such as the Wunambal of the northwestern part of the continent, judge as "very greedy" a man who would refuse to lend his wife to other potential husbands during the ceremonies: that is, he would be trying to keep for himself a privilege that, in the eyes of the group, could be shared by all those, however many they might be, who are equally entitled to it. As this attitude exists along with an official denial of physiological paternity, these groups doubly deny any bond between the husband and his wife's children. The family is no more than an economic association to which the man brings the products of his hunt and the woman those of her collecting and gathering. The theory that this social unit, founded on loans of reciprocal services, proves that the family exists everywhere, is no sounder than the theory that the "family" thus defined has little but its name in common with the family in today's accepted meaning of the term.

It is advisable to be prudent also in respect to the polygamous family: that is to say, where there prevails sometimes *polygyny* (the union of one man with several wives) and sometimes *polyandry* (the union of one wife with several husbands). These general definitions must be examined in detail. Sometimes the polygamous family consists of several monogamous families side by side: the same man has several wives, each living in a separate dwelling with her children. This situation has been observed often in Africa. On the other hand, among the Tupi-Kawahib of central Brazil, a chief may marry, simultaneously or in sequence, several sisters or a mother and her daughters by a former marriage. These women raise their respective children together without seeming to mind very much whether they are caring for their own children. Also, the chief willingly lends his wives to his younger brothers, to his companions, or to passing visitors. Here we have a combination of polygyny and polyandry, which the kinship ties between the co-wives complicate further. I have witnessed, among the Indians, a mother and her daughter, married to one man; together they took care of children who were, at the same time, stepchildren to both, grandchildren to one, and half-brothers or half-sisters to the other.

As for polyandry proper, it may sometimes take extreme forms, as among the Toda of India, where several men, usually brothers, shared the same wife. At the time of a birth, the legal father was the one who performed a special ceremony, and he remained the legal father of all the children to be born until another husband decided, in his turn, to fulfill the rites of paternity. In Tibet and Nepal, polyandry seems to be explained by sociological reasons of the same type as those already encountered among the Nayar: for men obliged to pursue the wandering life of guides or bearers, polyandry offers the opportunity for there to be, at all times, on the spot, at least one husband to take care of domestic affairs.

Neither polyandry nor polygyny prevents the family from keeping its legal, economic, or even sentimental identity. What happens when the two patterns coexist? Up to a certain point, the Tupi-Kawahib illustrate this concurrence. The chief, as we have seen, exercises the right of polygamy and lends his wives to several categories of individuals who may or may not be members of his tribe. The bond between the spouses differs more in degree than in kind from other bonds, which can be arranged in descending order, from regular, to semipermanent, to occasional ones. However, even in this case, only true marriage determines the children's status, starting with their clan membership.

The evolution of the Toda during the nineteenth century comes closer to what has been called "group marriage." The Toda practiced a form of polyandry facilitated by the custom of female infanticide, which created from the start an imbalance between the sexes. When this custom was prohibited by the British administration, the Toda continued to practice polyandry, with the differences that, rather than sharing one wife, it became possible for them to marry several. As in the case of the Nayar, the types of organization that seem remotest to the conjugal family occur not in the more savage and archaic societies but in the relatively recent and extremely sophisticated forms of social development.

It would thus be wrong to approach the study of the family in a dogmatic spirit. At each instant, the object that one thinks is in one's hands slips away. We do not know anything important about the types of social organization that prevailed in the very early stages of the history of humanity. Even for the Upper Paleolithic, ten thousand to twenty thousand years ago—aside from works of art, which are difficult to interpret—skeletal remains and stone implements provide little information about social organization and customs. Also, when one considers the immense range of human societies about which, since Herodotus, we have data, all that can be said from the perspective that concerns us here is that the conjugal family occurs frequently and that it seems absent, in general, in highly evolved societies and not, as one might have expected, in the most rudimentary and simple ones. On the other hand, there do exist types of non-conjugal family (whether polygamous or not); this fact alone can persuade us that the conjugal family does not emerge from a universal necessity; a society can conceivably exist and be maintained without it. Hence, the problem: if the universality of the family is not the effect of a natural law, how are we to explain that the family is found almost everywhere?

To progress toward a solution, let us try to define the family, not in an inductive way, by adding information gathered from the most diverse societies, nor by limiting ourselves to the situation that prevails in our own, but by constructing a model reduced to a few invariable properties, or distinctive characteristics, that a rapid survey has allowed us to discern.

1. The family originates in marriage.
2. It includes the husband, the wife, and the children born of their union, forming a nucleus around which other relatives can eventually gather.
3. The members of the family are united among themselves by:
   a. Legal bonds.
   b. Rights and obligations of an economic, a religious, or some other nature.
   c. A precise framework of sexual rights and prohibitions, and a variable and diversified group of feelings, such as love, affection, respect, fear, and so on.

I shall examine these three aspects of the family in order.

I have distinguished between two broad types of marriage—monogamous and polygamous; and it must be emphasized that the first, by far the most common, is still more so than a rapid survey would lead one to think. Among the so-called polygamous societies, a fair number are so in the full sense of the term; but others distinguish between the "first" wife, who alone enjoys all the prerogatives of the matrimonial state, and "secondary" wives, who are scarcely more than official concubines. Moreover, in all polygamous societies, few men can, in fact, have several wives—as is easily understandable since, in any population, the number of men and women is approximately the same, with a difference of about ten percent in favor of one or the other sex. Polygamous practice thus depends on certain conditions: either the children of one of the two sexes are deliberately destroyed (a custom recorded in some cases, as in female infanticide among the Toda); or life expectancy differs according to sex (for example, among the Inuit or in several Australian tribes where men, exposed to the dangers of whale hunting or even war, die younger than women. It is necessary also to consider those exceedingly hierarchical societies where a class, privileged by age or wealth or having magico-religious prerogatives, claims for itself a substantial fraction of the group's women at the expense of younger members or those less well-off.

We know societies, especially in Africa, where it is necessary to be rich to have many wives (as a bride-price must be paid), but where, at the same time, having several wives allows a man to enrich himself still more: he disposes thus of any surplus of manual labor, which is provided by the wives themselves and their children. Sometimes it is clear that the systematic practice of polygamy would be limited automatically by the structural modifications it imposes on society.

The predominance of monogamous marriage is thus not surprising. That monogamy is not an attribute of human nature is adequately attested by the existence of polygamy in many societies and under diverse forms. But if monogamy constitutes the most common form, it does so simply because, in a normal situation and in the absence of any disparity deliberately or accidentally introduced, every human group has about one woman for one man. For moral, religious, and economic reasons modern societies have institutionalized monogamous marriage (not without contriving all sorts ways of getting around the rule: premarital freedom, prostitution, adultery). In societies where no prejudice against polygamy exists, or that even honor it, the lack of social standing or economic means can lead to the same result: each man has neither the means nor the power to acquire for himself more than one wife; he must therefore make a virtue of necessity.

Whether marriage is monogamous or polygamous (and in the latter case, polygynous or polyandrous, or even both at once); whether one union is the result of free choice, accords with a prescriptive or preferential rule, or obeys the will of ancestors: in every case, a distinction is clearly determined between marriage as a legal bond, socially approved, and temporary or permanent unions resulting from violence or consent. It matters little whether group intervention is explicit or tacit; what matters is that each society has at its command a means of differentiating between *de facto* unions and legal ones—a means arrived at in several ways.

On the whole, human societies put a high price on the conjugal state. Wherever there exist age rankings, under a loose or an institutionalized form, the tendency is to assign to one category the young adolescent boys and the adult bachelors; to another, older adolescents and childless husbands; to a third, married adults in full possession of their rights, generally after the birth of the first child. This threefold distinction has been recognized not only among many so-called primitive peoples but also by peasant communities of western Europe, if only on the occasion of feasts and ceremonies, up to the beginning of the twentieth century. Even today, in the south of France, the terms *jeune homme* ("young man") and *célibataire* ("bachelor") are often taken as synonyms (as are, in standard French, the terms *garçon* ["boy"] and *célibataire*, with the result that the current, but already significant, expression *un vieux garçon* ["an old boy"] becomes, still more revealingly, *un vieux jeune homme* ["an old young man"]).

In most societies, the bachelor appears repugnant and even contemptible. It is scarcely an exaggeration to say that bachelors do not exist in illiterate societies, for the simple reason that they could not survive. I remember having one day noticed, in a Bororó village of central Brazil, a man about thirty years old, who was carelessly dressed and appeared to be badly nourished, sad, and solitary. I thought at first he was sick. "But no," was the answer to my question, "he is a bachelor." And it is true that, in a society where work is apportioned between the sexes, and where only the conjugal state permits a man to enjoy the products of women's labor—including delousing, other care of the hair, and body painting, in addition to gardening and cooking (since the Bororó woman cultivates the soil and makes the pots)— a bachelor is half a human being.

What is true of the bachelor is true also, to a lesser degree, of the childless couple. Without doubt the spouses can lead a normal life and provide for their needs; but many societies deny them full status not only in the bosom of the group but beyond the group, in that society of ancestors as important as, if not more so than, the living; because no one who lacks the cult of self provided by descendants can hope to achieve the rank of ancestor. Finally, the orphan shares the lot of the bachelor. Some languages make the two words their most serious insults; bachelors and orphans are sometimes equated with cripples and sorcerers, as if their conditions resulted from the same supernatural curse.

Society has come to express in a solemn manner its interest in the marriage of its members. So it is among us, where prospective spouses, if of legal age, must first publish banns and next secure the services of an authorized representative of the group to celebrate their union. Our society is certainly not the only one that subordinates agreement between individuals to public authority; but more often, marriage concerns not so much private persons, on the one hand, and the whole society, on the other, as more or less inclusive communities upon which each individual depends—families, lineages, clans; and it is between these groups, not between individuals, that marriage creates a bond. There are several reasons for this situation.

Even societies on a very low technical and economic level attribute so great an importance to marriage that parents are very soon concerned to find a match for their children, who are thus promised from their early youth. Moreover, by a paradox to which I must return, if each marriage gives birth to a family, it is the family or, rather, families that promote marriage as the principal socially approved device by which they are prepared to ally themselves with each other. As they say in New Guinea, the aim of marriage is not so much to acquire a wife for oneself as to obtain brothers-in-law. As soon as one recognizes that marriage unites groups rather than individuals, one is enlightened about many customs. One understands why, in several regions of Africa which trace descent according to the paternal line, marriage becomes final only when the wife has given birth to a son: under this condition only has the marriage fulfilled its function, which is to perpetuate the husband's line. The levirate and the sororate spring from the same principles: if marriage creates a bond between groups, a group can be logically required to replace, with a brother or a sister, the defaulting spouse it has originally furnished. On the death of the husband, the levirate provides that his unmarried brothers have a preferential right to his widow (or, as it is sometimes expressed, a duty, shared among the surviving brothers, to take charge of the widow and her children). Likewise, the sororate provides the sisters of the wife a preferential right if the marriage is polygamous or, in a case of monogamy, permits a husband to demand a sister in place of his wife if the latter is sterile, if her conduct justifies divorce, or if she dies. But, in whatever way society affirms its investment in the marriage of its members—through the channel of particular groups to which they belong or, more directly, through the intervention of the state—it remains true that marriage is not, never has been, and cannot be a private affair.

It is necessary to refer to cases as extreme as that of the Nayar in order to find societies where there does not exist, at least temporarily, a *de facto* union between husband, wife, and children. But let us be careful to note that while this nucleus constitutes the legal family among us, many societies have decided otherwise. Whether by instinct or by ancestral tradition, the mother takes care of her children and is happy to do so. Psychological tendencies also probably explain why a man, living in intimacy with a woman, feels affection for the children who are born to her, and whose physical and mental development he follows with interest even if he is officially denied any role in their procreation. Some societies seek to incorporate these feelings through such customs as the *couvade:* that the father shares symbolically in the indispositions (natural or imposed by custom) of the woman who is pregnant or in labor has often been explained by the need to integrate tendencies and attitudes that, in and of themselves, do not seem particularly homogeneous.

The great majority of societies, however, do not waste much interest on the nuclear family, which is important among some of them, including our own. As a general rule, as we have seen, it is the groups who count, not particular unions between individuals. Moreover, many societies are committed to assigning children either to the father's kinship group or to the mother's and succeed in sharply distinguishing the two types of bond, in order to recognize one to the exclusion of the other or else to allocate to them distinct areas of rights and obligations. Sometimes property rights are inherited in one line, religious privileges and obligations in the other; sometimes social status and magic lore are distributed in parallel fashion. There are countless examples of such patterns, from Africa, Asia, America, or Oceania. To cite but one, the Hopi Indians of Arizona carefully distribute different types of legal and religious rights between the paternal and the maternal lines; but at the same time, the frequency of divorce renders the family so unstable that many fathers do not live under the same roof as their children, because the houses belong to the wives, and the children's property rights follow the maternal line.

The brittleness of the conjugal family, apparently very common in societies that anthropologists study, does not prevent these societies from attaching some value to marital fidelity and to affection between parents and children. But these moral ideals are accounted for in another way than are the rules of law, which often trace kinship exclusively in the paternal or the maternal line, or else distinguish rights and obligations as respectively affected by each line. We know extreme cases, such as that of the Emerillon, a little tribe of French Guiana, which about thirty or forty years ago had no more than about fifty members. At this time, marriage was so precarious that each individual could, in the course of life, have married in succession every one of the other sex: it was also reported that the language had special names to distinguish from which of at least eight consecutive unions the children had issued. This was probably a recent phenomenon, explainable by the lack of an effective group and by living conditions that had been profoundly altered for one or two centuries. But it is obvious from such examples that the conjugal family can become practically imperceptible.

On the other hand, other societies provide a broader and firmer base for the institution of the family. Thus, sometimes as late as the nineteenth century, there were several European regions where the family, the basic unit of society, was of a type that could be called domestic rather than conjugal. The eldest living male, or a community of brothers born of the same dead ancestor, held all the property rights, exercised authority over the whole family group, and oversaw agricultural tasks. In the Russian *bratsvo*, the *zadruga* of the Slavs of the south, and the French *maisie*, large families consisted of a dominant elder and his brothers, his sons, nephews, and grandsons and their wives, his unmarried daughters, nieces, and granddaughters, and so on down to the great-grandchildren. Such arrangements are called, in English, "joint families" and, in French, *familles étendues* ["extended families"] and include up to several dozens of people who live and work under a common authority: these are convenient but deceptive terms, because they imply that these large units are, from the beginning, composed of several little conjugal families in association. But, even among ourselves, the conjugal family has been legally recognized only after a complex historical evolution, attributable in part only to the gradual recognition of its natural base; because this evolution has, above all, consisted of the dissolution of the extended family, so that of it there remains only a nucleus which has little by little acquired a legal status that used to be vested in much vaster conglomerations. In this sense, such terms as "joint" or "extended" family might be appropriately discarded. It is rather the conjugal family that could be called "restricted."

We have seen that when the family fills a tenuous functional role, it tends to descend even below the conjugal level. In the opposite case, it is effective above that level. So far as it exists in our societies, the conjugal family is thus not the expression of a universal need and is no longer inscribed in the depths of human nature: it is a halfway measure, a certain state of equilibrium between patterns that are in opposition to one another and that other societies have positively preferred.

To complete the picture, it is necessary finally to consider the cases where the conjugal family exists, but under forms that we would doubtless not be the only ones to judge incompatible with the aims that human beings conceive as the basis of the household. The Chukchee of eastern Siberia do not view as unsuitable a marriage between a girl about twenty years old and a baby boy of two or three years. The young woman, often already a mother if she has lovers, raises her child and her little husband together. In North America, the Mohave observe the opposite practice: an adult man marries a baby girl and cares for her until she is old enough to fulfill her marital duties. Such marriages are considered very sound: the memory of the paternal attention lavished by the husband on his little wife reinforces, it is believed, the natural affection between the spouses. Similar cases are known in the Andean and the tropical regions of South America and also in Melanesia.

However bizarre they appear to us, these types of marriage still respect the difference between the sexes, an essential condition in our eyes (although homosexual demands are beginning to undermine it) for the establishment of a family. But, in Africa, women of high rank often had the right to marry other women whom authorized lovers made pregnant. The noblewoman became the legal "father" of the children and, rigorously following the patrilineal rule, passed on to them her name, her rank, and her property. In other cases, the conjugal family served to procreate children but not to raise them, because families competed among themselves to adopt children (from a higher rank, if possible); a family thus sometimes bespoke the child of another family from before its birth. The custom was common in Polynesia and in a region of South America. The practice is comparable to that of entrusting boys to a maternal uncle, which has been recorded as occurring, up until recently, among the people of the northwestern coast of North America, and among the European nobility of the Middle Ages.

Over the centuries, Christian morality has considered sexual intercourse to be a sin unless it occurs within marriage and with the aim of founding a family. Here and there, other societies have assigned the same limits to legal sexuality, but these are rare. In most cases, marriage has nothing to do with sensual pleasure, because all sorts of possibilities for its satisfaction exist outside of marriage and sometimes in opposition to it. In central India, the Muria of Bastar put pubescent boys and girls into communal houses where they enjoy complete sexual freedom; but when the time comes for marriage, it is forbidden between those who were once lovers, so that, within the village community, each man marries a woman known to have been the mistress of one or even several of his neighbors.

In general, thus, sexual considerations interfere little in matrimonial plans. On the other hand, economic considerations are paramount, because it is above all the division of labor between the sexes that makes marriage indispensable. But, as with the family, the sexual division of labor rests on a social, rather than a natural, basis. Doubtless, in all human groups, women bring children into the world, nourish them, and care for them, while men are employed in hunting and going to war. Even this apparently natural separation of tasks, however, is not always rigid: men may not have babies but may, in societies that practice the *couvade,* act as if they do. And there is a great difference between a Nambikwara father who watches tenderly over his baby, cleaning it when it soils itself, and the European aristocrat whose children were, not so long ago, brought to him ceremoniously, for a few moments, from the women's quarters, where they were kept until they were old enough to learn horseback riding and fencing. On the other hand, the Nambikwara chief's young concubines disdain domestic work and prefer to accompany their husband on his adventurous expeditions. It is possible that a similar custom, notable among other South American tribes where a particular class of women—

half-courtesans, half-servants—remained celibate and followed the men to war, was the source of the legend of the Amazons.

When we turn to occupations that are less significantly contrasted than child rearing and war, it becomes still more difficult to make out the general rules that govern the division of work between the sexes. Boróro women till the soil; but among the Zuñi, the men do it; it varies from tribe to tribe whether the construction of houses, huts, or shelters, pot making, weaving, and basket making are the duties of one or the other sex. It is necessary thus to distinguish the *fact* of the division of labor, which is practically universal, from the *criteria* according to which, in one place or another, tasks are assigned to either sex. These criteria, too, spring from cultural factors: they are no less artificial than the forms of the family itself.

Again, we are confronted with the same problem. If natural reasons, which could explain the sexual division of labor, do not appear decisive once one leaves the solid ground of biological difference; if criteria for the division of labor vary from one society to another—why does it exist? I have already posed the same question in regard to the family: the fact of the family is universal; the forms it takes are scarcely relevant, at least in respect to any natural necessity. But, after having considered the different aspects of the problem, we are perhaps better able to perceive what they have in common and to discern some general characteristics that will begin to answer it. In the realm of social organization, the family appears to be a positive reality (some people would say the only one); and owing to this fact, we are persuaded to define it exclusively by its positive qualities. But each time we try to show what the family is, we are at the same time obliged to imply what it is not; and these negative aspects may be as important as the others. The same is true of the division of labor: to state that one sex is appointed to certain tasks amounts to stating that these are forbidden to the other sex. Viewed from this perspective, the division of labor establishes an interdependence between the sexes.

This reciprocity evidently also belongs to the sexual aspect of family life. We are not allowed to reduce it to this aspect, because, as we have seen, most societies do not establish between family and sexuality the intimate connection characteristic of our own. But, like the division of labor, the family can be defined by a negative function: always and everywhere, the existence of the family involves prohibitions that render certain unions impossible or at least condemned.

Restrictions on freedom of choice vary considerably from one society to another. In ancient Russia, there existed the custom of *snokatch-*

esvo, which accorded the father sexual rights over the young wife of his son. In other societies, the son of a sister exercised a symmetrical right over the wife of his maternal uncle. We ourselves no longer object to the remarriage of a man to his wife's sister, an incestuous practice under English law throughout the nineteenth century. At the very least, all known societies, past or present, assert that if the relation between spouses (and eventually several others, as we have just seen) implies reciprocal sexual rights, other kinship bonds—also serving the function of a family structure—make sexual relations immoral, subject to legal sanction, or simply inconceivable. The universal prohibition against incest specifies that individuals in the relation of parent and child or of brother and sister cannot have sexual relations or, even less, marry one another. Some societies—ancient Egypt, pre-Columbian Peru, several kingdoms in Africa, southeast Asia, and Polynesia—defined incest less strictly and permitted it (or even prescribed it), in certain forms, to the reigning family (in ancient Egypt, it was perhaps more common), but not without setting limits: the half-sister to the exclusion of the true one or, in the case of marriage with the true sister, the oldest to the exclusion of the youngest.

Since the original publication of this chapter in 1956, specialists in animal ethology have wished to find a natural basis for the incest prohibition. It seems that diverse species of social animals avoid mating with close kin, or that such unions rarely take place. This condition stems perhaps from the fact that the older males of the group expel the younger ones as soon as they become adults.

Assuming this data, unknown or incompletely published a quarter of a century ago, to be correctly interpreted by the observers, one would misunderstand, in extrapolating from it, the essential difference that separates animal behavior from human institutions: only the latter can systematically set up negative rules to create social bonds. What I have said about the sexual division of labor can help us grasp this point: just as the principle of the division of labor establishes an interdependence between the sexes, compelling them thereby to work together within the family, so the prohibition of incest establishes an interdependence between biological families and forces them to produce new families; and through these alone will the social group succeed in perpetuating itself.

One could have better understood the similarity between these two processes if they had not been labeled with such dissimilar terms as "division," on the one hand, and "prohibition," on the other. Had we called the division of labor "prohibition of tasks," only its negative aspect would have been perceived. Inversely, we would highlight the positive aspect of the incest prohibition if we defined it as "division of the rights of marriage between families," because the incest prohibition was established only so that families (however defined by each society) could intermingle, rather than each family, for its own benefit, with itself.

Nothing could thus be more wrong than to reduce the family to its natural base. It cannot be explained by either the instinct for procreation, or by the maternal instinct, or by ties of affection between husband and wife and between father and children, or by the combination of all these factors. As important as they are, these elements could not by themselves give rise to a family, and for a very simple reason: in all human societies, the absolute requirement for the creation of a new family is the previous existence of two other families, each prepared to furnish a man or a woman whose marriage would give rise to a third family, and so on indefinitely. In other words, what differentiates man from animal is that, in humanity, no family could exist if there were not first a society: a number of families who recognize that there exist other bonds than the blood tie, and that the natural process of filiation can be carried on only as integrated into the social process of marriage.

We shall probably never know how men came to recognize this social dependence of the natural order. Nothing permits the assumption that humanity, from the time it emerged from the animal condition, was not endowed with a form of social organization which, in its fundamental structure, scarcely differed from later ones. Indeed, it would be difficult to imagine any elementary social organization that lacked the incest prohibition. Because it remodels the biological conditions of mating and procreation, it allows families to perpetuate themselves only confined within an artificial framework of prohibitions and obligations. It is there alone that we can place the passage from nature to culture, from the animal condition to the human condition; and it is there alone that we can grasp their elaboration.

As Edward Burnett Tylor understood a century ago, the ultimate explanation is probably found in the fact that man knew very early that he had to choose between "either marrying-out or being killed-out" (1889, p. 267): the best, but not the only, way for biological families not to be driven to reciprocal extermination is to link themselves by ties of blood. Biological families that wished to live in isolation, side by side with one another, would each form a closed group, self-perpetuating and inevitably prey to ignorance, fear, and hatred. In opposing the separatist tendency of consanguinity, the incest prohibition succeeded in weaving the web of affinity that sustains societies and without which none could survive.

Although we do not yet know what exactly the family is, we have glimpsed so far its conditions of existence and the possible laws that govern its reproduction. In order to ensure the social interdependence of biological families, so-called primitive peoples have rules, which are simple or complex but always ingenious, and which are sometimes hard for us to understand, with our habit of thought being adapted to societies incomparably more dense and more fluid than theirs.

In order for us to ensure that biological families will not close in upon themselves and become so many isolated cells, it suffices to forbid marriage between very close relatives. Our large societies provide each individual with many opportunities for contacts beyond the restricted family and satisfactorily guarantee that the hundreds of thousands or the millions of families constituting a modern society will not run the risk of congealing. The freedom of choice of mate (except that one has to be outside the restricted family) ensures that the flow of exchanges between families will be kept open. An uninterrupted mixing will take place; and, from all those shuttlings, a homogeneous and well-blended social fabric will result.

Very different conditions prevail in so-called primitive societies. The overall population may vary from a few dozen to several thousand, but it remains small compared with ours. Moreover, a minimal social fluidity prevents each individual from meeting many others beyond the village or in the hunting grounds. Many societies try to multiply the opportunities for contact during feasts and tribal ceremonies. But these encounters remain, in general, circumscribed by the tribal circle, where most so-called primitive people see a sort of extended family at whose limits social relations stop. Often these people even go so far as to deny human dignity to their neighbors. There doubtless exist, in South America and in Melanesia, societies that prescribe marriage with foreign tribes and sometimes enemies; in such a case, explain natives of New Guinea, "one looks for a wife only among those with whom one is at war." But the network of intermarriage thus extended remains frozen in the traditional mold; and even if it includes several tribes instead of one, its rigid frontiers are rarely crossed.

Under such an arrangement, biological families can establish among themselves a homogeneous society through procedures similar to ours: that is to say, simply by prohibiting marriage between close relatives and without recourse to positive rules. Sometimes, in very small societies, this method is effective only if the inadequate size of the group and the lack of social mobility are compensated for by increasing the impediments to marriage. For a man, these will extend beyond mother, sister, and daughter to include all women with whom, however remotely, a kinship tie can be traced. These small groups characterized by a rudimentary cultural level and a relatively unstructured social and political organization (as are certain peoples of the semi-desert regions of the Americas) provide examples of this solution.

The great majority of so-called primitive peoples have adopted another method. Instead of trusting to probability again, so that there are enough impediments to marriage automatically to ensure exchanges between biological families, they have preferred to enact positive rules, constraining individuals and families, so that the one or the other form a particular kind of union.

In this case, the entire field of kinship becomes a kind of chessboard on which a complicated game unfolds. An adequate terminology assigns the members of the group to categories in accordance with these principles: that the category or categories of the parents determines directly or indirectly those to which their children belong; and that, following their respective categories, the members of the group can or cannot intermarry. Peoples who appear ignorant or savage have thus invented codes that we have trouble deciphering without the help of our best logicians and mathematicians. Rather than going into detail about these calculations, which are sometimes so long that one has to have recourse to computers, I shall limit myself to a few simple cases, beginning with marriage between cross-cousins.

This system separates collateral relatives into two categories: "parallel" collaterals, if their kinship is through siblings of the same sex (two brothers or two sisters); and "collateral" cross-cousins, if through siblings of opposite sexes. My paternal uncle and my maternal aunt are for me parallel relations; my maternal uncle and my paternal aunt, cross-relatives. The cousins issuing, respectively, from two brothers or two sisters are parallel to each other; those issuing, respectively, from a brother and a sister are crossed. In the following generation, the children of the sister (for a man) and those of a brother (for a woman) are cross-nephews and cross-nieces; they are parallel nephews and nieces if (for a man) they are born to his brother or (for a woman) to her sister.

Almost all the societies that apply this distinction equate parallel relatives with the closest relatives of the same generation: the brother of my father is a "father," and the sister of my mother, a "mother"; I call my parallel cousins "brothers" or "sisters," and I look on my parallel nephews as my own children. With all parallel kin, a marriage would be incestuous and, hence, forbidden. On the other hand, cross-relatives receive distinctive names; and it is among them that, as a duty or through a preference for non-relatives, that one chooses a spouse. Furthermore, often only one single word exists to designate one's female cross-cousin and one's wife as well as one's male cross-cousin and one's husband.

Certain societies push the distinction still farther. Some forbid marriage between cross-cousins and impose or authorize it only between their children—cross-cousins also, but in the second degree. Other societies elaborate on the notion of cross-cousins and subdivide these relatives into two categories: one including unions permitted or prescribed; the other, prohibited unions. Although the daughter of the maternal uncle and that of the paternal aunt are equally entitled to be cross-cousins, tribes have been found, established sometimes side by side, that forbid or prescribe either the one or the other. Certain tribes of India believe death preferable to the crime that, according to them, would be constituted by a marriage conforming to the rule of a neighboring tribe.

These distinctions, and others that could be cited, are difficult to explain by biological or psychological reasons and seem senseless. They are illuminated, however, by my previous discussion, and also when one remembers that the essential aim of impediments to marriage is to establish an interdependence between biological families. To put it in stronger terms, these rules express society's refusal to acknowledge the family as an exclusive reality. For all systems, complicated as they are by distinctions of terminology, by prohibitions, by prescriptions, or by preferences, are no more than processes for dividing families into rival or allied camps, who can and must take part in the great game of marriage.

Let us consider briefly the rules of this game. Every society first desires to reproduce itself; it must thus possess a rule to assign children the same status in the social structure as that of their parents' occupation. The so-called unilineal rule of descent is, in this respect, the simplest: it makes children members of the same subdivision of the whole society (family, line, or clan) as either their father and his male ancestors (patrilineal descent) or their mother and her female ancestors (matrilineal descent). The two functions can also be considered simultaneously or can be combined to define a third into which children are placed. For example, with a father from subdivision A and a mother from subdivision B, the children would belong to subdivision C; they would be in subdivision D if the situation were reversed. Individuals C and D could marry one another, and their children would be either A or B according to the status of their (the parents') respective assignations. One could spend one's spare time thinking up rules of this kind, and it would be surprising not to find at least one society that practiced them.

After the rule of descent has been determined, another question presents itself: Of how many exogamous groups is a particular society comprised? With marriage being forbidden by definition within the exogamous group, there must be at least one other group to which members of the first can apply to obtain a spouse. Each restricted family in our society constitutes an exogamous group; there are so many groups that the choice of spouse of each of its members can be left to chance. In so-called primitive societies, there are many fewer groups—partly because of the limited dimensions of the societies themselves, and also because the recognized ties of kinship stretch much farther than they do among us.

Let us first examine a society with unilineal descent and comprising only two exogamous groups, A and B. One solution is possible: the men from A marry the women from B; the women from A marry the men from B. One can thus imagine two men—from A and B, respectively—exchanging their sisters, each of whom would become the wife of the other man. If the reader is willing to use a piece of paper and a pencil to construct the hypothetical genealogy resulting from such an arrangement, he would establish firmly that, whatever might be the patrilineal or matrilineal rule of descent, the siblings and the parallel cousins will fall into one of two exogamous groups and the cross-cousins into the other. Hence, only cross-cousins (if the game is played between two or four groups) or the children of cross-cousins (for a game between eight groups; a game between six constitutes an intermediate case) will satisfy the initial condition that spouses must belong to distinct groups.

So far I have limited myself to examples of exogamous groups in even numbers—two, four, six, eight—and opposed two by two. What will happen if the society is composed of an odd number of groups?

According to the preceding rules, one group will remain, I dare say, "on the board," without a partner with whom to trade. It is necessary then to introduce other rules, capable of dealing with any number, odd or even, of parties engaged in matrimonial exchange.

These rules can take two forms: either the exchanges will remain simultaneous while becoming indirect, or they will remain direct but will then stretch out over time. Take the first type: group A gives its sisters or its daughters in marriage to group B; B to C; C to D; D to n; and finally n to A. When the cycle is completed, every group has given a woman and has received one, although it has not given to the same group as that from which it has received. An easy-to-follow scheme shows that, with this formula, one's parallel cousins fall as before into the same group as one's brothers and sisters; thanks to the rule of exogamy, they cannot marry each other. But—and it is the essential fact—cross-cousins subdivide into two categories according to whether they come from the mother's or the father's side. Thus, the female cross-cousin on the mother's side (that is, the mother's brother's daughter) will always fall into the group that provides wives (A, if I am B; B, if I am C; and so on); and, inversely, the female cross-cousin on the father's side (the father's sister's daughter) will always fall into the other group, to which my group gives wives, but from which it does not receive any (B, if I am A; C, if I am B; and so on). Thus, in such a system, it is normal for a man to marry a cross-cousin of the first type but against the rule to marry one of the second.

The alternative system keeps the exchange direct, but through consecutive generations: group A receives a wife from group B; in the following generation, group A returns to group B the daughter born from the previous marriage. If groups continue to be arranged in conventional order—A, B, C, D, n—in any generation, C, let us say, gives a wife to D and receives one from B; in the following generation, C repays B, so to speak, and gets its own return from D. Here again the patient reader will find out that cross-cousins are subdivided into two categories, but the reverse of the preceding way: the daughter of the paternal aunt is the permitted or prescribed spouse, while the daughter of the maternal uncle is prohibited.

Beside these relatively simple cases, all over the world there are still kinship systems and marriage rules about which we continue to speculate—such as those of the Ambrym in the New Hebrides and the Murngin or Miwuyt of northwestern Australia; and the whole complex of systems, principally North American and African, known as Crow-Omaha, named for the populations where those systems were first observed. But to decipher these and other codes, it is necessary to proceed as I have just done by considering that the analysis of kinship terms and of permitted, prescribed, or prohibited degrees reveals the mysteries of that very special game which consists, for members of an actual or reputed biological family, of exchanging women with other families—that is, breaking up families already established to create out of them others which, in time, will be broken up for the same ends.

This incessant work or destruction and reconstruction does not imply that descent is unilineal, as I assumed at the beginning in order to facilitate my exposition. It is enough that, by virtue of any principle —which may be unilineal descent but also, in a vague sense, ties of blood or other sorts of tie—a group that is losing a woman over whom it assumes authority considers itself owed a substitute woman, who comes from the same group as that to which it has ceded a daughter or a sister, or from a third group; in more general terms, the social rule provides that any individual can, in principle, marry beyond the prohibited degrees so as to establish and perpetuate among all the biological families interconnections that, in terms of the whole society, are approximately balanced.

Women readers, who may be shocked to see themselves reduced to being objects of exchange between male partners, can be reassured that the rules of the game would remain unchanged were the opposite convention adopted, with men being exchanged by women's groups. As a matter of fact, a few societies of a highly developed matrilineal type have, to a limited extent, expressed things that way. And both sexes can accommodate themselves to a slightly more complicated description of the game, which says that groups consisting of both men and women exchange among themselves kinship relations.

But from whatever perspective, the same conclusions must be drawn: the restricted family is no more the basic element of society than it is its product. It is more precise to say that society can exist only in opposition to the family while respecting its constraints: no society can maintain itself through time if women do not give birth to children; and if they do not benefit from male protection while carrying, nursing, and raising their children; and, finally, if precise sets of rules do not exist to perpetuate the basic pattern of the social fabric throughout the generations.

The Family

Society's primary social concern regarding the family, however, is not to honor it or to perpetuate it. Everything shows rather that society mistrusts the family and contests its right to exist as a separate entity. Restricted families are permitted to endure only for a limited time, either long or short according to the case, but on the strict condition that their component parts be ceaselessly displaced, loaned, borrowed, given away, or returned, so that new restricted families may be endlessly created before disintegrating in their turn. Thus, the relation between society as a whole and restricted families is not static, as is a house and the bricks it is built of; it is rather a dynamic process of tensions and oppositions which are always in precarious equilibrium. The point of equilibrium and the chances of its lasting vary endlessly according to time and place. But, in every case, the word of the Scriptures, "You will leave your father and your mother," provides the golden rule (or, possibly, the iron rule) for the establishment of any society.

If society belongs to the realm of culture, the family is, in the heart of social life, the emanation of those natural requirements without which there could be no society, and hence no mankind. As Bacon said, one can overcome nature only by submitting to its laws. Therefore, society has to give the family some recognition. And it is not so surprising that, as geographers have also shown in respect to the use of natural resources, the greatest compliance with the natural laws is likely to be found at both extremes of the scale on which one can order the economic and technological development of cultures. Those at the lower extreme are not in a position to pay the necessary price of breaking away from the natural order; those at the other end, instructed by past errors (at least one hopes they are), know that the best policy is the one that recognizes nature and its laws. Thus, the small, relatively stable, monogamous family occupies, both in societies judged very primitive and in modern societies, a bigger place than it does in what may be called (for the sake of argument) the intermediate levels.

Nonetheless, these shifts in the equilibrium point between nature and culture do not affect the whole picture. When one travels slowly and with great effort, halts should be long and frequent. And when one can travel often and fast, one should also stop often to catch one's breath. It is also true that the more roads there are, the more they are likely to intersect. Social life imposes on its individual members, and on the groups to which they are kin, an incessant changing of places. From this point, family life is little else than the expression of the need to slacken the pace at the crossroads and to take a little rest. But the orders are to keep on marching; and society can no more be said to consist of families than a journey is made up of the stopovers that break it into stages. One can say that families in any society are both its condition and its negation.

Chapter 4

An Australian "Atom of Kinship"

A NEW FASHION has been spreading among our English-language colleagues as they repudiate all the achievements of our discipline, revile its founders and the scholars who succeeded them, and insist that it is necessary to "rethink" anthropology from top to bottom, that nothing from its past remains valid. This rancor has been vented by turns on Frazer, Malinowski, Radcliffe-Brown, and several other anthropologists. Because of his position in Australian studies, Alfred R. Radcliffe-Brown has been a favorite target of young Australian anthropologists. It is sometimes amazing how his analyses and conclusions have been challenged in toto, and quite sharply, by investigators who, though often of the highest caliber, are condemned by current conditions to know only aboriginal groups whose traditional culture has greatly deteriorated. These groups are cooped up in missions, whose influence they have been absorbing for decades; or they lead precarious lives on the outskirts of cities, camping in vacant lots or between the tracks of some railroad yard. To such reservations, the detractors of Radcliffe-Brown cuttingly retort that the aborigines he met were as acculturated as those of today. Maybe so—but, even without any experience of Australian reality, we have the right to conjecture that a state of acculturation in 1910 was very different from one forty years later. For during these forty years, even in the absence of direct contact (which has been rare), Western civilization has been having an ever stronger impact on the aborigines. Throughout this period, the ecology, the demography, and the societies themselves have changed.

I shall try to show through a concrete example that, far from being invalidated by more recent research, old and new research can be used in a complementary way and that they enrich each other. In a paper published some years ago, a talented young anthropologist, David McKnight, confirmed at least on one point U. H. McConnel's account of the marriage rules among the Wikmunkan,* which remains of special interest to me as in the past I have relied extensively upon her work. McKnight (1971, p. 163) states that, beside marriage with a cross-cousin, marriage with a classificatory daughter's daughter may also take place. Limiting oneself to misapprehensions over McConnel's work (and leaving aside at this time misapprehensions over my own work),† some of the former stem from the fact that, in an alternate generation system (of which there are several indications in Wikmunkan nomenclature), terminological equations recur at intervals. Therefore no logical contradiction is involved in the statement that a man marries either a cross-cousin or a daughter's daughter—not the true granddaughter, of course, as I was careful to point out after McConnel when I wrote: "When Ego marries his grandson's cousin, . . ." (1969a, p. 209)—that is, a parallel cousin, not an actual sister. There is no incompatibility between the two marriage formulas since, on account of the trend toward an alternate generation terminology, individuals who are not at the same genealogical distance from Ego may nevertheless find themselves in an identical category; and despite the "spiraling" of the marriage system (where according to McConnel, men marry "down" while women marry "up"), genealogical links and kinship categories may become readjusted periodically.

When stating that "Ego marries a woman of a younger generation in an older line who, for this reason, is taboo to Ego's son's son because

---

*The Wikmunkan are a tribe on the Cape York Peninsula in Queensland. (Ed.)
†For instance, I have never written that the "atom of kinship" is to be found in all societies provided they are either patrilineal or matrilineal. As a matter of fact, I have stated just the opposite: "The avunculate does not occur in all matrilineal or all patrilineal systems, and we find it present in some systems which are neither matrilineal nor patrilineal" (Lévi-Strauss 1963, p. 41). And the "two groups," misunderstood as meaning patrilineal and matrilineal societies respectively, designate, in my text, without any conceivable equivocation, two particular societies—the Cherkess and the Trobriand —and certainly not patrilineal and matrilineal societies, broadly speaking. On such misunderstandings, see my *Structural Anthropology*, vol. II (1976, pp. 82–112), or preferably the French original as the English translation contains errors and misprints.

the latter may only marry a woman of a younger line in his own generation" (1940, p. 436), McConnel was not involved in a contradiction either, contrary to the claim that the marriage chart may have been drawn in reference to Ego's grandson as well as to his grandfather and that what one is permitted to do may also be done by the other. It is obvious that Ego's son's son could also marry a woman in an older line in a younger generation; but in fairness to McConnel, one should recognize that the point she was making was quite different. What she was trying to explain is that, since the two women referred to are both Ego's classificatory daughter's daughter and Ego's son's son's classificatory father's sister's daughter who are equally marriageable for the two men, those men could well enter in competition—as McKnight rightly points out (1971, p. 163)—*unless* the system puts those women in different categories by distinguishing the woman coming from an older line, forbidden to Ego's son's son, and the woman coming from a younger line, forbidden to Ego. As I understood it (1969a, p. 209), that was the gist of McConnel's argument.

However, there remain such discrepancies between McConnel's account and that of D. F. Thomson, who was an observer of the highest quality, that unless we decide to throw them both overboard (something that, I confess, I am not ready to do), we must resign ourselves to the idea that the enigmas raised by the Wikmunkan system will not be readily solved. The only point clear in my mind is that the Wikmunkan could not have been a two-line society. This would not fit McConnel's account where at least three lines are needed; and this would not fit Thomson's account either, since for him the correct marriage is with a daughter of a classificatory father's sister who is at the same time a parallel second cousin, so that a structural distinction is needed between own father's clan and wife's mother's clan, as well as between own mother's and husband's father's clans (Thomson 1955, p. 40). While McConnel's charts undoubtedly remain controversial, one should not overlook that B. Spencer and F. J. Gillen have described the Arabana system in strikingly similar terms despite obvious differences, such as the allowed marriage between actual father's sister and actual mother's brother—but this is precisely a marriage possibility that, according to McKnight, McConnel should have included in her charts. The Arabana have a system of two exogamous moieties where spouses permitted to a man would in principle include women belonging to a superior or an inferior generation as well as to his own generation. Actually Ego can, however, marry only a girl in the category of father's elder sister's daughter, so that "if we draw a genealogical tree in the Urabunna tribe, placing the elder members on the left side and the younger members on the right side, then every women's *Nupa* [possible spouse] lies to the right, and every man's to the left side of his or her position in the genealogical tree" (Spencer and Gillen 1938, p. 65).

It is true that, when visiting the Arabana over thirty years later, A. P. Elkin could not find anything of that sort. And yet it would be surprising if Spencer and Gillen on the one hand and McConnel on the other had made the same mistake over the system of descent of tribes located in widely distant areas. One cannot help suspecting that prior to their "broken down condition," as Elkin says of the Arabana, something peculiar to the kinship system and marriage rules of both tribes had induced different observers to describe them in the same way (although McConnel's so-called spiral was inverted among the Arabana). And all the more so as that unknown something still made itself felt in 1930 with the distinction of three lines of descent and a lasting asymmetry in the marriage rules: whereas mother's father may marry father's father's sister, the reverse does not occur: father's father marries into a different classificatory group (Elkin 1938a, pp. 438-50).

In order to explain the anomalies of the Arabana system, Elkin has assumed it to be a system in transition. In 1949, I tried likewise to reconcile Thomson's and McConnel's conflicting accounts of the Wikmunkan by hypothesizing a hybrid system halfway between restricted exchange and generalized exchange. Therefore I shall avail myself of the present opportunity to clarify a minor point that has sometimes been misunderstood. While restricted exchange can also be called "direct," and generalized exchange "indirect," I have purposely inverted those labels in respect to the Wikmunkan because McConnel explained that among them one can marry a (unilateral) cross-cousin (generalized exchange), sister of a man to whom one gives in (restricted) exchange a half-sister from his own family or clan. Therefore, in that case, it is general exchange that is the more direct (one marries straightway a unilateral cross-cousin) and restricted exchange the more indirect: instead of directly giving away a sister, one borrows a woman from a parallel line.

Discussions about the number of lines have turned on the number of terms in the grandparents' generation, following the alleged principle that the number of basic descent lines depends upon how many different kinds of relatives are recognized in the grandfather's generation. But whatever value it may have elsewhere, this principle certainly does not hold for Australia. For instance, the Andigari and the Kokata marry a second cousin and should accordingly distinguish four lines although they have only two terms in the grandfather's generation. The Gunwinggu have three terms, but their marriage system implies that four lines are actually distinguished. Similarly, in Arabana terminology, "there are three lines of descent, and in actual marriage and descent there are four lines" (Elkin 1938a, p. 447). The Ungarinyin acknowledge four lines of descent, although they have five terms in the grandfather's generation. Even among groups with an Aranda system of kinship and marriage, and who accordingly distinguish four lines each with a special term in the grandfather's generation, a fifth line is actually added (on this point, see Meggitt 1962, pp. 195-96, 202).

However, and as I have said already, the data presently available on the Wikmunkan remain laden with so many uncertainties that until McKnight succeeds in clearing them up on the basis of his own fieldwork, it would not be profitable to carry on with their discussion. Rather, I shall concentrate upon a problem with both theoretical and methodological implications: namely, whether the notion of the "atom of kinship" is applicable to the Wikmunkan.

Once all the misunderstandings have been dispelled (I have never claimed that the so-called law of the atom of kinship is universal, especially since in my first paper on that topic I was careful to point out that the phenomenon was frequent enough to make its study valuable, et cetera; see second footnote on page 64), an interesting problem remains. McKnight has convincingly demonstrated that the system of attitudes is partly structured:

> I can converse and interact freely with my mother's older brother but not with my mother's younger brother. My mother and my mother's older brother cannot interact directly, they usually do so through me and my siblings. In contrast, while I cannot interact directly with my mother's younger brother, my mother and mother's younger brother may interact quite freely. [1971, p. 169]

So far so good. But a first difficulty arises when we consider the attitudes of Ego on the father's side. According to McKnight, the father and son relationship is positive: "I would summarize this with a plus" (1971, p. 174)—a conclusion that his own observations hardly support:

> On the one hand, it [the relationship] does not have the deference and distance as with a mother's younger brother, but neither does it have the freedom, familiarity and indulgence characteristic of the mother's older brother and younger sister's son relationship . . . as [children] grow older they learn that a father must be treated with respect. [1971, p. 167]

McKnight's subsequent remarks must be added: "As one should respect a father, so one should respect his sister. . . . Just as there are pollution and food taboos separating father and son, so we find similar taboos separating a woman and her brother's son" (1971, p. 168). It follows that the father and son relationship, while not being as negative as the relationship of mother's older brother and sister's son, is certainly not as positive as that of mother's younger brother and sister's son; so the first relationship cannot be equated with the third. In due regard to McKnight's own account, I would call it ambivalent and represent it diagrammatically with two signs, plus and minus.

Now, and as we have just seen from McKnight's last quotation, the father's sister and brother's son relationship is very much the same, and McKnight himself calls it ambivalent (1973, p. 196). Therefore it is legitimate to represent the father's sister and brother's son relationship with the same symbols as the father and son relationship: that is, two signs, plus and minus. Indeed, McKnight himself has given evidence that we are dealing here with the same relationship:

> The Wikmunkan themselves recognize that it is a near thing that one's own father's sister is not one's actual father. It was an accident of birth that she was not born a man; as one male informant put it: "If my father's sister had been a man I would have called her father too." . . . In a sense he does for the same term, *pinya*, is used for father's sister and father's older brothers. Thomson (1936 p. 384) suggests that *pinya* is little more than a variation for the kinship term for father, i.e. *pipa*. [McKnight 1973, pp. 208-9]

Another moot point is how the husband and wife relationship should be rated. McKnight considers it to be positive; but in his 1971 paper, he acknowledges that he had at that time not enough data to draw a definite conclusion because "such an intimate relationship is not easily understood" (1971, p. 169). His fascinating paper of 1973 hardly touches upon the matter. However, even in the lack of direct evidence, several inferences may be drawn. If, as I still believe, there is a structural relationship between the husband and wife relationship and the brother and sister relationship, and since among the Wikmunkan the latter should be distinguished into two relationships, one positive and the other negative according to relative age, it follows that the same duality should reflect itself upon the husband and wife relationship. This is all the more likely as the same duality is actually reflected on the mother's sisters, the elder being assimilated both in attitudes and terminology to elder mother's brother, and the younger to mother. Furthermore, the husband makes a similar distinction between his wife's sisters, the elder (but not the younger) being considered as a wife giver (McKnight 1973, pp. 197-98). The problem is then to understand how a distinction of attitudes based on relative age can be reflected upon a single individual—namely, the wife in relation to her husband. My guess is that it is reflected diachronically, according to periods when the woman is considered only as one's wife and to periods when she is considered as one's child's mother. During the first periods (and although there seem to be at all times some restrictions of behavior between husband and wife; see McKnight 1973, p. 197), the husband and wife relationship may be an easy one (McKnight 1971, pp. 169-70). However, this was certainly not the case in the past whenever the wife gave birth to a child and for some time thereafter. Thomson has described, and published photographs of, an impressive ceremony for the presentation of the child to his father. He explained that, following the birth of the child, the woman "remains in isolation for a period of from two weeks to a month, and that during the whole of this time neither the father nor any other man may see the mother or baby." During her seclusion the woman is attended only by female relatives; and the formal presentation of the child to its father, which marks the end of the seclusion, unrolls with great decorum (Thomson 1936, pp. 381-83). Taking into account all those data, it seems that the husband and wife relationship should also be rated as ambivalent, the difference with the other attitudes in the same generation level being that, instead of a synchronic ambivalence expressed by way of contrasting attitudes with respect to two distinct individuals (elder and younger siblings), we have here a diachronic ambivalence whereby the same contrasting attitudes are being expressed in alternation toward one and the same individual—that is, one's spouse.

The network of formalized attitudes among the Wikmunkan seems so complex and so ramified that a complete representation should probably be extended to the grandparents' and the grandchildren's generations. Keeping this in mind but limiting ourselves to a narrower field for lack of sufficient data, we end with the diagram in figure 4.1 to illustrate the Wikmunkan atom of kinship:

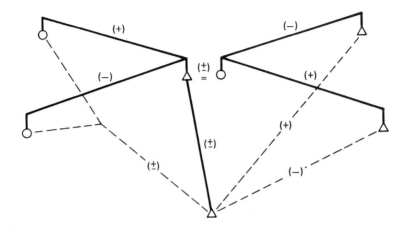

This diagram exhibits special features. In the first place, it calls for three types of connection: $(+, -, \pm)$ instead of the two that I mostly used in the past. But the case is not unique: in more recent work, I have shown that the Mundugomor atom of kinship, too, is three-valued (Lévi-Strauss 1976, pp. 88-94). In the second place and far more puzzling, the Wikmunkan diagram appears both equilibrated and asymmetrical. Equilibrated as it includes the same number of plus and minus signs which, so to speak, cancel each other. And it is also asymmetrical since the relationships on the father's side are neither expressed nor connected in the same way as those on the mother's side.

This anomalous situation calls for four remarks. (1) The asymmetry of the diagram has its roots in the asymmetry of the nomenclature:

> The Wikmunkan make no distinction in behavior nor, as far as I know, in kinship terminology between father's elder and younger sister. . . . All father's sisters, both actual and classificatory, regardless whether they are older or younger than one's father, are called *pinya*. There is therefore not a neat division of some father's sisters belonging to an affinal category, and others not, as happens with mother's brothers. As we shall see, this makes her treatment somewhat ambivalent. [McKnight 1973, pp. 195-96]

(2) The attitudes between affines are equally asymmetrical. On several occasions, McKnight has emphasized that, among the Wikmunkan, wife givers are in a superior position to wife takers, and that accord-

ingly sister's husband is subordinated to brother's wife. (3) For his part, Thomson has devoted a lengthy paper (1935) to the interplay among all tribes of the same geographical area, and particularly the Wikmunkan, of the nomenclature and of the system of attitudes. Either the nomenclature or the attitudes, and eventually both, become modified whenever due to special situations a contradiction between the nomenclature and the attitudes does occur. (4) Under its suggested form, the Wikmunkan atom of kinship would seem to support the interpretation of their marriage system as a blend of restricted exchange and of generalized exchange. In that case the equilibrated aspect would correspond to the former and the asymmetrical aspect (together with the asymmetrical attitudes between sister's husband and wife's brother) to the latter.

No less stimulating are McKnight's comments on the Walbiri. Should I have asserted that the atom of kinship may be found in all societies provided they are either patrilineal or matrilineal, the Walbiri could not be quoted as a valid objection since they are neither the one nor the other: they are ambilineal. But as pointed out earlier in this chapter, I have never made such an assertion. Therefore I am quite willing to include the Walbiri among the societies that one should consider, if only to point out that with the Walbiri, the actual mother's brother, never being a wife giver, has no place whatsoever in the atom of kinship. The only positions eligible for wife giver are those of classificatory mother's mother's brother (the preferred marriage is with the classificatory mother's mother's brother's daughter's daughter) and of classificatory mother's brother. Atoms of kinship may be "light" or "heavy" depending on the number of positions they include. When considering only light examples, as I did in my first paper on that topic, the position of wife giver could be appropriately allotted to the mother's brother. But even then I emphasized that a provision should be made for more complex cases (Lévi-Strauss 1963, p. 48) in which the position of wife giver will be taken by other or more distant relatives—for instance, the wife's father or, as among the Walbiri, a classificatory grandfather or a classificatory (and not actual) mother's brother. McKnight was perhaps right in reproaching McConnel for not having distinguished between actual and classificatory relatives, but this is not valid only in the case of the Wikmunkan.

Considering those more distant individual positions among the Walbiri, their relationships to Ego are certainly not positive. As *djuraldja* "the mother's father who is also the W.M.M.B. . . . is treated circumspectly, for he shares with the wife's father and mother's brother the right to dispose of the woman" and "the mother's mother's brother . . . take[s] a larger part in disciplining a youth than does his father or brother" (Meggitt 1962, pp. 146, 82). About the need to expand and develop the atom of kinship whenever it includes more positions than in the simpler forms, I shall refer the reader to my discussion of the Lele, an African tribe where the position of wife giver also belongs to the mother's mother's brother (Lévi-Strauss 1973, pp. 116-27).

Nothing could be farther from my mind than to claim that an elementary system of attitudes will be discovered in each and every society. On the contrary, I have many times taken the opposite stand: "It would be incorrect to assume that the kinship system constitutes the principal means of regulating interpersonal relationships in all societies. Even in societies where the kinship system functions as such, it does not fulfill that role everywhere to the same extent" (Lévi-Strauss 1963, p. 38). Furthermore, I have pointed out the cases where we may expect the system of attitudes to become inconspicuous because the atom of kinship "may be submerged within a differentiated context" (p. 48), or because "the system is undergoing rapid transformations . . . or . . . is in the throes of a mortal crisis" (p. 49).

However, when one looks at the situation prevailing with Australian tribes "unless their old rules have been forgotten" (Elkin 1938*b*, p. 115), one cannot fail to be struck, as Elkin himself was, by the complexity and subtlety of the negative attitudes between family groups: "One is a few yards from the others, facing away from them and saying nothing to them; two families are sitting near and talking to each other, but facing in different directions; while another family may be facing one of these two" (pp. 115-16). That there are "kinship rules of avoidance and familiarity" (pp. 115-16) derives from "general principles" which remain valid throughout Australia notwithstanding "some variations" that may happen "here and there" (p. 122). Although, for reasons already stated, the quest for the atom of kinship will not always be successful, it offers an efficient approach to an analysis in depth of the rules of avoidance and familiarity. It helps us to explore how these rules are correlated and become meaningful as parts of an integrated whole which includes the attitudes, the kinship nomenclature, and the marriage rules together with their dialectical relations.

Chapter 5

Cross-Readings

WRITTEN in the eleventh century, the *Genji Monogatari* by Murasaki Shikibu is not only one of the purest masterpieces of world literature in its poetic inspiration, in the poignant melancholy of the people and objects it brings to life, and in psychological analyses so deep and subtle that it took the West seven or eight centuries to achieve their equal. But this dense, slow narrative, attentive to the finest details of Japanese court life during the Heian period, also offers a mass of precise anthropological data, especially about a social change that certainly took place elsewhere, too, but about which we have little information outside of this invaluable source.

Anthropologists are familiar with many societies that recommend or prescribe marriage between cousins—as did ancient China, which strongly influenced the laws and customs of medieval Japan. We also know of societies that condemn marriages between close relatives and authorize only those between more distant kinfolk or between people with no discernible blood tie. But, if we grant that, at some point in their history, these cultures have been induced by circumstances to give up one marriage form for another, we know almost nothing about how individuals experienced this change, or about how it affected their sensibilities, or about their motives for encouraging or accommodating themselves to it.

The *Genji Monogatari*, however, introduces us into a society that is not unaware of, and often practices, marriage between cousins, but that, at a certain point in its history, is beginning to wonder about and question this custom. The witnesses to subjective attitudes accompanying such an evolution are so rare that it is worthwhile reviewing them—just as the author of this work makes a point of noting them whenever they crop up. Throughout this chapter, I have quoted from the recent English translation by Edward G. Seidensticker (1976), the only complete version in a Western tongue until Professor René Sieffert publishes his French translation.

Mulling over the advantages and the disadvantages of a match between his daughter and his uterine nephew (who are thus cross-cousins), Tō no Chūjō reflects: "A marriage between cousins was not wholly unacceptable, of course; but, people would think it at best uninteresting" (p. 368). Several days later, he discusses the plan with his mother and tells her his exact feelings about it:

> He [the bridegroom] may be a talented and erudite young man who knows more about history than anyone else at court, but even the lower classes think it a rather dull and common thing for cousins to marry. It will do him no more good than her. He would do far better to find a rich and stylish bride a little farther afield. [P. 369]

The same note is struck when a different character, Yūgiri, is planning to marry his daughters to two men: one supposedly his half-brother, but actually the son of his wife's brother; the second, the son of his father's daughter (by a different mother). Indeed, the kinship relationships are so complicated that these ties do not exclude others. In any case, even though Yūgiri himself is married to his matrilateral cross-cousin, his first thought now is: "Marriage to a near relative is not usually held to be very interesting" (p. 741). One of the possible bridegrooms is even more reticent: "There was no mystery, no excitement in the proposal" (p. 819).

These few examples suffice to shed light on why the characters of this novel contrast a marriage between cousins with a marriage between distant relatives. The former brings security but also monotony: from one generation to the next, the same or similar unions are repeated, and the familial and social structure is simply reproduced. On the other hand, while a match between distant relatives is subject to risk and adventure, it also permits speculation: it creates unprecedented alliances, and new coalitions stir up the dynamics of history. The protagonists, however, feel that these exciting experiences (as they put it) unfold on a stage whose backdrop is marriage between cousins.

This interpretation is confirmed *a contrario* by apparently the one case in which the author of the *Genji* places in the mouth of one character a plea in favor of marriage between cousins. But this character, who is none other than the reigning emperor, is attempting to solve a highly delicate predicament. As heir apparent, he has married the daughter of a mere minister. Although he loved her tenderly, her modest station prevented him from bestowing on her the dignity of an empress. Eventually she gave birth to an only daughter, whom her father could elevate to the rank only of Second Princess. Rich, but without adequate maternal background, the daughter is just "slightly above her mother" in rank, because of a blending of the status inherited in each line, as has also been observed in Polynesia, from the Fiji Islands to Tahiti and Hawaii. When her mother dies, the girl's future seems jeopardized, for, as the novel says, "She had no maternal uncles to whom she could turn for support" (p. 886). The emperor wants to get her married while he is still on the throne; but he has to find an acceptable husband for a daughter who is of his blood but not noble on her mother's side.

Now, during the reign of the present emperor's father, the latter gave one of his daughters, a Third Princess, in marriage to Genji, his half-brother, a commoner also owing to his mother's humble origins and his consequent lack of matrilateral support (his story is told in detail in chapter 34). This hypogamic union was greatly criticized; it would have been normal for the Third Princess to remain unwed. In fact, imperial daughters who were unable to find a husband of the proper rank frequently had no other recourse than to become nuns or priestesses.

Kaoru, actually conceived in adultery, was supposedly born to this couple, whose age difference made the match even more unequal. The emperor considers this uterine nephew a possible husband for the Second Princess, because "where could he find a more appropriate candidate for her hand . . . a better solution than to follow in the second generation the precedent of the first?" (p. 886). (Let it be said in passing that this is a technically impeccable definition of a marriage with the matrilineal cross-cousin.) In this case, thus, the concern for security wins out; by uniting two cousins, the emperor hopes to re-establish a certain balance between a hypergamic marriage (to a woman of common birth) and a hypogamic marriage (to a man of common birth), whose antithetical characteristics are due, in both cases, to the fact that one of the partners, already deprived of support on the maternal side, is also a younger son or daughter on the paternal side. In sum, the emperor's anxieties are scarcely different from those of Louis XIV of France when he finally decided to marry one of his illegitimate daughters, Mademoiselle de Blois, to his nephew in the younger branch, Philippe d'Orléans, the future regent.

Marriage between cousins thus enables a group to deal with strains inflicted on the social order and to protect it against possible danger. As an attenuated form of endogamy (in societies that do not fear matches between close relatives), marriage between cousins fulfills the function of endogamy or else alternates (and also harmonizes) with exogamous marriage by consolidating collateral lines when a gap seems to be emerging between them (with the consequent risk, moreover, of their becoming too equal through this consolidation and of their beginning to compete with each other). In contrast, exogamy, through well-chosen matches, allows a collateral line to distinguish itself from the others and forge its own destiny. Either tendency will prevail, depending on the time or the occasion. Without specifying dates or examples, W. H. McCullough (1967, pp. 136, 164 n. 268) believes that marriage with a female cross-cousin on the mother's side was very frequent during the Heian period, especially in the imperial family. And it is clear that, in precarious situations like the one I have just described, prudence, the mother of security, dictates matrimonial choices. On the other hand, more peaceful circumstances can encourage families to take a chance and seek new connections.

Therefore it looks as if, during the tenth and eleventh centuries, Japan developed a disaffection for marriage between cousins which may have been temporary, and whose psychological sources are revealed in the literature of that time. Barring exceptional circumstances, a society confronted with history will enter it consciously. Earlier I mentioned Polynesian data on social rank, which is determined for each individual by the rank of both parents. And one cannot help being struck by a remarkable symmetry between the social and mental state I have just described in ancient Japan, and what anthropologists have observed only recently in the Fiji Islands.

Before tackling this issue, I must first anticipate a possible misunderstanding. The existence of works as grand as the one from which I have quoted is enough to convince us that an abyss separates the Japan of the Heian period, with an élite that had been literate for several centuries, from an unlettered society like the Fijian. We therefore have to make sure not to repeat, in regard to the Far East, the mistakes made by Western "primitivists" when they claim to recognize, in obscure customs of ancient Greece and Rome, vestiges of archaic institutions on the basis of comparisons with the lives of illiterate peoples.

When cultures are different from, and cannot be compared with, one another, it is an altogether different matter to pick out patterns of activity that recur because of their fundamental roles, and that are thus independent of what might be called states of civilization—states with which a positive or a negative attitude toward certain types of marriage has, strictly speaking, nothing to do. F. Zonabend (1980, p. 221) has pointed out the paradox that, in rural France today, marriage between cousins is reappearing not despite the development of automobile travel, but because of it: easier communication is reintegrating into a person's circle of acquaintances collateral lines that had long been lost from sight. The old matrimonial policy that wanted "marriages to concatenate" (p. 152)—doomed, one might have thought, by the mingling of populations and the dispersal of relatives—is now being revitalized.

In human societies as in biological species, elementary mechanisms operate identically, no matter how complex each type of organization may be: on a molecular level, physicochemical processes are the same everywhere. The legitimacy of the comparative method does not rest on massive and superficial resemblances. Analysis has to take place on a level deep enough to allow us to discern, at the base of all social life, the simple features that combine into rudimentary systems, which may eventually become the stuff of more complex and more completely integrated systems with entirely new characteristics. It is in this spirit and with these reservations that one has the right to compare, in order to contrast, the attitudes toward marriages between cousins in ancient Japan and on the Fiji Islands.

Marriage between true cross-cousins was permitted but not, it seems, preferred in certain regions of the Fijis; it was prohibited elsewhere because, it was said, it would have confused descents (Sahlins 1962). Yet the kinship system is of the Dravidian type, which divides all individuals into two categories—those related by blood and those by marriage—as if the entire society were reduced to two exogamic sections practicing cross-cousin marriage with the exchange of sisters. The reality was entirely different: the Fijians did not exchange their sisters, and the society counted a great number of lines. Some lines tried to maintain the same alliances for several generations, but nothing forbade any line from contracting simultaneous or successive marriages with any number of other lines (Nayacakalou 1955-57, pp. 64, 66; Groves 1963, p. 72.)

Contrary to actual practice, once a marriage was consummated, the husband and the wife became, nominally, each other's cross-cousin, and all the kinship terms changed accordingly. Each spouse's siblings became the cross-cousins of the other spouse, and each set of parents-in-law became cross-uncle and cross-aunt. For a husband, the children of his wife's sister became parallel children; the children of his wife's brother became cross-children; and vice versa for the wife.

Unlike ancient Japan, where, if we are to believe the *Genji Monogatari*, marriage between cousins was practiced despite ambiguous feelings about it, Fijians pretended that such marriages were the rule in their society, even if they did not conform to it. It could be said that societies poised at the same unstable point between two practices tilt in opposite directions. Medieval Japanese society decried marriage between cousins when perceived as an obstacle to the spirit of adventure, but preserved the practice or returned to it for reasons of security. Fijian society, being less enterprising, may go so far as to proscribe cousin marriage but, as if inconsolable, keeps its ghost in a verbal and fictitious form. Haunted by an elementary structure whose roots probably are deep in their respective pasts, Fiji preserves nostalgia and is unable to let go of it, at least in words; while ancient Japan perceived the limits, making the typically "medieval" discovery (but one perceptible throughout the Pacific) that a society that aspires only to reproduce itself, and endures rather than desires change, can, without leaving the paths of kinship, find in the great game of matrimonial alliances the means of opening itself to history and the conditions for a planned development.

We will now be led to another region of the Austronesian world by a further comparison inspired by the *Genji Monogatari*. The reader has already had the chance to note the importance placed on maternal relatives in a cognate or—as W. H. McCullough terms it (1967, p. 113) —bilateral society, as reflected by a very simple kinship nomenclature which seems scarcely to have changed since the tenth century. In ancient times, this terminology separated cousins from siblings and subdivided the latter into older and younger. In the first ascending generation, it separated parents from uncles and aunts and, in the first descending generation, children from nephews and nieces. Without further distinguishing the lines, the same word, *itoko*, was applied both to first cousins and to other, distant ones.

The *Genji Monogatari* keeps recurring to the same theme, as a sort of leitmotif: both at the edge of and within the imperial family, a person's rank depends not only on his paternal forebears but also on the recognized influence of his maternal relatives (pp. 13, 15).

> Even when a child has the emperor himself for its father, the mother's station in life makes all the difference. Look at the case of His Lordship [Genji]. He was the handsomest and the most gifted of them all, and still he was made a commoner. His maternal grandfather was just not important enough, and his mother was one of the lesser ladies at court. . . . Even the daughter of a prince or a minister is at a great disadvantage if her mother's family does not have influence. Her father cannot do the things that one might expect from his rank. [P. 332]

Indeed, what is true for one sex is not less so for the other: even a princess of the blood would have no future if "she had no maternal uncles to whom she could turn for support" (p. 886). Hence, there is nothing astonishing about a young man's being exhorted to "Go get yourself a wife, . . . and useful in-laws" (p. 941).

This point is faithfully echoed by the *Eiga Monogatari*, a Japanese historical chronicle written shortly after the *Genji:* "A man's career depends on his wife's family" (W. H. and H. C. McCullough 1980, I, p. 296). Translators and commentators emphasize: "One of *Eiga*'s constant themes is the dependence of Princely fortunes on the support of maternal relatives" (I, p. 35; see also W. H. McCullough 1967, pp. 126-27).

During this period of Japanese history, the Fujiwara clan knew how to make the most of these principles. It ensured for itself real power by systematically marrying its sisters and daughters to the heirs to the imperial throne. The Fujiwaras thus turned to their advantage the reigning emperor's custom of retiring after the birth of a son, and giving the dowager empress and her family free rein during the son's childhood and adolescence. It is, moreover, not certain that his relatives by marriage had to force the emperor into early retirement (even though it was greatly to their benefit), for examples of the same custom have been found in other parts of the Pacific, notably in the Society Islands. Here, a ruler became his son's subject the moment the child was born (although he wielded power on the child's behalf and subsequently became his feared rival) through the principle, consistent with our initial reflections, that the child was superior to both his father and his mother through combining in himself the *mana* of both parents.

If we look farther afield (without leaving the Austronesian world to which, except for language, Japan belongs in many ways), certain analogies do not fail to appear between such practices and, several centuries later, the dynastic customs of Imerina, a region in central Madagascar. To calm any anxieties aroused by this leap through space and history, let me note that the practices in question have survived up to the contemporary era. Princess Yi Pangja, a native Japanese, who granted me an audience at her palace in Seoul in 1981, writes in her autobiography: "The tendency in modern Korean history was for the queen's family to grasp power and become the actual rulers until they were supplanted by another family" (1973, pp. 67-68). The princess explains why reasons of state required her to marry the last crown prince of the kingdom of Korea after the Japanese conquest: through her marriage, the Japanese government became the "father-in-law" of the future sovereign. We can therefore introduce into our discussion Madagascan facts that, although more recent than the Japanese ones, antedate by a century the situation still prevalent in Korea only seventy years ago.

We know that Imerina, then divided into four small kingdoms, was reunified in the late eighteenth century by the sovereign of one of them—Andrianampoinimerina—who immediately extended his hegemony over the major part of the island. The reign of this powerful monarch had two paradoxical features. First of all, he reformed the order of succession to the throne, which had previously gone through the males, but was now reserved for the offspring of his sisters. Second, although he did not cease insisting on the primacy of monarchic power, he seems to have governed by relying on popular support or, more precisely, by sharing his power with an oligarchy: "It is remarkable to see how, during his reign, the most capable men in his entourage always acted in harmony with him and frequently even took the lead, as it were, by adopting the most useful, most just, and sometimes most severe measures" (Malzac 1912, p. 136).

Father Malzac, whose opinion was corroborated by other sources, also hypothesized that these two paradoxes might be linked. He wondered whether Andrianampoinimerina's predilection for the female line might not fit in with the idea that "a woman, being by nature more open than a man to the advice of experienced leaders, would more surely procure the happiness of her people." And the author then added:

> According to certain old Madagascans, who were well informed about the genealogies and practices of the court, he had formally transmitted this very strange idea to the nation. . . . This idea could only appeal to the

grandees of the realm, who, with a queen, could hope to rule as they wished. [Malzac 1912, p. 136]

No one would dream of believing all the tales about the beginnings of the Merina dynasty. Collected in the Madagascan language by Father Callet in his *Tantaran' ny Andriana*, these tales have a patently legendary, often mythical character. Nevertheless, they are extremely interesting because they illustrate if not real events, then at least the way in which the Madagascan sages thought of and, to a large extent, reconstructed a distant past, in order to reconcile it with—and, if necessary, even justify—a well-attested recent history. Therefore, one does not look for hard facts in the first part of *L'Histoire des rois* ("The History of Kings"; the translation of the original title) but only for an ideological schema filling the need to conceptualize the social order: not true history, but the model suggested by memorialists and political thinkers in the mid-nineteenth century.

According to this model, the Merina dynasty originated among the Vazimba, the earlier if not earliest inhabitants of the country, and masters of the soil, *tompotany* (Callet 1953-58, I, p. 8). Two queens of this race, either mother and daughter or sisters (depending on the version), married newcomers and gave birth to the first kings, who passed the throne at first from brother to brother, then from father to son. In their successive marriages, we note a remarkable alternation of endogamous and exogamous unions. Toward the middle of the seventeenth century, it seems, one of these sovereigns, Andrianjaka, expelled the Vazimba from Tananarive, where they had reigned for several generations. In compensation, he granted them estates and conferred great privileges on them: they were the only people who could officiate at certain rituals and preside at the circumcision of a king's sons; and henceforth their dead would be considered "sacred remains" and would be objects of worship.

Now, if the Merina dynasty claims descent from the Vazimba queens as traditions state, then the Vazimba and their descendants constitute, in regard to it, a line of mothers' brothers. And in the privileges accorded them in exchange for renouncing the throne, we easily discern an analogy to the privileges that are often granted throughout the world to kinsmen on the mother's side: they are deified, granted ritual prerogatives with respect to their uterine nephews, and play an important role at the latter's circumcision. It is worthy of note that, in Madagascar, the original unions between the two lines were renewed throughout the generations. When, in the late

eighteenth century, Andrianampoinimerina finally subdued the Antehiroka, the last descendants of the Vazimba (Callet 1953-58, I, p. 8), he
treated them favorably because they were descended from one of the
wives of his ancestor Ralambo, and he from the other: " 'You and I,'
he said to the Antehiroka, 'are one person, for I am the son of
Ralambo's first wife, and you are the sons of his second wife' " (III, p.
98). There is some doubt about the rank of these wives, for we read
elsewhere that Ralambo chose as successor his younger son Andrianjaka, because the boy's mother, daughter of a powerful Vazimba chief,
was the king's first and principal wife. Perhaps it was even because of
his maternal ancestry that Andrianjaka, behaving more like a genuine
Polynesian *vasu** than a natural child, undertook to dispossess the
Vazimba, as I have said, and drove them from the north of Imerina.

About 1787, Andrianampoinimerina succeeded his maternal grandfather, who had designated him over his own—still childless—son. A
female link was thus introduced into the dynastic succession; and
throughout his life, Andrianampoinimerina actually claimed descent
—through his mother—not from his grandfather but from his grandmother, Rasoherina, as if she had been the real founder of his line. This
fact does not adequately explain his turning over the order of succession by making his sisters "the great source" of the future sovereigns
of Imerina. Even his son, who succeeded him under the name of
Radama I, merited this right in his eyes, less by his paternal descent
than because he was the offspring of Ramorabe, queen of Ambohidratimo, and the adopted son of Ralesoka, his older sister, the childless
wife of the king of Tananarive (Malzac 1912, p. 158). Andrianampoinimerina thus used cognate (or bilateral) links in order to reunite
the kingdom, which his great-grandfather, loyal to the agnate (or paternal) succession, had split up among his four sons in the late seventeenth century.

The stages of this reunification were marked by significant episodes.
We do not know precisely who Rasoherina was, but the chronicles give
her a strategic importance: she is the only princess in the *Histoire des
rois* to be the heroine of a romance that is narrated in detail. Furthermore, her descent is controversial. She is said to have been closely
related to the sovereigns of Ambohimanga, whose son, heir to the
throne, supposedly became infatuated with her even though she was
married to a foreign prince (Callet 1953-58, II, p. 702). Elsewhere, she is
called the daughter of a foreign prince, the sister of Ramorabe, grand-

*A *vasu* is a sister's son who is entitled to exercise rights over his uncle. (Ed.)

mother of Andrianampoinimerina, and wife of the king of Ambohidratimo (p. 700 n. 5). In either theory, Rasoherina combines endogamous and exogamous traits.

I have just mentioned Ramorabe. This ancestress played a decisive role in the process that brought her grandson to the throne and ended with the reunification of Imerina. During the period when this territory was still divided into four kingdoms and Andrianampoinimerina was still only the grandson—through his mother—of the king of Ambohimanga and, since the grandfather had a son, had no dynastic hopes, Andrianampoinimerina went to visit his grandmother in Ambohidratimo. It was she who revealed his future to him and began to work for his success (Callet 1953-58, II, pp. 737ff). For this princess was in league with the Antehiroka, whose help she obtained against her own sons, in order to put Andrianampoinerina on the throne, by promising to respect their ancestral customs. At another point, she had the reigning sovereign, her own grandson, put to death because he had committed extortion against the Antehiroka (p. 759). For his part, the future Andrianampoinimerina needed wide popular support in order to replace his uterine uncle, Andrianajafy. The part played by the Antehiroka is described in a local chronicle (Délivré 1974, p. 334).

Thus, everything leads us to believe that Andrianampoinimerina's disputed ascent to the throne and his reunification of Imerina were made possible only by the return to a socio-political configuration temporarily set aside for the benefit of agnate succession—a union of two (sometimes also three) lines, who put ahead of common ambitions both antagonistic and complementary relations, insofar as they are, in regard to each other, paternal or maternal, takers or givers of wives, wielders of temporal or spiritual power, conquerors or aboriginals— or even, as was said in the Middle Ages, insofar as they stemmed from the "race" or from the "earth." The cognate lines thus became the keystone of the system.

The historians of Madagascar seem to have paid no attention to the similar upheaval that took place at exactly the same time in the kingdom of Lovedu in southern Africa. Since at least the beginning of the seventeenth century, the throne had been occupied by males, the succession going from father to son. About 1800, the reigning sovereign decreed his sons to be unfit and transferred the royal power to his daughter; the succession passed henceforth from woman to woman (Krige 1975*b*). E. J. Krige, who supplied this information, interprets this change of descent in almost the same terms as Father Malzac in regard to Madagascar (see pages 80-81). Let me add that, owing to a secret incestuous rule, the Lovedu queens were always fathered by a brother or a half-brother of their mother; and that a queen's chief adviser was usually a maternal uncle who wielded temporal power. The Lovedu practice thus combines in the same person the functions performed in ancient Japan by the maternal relatives and in Madagascar—as we shall see—by the prime ministers, who were also the consorts of the female sovereign.

Krige attributes the reform to the fact that, by his many wives, the last king had rebellious sons who tried to oust him and fought ferociously among themselves to seize power. Female succession prevented the disintegration of the kingdom by creating a lasting equilibrium between the ritual functions devolving on the queen and the political functions assumed by her adviser coming from the maternal side.

Among the Lovedu and the Merina, it was thus as a remedy for the rivalry among agnates that matrilineal succession appeared in its two conceivable forms: in Japan, the exercise of power by the maternal family; and, among the Lovedu and the Merina, the succession from mother to daughter. Furthermore, these two modalities may partly overlap, as happened among the Lovedu. And ancient Japan, which clearly illustrates the first modality, seems to have repeatedly touched upon the second. Witness this reflection by Emperor Go-Ichijô (early in the eleventh century) upon the birth of his daughter Shôshi (the same name as his paternal grandmother, who was also his mother's sister), as quoted in the *Eiga Monogatari:* "It is absurd to complain about the child's being a girl. It might be different if the wise Emperors of the past had never installed a woman sovereign" (McCullough and McCullough 1980, II, p. 725). W. H. McCullough has clearly shown that, in Japan at the same period, a noblewoman brought her husband, if not always lands, then at least a palace, and that these princely dwellings were usually passed down the maternal line. The wife would normally live there, and her husband would visit her there or even in her parents' home (1967, pp. 105-27).

The Lovedu pushed these principles much farther, since their queen had no right to have a husband, but could have only lovers. It is, on the other hand, striking that her right to marry women and be the legal "father" of their children led to a sort of reverse patrilinealism. Likewise, the queens' mode of reproduction by incestuous unions constituted what might be called a reverse matrilinealism. These two modes of reproduction created, moreover, a balance between the extreme endogamy of one and the exogamy of the other, for the queen married women chosen from outside the royal line.

A comparison between the royal institutions of Madagascar and the customs of ancient Japan will provide a further example of these reverse structures. Beyond the psychological and political interpretations offered by Malzac and Krige, such a comparison seems to lead to an underlying pattern that was common to several archaic royal lines and reveals how kinship structures are organized or reorganized when rudimentary forms of a political state emerge in their midst. Far from being obliterated, people are keenly interested in these ties and manipulate them. As W. H. and H. C. McCullough note about medieval Japan, "For success at the Heian Court, there was no substitute for kinship ties" (1980, II, p. 827). Closer to us in time is the incredibly complicated game of matrimonial alliances that Blanche of Castille worked out, in the thirteenth century, to carry out her political plans.

Let us return to Madagascar, whose situation seems very like that of Japan during the Heian period, except that the balance of power was different. Anthropologists are well aware that the avuncular relationship (the first rough form of such systems in illiterate societies) already testifies to great instability: depending on the case, identical privileges belong to either the maternal uncle or the nephew. In Fiji and on the neighboring islands, a nephew seizes his uncle's property with impunity. The reverse custom prevails among the Tsimihety in northern Madagascar: "Whenever a major sacrifice is offered, the *fokondreny* of the individual giving the feast must be invited, and the mother's brother (*zama*) plays an important, symbolic role, guarding the displayed head of the sacrificial animal. He is also permitted to demand anything in the way of food and drink from his nephew" (P. J. Wilson 1967, p. 149). When Andrianampoinimerina created a body of personal representatives to supervise the execution of his orders in the provinces, he revealingly called them *vadintany*, "husbands of the soil." This term is quite in keeping with the original nature of the Merina dynasty, which stemmed from newcomers who "married the earth" in the persons of the sisters or the daughters of the original inhabitants, the husbands of the soil. It was most likely not just during the era evoked by Andriamasinavalona, the great-grandson of Andrianjaka, that some Antehiroka were intimately linked to the sovereigns "who had made them their advisers and associated them with him to keep watch over the state" (Callet 1953-58, I, p. 571).

The preceding discussion sheds light on the seemingly aberrant forms of power during the last half-century of the Merina dynasty. The throne was occupied almost exclusively by women, descendants of the sisters of Andrianampoinimerina, as he had wanted; while a line of prime ministers wielded the actual power, and one of these was even the titular lover of the last three queens. These ministers descended from Andriantsilavo, whom Andrianampoinimerina had already made his intimate counselor (Chapus and Mondain 1953, p. 9). Thus, the role of this line, which originated in Avaradrano, the oldest district in Imerina, lasted for more than a century. But it boasted not only its ancestors Tsimiambolahy and Tsimahafotsy, who had helped Andrianampoinimerina seize the throne, but also Antehiroka, hence Vazimba, ancestors. As late as the nineteenth century, this line still held some of the lands that had been originally granted to the latter forebears (Callet 1953-58, I, pp. 569-74; 571 n. 5).

However, rather than restoring the old alliance by giving it its original shape, Andrianampoinimerina's reform shifted, to the other side of the balance, the system that had temporarily replaced the old alliance. The succession was changed from agnatic to uterine, and the roles of the two lines were accordingly transposed. Even if the last few Antehiroka could marry queens only in left-handed marriages, the sexual connotations of "race" and "earth" were exchanged. It was still the same system, but its mirror image.

This final state of the system brings it closer to the one prevailing in Japan during the Heian period—with one difference, however, which I need only describe in order to make clear the symmetry of the two structures. The Fujiwara married their sisters or daughters to emperors who were forced to abdicate in favor of infant heirs, in whose name their grandfather or maternal uncles then wielded power. On the other hand, when necessary, the Antehiroka (whether truly so or not) physically eliminated the occupants of the throne (such was the fate of Radama II) and replaced them with female heirs upon whom the Antehiroka forced themselves as favorites in order to exercise power in their name as "royal consorts . . . such being the title of the leading politician, who is in command and performs the functions of prime minister" (Callet 1953-58, II, p. 718). In Japan, according to the Ōkagami (H. C. McCullough 1980), the regent Fujiwara Michinaga (966-1027) was the father-in-law of three successive emperors. Eight centuries later, in Madagascar, the minister Rainilaiarivony married three queens in succession.

In the time of Ramorabe, the Antehiroka, descendants of the Vazimba, helped the future Andrianampoinimerina obtain royal power. Similarly, in seventh-century Japan, the historical founder of the Fujiwara clan greatly contributed to establishing the absolute monarchy for the imperial line. Like the Vazimba, the Fujiwara held hereditary religious offices, entitling them to celebrate the rites of the court and preside at great ceremonies. And, like the Antehiroka, who claimed descent from the Vazimba, the Fujiwara claimed descent from a largely mythical clan, the Nakatomi.

It is thus revealing that the most ancient Japanese texts offer a sort of rear view, enlarged to mythic dimensions, of this dual relationship, attested to by history, between the two lines. Once, when the sun goddess Amaterasu, ancestor of the imperial line, was offended, she locked herself up in a cave and deprived the gods of her light. The gods resorted to a trick to get her out of her retreat, but they also had to prevent her from returning to it. The ancestral god of the Nakatomi and an ally barred the entrance with a rope while singing a religious hymn (Aston 1896, I, pp. 45-49; Shibata and Shibata 1969, pp. 84-85). These two methods, one negative and the other positive, prefigured the Fujiwara clan's dual approach to the imperial family. It is also tempting to recognize the blend of seduction and violence that, according to authentic tales, the nineteenth-century Madagascan ministers used against their queens in various circumstances.

Chapter 6

On Marriage between Close Kin

DESPITE the accumulation of knowledge and lengthy theoretical reflection, an old problem still preys on the minds of specialists in kinship and marriage—the historians of institutions and anthropologists. Why do highly diverse societies, which tolerate or discourage marriage between close relatives, allow it between children born to the same father but to different mothers, and proscribe it in the reverse situation, even though their descent system is patrilineal or at least their conduct or ideology tends to be patrilineal?

A classic example of this apparent contradiction is offered by ancient Athens, yet the centuries seem to have brought us no closer to a solution. In 1748, Hume posed the question, "What is the reason, why, by the Athenian laws, one might marry a half-sister by the father, but not by the mother?" (1965, pp. 56-57)—and gave an answer that we find inadequate today.* The question has resurfaced, almost in the same terms, after two hundred and thirty years: "If all that counts is paternal heredity, how can we explain the existence of an Athenian law forbidding any union between children born to the same mother but with different fathers?" (Loraux 1981, p. 130). In contrast to Athens, we know little about the mode of descent among the ancient Semites,

*Hume's answer was, "Public utility is the cause of all these variations." (Ed.)

about its evolution or its fluctuations from ancient times up to Ezekiel and beyond. For a long time, however, specialists have been asking the same question of the several Biblical passages (such as *Genesis* 20:12; *Samuel* 13:13; and *Ezekiel* 22:11) that distinguish between two half-sisters, the one marriageable and the other not (Westermarck 1922, pp. 95-97).

The same difficulty confronts anthropologists dealing with illiterate societies. The Kwakiutl Indians of British Columbia—who have generally seemed to be patrilineal despite their hybrid rules about the transmission of ranks and titles—authorized marriage between siblings born to the same father but not between those born to the same mother. They took this principle so much for granted that, when informing Boas about it, George Hunt felt it necessary to add, "I have never seen anyone do this, and also nobody told me that it was done by any tribe" (Boas 1921, pp. 1, 345). It is this custom, which recurs in time and place, that—without claiming to elucidate it completely—I would like to discuss, with the aim of answering the question posed by Nicole Loraux in her fine book *Les Enfants d'Athéna* (1981).

First of all, the Athenian rule is a particular case of a more general situation: that of societies that are oriented unequally but always predominantly toward the patrilineal rule, but in which, as J. P. Vernant aptly says of Greece, "the incest prohibition rules are more strict for the maternal side" (1974, p. 112). Direct and indirect examples are so numerous throughout the world that it suffices to cite a few at random, without weighing down with references a list whose impressionistic character I will not try to hide.

In Sumatra, the Karo Batak have a special term for cousins whose mothers belong to the same clan, but not for cousins whose fathers belong to the same clan and who are the only ones who can, in a strict sense, marry one another. The Buna of Timor formally prohibit a man from marrying a matrilateral parallel cousin. The same holds almost everywhere in Madagascar.

In Tonga, in Polynesia, half-siblings with the same father are considered rivals and are therefore more distantly related to each other than half-siblings with the same mother, who are said to be "of the same cord." Palau, in Micronesia, forbade marriage between the children of sisters.

Three spotchecks in Africa—from Nigeria to Ghana, among the central Bantus, and among the Nilotics—reveal comparable practices. As in Tonga, the Yoruba feel that children of the same mother are closer to one another than those of the same father. The Itsekiri outlaw marriage between *omere,* people having a woman as a common ancestor, but tolerate it between *egusa*, people whose common ancestor is a man. The kinship terminology of Benin makes uterine siblings equal to full siblings. The Edo of northwestern Africa authorize marriage between half-siblings born of the same father. Several groups in northern Nigeria ban marriage to any kin on the mother's side but allow it to distant kin on the father's side. In Ghana, the Gonja prohibit a man from marrying his parallel matrilateral cousin; while their neighbors the LoWiili prohibit marriage between the descendants of sisters. The Luapula of Zambia forbid marriage within the mother's descent group and even within her clan. Among the patrilineal Bantus, whose king marries his half-sister, only the agnate, not the uterine, are allowed. Thus, the Baganda, who proscribe marriage within the mother's clan, restrict royal incest to the agnate half-sister. In contrast, the matrilineal Bantus allow it only with a uterine half-sister, but the sons of this half-sister cannot succeed to the throne because they are classified as ordinary sons of the king. The Tswana disapprove of marriage to a matrilateral parallel cousin, regarding her as "too similar to the sister." The Venda outlaw marriage to the daughter of the mother's sister. Finally, among the Nuer of the Upper Nile, there is no worse form of incest than that with a female relative on the mother's side. Taking a more general point of view, F. Héritier notes that the Omaha kinship systems of the type frequent in Africa "do not permit marriage to the daughter of the mother's sister" (1981, p. 104).

Let us now approach the problem from a different angle. Africa and New Guinea offer many examples of kinship systems that allow the transformation of agnates into non-agnates and vice versa, sometimes *de jure*, sometimes only *de facto*. In New Guinea, the systems of the Mae Enga, the Tombema Enga, and even the Manga have been described, analyzed, and discussed more than enough, so that it is not necessary to go into them. We know that in Africa, too, a female link in a genealogy is often counted as a male link after two or three generations, so that, even among the Nuer, cognates are transformed into agnates.

On the other hand, the royal lineages of the Yoruba manage to limit their membership by means of two complementary processes: they expel from their midst overly powerful collaterals, and they urge overly poor collaterals to join the maternal line, in the hope of obtaining land while at the same time giving up their dynastic rights. After two or three generations, these former agnates-become-cognates turn into commoners (Lloyd 1960). Similarly, among the Basuto and in Buganda, there has been observed regular movement within the social structure in which royal collaterals are pushed to the periphery and replaced with direct descendants of the sovereign, and commoners are pushed even farther to make room for the displaced royal collaterals. A special category is thus formed of "peasant princes" or "rejected princes," who doubtless remain collaterals in an agnate line but lose the prerogatives of that state, starting with the chief one: they can no longer succeed to the throne. The same mechanisms are observed among the Shilluk as well as in Cameroon, and also in Bali. The Swazi in southern Africa limit the power of the royal house by creating new sub-clans whose members cannot succeed to the throne, and to which the reigning sovereign gradually shifts any collaterals too close to the throne. The same was true in ancient Japan: according to the Taihô Code, which was promulgated in 701, descendants of the emperor were to forfeit their princely quality in the sixth generation (as they apparently actually did in the third or fourth generation); given new names, these descendants founded lines within the ordinary nobility. In all these cases, moreover, these *ad hoc* non-agnates—if we may call them that—began again to procreate agnates for their original line every time a sovereign married one of their daughters.

Let us go one step farther. In New Guinea and Africa, there are kinship systems that experts on New Guinea have dubbed "partial Omaha systems," because the characteristic obliquity of the Crow-Omaha nomenclatures appears on only one side instead of both. Specialists on Africa use almost the same terms. Witness J. H. M. Beattie, who writes that the principle of the unity of lineage, posed by Radcliffe-Brown, applies here only unilaterally (1958, p. 14), in regard to a system where the female cross-cousin on the mother's side and her brother's daughter are, like the maternal aunt, called "little mother"; and where a man calls his wife's agnates—whatever their generation level—"father (or mother) of my wife," although there is no overall term for the husbands of female agnates without distinction of generation.

The analysis of New Guinean terms suggests that nomenclatures where the female cross-cousin on the mother's side is known by the same word as the mother, may aim at—or, at least, result in—hindering too prompt returns to marriage with the mother's clan or line. In other words, in these systems, a man meets fewer obstacles to marrying the same way as his female agnates than he does to marrying the same way as his male agnates. Beattie explains the asymmetry of marital nomenclature among the Banyoro by the fact that each male member of Ego's agnate group is led to establish ties with a different line of kin (1958, p. 13). In the same way, the matrimonial prohibitions of the Tullishi, whose asymmetry has been demonstrated by S. F. Nadel (1950, p. 350), become clear in light of the rule that Ego, who is forbidden wives from his own or his father's matrilineal clan, cannot contract the same type of marriage as his father or father's father.

Thus, many of the societies we are dealing with reject long cycles —in preference either to short cycles (from marriage by exchange through marriage with a patrilateral female cross-cousin, to royal incest with an agnate half-sister) or to entirely new alliances, which may therefore be considered as limited instances of such long cycles as to exceed the very notion of cycle. Thus, depending on time and occasion, these societies give themselves the freedom to choose between extremely short cycles of alliance and cycles that are so long that alliances become systematically dispersed (think of the Itsekiri, who prohibit marriage between people having a common ancestor as far back as the seventh generation).

Even the marital customs of the Lovedu, about whom E. J. Krige (1975a) and E. Leach (1961) have stirred up or maintained much uncertainty, must be interpreted in the same way. Preferential marriage with matrilateral cross-cousins pertains to generalized exchange. However, the Lovedu narrow it down, so to speak, to restricted exchange because of their inability to conceive of matrimonial transactions on any but a cash-and-carry basis. In such a system, women are exchanged not for other women but for cattle; more precisely, one gives cattle to have a wife and then gives a woman to recover the cattle. The cycles (which would close only if complete equivalence were assumed between woman and cattle) come apart as soon as a father's sister gives up her right to have her son marry her niece—as can happen for various reasons pointed out by Krige herself. On such an occasion, another social unit, the cognate but lasting *moloko* takes over for the unstable house. Haunted, owing to its very precariousness, by the short term and the "give-and-take" rule, the house must sooner or later give in to the *moloko*, which enjoys more freedom in the choice of its matrimonial strategies. Thus, the Lovedu case is somewhat analogous to that of the Mambila in western Cameroon, who practice two types of marriage: by exchange, in which the partners receive the exact equivalent of what they give; and by purchase, which allows each side to speculate entirely for its own profit, the goal being to acquire, at the other's expense, the greatest number of new members before giving up the procreative power of its daughters (Rehfisch 1960).

In these conditions, how are we to interpret the patrilineal predominance attributed to groups that allow marriage in a closer degree on the father's side than on the mother's? First of all, practically all these groups are part of territorial ensembles in which a transition from a patrilineal to a matrilineal trend (or vice versa) can be observed. This is the case among the Kwakiutl on the northwestern coast of North America as well as among the groups dwelling on the coast and in the interior of the Gulf of Guinea, and among the central Bantus.

Anthropologists, especially in England, have gone to great pains to identify and tag extreme and intermediate types of marriage with the help of a terminology that is probably too analytical: it distinguishes between filiation and descent and characterizes the one or the other, or even both, with such terms as "unilineal," "bilineal," "ambilineal," "multilineal," "utrolateral," or "dual descent." One may nevertheless wonder whether the choice of these labels and their attribution might not depend on an individual researcher's particular point of view rather than on distinctive traits attributable to the societies themselves. An unbiased perusal of the literature shows that often different names are applied to the same or to very similar rules, and that the question whether a rule belongs to a specific type can rarely be answered with a simple yes or no. Between societies or even within a single society, variations are perceptible—albeit in degree and not in nature.

By refining the details and trying to pigeonhole every discernible nuance in these systems, one overlooks the essential: namely, that the societies in question are not distinguished from one another by intrinsic modes of filiation or descent. In varying degrees, these societies follow what, to avoid the equivocal English terms *non-unilineal* and *bilineal* (and their literal French translations), I have repeatedly suggested calling "undifferentiated systems": that is, a system where the elements of personal status and hereditary rights and obligations are handed down indifferently in either line or both, which does not prevent people from thinking of them as distinct. In calling these systems now unilineal and now bilineal (whatever their criteria), our British and American colleagues pull them, so to speak, on the side of systems of dual descent—and sometimes even include them in that category; when, as is proved by the frequency of sexual affiliation in undifferentiated systems, it is rather the systems of dual descent that refer to a particular case, as if it were pushed to the limit, of undifferentiated systems.

In such systems, the point is not to identify a mode of filiation or descent characterizing each one. As has already been touched on explicitly or implicitly, in the interpretations proposed by Audrey I. Richards in a chapter in *African Systems of Kinship and Marriage*, by E. E. Evans-Pritchard in the Frazer Lecture of 1948, and by G. Lienhardt in an article (1955), the truly pertinent factor is to seek in respective power—"respective pull," according to Richards—of the paternal and the maternal kin or, more precisely, of the wife takers and the wife givers.

Indeed, as a taker, a group uses its men to strengthen its position; as a giver, it uses its women, whatever its mode of filiation may be. It happens only that in certain societies—or in the same society at different periods, or even in different milieus of a society during the same period—this relationship may become strained, and the tension may leave its mark on customs. This relationship may be ambiguous; or, to put it differently, the position of either taker or giver seems superior in certain respects and inferior in others. A recent article by E. Bott on the kingdom of Tonga shows that, in an intricately hierarchical society with undifferentiated descent, the exchange cycles may nevertheless link up owing to two parameters, rank and position, which vary inversely to one another; as a result, the instant the cycle closes, "political power was eventually converted into high rank" (1981, p. 57).

It is from this relationship—strained, or unstable, or both at once—that cognation arises. Paul Vinogradoff, the great legal historian, writes that even where blood ties are recognized, relations are organized from house to house, so that cognation appears as the result of an alliance between families organized in a patriarchal way (Vinogradoff 1920). Nevertheless, the patriarchal aspect that Vinogradoff sees in houses related by marriage does not necessarily derive from the old blood ties which, according to him, precede cognation. It would be better to assert that, within the alliance, the relationship uniting and opposing takers and givers wavers between two poles. This oscillation may take place in time, because of demographic fluctuations within the society itself; it can also put societies in lasting opposition to one another for deeper reasons, rooted in their structures. In either case, the wavering engenders what one might call pseudomorphs: that is, aspects of the social structure that are superficially perceived as patrilineal or matrilineal, and that lead to mistaken definitions of systems that are neither, because even if the rule of filiation or descent exists, it is not the operative factor. All debates on Indo-European kinship systems are still burdened by this misapprehension.

The primacy of the exchange relationship over the unilineal criterion and of alliance over filiation explains that groups practicing exchange can, if they like, practice both exogamy and endogamy simultaneously or successively. Exogamy enables them to diversify alliances and to gain certain advantages (at the price, however, of certain risks); while endogamy consolidates and perpetuates previously acquired advantages (though not without exposing the momentarily more powerful line to dangers in the form of collaterals who have become rivals). This is a twofold dynamic of opening and closing, whereby one movement corresponds to a statistical model, and the other to a mechanical model: by means of the one, a group opens itself to history and exploits the resources of chance; while the other assures the preservation or the regular recovery of patrimonies, ranks, and titles.

Thus, the question with which this chapter opened was badly stated. The issue is not why certain societies favor unions closer to the father's side than the mother's, *even though* the paternal right seems to dominate. On the contrary, it is *because* paternal relatives occupy the stronger position as takers of wives that endogamy is of interest to them and that they practice it to their advantage. Historians tell us that in France, up to the time of Philip Augustus (1165-1223), the daughters of kings could inherit appanages. In the thirteenth century, Philip the Fair restricted this privilege to male heirs, in order to return appanages to the crown sooner and to prevent them from passing through the women into foreign or enemy houses. Patrilinealism is thus introduced as a mode of endogamy or, more precisely, as its replacement, since endogamy in undifferentiated filiation also assures the preservation of patrimonies. In these terms, the results are equivalent whether the group practices undifferentiated filiation *plus* endogamy or patrilineal filiation *plus* exogamy: the former constitutes a rampart against the possible dangers inherent in the latter. It is striking that, among royal families in early France, or among those close to the throne, exogamic unions regularly enabled paternal relatives or wife takers to obtain landed patrimonies brought as a dowry by wives procured from the outside.

The imbalance between takers and givers also works in the opposite direction. It is not quite clear why the Lozi of present-day Zambia (formerly Northern Rhodesia) "say that a man should not marry a woman with whom he is linked only by patrilineal ties," according to M. Gluckman, who adds, "Most Northern Rhodesian tribes have matrilineal exogamous clans but also forbid intermarriage with ortho-cousins on the father's side" (1950, p. 173). The Lozi are not matrilineal, however; and, while Gluckman is sometimes unsure of the ultimate nature of their system, everything points to undifferentiated descent.

Furthermore, according to a great deal of data supplied by Gluckman, the respective positions of the takers and the givers differed, in the past, from what has been observed in societies where the paternal right is merely a way of affirming the superiority of the takers: even after the wedding (whose all but normal outcome is divorce), the wife is attached first and foremost to her parents; the cattle the man has paid for the marriage do not give him an automatic right to his wife's children; her sterility does not terminate the contract; after a husband's death, his kin have no claims on the widow; the children automatically belong not to the legal husband's family but to the family of their mother or of the man who actually fathered them; the marriage rites express the hostility and the conciliation of the two lines involved. Gluckman contrasts the pull of agnate lineage ties, in actual or supposed patrilineal societies, with the territorial or economic motives that may "pull a man to settle" amid his wife's kinfolk, whether on her father's or her mother's side (p. 201).

More conclusive appears medieval Japan, where the wedding banquet, *tokoroarawishi*, was a public act by which the wife's family demonstrated its acceptance of the husband as a new member, who would now be living with it. Before the feast, the wife's mother or some other older woman in the family would serve rice cakes to the young couple lying in the nuptial bed, symbolically discover the husband's presence, and make him part of the new household by having him eat food cooked on the domestic hearth (McCullough and McCullough 1980, I, p. 297 n. 158).

It is true that the Kwakiutl, cited at the beginning of this chapter, also celebrated the bridegroom's entrance into his father-in-law's house; likewise, certain facts suggest that, in ancient times, a Japanese man could marry his half-sister by the same father but not by the same mother (Aston 1896, I, p. 323). Nevertheless, during these periods, political sovereignty was transmitted through the paternal line in both societies; and we may wonder whether the ambiguity of the respective positions of bride takers and bride givers might have resulted from the coexistence of two antagonistic principles, providing the same kind of difference as that traced by historians of the European Middle Ages between royal power and the ties of vassalage. Both the Japanese imperial throne and the Kwakiutl chieftainry were *de jure* hereditary in the agnate line, but ties of another sort made a son-in-law subordinate to his father-in-law. Thus, depending on the case, the time, or the occasion, the scales may tilt to either side. From the seventh to the eleventh centuries, Japanese emperors were strictly dependent on their maternal relatives, because one group of wife givers, the Fujiwara, had ensured real power for themselves by systematically marrying their sisters and daughters to the reigning sovereign and his possible successors. The closest unions here were on the mother's side, contrary to the cases that we have been studying: between the eighth and the eleventh centuries, at least three Japanese sovereigns married a younger sister of their mother.*

We cannot exclude the possibility that the rule of Sparta, which offers a symmetrical image to that of Athens (marriage being permitted between children of the same mother and of different fathers), may be interpreted on the same basis. The perplexity of Athenian authors about the privileged position of Spartan women, which these writers considered outrageous, and about the freedom of their morals would spring from the distorted view of a society where the wife givers outranked the wife takers in status, prestige, and power. Such was doubtless the case in Troy, where Priam gathered in his palace his sons and sons-in-law along with their wives and children. J.-P. Vernant finds, in the *Iliad* and in Apollodorus, several examples of legendary marriages between a man and his maternal aunt, which, Vernant notes, could not have failed to astonish the Greeks (1974, p. 74). The Fujiwara case, which has been documented down to the slightest detail for several centuries, seems likely to illuminate, from the point of view that I have taken, the sociological conditions favoring this type of match or, reasoning in reverse, the Athenian type, on which attention has been focused for a longer period.

---

*A form of marriage whose prototype is the marriage of the two deities—the son of a mother's elder sister and of a mother's younger sister—who produced Jimmu Tennô, the first Japanese emperor endowed with a properly human nature (Aston 1896, I, p. 108).

PART III

THE ENVIRONMENT

AND ITS

REPRESENTATION

Les êtres particuliers intelligents peuvent avoir des lois qu'ils ont faites: mais ils en ont aussi qu'ils n'ont pas faites. Avant qu'il y eût des êtres intelligents, ils étaient possibles; ils avaient donc des rapports possibles, et par conséquent des lois possibles.

MONTESQUIEU

L'Esprit des Lois

Chapter 7

Structuralism and Ecology

IT IS INDEED a pleasure to be back at Barnard College after almost thirty years* and to be given this opportunity to honor the memory of Dean Virginia Gildersleeve. I can still remember her gracious welcome when, living as a refugee in New York during the war years, I paid her my respects and thanked her upon my appointment to teach during a summer session. The invitation had come unexpectedly owing to the kindness of Dr. Gladys A. Reichard, to whose memory I also wish to pay tribute. A fine woman and a great anthropologist, she taught for more than thirty years at Barnard College. We became acquainted at the informal meetings that led to the foundation of the Linguistic Circle of New York; and I was often at her house near Barnard where she liked to invite colleagues and friends. She had already written her major work, *Navaho Religion* (1963), whose structural bent may owe something to the friendly discussions she had with Roman Jakobson and myself—a small fact that she generously recalled in her preface.

I shall never forget my fright when I gave my first lecture at Barnard in the early 1940s. I had already been teaching at the New School for

---

*This chapter was originally a talk that I gave in English to alumnae of Barnard College in New York in 1972.

Social Research; but this was different. Most of the people attending the evening classes at the New School were adults leading a professional life, who came to brush up their general knowledge or to learn about a specialized field. Most of them, too, were foreign-born and refugees like myself, and their English was not much better than mine. At Barnard, I was admitted for the first time into the traditional American academic system—one where the great Franz Boas himself had taught for many years. It is even said that his class at Barnard, consisting of débutantes, was the one he liked best.

When I settled myself behind the table and started lecturing on the Nambikwara Indians, my fright changed to panic: no student was taking notes; instead of writing, they were knitting. They went on knitting until the hour was over as if they were paying no attention to what I was saying—or, rather, trying to say in my clumsy English. They did listen, though, for after the class was over, a girl (I can still see her: slender, graceful, with short and curly ash-blond hair, and wearing a blue dress) came up to me and said that it was all very interesting but she thought I should know that *desert* and *dessert* are different words. Her remark, which left me quite dismayed, deserves recalling because it shows that, in those remote years, I was already interested in ecology and mixing it, on a linguistic level at least, with the culinary art which later served to illustrate some of the structural workings of the human mind. And since my present topic happens to be "Structuralism and Ecology," the chiding of a former Barnard student is not irrelevant.

The structural approach I have followed for over a quarter of a century has often been assessed by my Anglo-Saxon colleagues as "idealism" or "mentalism." I have even been labeled as Hegelian. Certain critics have accused me of seeing structures of thought as the cause of culture, sometimes even of confusing them. Or else they believe that I claim to tackle the structure of the human mind directly in order to seek what they ironically call "Lévi-Straussian universals." If this were the case, study of the cultural contexts within which the mind operates, and through which it manifests itself, would, indeed, be of little interest. But were that so, why should I have chosen to become an anthropologist instead of following the philosophical career for which my academic training destined me? And why do I, in my books, pay so much attention to the most minute ethnographical details? Why do I try to identify precisely the plants and the animals known by each society; the different technical uses to which they are put; and, if these plants or animals are edible, how they are prepared

—that is, boiled, stewed, steamed, roasted, grilled, fried, or even dried or smoked for curing? For years, I have worked surrounded by globes and celestial maps that have allowed me to track the position of the stars and constellations in different latitudes and seasons; by treatises on geology, geography, and meteorology; by works on botany; by books on mammals and on birds.

The reason is very simple: one can undertake no research whatever without first collecting and verifying all the data. As I have often pointed out, no general principle or deductive process allows us to anticipate the chance events that constitute the history of each group, the peculiar features of its environment, or the unpredictable way each has chosen to interpret particular historical events or aspects of its habitat, out of the many possible events or aspects that it could have endowed with meaning.

Anthropology is, above all, an empirical science. Each culture is a unique situation which can be described and understood only at the cost of the most painstaking attention. Such scrutiny alone reveals not only the facts but also the criteria, which vary from one culture to another, and according to which each confers significance on certain animal or vegetable species, certain minerals, certain celestial bodies and other natural phenomena, in order to make a logical system out of a finite set of data. Empirical study allows access to structure. For, even if the same elements have been retained here and there, experience proves that these identical elements can be accounted for by way of different reasons; and that, inversely, different elements sometimes fulfill the same function. Each culture settles on a few distinctive features of its environment, but no one can predict which these are or to what end they will be put. Furthermore, so great is the wealth and diversity of the raw material offered by the environment for observation and reflection that the mind is capable only of apprehending a fraction of it. The mind can put it to use for elaborating one system among an infinity of other, equally conceivable ones: nothing predestines any one among them for a privileged fate.

Thus, at the outset, we run into an arbitrary factor from which spring difficulties that experience alone can solve. However, although the choice of elements may appear arbitrary, these become organized into a system, and the connections between them form a whole. In *The Savage Mind*, I wrote that "the principle underlying a classification can never be postulated in advance; it can only be discovered *a posteriori* by ethnographic observation—that is, by experience" (1966, p. 58). The coherence of each system of classification depends strictly on constraints specific to the functioning of the human mind. These constraints determine how symbols are formed, and explain their opposition and how they connect.

Ethnographical observation does not, therefore, oblige us to choose between two hypotheses: either a plastic mind passively shaped by outside influences; or universal psychological laws that everywhere give rise to and invite the same properties regardless of history and of the particular environment. Rather, what we witness and try to describe are attempts to realize a sort of compromise between certain historical trends and special characteristics of the environment, on the one hand, and, on the other, mental requirements that in each area carry on previous ones of the same kind. In adjusting to each other, these two orders of reality mingle so as to make a meaningful whole.

There is nothing Hegelian in such a conception. Instead of coming from nowhere at a philosopher's discretion who likely would have made only a rapid survey, limited to a small part of the globe and to a few centuries of the history of ideas, these constraints of the human mind are found by an inductive process. We are able to reach them only by patient examination of how, in like or unlike ways, they are reflected in the ideology of dozens or even hundreds of societies. Besides, we do not judge these constraints as acquired once and for all or take them as a key that, in psychoanalytical fashion, will allow us henceforth to open all locks. Instead, we are guided by the linguists, who are well aware that all the world's grammars exhibit common properties, and who hope to be able to find language universals. But linguists know that the logical system formed by these universals will be much poorer than any particular grammar and can never replace one. They know, too, that it is an endless task to study language in general and particular languages that have existed or still exist, and that a finite set of rules will never exhaust their common properties. If and when universals are reached, they will appear as open structures: one will always be able to add definitions and to complete, enlarge on, or correct earlier ones.

Therefore, two kinds of determinism are simultaneously at work in social life; and it is no wonder that, being different in nature, each may appear arbitrary from the point of view of the other. Behind every ideological construct, older constructs stand out; and they echo back in time to the hypothetical moment when, hundreds of thousands of years ago and maybe more, a stammering mankind thought out and expressed its first myths. And it is also true that, at each stage of this complex process, each ideological construct becomes modified by prevailing technological and economic conditions; they warp and deform it in several ways. Any common mechanism that may underlie the various ways in which the human mind operates in different societies, at different stages of historical development, does not operate in a vacuum. These mental cogwheels must be put in gear with other mechanisms; observation never reveals the isolated performance of a single mechanism; we can affirm only the results of their interaction.

These views, which are not at all philosophical, are forced upon us by the most rigorous ethnographical examination of each particular problem. I shall try to illustrate this practice with samples taken from the mythological analysis on which I have been working for some twenty years.

The Heiltsuk or Bella Bella Indians are closely related to their southern neighbors, the Kwakiutl, on the coast of British Columbia. Both groups tell the story of a child—a girl or a boy according to different versions—who is kidnapped by a cannibalistic supernatural being, generally female, who is called Kāwaka by the Bella Bella and Dzōnokwa by the Kwakiutl. As in the Kwakiutl tales, the Bella Bella explain that the child succeeds in escaping; the ogress is killed or put to flight. Her considerable fortune falls to the father of the hero or the heroine, and he distributes it around. Thus is explained the origin of the potlatch.

Sometimes, the Bella Bella versions differ from those of the Kwakiutl in a curious incident. A supernatural helper instructs the girl or the boy how to get free from the ogress: when the ogress, according to habit, goes to gather clams at low tide, the child must collect the siphons, a part of the mollusk that the ogress does not eat and that she discards. The child is to put these organs on the tips of his or her fingers and brandish them at the ogress, who will become so frightened that she will fall backward into an abyss and be killed.

Why should a powerful ogress be frightened by something as harmless and insignificant as clam siphons—these soft, little trunks by means of which mollusks take in and expel water, and which are conspicuous in some species of clam? (These siphons are also very handy for holding the steamed shellfish and dipping it in drawn butter, a famous specialty of a restaurant near Times Square when I lived in New York.) This point is not dealt with by the Bella Bella myths.

In order to solve the problem, we must apply an essential rule of structural analysis: whenever a version of a myth contains a detail that seems anomalous, one asks oneself whether, in deviating from the normal, this version is contradicting another, which is usually not far away.

The terms *deviating* and *normal* are to be understood here in a relative sense. A version chosen for reference will be called "straight"; and in respect to it, the others will appear "inverted." But one could equally well proceed in the other direction, except for certain cases (examples of which I have provided in my Science of Mythology series [1969, 1973, 1979, 1981]) where the transformation can take place only in a certain direction. In the present case, the "straight" version is easily located. It is found among the Chilcotin, who lived inland, east of the coastal mountains. But they knew the Bella Bella well and often visited them on the other side of the mountains. Their languages were undoubtedly different, the Chilcotin belonging to the Athapaskan family. In everything else, the Chilcotin resembled the coastal tribes, from whom they borrowed many features of their social organization.

What do we learn from the Chilcotin myth? It says that an infant boy who cries all the time (like the little girl in one of the Bella Bella versions) is kidnapped by Owl. This powerful sorcerer treats him well, and the child grows up satisfied with his lot. When, after years, his friends and parents discover his retreat, he refuses to follow them. He is finally persuaded. When Owl gives chase to the little band, the boy frightens him by putting mountain-goat horns on his fingers and brandishing them like claws. He has taken with him all the dentalia shells (little white univalves, looking like tiny elephant tusks) of which, until this time, Owl has been sole owner. It is in this way that the Indians obtained these shells, which are their most precious possession.

As the rest of the Chilcotin myth does not relate to this discussion, I shall omit it, along with the versions coming from the Bella Coola, who were Salish-speaking neighbors of both the Bella Bella and the Chilcotin. These versions retain the incident of the mountain-goat horns and transform the Bella Bella myth by attributing to the ogress, whom the Bella Coola call Sninik, characteristics the exact reverse of those of both the Bella Bella and the Kwakiutl ogress. It is from this particular perspective that one must analyze these versions.

Let us limit ourselves to the Bella Bella and the Chilcotin myths. It is obvious that so far they are organized in the same way, and that only the respective connotations attributed to each element are inverted. A crying boy among the Chilcotin, a crying girl in the more developed

Bella Bella version, is kidnapped by a supernatural being: a female ogress in human form, in one case; a benevolent male sorcerer in the form of a bird, in the other. To escape this captor, the hero or the heroine resorts to the same strategem: they fit their fingers with artificial claws. But these claws are either the horns of goats or the siphons of clams—that is, either something hard and harmful coming from the land, or something soft and harmless coming from the sea. As a result, the Chilcotin owl falls in the water and does not drown, while the Bella Bella ogress crashes on the rocks and dies. Horns and siphons, thus, are *means* leading to an *end*. Of what exactly does this end consist? The hero or the heroine becomes the first owner of either the dentalia shells or the treasures belonging to the ogress. Now all the mythological and ritual data that we have concerning this Kāwaka—or Dzōnokwa, as the Kwakiutl call her—attest that her treasures all come from the land, as they consist of copper plates, furs, dressed skins, and dried meat. In other Bella Bella and Kwakiutl myths, this same ogress —land dweller, denizen of forests and mountains—continually steals salmon from the Indians but does not fish.

Each myth explains, thus, how a determined end was reached by an equally determined means. And, since we are considering two myths, each has a different means and a different end. It is remarkable that one means shows an affinity with water (the clam siphons) and the other with land (the goat horns); the first means leads to an end of a terrestrial nature (the treasures of the ogress), and the second leads to an end of a marine nature (the dentalia shells). As a result, the "water means," so to speak, leads to a "terrestrial end"; and, conversely, the "terrestrial means" to a "water end."

Moreover, two supplementary relationships emerge between the means in one myth and the end or result in the other. That clam siphons, *means* of the Bella Bella myth, and dentalia shells, *end* of the Chilcotin myth, have something in common is obvious: they both come from the sea. Nevertheless, the role vested in them in native cultures opposes them: for the Chilcotin, dentalia shells are by far the most precious objects the sea has to offer; while the Bella Bella myth accords no value to clam siphons, not even as food, since the ogress throws them away without eating them.

Now what about the mountain-goat horns, the *means* in the Chilcotin myth, and the earthly treasures of the ogress, whose acquisition is the *result* in the Bella Bella myth? Unlike seashells, these both belong to the terrestrial world. Goat horns, however, though unfit to eat, serve to make ceremonial objects: those marvelously wrought and sculpted spoons that we admire in museums are works of art and emblematic objects; they are treasure. Moreover, if not edible, the spoons provide, like the clam siphons, a convenient means (cultural instead of natural) to carry the food to the mouth of the eater. If, therefore, despite their common origin, the means in one myth and the result in the other are opposed, a parallel is established between the result in the first myth and the means in the second, which also have a common origin but (terrestrial instead of marine) exactly opposite.

I have simply outlined the dialectical relationship between two myths of neighboring tribes—an outline that could easily be enriched and refined. It will, however, suffice to demonstrate that rules exist allowing the transformation of one myth into another, and that these complex rules are nonetheless coherent. Where do these rules come from? We do not invent them in the course of analysis. They are, so to speak, liberated by the myths. When formulated by the analyst, they rise to the surface as visible manifestations of laws governing the mind of the people when they hear neighbors narrate one of their myths. For the listeners may borrow the myth, but not without deforming it through mental operations that they do not control. They will appropriate it in order not to feel themselves to be inferior, while remodeling it consciously or unconsciously, until it becomes their own.

These manipulations are not random. The inventory of American mythology which I have been engaged upon for many years apparently shows that different myths result from a transformation that obeys certain rules of symmetry and inversion: myths reflect each other according to axes on which one can construct the list. To account for the phenomenon, we cannot escape the conclusion that mental operations obey laws not unlike those operating in the physical world. These constraints, which keep ideological constructs within an isomorphism where only certain kinds of transformation are possible, exemplify the first type of determinism I have mentioned.

This is, however, only half of the story: other questions remain to be answered. If we decide to select the Chilcotin myth as our reference, we must wonder why these Indians needed to explain the origin of dentalia shells, and why they did it in such a bizarre way, by giving them a terrestrial instead of an oceanic origin? And, supposing that some necessity required the Bella Bella to alter the image of mountain-goat horns used as claws, why had they to pick clam siphons out of the many objects in their natural environment which could have fulfilled the same function? Why, finally, did the Bella Bella seem uninterested in the origin of dentalia shells, reserving all their attention for a different kind of treasure? These questions oblige us to turn toward a second type of determinism which brings external constraints to bear on ideology. But neither the characteristics of the natural environment, nor the modes of life, nor even social and political conditions were exactly the same among the inland tribes and the coastal tribes.

Dentalia shells were highly valued among the inland tribes, eastern neighbors of the Chilcotin and belonging to the Salish linguistic stock. They obtained these shells from the Chilcotin and hence called them the "dentalia people" (Teit 1909, p. 759). Hence, in order to protect their monopoly and to give it more prestige in their neighbors' eyes, the Chilcotin had a vested interest in making others believe that they possessed an inexhaustible quantity of dentalia shells, which originated in their own land as a result of supernatural events that specially favored them.

In this way, they hid an utterly different reality: the Chilcotin, in fact, got the dentalia shells by trade, through the mountain passes, with coastal tribes, which alone had direct access to the products of the sea. According to old accounts, these coastal tribes were on friendly terms with the Chilcotin, whom they never made war on "as they seldom ventured far from their home on the seacoast or on the lower reaches of the rivers, and seem to have had great awe of entering the forbidden and unknown fastness of the mountains" (Teit 1909, p. 761). Indeed, inland Salish like the Thompson and the Coeur d'Alene tribes who, unlike the Chilcotin, were unaware of the actual origin of dentalia shells, had a series of myths that is both symmetrical with and the invented form of those of the purveyors of these shells. They recount that, in former times, dentalia shells existed in their territory, and that they disappeared in the wake of certain events, so that today the Indians can obtain these precious articles only by trade.

Quite other was the situation of the coastal tribes in respect to the products of both land and sea. For them, products of the sea belonged to technological and economic activities: fishing or gathering clams was the usual occupation of the coastal Indians, who ate these products themselves or sold them to the Chilcotin. As my neo-Marxist colleagues would say, these goods were part and parcel of their praxis. On the other hand, for products of the land, the Indians were tributaries of those mountains where they dared not venture, and whose inhabitants visited them in order to barter land products for sea products. These inverted relationships provide a formal analogy with those we have discerned between the respective myths on the ideological level: that is, the fact that, in the myths, a means connected with the land leads to a result connected with the sea; while, in the second case, it is the other way around. Hence, we understand why the coastal tribes do not need to "mythologize" the seashells—these belong to their praxis; and also why, if the mythical transformation takes the form of a chiasmus as is often the case, the shift of the marine element from the category of result to that of means can be appropriately achieved by substituting the clam siphons for the dentalia shells. They stand to each other in the same doubly inverted relationship that prevails between the respective ecologies of the two types of peoples.

Let us first consider the horns of the mountain goat. It is their *pointed tip*—curving out and, in this sense, *convex*—that makes dangerous weapons of them; while their *concave* and *hollow base* allows them to be carved into spoons and thus be part of a treasure. On the contrary, it is their *convex, hard exterior* that makes dentalia shells a treasure; as for the interior of these univalves, it contains an insignificant mollusk that is unfit to eat. In all these relationships, the dentalia shells are thus opposed to the clam siphons: hollow, soft tubes, internal appendages of bivalves that play a major role in the diet of coastal people. The Bella Bella myth, however, denies any food value to the clam siphons, which appear, paradoxically, as conspicuous organs but lacking in interest. Thus, they can easily be "mythologized" for a reason opposite to the one that leads the people of the interior to explain the origin of the dentalia shells: people value them highly but do not have them; the coastal people have the clams but do not particularly value their siphons.

When confronted with technological and economic conditions linked with the natural environment, the mind does not stay passive. It does not merely reflect upon these conditions; it reacts to them and works them into a logical system. Furthermore, because the mind does not react only to its own environment, it is also aware that there exist different environments, to which their inhabitants react in their own way. All these environments, whether present or absent, are integrated into ideological systems which yield to other, mental constraints, which compel groups of a different mind to follow the same development. Two examples will allow me to demonstrate this idea.

The first comes from the same area as the previous ones: the Seechelt Indians, a Salish-speaking group settled north of the Fraser River delta. These Indians distort in a strange way a myth that extends west of the Rocky Mountains from the Columbia River basin to that of the Fraser. In its usual form, this myth is about a Trickster who persuades his son or grandson into climbing a tree to get the feathers of the birds nesting at the top. By magical means, he makes the tree grow up so that the hero cannot descend and is finally stranded in the sky world. After many adventures there, he succeeds in coming back to the earth, where the Trickster has taken the hero's physical appearance in order to seduce his wives. In revenge, the hero causes his evil parent to fall into a river whose current carries him to the sea where selfish supernatural women keep the salmon imprisoned. These women save the Trickster from drowning and welcome him; he takes advantage of them to destroy their dam and free the fish. Since that time, the salmon travel freely and, each year, swim up the rivers where the Indians catch and eat them.

It is a fact borne out by experience that salmon are fished during their yearly run when they return from the ocean and ascend the rivers to spawn in fresh water. In this regard, the myth reflects objective conditions, which are vital for the native economy and which the myth purports to explain. But the Seechelt tell the story differently. The father falls into water at the outset, under unknown circumstances; a woman rescues him and sends him back home. There he wants to avenge himself on his son, whom he considers responsible for his mishap, and dispatches the boy up to the sky world by the same magical means as in the other versions. In the sky, the hero meets two old women to whom he discloses that salmon abound near their dwelling place. As a sign of their gratitude for this revelation, they help him return to the earth.

Hence, in the Seechelt version, the Trickster's drowning and rescue by a woman living downstream replaces the first sequence of the other versions; and thus the episode of the drowning no longer makes sense. Inversely, the salmon episode is pushed back among the adventures in the sky world; and this celestial sequence comes after the aquatic sequence instead of before it. Finally, in the sky, it is a question no longer of liberating the fish but only of discovering that they are there.

How to explain all these aberrations? It is conceivable that the Seechelt have tried to repeat a story first heard from their neighbors, the Thompson Indians, who had a very full and detailed version of the myth; and not understanding it, the Seechelt made a complete mess of it. This theory would not take account of a crucial fact: the Seechelt lived in a different geographical area from their neighbors who lived further in the interior; salmon could not be fished in their territory as there were no rivers suitable for the salmon runs. In order to fish, the Seechelt had to venture among the Stseelis on the middle course of the Harrison River—invasions that sometimes led to bloody conflicts.

Since the Seechelt did not have salmon, they could not reasonably attribute their liberation to one of their cultural heroes; or, if they did, this liberation could occur not here on earth but in the sky, an imaginary world where experience has no claim. This shift makes the liberation episode meaningless: the Seechelt did not ask how the salmon became free to run up the rivers, a phenomenon contradicted by local experience; since their domain lacked salmon, the Seechelt preferred to attribute to them a metaphysical abode, rather than recognize their actual ecological inferiority compared with their neighbors.

Should the local ecology lead to change in one part of the story, mental constraints require that other parts be changed accordingly. Hence, the strange turn the tale takes: the son revenges himself for no apparent reason for a persecution that has not taken place; the father visits the sea-dwelling women without liberating the salmon; the son's discovery of the salmon in the sky replaces the father's liberation of them in the ocean; and so on.

There is another lesson in the previous example. If a simple one-way relationship, as between cause and effect, did prevail between the techno-economic infrastructure and ideology, we could expect the Seechelt myths to explain why their territory lacked salmon, or why, having once possessed them, they had lost them, to their neighbors' advantage; or they could have no myth at all about salmon. What we actually find is quite different: the absent salmon is made present by the myth—and in a way that accounts for the fact that, though present elsewhere, the salmon is nevertheless absent where it should be present. A mythical pattern contradicted by experience does not simply disappear; neither does it undergo a change that would bring it closer to experience. It goes on living its own life, and any transformation satisfies not the constraints of experience but those mental constraints wholly independent of the former. In our case, the axis whose poles are land and sea—the only "true" axis from the point of view of the environment as well as of techno-economic activity—oscillates from the horizontal to the vertical. The sea pole becomes a sky pole; the land pole connotes the low, instead of the near; an empirical axis becomes an imaginary one. This shift entails other shifts that have no conceivable relationship to experience but are also the outcome of a formal necessity.

The Seechelt myth thus strikingly illustrates the two kinds of influence that operate on mythic thought, and of which there are many other examples. I shall limit myself to one example which is particularly telling because, in another ecological and cultural context, a problem like the one I have just discussed is treated in the same way.

For the peoples of the Algonkian linguistic family who lived in the Canadian ecological zone, the porcupine was a real animal. They hunted it assiduously for its flesh, which they relished, and for its quills, which the women used in embroidery. The porcupine also played a conspicuous part in mythology. One myth speaks of two girls who, while traveling on foot to a distant village, find a porcupine nested in a fallen tree. One of the girls pulls out the poor animal's quills and throws them away. The tormented porcupine conjures up a snowstorm, and the girls perish of cold. Another myth has two lonely sisters for heroines. One day, while wandering far from their home, they find a porcupine nested in a fallen tree, and one of the girls is fool enough to sit on the rodent's back so that all its quills get stuck in her rump. It takes her a long time to recover from her wounds.

Now, the Arapaho, also members of the Algonkian linguistic stock, make the porcupine the hero of a quite different tale. According to them, the brothers Sun and Moon quarrel about the kind of wife each would like to marry: which would be better—a frog or a human girl? Moon, who prefers the latter, transforms himself into a porcupine in order to entice an Indian girl. So covetous is she of the quills that she climbs higher and higher up the tree in which the porcupine is pretending to take refuge. The porcupine succeeds by this ruse in luring her to the sky world, where Moon resumes his human form and marries her.

How are we to account for the differences between stories that, apart from the presence of the porcupine in both, seem to have nothing in common? Although widespread in the Canadian ecological zone, the porcupine was rare in, if not absent from, the Plains where the Arapaho moved a few centuries ago. In their new environment, they could not hunt the porcupine; and to get quills, they had to trade with northern tribes or undertake hunting expeditions of their own in foreign territory. These two conditions seem to have had an effect both on the technological and economic levels and on the mythological one. The Arapaho quillwork ranks among the best in North America, and their art was profoundly imbued with a mysticism that can scarcely be matched elsewhere. To the Arapaho, quillwork was a ritual activity; their women undertook no work of this kind without fasting and praying, in the hope of supernatural help which they deemed essential for the success of their work. As for Arapaho mythology, we have just seen that it radically modifies the characteristics of the porcupine. From a magical land-dwelling animal, master of the cold and the snow, it becomes—as in neighboring tribes—the animal disguise of a supernatural being in human form, a sky dweller responsible for a biological periodicity instead of a meteorological and physical one. The myth specifies, indeed, that Moon's wife becomes the first of her sex to have regular menses every month and, when pregnant, to be delivered after a fixed time span.

Therefore when we shift from the northern Algonkian to the Arapaho, the empirical axis—horizontal, uniting the near and the far —shifts to an imaginary axis—vertical, uniting the sky and the earth. This is exactly the same transformation we have witnessed among the Salish: it occurs when an animal, important both technologically and economically, is lacking in a particular geographical situation. Also, as with the Salish, there follow other transformations, which are inwardly, not outwardly, determined. Once it is understood that, despite their different origins, all these transformations are related, that they are structurally part of the same set, it is clear that the two stories are actually one and the same; and that coherent rules permit the conversion of one to the other.

In one case, the two women are sisters; in the other, they belong to different zoological species—human and amphibian. The sisters move on a horizontal plane from near to far, while the two other females move on a vertical plane from low to high. Instead of pulling out the porcupine's quills like the first heroine, the second is pulled out of her village, so to speak, by the quills she covets. One girl recklessly throws away the quills; the other girl desires them as precious objects. In the first group of stories, the porcupine nests in a dead tree that has fallen to the ground, while the same animal in the second group climbs up an endlessly growing tree. And if the first porcupine slows down the traveling sisters, the second lures the heroine into climbing up faster and faster. One girl crouches down on the porcupine's back; the other girl stretches out to grab it. The first porcupine is aggressive; the second is a seducer. While the former lacerates the girl from behind, the latter deflowers—that is, "pierces" her—in her foreparts.

Considered separately, none of these changes is attributable to environmental peculiarities; they result together from a logical necessity which links each to the other in a series of operations. Should an animal as important as the porcupine for the technology and the economy be lacking in a new environment, it could keep its role only in another world. As a result, low becomes high, horizontal swings to vertical, the internal becomes external, and so on. All these shifts proceed from an obscure wish: to maintain the coherent relationships conceived by men in a previous environment. So strong does the need for coherence appear to be that, to preserve the unvarying structure of relationships, people prefer to falsify the image of the environment rather than to acknowledge that the relationships with the actual environment have changed.

All these examples show how the two kinds of determinism to which I have referred are expressed: the one imposed on mythic thought by the constraints inherent in a relationship to a particular environment; the other drawn from persistent mental constraints which are independent of the environment. This interaction would be hard to understand if human relationships with the environment and the mind's inherent constraints arose from irreducibly separate orders. It is fitting to examine those mental constraints whose pervasiveness induces the assumption that they have a natural basis. If not, we risk falling into the snares of an old philosophical dualism. That one seeks to define man's biological nature in terms of anatomy and physiology in no way changes the fact that this corporal nature is also an environment in which humans exercise their faculties; this organic environment is so closely tied to the physical environment that man apprehends the second only through the mediation of the first. A certain affinity, thus, must exist between sensory data and their processing in the brain—the means of this apprehension—and the physical world itself.

The point I am trying to make can be illustrated by referring to the distinction in linguistics between the "etic" and "emic" levels. These convenient terms, coined from *phonetic* and *phonemic,* denote two complementary ways of approaching language sounds: either as they are perceived (or, rather, are believed to be perceived) by the ear, even if aided by acoustic devices, or as they are revealed after they have been described and analyzed by going behind phonic raw material to its constituent units. The anthropologist, following the linguist, seeks to restore empirical ideologies to the interplay of binary oppositions and transformation rules.

Convenient as the distinction may be in practice, it would be wrong to push it too far and grant it objective status. The work of the Russian neuropsychologist A. R. Luria (1976) has succeeded in convincing us that articulate language is not made up of sounds. He showed that the cerebral mechanisms for the perception of noises and of musical sounds are quite different from those that allow us to perceive the so-called sounds of language; and that a lesion of the left temporal lobe destroys the ability to analyze phonemes but leaves musical hearing intact. To explain this apparent paradox, one must acknowledge that, in linguistic attention, the brain isolates not sounds but distinctive features. Moreover, these traits are both logical and empirical, as they have been recorded on a screen by acoustic machines, which can be suspected of neither mentalism nor idealism. It follows that the only true "etic" level is the "emic" one.

Current research on the mechanisms of vision suggest similar conclusions. The eye does not merely photograph objects: it encodes their distinctive characteristics. These consist not of the qualities that we attribute to the things that surround us, but of an ensemble of relationships. In mammals, specialized cells in the cerebral cortex perform a kind of structural analysis, which, in other animal families, retinal and ganglion cells have already undertaken and even achieved. Each cell —whether in the retina, in the ganglions, or in the brain—responds only to a stimulus of a certain type: contrast between motion and immobility; presence or absence of color; changes in light or dark; objects whose contours are positively or negatively curved; direction of motion either straight or oblique, from right to left or the reverse, horizontal or vertical; and so on. Out of all this information, the mind reconstructs, so to speak, objects that have not been actually perceived as such. The analytical function of the retina prevails mostly in species devoid of a cerebral cortex, such as the frog; but it also exists in the squirrel. And among higher mammals in which the analytical function is largely taken over by the brain, cortical cells merely pick up operations that the sensory organs have already registered. There is every reason to believe that this encoding and decoding mechanism, which translates incoming data by means of several grids inscribed in the form of binary oppositions in the nervous system, also exists in man. Therefore, the immediate data of sensory perception are not raw material, an "etic" reality that, strictly speaking, does not exist; they are, from the beginning, distinctive abstractions of reality and thus belong to the "emic" level.

Should we insist on sticking to the "etic" /"emic" distinction, we would have to reverse the meanings that are ever more often given to these terms. It is the "etic" level, taken as sole reality by authors imbued with mechanistic materialism and sensualist philosophy, which is reduced to an appearance, an accidental figure, one we would call an artifact. On the other hand, the "emic" level is the one where the operation of perception and the most intellectual activities of the mind can meet and, mingling, can express their common subservience to the nature of reality itself. Structural arrangements are not a pure product of mental operations; the sense organs also function structurally; and beyond us, there are analogous structures in atoms, molecules, cells, and organisms. Since these structures, both internal and external, cannot be apprehended on the "etic" level, it follows that the nature of things is "emic," not "etic," and that the "emic" approach is the one that brings us closer to it. When the mind processes the empirical data that has been previously processed by the sense organs, it continues to work out structurally a material that it has received structured. And it can only do so if the mind, the body to which the mind belongs, and the things perceived by body and mind are part and parcel of one and the same reality.

If the stereochemical theory of odors developed by John E. Amoore (1970) is right, then a qualitative diversity, which—on the sensory level —is impossible to analyze and even to describe adequately, can be reduced to differences between geometrical properties of odoriferous molecules. Let me add one last example: in their important book *Basic Color Terms* (1969), Brent Berlin and Paul Kay should not, in my opinion, have equated opposition of black and white with that of consonant and vowel. Indeed, the cerebral maps of the visual and the auditory systems seem, each on its own account, to be broadly homologous with both the consonant and the vowel systems. In making use of the work of Wolfgang Köhler (1910-15) and Carl Stumpf (1926), Roman Jakobson has demonstrated that the dark and light opposition corresponds to the phonemes p and t, which, in the phonic point of view, oppose each other as grave and acute, and that, in the vowel system, the same opposition is shifted to u and i. To these two vowel phonemes a third, a, is opposed; and it, being more intensely chromatic—"less susceptible to the opposition of light and dark," says Jakobson (1962, p. 324)— corresponds to the color red whose name, according to Berlin and Kay, immediately follows, in a language, the names for black and white. In imitation of physicists, Berlin and Kay distinguish three dimensions of color—hue, saturation, and value (or luminosity). It is thus striking that their initial triangle—including white, black, and red—as compared with the consonant and the vowel triangles is comparable to the two linguistic triangles insofar as none requires hue—that is, the most "etic" dimension of the three (in the sense that one can determine a hue only by a criterion of fact: the length of light-waves). On the contrary, to say of a color that it is saturated or not saturated, that it has a dark or a light value, one must consider it in relation to another color: the perception of relationship, a logical act, precedes individual knowledge of objects. But the place of red in the basic triangle of colors does not involve hue; red is merely situated at the extremity of an axis whose poles are respectively defined by the presence or the absence of chromatism, which characterizes the whole axis of black and white. One can thus always define the saturation of a color, or its luminosity, by means of binary oppositions, in asking whether, in regard to another color whose hue no longer needs to be determined, the characteristic is present or absent. Here, too, the complexities of sensory perception presuppose a simple and logical underlying structure.

Only a close collaboration between the natural and the human sciences will permit the rejection of an outmoded philosophical dualism. Instead of opposing ideal and real, abstract and concrete, "emic" and "etic," one will recognize that the immediate data of perception cannot be reduced to any of these terms but lies betwixt and between: that is, already encoded by the sense organs as well as by the brain, in the manner of a *text* which, like any text, must be decoded so that it can be translated into the language of other texts. Furthermore, the physico-chemical processes through which this original text was primitively encoded are not substantially different from the analytical procedures that the mind uses in decoding. The ways and means of understanding do not pertain exclusively to the highest intellectual activity, because the understanding takes over and develops intellectual processes already operating in the sensory organs themselves.

Vulgar materialism and sensual empiricism put man in direct confrontation with nature, but without seeing that the latter has structural properties that, while undoubtedly richer, do not differ essentially from the codes by which the nervous system deciphers them or from the categories elaborated by the understanding to return to reality's original structure. It is not being mentalist or idealist to acknowledge that the mind is able to understand the world only because the mind is itself part and product of this world. It is verified a little more each day that, in trying to understand the world, the mind operates in ways that do not differ in kind from those that have unfolded in the world since the beginning of time.

Structuralists have often been accused of playing with abstractions having no bearing upon reality. I have tried to show that, far from being an amusement for sophisticated intellectuals, structural analysis gets going in the mind only because its model already exists in the body. From the very start, visual perception rests on binary oppositions; and neurologists would probably agree that this statement is also true of other areas of cerebral activity. By following a path that is sometimes wrongly accused of being overly intellectual, structuralism recovers and brings to awareness deeper truths that have already been dimly announced in the body itself; it reconciles the physical and the moral, nature and man, the mind and the world, and tends toward the only kind of materialism consistent with the actual development of scientific knowledge. Nothing could be farther from Hegel—and even from Descartes, whose dualism we try to overcome while adhering to his rationalist faith.

The misunderstanding is related to the fact that only those who practice structural analysis every day can clearly conceive the direction and range of their undertaking: that is, to unify perspectives that the narrow scientific outlook of the last few centuries has believed to be incompatible—sensibility and intellect, quality and quantity, the concrete and the geometrical, or, as we say today, the "etic" and the "emic." Even ideological works whose structure is very abstract (everything that can be included under the label *mythology*), and that the mind seems to elaborate without unduly submitting to the constraints of the techno-economic infrastructure, remain rebellious to both description and analysis if minute attention is not paid to ecological conditions and to the different ways each culture reacts to its natural environment. Only an almost slavish respect for the most concrete reality can inspire in us confidence that mind and body have not lost their ancient unity.

Structuralism knows of other less theoretical and more practical justifications. The so-called primitive cultures that anthropologists study teach that reality can be meaningful on the levels of both scientific knowledge and sensory perception. These cultures encourage us to reject the divorce between the intelligible and the sensible declared by an outmoded empiricism and mechanism, and to discover a secret harmony between humanity's everlasting quest for meaning and the world in which we appeared and where we continue to live—a world made of shapes, colors, textures, flavors, and odors. Structuralism teaches us better to love and respect nature and the living beings who people it, by understanding that vegetables and animals, however humble they may be, did not supply man with sustenance only but were, from the very beginning, the source of his most intense esthetic feelings and, in the intellectual and moral order, of his first and even then profound speculations.

Chapter 8

Structuralism and Empiricism

MARVIN HARRIS, then professor at Columbia University (of which Barnard College is a part), was not present at the lecture that constitutes the preceding chapter; but when the original text was published in the United States, he was inspired to write a vigorous criticism. He wished his article to be published first in *L'Homme*, a French journal of anthropology, and even went to the trouble of providing the editor with a French translation. The English text was later published in his book *Cultural Materialism: The Struggle for a Science of Culture* (1979).*

L'Homme published Harris's article under the title he himself had chosen: "Lévi-Strauss et la palourde. Réponse à la Conférence Gildersleeve de 1972" (Lévi-Strauss and the Clam: A Response to the Gildersleeve Lecture of 1972). My rejoinder, published in the same issue, constitutes this chapter. It is not necessary to give a résumé of Harris's article, since here I take up his arguments one by one. This is my text as it originally appeared, with three or four references added.

When the editors of *L'Homme* asked my opinion of Marvin Harris's article, I recommended that they publish it even though his tone is very different from what we are used to in discussions among col-

*All the following references to and quotations from Harris's article are translated from the article in *L'Homme*. (Ed.)

leagues. For, while his arguments may miss the point, I find his article refreshing as one of the rare ones, among the many attacks against the structural analysis of myths, to place the problem on its real terrain —that of facts and our ability to deal with them. Most criticisms resort to often abstract prejudicial objections as a basis for the *a priori* rejection of structuralism, with no concern for whether this method successfully reveals how apparently arbitrary mythical representations link up into systems that link up with reality, natural as well as social, in order to reflect, obscure, or contradict it. Cutting short the preliminaries, I shall follow my critic on the terrain of his choosing.

Like him, I regret that we do not have the native-language versions of Franz Boas's *Bella Bella Tales* (1932), from which I drew my examples. In fact, we do not even know in which tongue or dialect some of these myths were gathered. The most highly developed version of the myth of Kāwaka (K.!ā'waq!a—I am simplifying for convenience' sake) as well as a different version from the ÅwīLīdEx^u (Uwit'lidox? In this case, a tribe from Ellerslie Lake [cf. Olson 1955, p. 321], which is an arm of Spiller Channel, northeast of the village of Bella Bella). The first version comes from George Hunt, Boas's Kwakiutl collaborator, who obtained it from a man named Otsestalis. There were several people with this name (Boas 1925, p. 260 n. 1; cf. Boas 1895b, p. 621; Curtis 1915, pp. 220, 242, 301). This Otsestalis was already an informant for Boas in 1895 (Boas 1932, p. 38 n. 1). He spent years living in the Kwakiutl milieu at Fort Rupert (p. *vii*) and spoke their language fluently, for he dictated a tale in that tongue to Hunt (p. 143). Thus, there is a good chance that this myth had originally been told to him in Kwakiutl. The next two myths in the collection are briefer. One was probably obtained by Boas in Owikeno (a hybrid dialect of Rivers Inlet, at the southern tip of the Bella Bella territory); the other was obtained by Boas and Hunt in a dialect closer to Bella Bella itself. Boas's glossary at the end of *Bella Bella Texts* (1928) distinguishes the two forms.

This linguistic problem is not essential, for, as Marvin Harris correctly emphasizes, Kwakiutl and Bella Bella each use separate terms (which are not the same in both languages) to designate ordinary clams and horse clams. I therefore fully agree that Boas or Hunt could not have spoken of clams (without specifying) when the original text had *horse clams*, or of *horse clams* when the original text had *clams*. The glossary of *Bella Bella Texts* even contains special verbs for actions pertaining to the biggest species: *tsātsE'mts!a*, "to get horse clams"; *ts.E'mtsī'la*, "to cook horse clams (?)." However, the conclusion that could be drawn to interpret these myths is the opposite of the conclusion reached by Harris, who apparently failed to see that his own argument turns against him.

In the three myths illustrating the incident of the siphons, shellfish are mentioned five times. But the word that had to be translated "horse clams" may have figured in only one of these instances, if we assume —as both Harris and I do—that Boas and Hunt were scrupulous translators. Hence, the other four "shellfish" could not be horse clams; if they were, Boas and Hunt would have used this word each time. The mention of horse clams, limited to this one case out of the five, should have made my critic (who is elsewhere fussy about statistical frequencies) reflective, as well as cautious about imprudent generalizations.

This is not all. Not only do horse clams appear only once in one of the three tales that I have cited for the incident of the siphons; but, apart from this single mention, they have no function in the plot. Furthermore, the development of the plot proves that the heroine could not have used their siphons.

To convince ourselves, all we need do is read the myth, which Harris has no qualms about fully reprinting, in the belief that it supports his reasoning. The young heroine, imprisoned by Kāwaka, is told by the supernatural protectress that the ogress comes down to the beach every morning to dig clams and, upon returning home, eats them, except for the siphons, which she throws away:

> "Pick these up," she adds, "and put them on your fingers." . . . The following day, while Kāwaka goes back up the steep slope with her big basket full of horse clams, the girl shows one finger. Kāwaka is so frightened that she staggers. When the girl shows all her fingers, Kāwaka tumbles to the bottom of the mountain and dies. [Boas 1932, p. 95]

As we see, the horse clams play no role in the plot. It is not *their* siphons that the girl uses, since the ogress has not yet come to her; it is the siphons she gathers in the house—these leftovers of earlier meals which are described as coming, quite simply, from clams, never from horse clams.

The other versions are still more vague. The one obtained in 1886 on Rivers Inlet does not even speak of clams: "The woman rooted to the floor advised the boy to get some shellfish and to put the siphons on the points of his fingers." In the next version, which was probably obtained in 1923, the protectress expresses herself thus: "Kāwaka goes always down to the beach to get mussels and clams. When she comes up the steep mountainside, put the siphons of the clams on the tips of your fingers, etc." (Boas 1932, p. 96). On four occasions, consequently, it is wholly inconceivable that shellfish, mussels, and clams (twice) translate the word for horse clams (tsī'mani in Bella Bella and tsē'manē in the Rivers Inlet dialect) when in the glossary of *Bella Bella Texts*, where Boas collected and analyzed the terms used by his informants, there is a whole series of words for mussel (k!wās, xawǘ'l), clam (ts!ekwa), and shellfish (ts!ē'ts!-), as well as verbs relating to the gathering of these mollusks. In passing, let me note that the native text used by Harris to illustrate the distinction between ordinary clams and horse clams designates the former by a word that, to Boas's informants, had the general sense of shellfish (ts!ē'ts!Ex*ᵘ*p!āt), "shell of shellfish" (Boas 1928, p. 233, referring to group 14, line 2). Everywhere, thus, the siphons used by the hero or the heroine are any siphons coming from any species of clam or even from unspecified shellfish. None of the texts that I have employed attributes any special role to the siphons of horse clams. And my humorous reference to the clams (any lecture before an American audience ritually demands a joke) that I had enjoyed when I was living in New York City was contrary to neither the spirit nor the letter of the myths that I cited.

It is true that Harris brings up two later versions in which the siphons come from very big clams. The first of these versions is among the tales gathered by R. L. Olson in 1935 and 1949, twelve and then twenty-six years, respectively, after Boas had noted *in situ* that "the whole culture of the Bella Bella had practically disappeared" (1928, p. *ix*)—a judgment that Olson himself said was "of course an understatement in terms of 1935 and 1949" (1955, p. 319). Hence, it would have been normal for the contents of the myth to evolve following this extinction. We know of other examples: thus, contemporary Kwakiutl sculptors depict the ogress Dzōnoqwa with bulging eyes. While such portrayals doubtless emphasize her ferocity, they are contrary to the ancient traditions attested by myths, masks, and other carvings, which depict her as almost blind with her eyes half-closed or deep in their sockets. Along the same lines, contemporary natives may have figured out that enormous bivalves are far more suitable for the diet of an ogress, who is also a giant. This is not the only peculiarity of this version, which is silent about the ogress's alimentary idiosyncrasies and which is the only version that attributes to clams the power to bewitch her victims. This is why the heroine takes care not to share her guardian's meal and uses, to terrify her, the shellfish siphons that, on her protectress's advice, she has hidden in a basket. Although the Olson version is unquestionably part of the same set as the others and must be placed along with them, its internal economy is so peculiar that it cannot be seen as representative of the group as a whole.*

The other version, an even later one, published one year after my lecture (which did not prevent Harris from wondering why I did not use it), has features not found elsewhere. According to the woman informant, it was necessary first to tear off the end of the siphons, then to turn these inside out, like the fingers of a glove, in order to expose the inside, which is colored red by toxic micro-organisms for part of the year. During this season, the clams or their siphons are inedible. But, if it was customary in this area to remove the part believed to be poisonous, then one would be rightly surprised that Hunt did not mention it among the Kwakiutl whose culinary techniques he describes with an extraordinary wealth of details. Such an omission is even more unlikely in that Hunt twice describes a similar treatment for the chiton, a very different mollusk: before eating it, the fisherman "scrapes it to remove the red color on the body of the chiton"; and then, further on, in regard to a woman performing the same task: "She scrapes off with the back of her knife what looks like red paint on its body, she scrapes it so that the body of the chiton comes off" (Boas 1921, pp. 485, 487). On the other hand, in regard to the occasional toxicity of clams, the Kwakiutl seem to have had very different views from those of the Bella Bella informant. According to one text, this toxicity was local, not seasonal: "The clams of Gē'g äqe are poisonous. That is the reason why the clams [from that place] are not eaten" (Boas 1910, p. 377). Coincidentally, the locality in question is near Rivers Inlet.†

---

*Especially since, through the bias of the material culture, there are traces of the group in Salish country more than 350 miles south of Bella Bella territory. For digging clams, the Puget Sound Indians used a special kind of basket called "cannibal," which, according to myth, was the one used by an old ogress to carry off children, whom she ate (Waterman 1973, pp. 8, 12–13, and plate Ic). Here too, consequently, clams (any species) are linked to the ogress. Closer to the Bella Bella, one could mention the Kwakiutl belief that Bukwus, the spirit of the woods, eats cockles, and that, according to a Niska informant, the Tsimshian used cockles to drive out land otters, other evil spirits (Halpin, n.d., p. 21 n. 14).

†Curiously, this is not the only case of supposedly poisonous shellfish being relegated to a northern region, even though it is not the same region: the Kwakiutl of the Nimkish group assert in a myth that the clams of Koā'qem (toward the northeast, in Tsawatenok territory) are poisonous (Boas 1895a, p. 135). "In the Tsimshian country [explains an informant] the shellfish are fine and the mussels are not poisonous as they are here [in Wrangell]. In April, Alaskans [the Tlingit] do not dare to eat shellfish, especially mussels, claiming that they are poisonous" (Swanton 1909, p. 130). Now the Bella Bella are

Hence, the second version cited by Harris seems to reflect not so much a real and widespread practice as one limited to a small group, if not to several individuals. This version might be a late blending of the traditional readings of the myth and the belief attributed to the Awī'LīdEx[u] (which produced two of these versions—see page 122). According to this belief, in order to ward off supernatural beings, one must bite into one's tongue and spit the flowing blood at them: this blood is as poisonous as menstrual blood, especially a virgin's (Boas and Hunt 1902-5, pp. 429-31; cf. Boas 1895a, p. 21; Boas 1916, p. 481; Swanton 1905, p. 148 n. 49). However this aberrant version may have taken shape, it—like the Olson version—belongs to the group but cannot represent it.

In order to put both versions in their proper places, I shall introduce a version that expands again, although in the opposite direction, the repertoire of mollusk appendages, which are given identical functions by the myths drawn from that repertoire. This third version offers the further interest of being one of the oldest known—published in 1895, in German, by Boas in *Indianische Sagen* (1895a, pp. 224-25). It comes from the Owikeno of Rivers Inlet, the southernmost Bella Bella group, considerably mixed with Kwakiutl in both language and culture. As Olson nostalgically points out (1954, foreword), their culture was still flourishing when Boas was working in the area.

In this version, the supernatural protectress tells a little boy, who has been carried off by the ogress, to gather shellfish (German, *Muscheln*), to cook them, then to clean and shred them, and make sheaths for his fingers out of the "beards" (*Bärte*). When the young hero shows the ogress his hand, she cries, "What do you have there? I've never seen anything like that, and I'm afraid." As he has been advised, the boy moves his fingers and yells, and the ogress drops dead.

What did Boas mean by the mollusk's "beard"? If we go back to the monumental ten-volume *Tierleben* (1864-69) by the German scholar Alfred Edmund Brehm, we will find the anatomical nomenclature for the Lamellibranchia, *Bart oder Byssus* (Schmidt 1893,

---

north of the Kwakiutl just as the Tlingit are north of the Tsimshian, who are themselves north of the Bella Bella. On the other hand, the Yakutat group, at the far north of Tlingit territory, regard its own shellfish as edible in all seasons, but sometimes consider them toxic in southern Alaska. Nevertheless, their shamans abstain from eating shellfish even in the months of March and April, when Dame Bounty comes to gather them on the beaches and eats them. Otherwise, they would fall ill (Laguna 1972, I, pp. 392, 393, 404; II, p. 683). As I have emphasized elsewhere, the Property Woman of the Tlingit and her Haida colleague have several traits in common with the ogress of the Kwakiutl and the Bella Bella (Lévi-Strauss 1982, II, pp. 52–54). Still, it might not be irrelevant here to mention that, according to Tlingit informants, Dame Bounty appears on the beaches to eat shellfish only after they have lost their toxicity, whose origin is mystical, not natural.

p. 450). A bart, or byssus, is a tuft of silky filaments with which certain bivalves fasten themselves to rocks temporarily or permanently. Unless Boas completely misunderstood his informant and translated "byssus" instead of "siphon," and "mussel" (or some other sedentary bivalve) instead of "clam" (but in this case he would not have failed to emend the text thirty years later in *Bella Bella Tales*, where he refers to that version without comment [1932, p. 95 n.1 and 2]),* we must rule out any possibility of horse clams. And—differently from the other versions—this version does not mention siphons (German, *Siphonen*) but speaks of an appendage that could not be a siphon, even if Boas understood *Barten* to mean something other than "byssus." Contrary to what Harris believed, myths—which are the furthest thing possible from the rampant empiricism that is the senile illness of so-called neo-Marxism—do not have a content fixed once and for all, nor one whose meaning would be rigidly determined by the properties attributed to a particular organ of a unique kind of bivalve. Myths operate on a gamut consisting of various empirical examples of the same organ as well as of other organs, which may differ from one another and even belong to distinct animal families. All the terms of this paradigm can be used by mythical thinking provided that—at the price of transformations it is our duty to restore—they allow the expression of significations of the same type, not each on its own account but in opposition to other terms, which vary simultaneously.

Now that the horse clams are back in their place, there is no need to dwell on Harris's discussion of the food value of their siphons, since the latter play no part in the myths on which my discussion was based. Indeed, I am not unaware that the siphons of other clams are edible, since I have always eaten them myself. The real issue is what place the myths assign them semantically, and what connections there are between that place and the native practice. The white American authors cited by Harris tell us nothing about this twofold question. On the other hand, it is useful to know that the old Heiltsuq informants (from the Bella Bella group least influenced by the Kwakiutl) regarded horse clams and their siphons as partly edible; while the Kwakiutl themselves rejected clams totally unless they had nothing else to eat. But once again, our myths do not refer specifically to the siphons of horse clams; they speak more generally of the siphons of clams and even, at times, unspecified shellfish. Of the data supplied by Harris, one should remember that, before the siphons of small clams are eaten, their

*Earlier, in "Sagen" (1895a, p. 243 n. 1), he had made a point of correcting a mistranslation.

purplish-blue sheaths should be stripped off; and that, according to his Bella Bella informants, an inedible part must be cut off all siphons—a part described as a blackish extremity in the small species and as reddish in the large. Even the enthusiastic eaters of horse-clam siphons, whom Harris cites as witnesses, acknowledge that only the inside is edible, but not the tough, repulsive-looking envelope or its horny extremity.

Let me sum up:

1. The ogress Kāwaka eats clams (once again, *any* clams) but throws away their siphons; for her at least, the latter are inedible.
2. Even the most resolute eaters of any species of clam siphons reject the envelope or sheath as well as the horny part, if there is one. Thus, they regard the siphons as partly inedible (and, after all, these may be the parts rejected by the ogress and used by the hero or heroine to terrify her).
3. It is, at the very least, surprising to suggest—as Harris does twice, several pages apart (1979, pp. 14, 16)—that the ogress shows her stupidity by throwing away the siphons which are the best part, and that the sight of these same siphons terrifies her because of their fatal toxicity.
4. The distinction between these two parts—one edible, the other inedible (the latter being first sliced off and thrown away)—bears a curious resemblance to the contrast the Kwakiutl make between the edible parts of a mountain goat and its inedible parts—the horns:

When the mountain-goat hunter goes out to hunt, the spoon-maker asks him to break off the horns of the goats that he will get, for the mountain-goat hunter only wants the tallow and the kidney fat and the meat. He does not want the bones and the horns. Therefore the spoon-maker asks him for these. . . . After he [the hunter] has killed a mountain-goat, he takes off the tallow, kidney-fat, and the meat, and finally he cuts the skin around the bottom of the horns; and when he has cut off the skin, he takes a hammer and pounds off the horns. Now they break off from the bone core. [Kwakiutl text by Hunt, translated by Boas 1921, pp. 104-5]

In sum, the goat horns, which the hero of the Chilcotin version uses to terrify his kidnapper, occupy in the hunter's praxis a place that is curiously analogous to that occupied wholly or partly by the clam siphons that his Bella Bella homologue uses to terrify his kidnapper. From this unforeseen angle, the precise details supplied by Marvin Harris reinforce my interpretation.

Let us move on to the second of Harris's crushing arguments—or so he believes them to be. He claims that I made up out of whole cloth the thesis that the ogress's treasures are exclusively of earthly origin. And my critic, who is here accusing me of inaccuracy, adds that any first-year student knows that, at a potlatch, fresh and dried fish, fish eggs and fish oil, and richly colored abalone shells were passed around. Whom is Harris making fun of? I am as well acquainted as he with the inventories drawn up by observers;* but nowhere in the last chapter do I speak of real potlatches (or, incidentally, of real ogresses). The only potlatches I mention are in myths, in terms both of what these myths say about them and of the rites commemorating events that are themselves mythical. Now the myths affirm categorically: (1) that the ogress who carries off children possesses only goods of earthly origin; and (2) that when appropriated by human beings, these goods are instantly used at a potlatch that has, as I shall presently show, the value of a model.

Which myths? When quoting me on this topic, Harris does not hesitate, the better to refute me, to amputate an essential phrase from my text. He has me say (in his translation) that "the mythological documents and rituals that we have on the subject of this Kāwaka tend to prove that her treasures all come from the interior of the earth." Yet in my original text, I had specified: "This Kāwaka, or Dzōnoqwa as the Kwakiutl call her." Everything is there. We know indeed that the Bella Bella texts published by Boas come mainly from Fort Rupert and Rivers Inlet—that is, from Kwakiutl country or an area where the Kwakiutl influence predominated. For this reason, moreover, the strict bearers of a "pure" Bella Bella culture, to whom Harris refers, have qualms about the Boas texts, which they do not feel properly represent it. Hence, in order to interpret these texts correctly, we must look toward the Kwakiutl myths and not toward myths originating farther north (which, in addition, do not say what Harris has them say: Crow has wings of copper; he did not "bring copper from the sky" (cf. Olson 1955, p. 330). In any case, a myth attributing a celestial origin to copper would reveal Tsimshian or even Tlingit influence. Actually, all the "Kāwaka" myths in Boas's collection, except for the episode of the siphons, are almost literal variants of Kwakiutl myths, whose texts are found in Boas (1895b, pp. 372-74; 1910, pp. 116-22, 442-45; 1935b, pp. 69-71), in Boas and Hunt (1902-5, pp. 86-93, 103-4, 431-36), and Curtis (1915, pp. 293-98); and so on. There is nothing astonishing about this, since the Bella Bella figure of Kāwaka is none other than the one known by the Kwakiutl as Dzōnoqwa (Boas 1928, p. 224; 1932, p. 95 n. 1). And in saying

*Who do not always confirm his list. According to S. Barrett, the ceremonial meals offered to the invited "tribes" did not include fish, shellfish, or land animals—all of them vulgar food. The hosts served only seal, whale, fruits, and other vegetable products (Ritzenthaler and Parsons 1966, p. 91). Now, to the Kwakiutl mind, the seal and the whale have a connotation less marine than chthonian.

with a smugness all the more shocking since he finds fault not with me but with Boas: "Even the title *Kāwaka Tales* leads to an error because, in the third Bella Bella version, the ogress is named Ts!E'lk.ig.ila or Adzi, the frog," Harris ignores the detailed note in "Sagen" (Boas 1895*a*, p. 226 n. 1) explaining that this is none other than the personage called Tsonō'k.oa (Dzōnoqwa) by the Kwakiutl and Snēnē'ik by the Bella Coola. Even within one language, there is nothing surprising about a plurality of names; in Kwakiutl, Dzōnoqwa has three names (Boas 1935*a*, p. 144).

Now what do the Kwakiutl say about Dzōnoqwa's treasure? When a heroine who has killed the ogress enters her victim's dwelling, she discovers great riches: "Oh, there was property! There was no river food among all these quadrupeds, for she [the ogress] had dried meat as means of inviting. . . . There was nothing from the river on account of the way she was" (Boas 1935*b*, p. 70). In the last that we know of his thinking, Boas still insisted on "Dzō'noq!wa [as] a being powerful but stupid. This race lives inland. Their only food is the meat of land animals. Therefore, one of them, generally a female, visits the villages to steal fish. . . . She is also the ogress who carries away crying children" (Boas 1966, p. 307).

There we have the exclusively earthly origin of the ogress's treasure. The fact that this treasure, obtained by human beings, also includes ritual objects such as copper, furs, and berry preserves—earthly products—and that the appropriation of the treasure permits for the first time the celebration of winter ceremonies and the giving of a potlatch, proceeds unequivocally from all the myths about Dzōnoqwa and in one that Boas collected (1932, p. 95) about her homologue Kāwaka.

Undoubtedly other Kwakiutl myths trace the origins of potlatch back to the adventures of a princess lost at sea. Kōmogwa, the master of riches, welcomes her into his kingdom in the other world. There, she bears children, who eventually return to their mother's homeland, bearing copper and other presents (Boas 1910, pp. 267-85). But Kōmogwa, who is also a cannibal, has certain affinities with Dzōnoqwa. Though a sea god, he is sometimes called a mountain spirit (Boas 1888, p. 55; 1895*a*, p. 164). A statue of Dzōnoqwa stands at the entrance to his dwelling (Boas 1895*a*, p. 146). Finally and most important, both possess copper, which is an essential element of the potlatch, and which human beings obtained from them. Nevertheless, Kōmogwa is the most remote master of copper; Dzōnoqwa, the closest mistress of copper: thus, receiving it from her is easier than receiving it from him.

This connection between copper and the ogress is confirmed by the rites; for, in order to celebrate a potlatch, the chief receives the copper objects from an assistant, who keeps them piled up in a basket usually carried on the back (a common accessory of Dzōnoqwa's); and, at the moment of distributing them, the chief puts on a mask of Dzōnoqwa. Nothing can demonstrate more strikingly that, for the Kwakiutl, the copper and the other articles distributed at a potlatch are the true facsimile of the wealth human beings wrested from Dzōnoqwa in mythical times. Every potlatch repeats its archetype, which was once made possible by the ogress's earthly treasures.*

Readers more familiar than my critic with the mythology of the northeastern coast may object that, unlike the Dzōnoqwa of the Kwakiutl, the Kāwaka of the Bella Bella does not sustain herself on earthly food alone, since shellfish are part of her daily fare. But, in addition to the fact that the Kwakiutl have a "Dzōnoqwa of the sea" (coming not so much from water *per se* as from the chthonian world, whose entrance is at the bottom of the ocean), the giantess's predilection for clams—or, more precisely, her need to eat them—is explained by a Kwakiutl myth that contrasts the life styles of two groups: the Nimkish of Vancouver Island and the Koeksotenok of the mainland. One day, the Nimkish chief's daughter, who is married to a Koeksotenok, comes to visit her family with her little boy. During the banquet given for the occasion, the child walks about eating cooked clams whose "heads" are full of a greenish juice that drips out of his mouth:

> When the children saw the green juice running out of [his] mouth, they shouted and said: "Let [the woman] come and see the green juice her son is vomiting." The children [of the Nimkish] made fun of him because the ancestors [of the Koeksotenok] had no great river. And therefore the [Koeksotenok] ate only mussels and large and small clams. Therefore [the Nimkish] made fun [of the Koeksotenok], because they had no great river in which salmon ascend, like the large river of the Nimkish, for various kinds of salmon ascend [it] and that is the food of all [the Nimkish]; and this was meant by the children. Therefore they made fun of him. [Boas and Hunt 1902–5, p. 134; cf. Boas 1895a, pp. 143, 154]†

*Harris once again must be joking when he accuses me of "ignoring that most of the metal used in copper for a potlatch came in fact from the bottom of European sailing ships." This is something that everyone knows (cf. Lévi-Strauss 1982, I, pp. 68–69, 95; II, pp. 35, 52–53, 137). It is actually Harris who seeks to keep the reader from knowing that, before the introduction of strip copper, the native metal (extracted from the ground) had a major place in coastal cultures.

†The original text has tribes' names in Boas's complicated spelling and, instead of "the child" or "the woman," their personal names which are very cumbersome. I have used brackets wherever I have suppressed the personal names or used the current spelling of tribes' names instead of Boas's.

The meaning of this episode is clear. Mussels and clams (here once again, whatever their species) are the little prized food of people who live close to water but have no salmon in their country. Making Kāwaka a shellfish eater is another way of saying—in "sea clef," if I may say so (as, in music, "bass clef" and "treble clef")—that she is deprived of fish and that, despite the seashores that she haunts, her inner nature remains landlocked like the mountaintop she lives on, even though she goes down to the beach every day to gather that most terrestrial of all seafood which one has to dig into the ground to find. It follows from this story that salmon eaters like the Nimkish and their neighbors disparaged shellfish—although they certainly ate it.

This attitude was shared by the Tsimshian (Boas 1935a, p. 173). The myths of other neighbors of the Kwakiutl—the Haida and the Tlingit —present shellfish as being eaten only in times of want (Swanton 1905, p. 48; 1909, p. 41). According to the Kwakiutl informants of Dr. Martine Reid, who knows the Kwakwala language and to whom I am obliged for this information, the word that currently denotes a clam siphon is a euphemism for "penis." Three quarters of a century ago, J. R. Swanton (1909, p. 21) made the same remark about the Tlingit language. Considered unseemly and censured by the Indians themselves, the direct expression suggests that they cared even less for the siphons than for the entire mollusk.

One cannot say everything in the one-hour lecture that chapter 7 originally was. One is forced to be schematic, and a foreign language is a further obstacle to communication. There are, thus, many aspects and problems that I had to leave out—indeed, far more than Harris imagines. As he is particularly harsh, however, in reproaching me for neglecting the motif of the good adviser, "who appears three times more often than the treasure" in the myths I have used, I will therefore take up his challenge and demonstrate that this, too, has its antithesis in the Chilcotin myth. Nevertheless, this motif is part of a vast system, within which it should first be located.

The good adviser (whom I dealt with at length in my courses at the Collège de France during 1974 to 1975) has an important place in the Kwakiutl myths where she appears in one of two guises: sometimes human, but incapable of moving because her lower body is stone, or because she is rooted in the ground like a tree or by a kind of umbilical cord filled with blood; sometimes a mouse, moving freely between the surface of the earth and the subterranean world. The former is thus immobile on the horizontal axis; often a daughter or sister of the human beings in the myth, she is astray in a remote and maleficent world with which she has unwittingly come to terms. Unable to return to her people, she restricts herself to helping them with her good advice when they themselves wander and are faced with the same danger. The Mouse Lady, on the contrary, is mobile on a vertical axis and plays the role of emissary from the supernatural world, being able to come and go between it and the human world. Her character is thus in correlation with, and in opposition to, that of the other woman, who represents the earthly world and is kept hostage in the beyond. According to their different ways, both the rooted woman and the Mouse Lady are mediators between the two worlds: the former, fixed, operates as a pivot around which move their respective protagonists, while the latter shuttles back and forth between them.

The Bella Bella and the Kwakiutl myths that I have so far examined tell the story of a child carried off by an ogress. In her dwelling, he is helped by a good adviser, who appears in either of the shapes I have just discussed. When the good adviser is a rooted woman, her advice enables the captive child to avoid the same fate, to escape from the ogress, and, as the child wishes, to return to his family. Now we need only read the Chilcotin myth to understand why the good adviser does not figure in it. Unlike the hero of the Kwakiutl and the Bella Bella myths, the Chilcotin hero has no desire to return to his village; he feels fine living with his kidnapper, who teaches him lofty things; and when his parents set out to bring him back, they have the most difficult time convincing him. It is, thus, he who is the rooted one, or is about to become so; while his parents, instead of remaining in their village or abandoning their quest, succeed in finding him and aiding him against his will. The figure of the helpful woman splits into two distinct functions: that of the rooted person, which is taken over by the hero himself; and that of the good adviser, which his parents, not without difficulty, manage to perform. The same functions appear in both groups of myths, but they are distributed among three agents in the one group and between two agents in the other, because each of the two agents in the Chilcotin myth assumes, in addition to his own function, one of the functions that, in the Kwakiutl and the Bella Bella myths, are combined in a third agent:

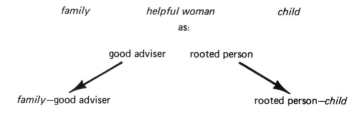

It would be interesting to find out how and why this equal distribution of functions operates in the Chilcotin myth. It is unlikely that the documents available on Chilcotin culture are rich enough to help us succeed. In any event, this is not the place to undertake an investigation that would require a systematic comparative analysis of the myths of both the Kwakiutl and their coastal and inland neighbors.

What remains to be said? It does not seem unreasonable to assume that, in the eyes of both the Canadian Indians and ourselves, the horns of wild goats had a more aggressive connotation than the siphons of bivalves. Goat hunters were not unaware that these animals occasionally come to blows with their horns. Furthermore, the Indians used horn chisels to split tree trunks (Curtis 1915, pp. 10-12) and war clubs made of antlers, called in Bella Bella "wōL!Em"—a word that denotes both the horns themselves and their wood. In a Bella Bella myth, a club of this name has the magic power of killing enemies by the dozen if it is merely waved in the air (Boas 1928, p. 191; 1932, p. 141).

As for the spoons of carved horn, contrary to what Harris may claim, I did not state that they were either part of the ogress's treasure or among the articles distributed at a potlatch; I said only that they were very precious objects that "may be made part of a treasure" and are, in this respect, comparable to the dentalia shells.

Rather than admitting that the Bella Bella myths are reworkings of the Chilcotin myth, Harris inclines toward a borrowing in the opposite direction. The issue remains moot and can be discussed, but with different arguments from those advanced by Harris. He claims, indeed, that, while the Bella Bella knew the goats they hunted in the coastal range (obviously: where else could they have found them?), the Chilcotin had only the vaguest notion about clams and may never have seen any. Now the Chilcotin, who dealt in marine shellfish, often frequented the coast, whence, according to a Kwakiutl tradition, they had even originally come (Boas 1935b, pp. 91-92). Without going back that far, we may note that, in the mid-nineteenth century, Chilcotin warfare extended all the way to Knight Inlet (Boas 1966, p. 110). During the same period, a good observer included them among the semi-nomadic tribes who spent half the year in the interior and the other half on the coast, and said that they spent much time at Bellhoula in Bentinck Inlet (Mayne 1862, p. 299), or some sixty kilometers as the crow flies both from the country of the Uwi'tlidox (to whom two of the Kāwaka myths are attributed) and from Rivers Inlet, where Boas collected some of his material and where we can be sure the Chilcotin came also.

I have devoted a good deal of time to refuting Harris's criticisms, of which nothing, finally, can stand up aside from two unimportant remarks, which should not, however, be neglected. Harris rightly points out that the adjectives "harmless" and "insignificant" could not apply to the siphons of the biggest clams (the siphons that have no part in the myths I cited) and that only a part of the clam siphons could with certainty have been regarded as inedible by the Indians. If I have held back on this subject, it is because I wished to profit by the occasion to emphasize the complexity of the problems involved in the structural analysis of myths—problems that I could only touch lightly upon, as I was using a language not my own, and my audience was made up mostly of non-specialists.

In conclusion, may I be permitted to list several of the problems that still await solution in the limited area of the myths I have discussed. First of all, the coastal and the inland versions transform the Chilcotin myth in not one but three ways. In regard to the goat horns in the Chilcotin myth and in certain Bella Coola versions (Boas 1898, p. 89; McIlwraith 1948, II, p. 446), we must put side by side not only the clam siphons but the byssuses of bivalves, of which I have already spoken, and also a third transformation in one of the Bella Coola versions (Boas 1895a, p. 248), where the girl imprisoned by the ogress Snēnē'ik terrorizes her by arming her fingers with eagle claws (by putting on the ogress's gloves, which shoot bolts of lightning [McIlwraith 1948, II, p. 448]). As tradition attributes to Snēnē'ik extremities like a bird of prey's, the "gloves" are doubtless the same as claws. Thus, all in all, there are four animal parts—two stemming from water (while nevertheless being opposed to each other), one from the earth, and one from the air—which have different anatomical functions but are nevertheless *commutable* and, thus, together constitute a mythical paradigm.

This paradigm includes the byssuses of bivalves, the siphons of various kinds of mollusk belonging also to this class, the eagle claws, and the goat horns: that is, the organs that are cut off from an animal, or from which a part is cut off, before either the animal or the part is eaten. The blood one spits out after biting into one's tongue (see page 126) could thus have its place in this system. Within the paradigm, the byssus has more affinity with the siphon (both come from shellfish). And it can also be said that although the claws belong to the sky-world and the lower body, and the horns to the land-world and the upper body, there is an affinity between them as they are both opposed to the sea-world to which byssus and siphon belong.* This is not the only respect in which the Bella Bella myths seem very close to the Chilcotin myth: some versions are practically identical; and the others also have the parents setting out and give a footbridge a strategic role in the narrative.

These oppositions are linked to others, which, strikingly enough, refer to wild goats in myths that do not emphasize their horns. In one of the Bella Bella versions "with the siphon," the good adviser, whose lower body is stone, tells the heroine that, in order to avoid the same fate, she must eat no berries in the ogress's home but only goat fat, which will do her no harm. Goat fat is also the harmless food in some Bella Bella versions (Boas 1898, p. 89; McIlwraith 1948, II, pp. 447, 449). On the other hand, in the Owikeno version "with the byssus," it is the same goat fat the hero must refuse if he also is not to become a rooted person (Boas 1895a, p. 224; cf. Olson 1954, p. 258); while in the Bella Coola versions "with horns" or "with claws," a cord of goat hair becomes the thread of Ariadne, enabling the heroine and her parents to return to the ogress's home (Boas 1895a, p. 248; McIlwraith 1948, II, pp. 447, 449). Thus, here too, a substance drawn from goats plays a role that is now positive, now negative. When it is not horns, the nature of this substance can be fat or hair; and, depending on the case, it operates inside or outside the body. As for the ogress's "slave," as Boas calls her in "Sagen" (1895a), we have seen that the condition to which she is reduced can take three different forms, and the myths also assign her different fates: she dies of a hemorrhage, or cannot be carried, or else is saved and goes back to her country.

The ogress herself poses a few problems. Aside from the fish that she steals from the Indians, the Kwakiutl Dzōnoqwa can eat only quad-

---

*In support of this reading, there is a myth of the Nootka (who recently changed their name to Westcoast People), where marine shellfish are converted to antlers (Boas 1895a, p. 98).

rupeds. The Bella Bella Kāwaka eats shellfish. But the Bella Coola Snēnē'ik contrasts in other ways with her Kwakiutl colleague: the former has a white throat; the latter is all black; Dzōnoqwa is afflicted with poor vision, Snēnē'ik's eyes emit lightning; one suffers from a speech problem, the other releases intestinal gas while walking. Finally, Dzōnoqwa is the protectress of pubescent girls, while Snēnē'ik dies asphyxiated by smoke from a brasier fed with old strips of bark soaked in menstrual blood. Hence, down to their finest details, the myths of neighboring peoples systematically contradict one another, and the opposition of siphons and horns is merely a particular case of these contradictions.

I could have gone on much longer in the same vein, but these brief remarks suffice to show that I have considered only a fragment of a highly complex network of oppositions. Exhaustive analyses of even a few myths would have been impossible within the limited framework of a lecture. I therefore limited myself to a few characteristic aspects—what I called "the more salient points"—to illustrate the structuralist approach and to demonstrate the mechanism and its operation.

However, even in enterprises of a broader scope, structural analysis does not claim to supply an answer to every question. Its ambitions remain modest: to pinpoint and determine problems, to arrange them in a methodical order, perhaps to solve a few of them, but especially to suggest a useful path to researchers who hope to tackle the mass of problems that are, and will probably long remain, unsettled.

Chapter 9

The Lessons
of Linguistics

A book bearing Roman Jakobson's name has no need of a preface,* and I would not have assumed the overwhelming honor of writing one had Jakobson himself not wished me to express my feelings as a member of his audience and, if I may be permitted to add, as a disciple. Indeed, these lectures, which go back a third of a century, were the first ones that I heard him give at the Ecole libre des hautes études, New York, during the 1942-43 year, when we began to attend each other's courses. Now their author has finally decided to publish them after often planning to do so but always being held up by more urgent tasks.

In reading these lectures today, I re-experience the excitement I felt so long ago. At that time, I knew almost nothing about linguistics, and I had never heard of Roman Jakobson. Alexandre Koyré, the Russian-born French philosopher and historian of science (1892-1964), enlightened me about his role and put us in touch with each other. Still feeling the impact of the difficulties, owing to my inexperience, that I had encountered three or four years earlier when trying to make an accurate notation of the languages of central Brazil, I looked forward to

---

*This chapter was published originally as the preface to Roman Jakobson's *Six Lectures on Sound and Meaning* (1978; originally published in France in 1976). All of Jakobson's quotations are, unless otherwise identified, from the American edition of this book.

acquiring from Jakobson the rudiments I lacked. His lectures, however, gave me something very different and, need I add, a great deal more than I had bargained for. This was the revelation of structural linguistics, which provided me with a body of coherent ideas where I could crystallize my reveries about the wild flowers I had gazed at somewhere along the Luxembourg border early in May 1940, and the ambiguous blend of enthusiasm and exasperation that, a little later in Montpellier—where, for the last time in my life, I briefly taught philosophy—I felt upon reading Marcel Granet's *Catégories matrimoniales et relations de proximité dans la Chine ancienne* (*Matrimonial Categories and Kinship in Ancient China* [1939]). This book had aroused these ambiguous feelings partly because of his attempt to organize seemingly arbitrary facts into a system, and partly because of an unlikely complication arising from his efforts.

Structural linguistics taught me, on the contrary, that instead of being led astray by a multiplicity of terms, one should consider the simplest and most intelligible relationships uniting them. In listening to Jakobson, I discovered that anthropology of the nineteenth and even the early twentieth century had been content, as was the linguistics of the neo-grammarians, to substitute "strictly causal questions for questions concerning means and ends" (p. 35). Without ever really describing a phenomenon, these anthropologists and linguists were content to refer to its origins (p. 6). Thus, the two disciplines were confronted with "a stunning multitude of variations"; whereas an explanation should always have the goal of "discovering the invariants among all this variety" (p. 10). *Mutatis mutandis*, what Jakobson said about phonetics was applicable also to anthropology:

> It is true that the phonic substance of language has been studied thoroughly, and that such studies, especially over the past fifty years, have produced an abundance of illuminating results. But for the most part the phenomena under consideration have been investigated in abstraction from their function. In these circumstances it has been impossible to classify, or even to understand, these phenomena. [P. 26]

As for kinship systems, which were the subject of my course during that same year, 1942-43, men like F. A. E. Van Wouden (1908–), whose work I was as yet unfamiliar with, and the French sociologist Marcel Granet (1884-1940) had managed to go farther—but were still focusing on terms instead of on the relations between them. Since they could not grasp the rationale for phenomena, they were condemned to the futile task of seeking things behind things, in the vain hope of attaining more manageable facts than the empirical data on which their analyses were stumbling. Yet one can say about any terms, real or imaginary, what Jakobson writes here about the phonic individuality of phonemes: "The important thing . . . is not at all each phoneme's individual phonic quality considered in isolation and existing in its own right. What matters is their reciprocal opposition within a . . . system" (p. 76).

These innovative views—toward which my own reflections were already tending although I was not yet bold enough, nor had the necessary conceptual tools, to give them shape—were all the more persuasive owing to the incomparable artistry of Jakobson's articulation of them. He was the most dazzling teacher and lecturer that I had ever been fortunate enough to hear. And his book fully retains his elegance and expository power. For those who did not have the good luck to attend his lectures, these pages have the added value of demonstrating what his courses and lectures were—and still are in this, his eightieth year.*

Served by an oratorical talent equally great in any language Jakobson chooses to employ (though we may assume it to be extraordinary in his native Russian), these lectures develop an argument that is both limpid and rigorous. Never does he prolong abstract and sometimes difficult reasoning without illuminating it with examples drawn from the most diverse languages and often also from contemporary poetry and the plastic arts. His systematic citing of the great thinkers—Stoics, scholastics, Renaissance rhetoricians, Indian grammarians, and others —reveals his unflagging concern with putting new ideas in perspective and with instilling in the minds of his audience a sense of continuity in thought and history.

In Jakobson, the order of the exposition follows step by step the process of discovery, giving his lectures a dramatic power that keeps his audience on tenterhooks. Rich in dramatic surprise, his digressions alternate with sharp insights all hurtling toward a dénouement that is sometimes totally unforeseeable and always convincing.

Along with the works that Jakobson aimed directly at a reading public, these six lectures will endure as samples of his spoken style, and publication has not deprived them of their flavor. The first lecture presents the state of linguistics at the end of the nineteenth century. It criticizes the views of the neo-grammarians, for whom sound and meaning were entirely separate categories. Jakobson concedes the re-

*Jakobson died in 1982 at the age of eighty-six. (Ed.)

sults of phonetic research; but, by distinguishing between motor and acoustic phonetics, he demonstrates that it is impossible to detach sound from meaning, or linguistic means from their ends.

If sound and meaning are inseparable, then what is the mechanism of their union? In the second lecture, Jakobson proves that the concept of the phoneme enables us to solve this apparent mystery. He defines this notion, tracing its genesis and discussing the interpretations that were originally suggested. Following this same line, the third lecture tackles the theory of phonology, which is based on the primacy of the relationship and the system. Jakobson refuses to delve into the nature of the phoneme, a useless and inconsequential issue; and, in a concrete analysis, he establishes the originality of this linguistic entity by comparing it with the morpheme, the word, and the sentence. As the only linguistic unit devoid of conceptual content, the phoneme, with no meaning of its own, is a tool to distinguish meanings.

Thus, we are faced with two problems, which are the topic of the fourth lecture. First of all, the definition of the phoneme as a distinctive value implies that phonemes play their part by reason not of their phonic individuality but of their mutual opposition within a system. Yet we do not discern any logical bond between opposing phonemes: the presence of one does not necessarily entail the presence of the other. Secondly, if the oppositions between phonemes are primary values permitting differentiation of meaning, how is it that these relations are far more numerous than the phonemes deriving from them? Jakobson shows that these two paradoxes stem from a misconception of phonemes as indissoluble units. Quite the contrary: once they are broken down into differential elements, there arise new types of relations that are both characterized by logical oppositions and less numerous in any language than the phonemes created by the interplay of these oppositions.

The fifth lecture illustrates these theoretical views by describing and analyzing the French consonant system. Here the notion of the combinatory variation is deepened, and the problem of the presence of phonemes on the axes of succession and simultaneity is solved in a positive way. This demonstration results in part from an original treatment of the notion of *morae** which, as I recall, delighted Boas (shortly before his death) at a dinner to which he had invited Jakobson and myself.

---

*In some languages, a *mora* is the smallest phonic segment that can bear the accent. On this particular point, see R. Jakobson's, "Franz Boas' Approach to Language" (1971a, p. 480).

The sixth lecture resumes and summarizes the argument of the entire course. Jakobson's conclusions, however, are never repetitive. They take the reader beyond the point where he might think he could stop. In this case, Jakobson leads us past the Saussurian principle of the arbitrary nature of the linguistic sign. This sign probably seems arbitrary in terms of resemblance—that is, when compared with the signifiers of the same signified in several languages. But, as the French linguist Emile Benveniste (1902-76) showed, for each language studied separately, the linguistic sign is no longer arbitrary in terms of the contiguity perceived necessary between signifier and signified (Benveniste 1966, vol. I, chap. 4). In the former case, the relation is internal; in the latter, external. Hence, a speaker tries to make up for the absence of the one by having recourse to the other and giving language a phonetic symbolism. On a terrain whose organic foundations Jakobson reveals, the union of sound and meaning recurs. This union is misunderstood by traditional phoneticians, not because they have reduced linguistic activity to its physiological substratum (a viewpoint criticized in the first lecture), but, as we now see, because they have treated this aspect too superficially.

Today more than ever, after the passage of years, I recognize the themes of the lectures that had the strongest impact on me. However irregular may be such notions as those of the phoneme and the incest taboo, my conception of the latter was ultimately inspired by the role linguists have assigned to the former. Like a phoneme, a device having no meaning of its own but helping to form meanings, the incest taboo struck me as a link between two domains.

The articulation of sound and meaning was thus answered, on a different level, by that of nature and culture. And, just as the phoneme *qua* form is accounted by all languages a universal device for establishing linguistic communication, the incest taboo, universally present so far as its negative expression is concerned, likewise constitutes an empty but indispensable form, making both possible and necessary the articulation of biological groups in a network of exchange that allows them to communicate with one another. Finally, the significance of marriage rules—incomprehensible when studied separately—can emerge only when they are contrasted with one another; just as the reality of the phoneme resides not in its phonic individuality but in the oppositive and negative relationships among the phonemes themselves.

"Saussure's great merit," says Jakobson, "was to have understood clearly that . . . something extrinsic is unconsciously brought into play" (pp. 10-11). It cannot be doubted that these lectures also make a major contribution to the human sciences by emphasizing the role of unconscious mental activity in the production of language (and also of all symbolic systems). Indeed, it is only when we recognize that language, like any other social institution, presupposes unconscious mental operations that we are ready to achieve, beyond the continuity of phenomena, the discontinuity of "those principles by which . . . language is organized" (p. 11), and which normally elude the conscious mind of the speaking or thinking subject. The discovery of these principles, and especially of their discontinuity, was to open the way for the rapid progress of linguistics and of the other sciences of man.

This point is important; for it has often been doubted whether, from its very birth and especially in the Russian linguist N. S. Trubetzkoy (1890-1938), the phonological theory involved a movement to the unconscious infrastructure. Now we need only compare Jakobson's critique of Ščerba to see that it coincides in every way with Trubetzkoy's critique. There is nothing astonishing about this similarity if we recall how intimately related their ways of thinking were: "Ščerba and some other disciples of Baudouin de Courtenay . . . , " writes Jakobson, "appealed to the linguistic intuition of the speaking subject" (p. 38), because they failed to understand that "the elements of language usually remain beneath the threshold of our conscious deliberation.* As the philosophers say, linguistic activity takes place without self-knowledge" (p. 39). And Trubetzkoy: "The phoneme . . . is a linguistic and not a psychological concept. Any reference to 'linguistic consciousness' must be ignored in defining the phoneme" (1969, p. 38). Trubetzkoy sensed that the phoneme could be broken down into distinctive elements—a breakdown first achieved by Jakobson in 1938; it was to enable linguists definitively to eliminate "quite objectively and unambiguously" any recourse to "the subjective intuition of speakers" (p. 85). The distinctive value of the elements constitutes the primary fact, and our more or less conscious attitude toward these elements is never anything but a secondary phenomenon (p. 38).

There is only one aspect of these lectures on which Jakobson would

---

*Lev V. Ščerba (1880–1944) was a Russian linguist and pupil of the great Polish linguist Jan Baudouin de Courtenay (1845–1929) who introduced the idea of the phoneme. See Jakobson 1979, p. 292, for a list of Ščerba's works. [Ed.]

most likely not maintain his position of thirty years ago. In 1942 and 1943, he felt he could say (and correctly at the time) that "language is the only system which is composed of elements which are signifiers and yet at the same time signify nothing" (p. 66). Since then, there has been a revolution in biology with the discovery of the genetic code— a revolution whose theoretical consequences were bound to affect all the human sciences. Jakobson understood this implication immediately and was one of the first to recognize and elucidate "the extraordinary degree of similarity between the genetic information system and that of verbal information" (1970, p. 526). After listing "all the characteristics which are isomorphic between the genetic code . . . and the architectonic pattern which underlies the verbal codes of all human languages" (1970, p. 529), Jakobson goes one step farther and asks whether "the isomorphism of these two different, genetic and verbal, codes can be explained by a simple convergence stemming from a similarity of needs, or whether the foundations of the manifest linguistic structures, intimately based on molecular communication, are not directly patterned on the structural principles of the latter" (1970, p. 530).

This is an immense problem, which may some day be solved through collaboration between biologists and linguists. For now, however, are we not in a position to formulate and solve, at the other end of the scale of linguistic operations, a similar problem, but one narrower in scope? I am referring to the relation between the analysis of language and the analysis of myths. In regard to the other side of language—the side involving the world and the society rather than the organism—the same question arises about the relationship between language and a system (one closer to language, of course, since it has to use it) that, in a different way from language, is made up of elements that combine among themselves to form meanings, but each of which has no meaning in itself.

In the third lecture, Jakobson, contrary to Saussure, establishes that phonemes differ from other linguistic entities—words and grammatical categories—by a set of traits that are never all present in any other entity. Certainly, grammatical categories are oppositive and relative entities like the phonemes; but, unlike the latter, they are never negative. In other words, their value is not purely discriminative: each grammatical category viewed by itself carries a semantic charge that is perceived by the speaking subject (p. 64). Now we may ask whether all the characteristics of the phoneme do not emerge in what we have dubbed "mythemes": elements in the construction of mythical discourse that are also oppositive, relative, and negative entities. To repeat the formula that Jakobson applies to the phoneme, a mytheme "is a purely differential and contentless sign" (p. 66). For we must always separate the meaning or meanings that a word possesses in its language from the mytheme that this word, in whole or in part, may help to denote. In everyday language, the sun is the star of the day; but in and of itself, the mytheme "sun" is meaningless. Depending on the myths that one chooses to consider, "sun" can cover the most diverse ideal contents. Indeed, no one who finds "sun" in a myth can make any assumptions about its individuality, its nature, or its functions there. Its meaning can emerge only from its correlative and oppositive relations with other mythemes within the myth. This meaning does not really belong to any of the mythemes; it results from their combination.

We are aware of the risks we run when trying to outline formal correspondences between entities of language and those we believe are revealed by the analysis of myths. These latter are doubtless part of language; but, within it, they constitute a separate category because of the principles that rule them. In any hypothesis, one would be wrong to put the mytheme in the same category as the word or the sentence —entities whose meaning or meanings can be defined, albeit ideally (for the very meaning of a word varies with the context), and arranged in a dictionary. The elementary units of mythical discourse certainly consist of words and sentences which—in this particular use and without overextending the analogy—are, however, more in the category of phonemes: meaningless units that are opposed within a system, where they create meanings precisely because of this opposition.

Thus, at best, mythic utterances reproduce the structure of language only by way of a shift in gear: their basic elements function like those of language, but their nature is more complex from the very start. Because of this complexity, mythical discourse unglues—if I may so phrase it—current language usage, so that one cannot make an exact parallel of the ultimate results achieved when units of different ranks combine with one another. Unlike a linguistic statement that commands, questions, or informs, and that can be understood by any member of a culture or a subculture who is familiar with the context, a myth never offers a determined meaning to those who listen to it. A myth proposes a grid, definable only by its rules of construction. For the participants in the culture to which the myth belongs, this grid confers a meaning not on the myth itself but on everything else: that is, on the images of the world, of the society, and of its history, of which the members of the group are more or less aware, as well as on the images of the questions with which these various objects confront the participants. In general, these scattered givens fail to link up and usually collide with one another. The matrix of intelligibility supplied by myth allows us to articulate those givens in a coherent system. It might be said in passing that this role of myth is like the role that Baudelaire ascribed to music.

Do we not also find here—though at the other end of the scale—a phenomenon analogous to the "sound symbolism" which Jakobson discusses at length in the sixth lecture? Even if phonetic symbolism derives from "the neuropsychological laws of synaesthesia" (p. 113)— and, moreover, because of these very laws—this symbolism, too, is not necessarily the same for everyone. Poetry has numerous ways of over-coming the divergence between sound and meaning, which Mallarmé deplored in the French words *jour* ("day") and *nuit* ("night"). But if I may be permitted a personal opinion here, I must confess that I have never perceived this as a divergence: it only makes me think of these periods of time in two ways. For me, the day is something that lasts, the night something that occurs or that happens unexpectedly, as in the expression "night falls." *Jour* denotes a state; *nuit*, an event. Rather than perceiving a contradiction between the signifieds and the phonic peculiarities of their respective signifiers, I unconsciously ascribe dif-ferent natures to the signifieds. *Jour* represents a durative aspect, con-gruent with a grave vocalism; *nuit* a perfective aspect, congruent with an acute vocalism; all this, in its way, makes for a small mythology.

At the two poles of language, we encounter the emptiness of which Jakobson speaks, and which calls for a content to fill it. Nevertheless, from one pole to the other, the present and the absent relations are turned around. At the lowest level of language, we have the relation-ship of contiguity, but not that of resemblance. In reverse, on the other level which could be called "hyperstatic" (because it manifests proper-ties of a new category), and where mythology bends language to its own needs, the relationship of resemblance is present: unlike their words, the myths of different nations resemble one another. On this level, the relationship of contiguity has disappeared, because, as we have seen, no necessary link exists between the myth, as signifier, and the concrete signifieds to which it can be applied.

Thus, in one case as in the other, the complement is neither prede-termined nor imposed. Phonetic symbolism can be expressed at the lowest level, where language is in the firm grip of neuropsychological laws that represent the properties of cerebral maps that are homologous to one another. Semantic symbolism finds its place at the very top, in the zone where language, transcended by myth, locks into external realities. But, however far apart they may be at the two ends of the scale of linguistic functions, these two symbolisms—the phonetic and the semantic—offer a clear symmetry. They correspond to mental demands of the same type, turned either toward the body or toward society and the world.

By means of these extensions of his theories—possibilities that Jakobson might challenge—we measure the breadth of the domain that he has opened to research and the fruitfulness of the principles that, thanks to him, can henceforth guide research. Although old, these lectures do not illustrate a state of knowledge at a moment in the past. Today as much as yesterday, they breathe new life into a great adventure of the mind.

Chapter 10

Religion, Language, and History: Concerning an Unpublished Text by Ferdinand de Saussure

AMONG the unpublished manuscripts of Ferdinand de Saussure stored in the library of the University of Geneva is a notebook (Ms. fr. 3.951: 10), written in 1894, which deals mainly with the American linguist W. D. Whitney (1827-94). Roman Jakobson, who knew of this notebook (see Jakobson 1971*b*, pp. *xxv-xlv*), sent me, for their eventual publication, photocopies of four pages in which Saussure raises a problem about the relations between language, history, and religion. His text contains so many deletions, blanks, additions, incomplete sentences, and abbreviated or practically indecipherable words that an attempt to restore it fully would require the services of an epigraphist. I shall therefore limit myself here to reproducing its main point.*

*In the following transcription of Saussure's notes, crossed-out words are placed

Saussure is slow in coming to the subject. He begins three sentences, crossing out each in turn: "The fundamental measure of the degree of divinification of a thing . . . "; "The moment in which a thing [becomes] passes clearly into [. . .] is linked by certain conditions . . . "; "It would be completely illusory to believe that the moment when. . . ." Then he takes hold as follows:

So long as there exists a community of name (simply of *name*) between an object that falls under the sense[s]* and the [. . .], there is a primary category of mythological beings worthy of being fundamentally opposed to others, as the primary classification of the mythological idea. Hence, the *name* is the [primary] decisive principle, not of the invention of mythological beings—for who would scrutinize that in its foundation?—but of the instant when these beings become *purely* mythological and sever their last tie with the earth in order to [populate] come [contribute to] populating Olympus after many [others?].

So long as the word *agni* designates in the confusion both the fire of everyday and the god Agni, so long as *djeus* is both the name of [. . .], it is impossible, no matter what one may do, for Agni or Djeus to be a figure in the same category as *Varuna* or 'Aπόλλων,† whose names [do not designate] have the peculiarity [(today)] of designating nothing on the earth at the same moment.

If there is a determined instant when Agni will stop participating [. . .], that instant does not consist [in anything but] in [an increase of its divine attributes in the minds of its] anything but the accident that will bring the rupture of *name* with the perceptible object: an accident that is at the mercy of the first fact of language and with no necessary connection with the sphere of mythological ideas. If one has called [said about] a *cauldron* successively [. . .], it can happen automatically that one calls the fire successively agni and [something?] else.

And at this moment, the god *Agni*, like the god Zεύς‡ will [would] be [is] INEVITABLY raised to the rank of inscrutable divinities like Varuna, instead of running in the final [general] sphere of divinities like Ushas.§ [But] [now the point] Thus, what is the cause of [the] such an important and positive change in mythology? Nothing, if not a fact [purely negative in linguistics] [purely linguistic] that is not only *purely linguistic*, but with no visible [special] [striking] importance in the course of the linguistic events of each day. It is in that that it is definitively true, not that the *nūmina* are *nōmina*, according to the celebrated expression, but that on the fate of the *nōmen* ("name") hangs [absolutely] very decisively [and at every minute] and, so to speak, from second to second that of the *nūmen* ("divine majesty").

It is true that now the largest category of beings placed in the Pantheon

---

within brackets, while blank spaces and omissions are indicated by ellipses. Any explanations are indicated in footnotes.
*That is, "is obvious." [Ed.]
†'Aπόλλων is the Greek for Apollo. [Trans.]
‡Zεύς is the Greek for Zeus. [Trans.]
§Ushas is the goddess Aurora.

of eac[h] ancie[nt] people stems, not from the impression made by a real object, such as *agni*, but from the infinite play of epithets revolving about each name and enabling [This is not peculiar to] at every instant the creation [the] [at will] of as many substitutes (for " ") as one wishes. . . . This will not properly dissuade us of the fundamental influence of names and of language on the creation of figures. If we agree that . . . the word is . . . , [here it is simply the word that is decisive] here the word is simply [decisive and] *determining*; there is [*illegible addition*] the first [the only and last] suggestor and the only explic. final [reason] of the new divinity [to be created] that is one day created beside the preceding one.

No doubt, this sketchy linguistic interpretation of the origin of deities is more or less a variation on a famous theme—that of mythology as an illness of language. For the anthropologist, however, it is striking that Saussure's notions have a reputation in areas as remote as the one from which he draws examples and as far from one another as Australia and North America. These examples, of course, do not directly concern the origin of the names of deities but concern the connected domain of the names of people, where the type of phenomenon cited by Saussure can be observed directly.

In *The Savage Mind* (1966, pp. 149-50, 167-68, 172-218), I had already drawn attention to certain peculiarities in the name systems of several Australian tribes. For various reasons, the Tiwi, on the islands of Melville and Bathurst, in northern Australia, have many personal names. Each Tiwi has several names that he alone can bear. When a woman remarries (a frequent occurrence), all her children receive new names. Finally, a person's death places an interdict on all his names and on those he himself has given to others. Hence, the need for a linguistic mechanism to create new names in response to the demand. This mechanism functions as follows. The prohibition on certain names extends automatically to any common nouns that resemble them phonetically. But, these nouns are not totally abolished; they pass into the sacred language, which is reserved for ritual, and there gradually shed their original meaning. Once this is completely forgotten, nothing prevents anyone from using a now meaningless word and adding a suffix to transform it into a personal name. Thus, personal names, devoid of meaning *per se*, acquire a simulacrum of meaning in contact with the common nouns that they contaminate; these nouns lose their meanings when passing into the sacred language, which enables them to become names once again.

We know of similar systems on the Pacific coast of North America. The one that best lends itself to comparison belonged to the Twana, who lived around the Hood Canal in the northwestern part of what is now the state of Washington. According to W. W. Elmendorf, who devoted a monograph (1960) and several articles to them (1951), the Twana distinguished between sobriquets for children, based on physical or mental traits, and adult or "complete" names. The latter were meaningless and impossible to analyze grammatically; they belonged to family lines, and such a name could be borne by only one person during a lifetime, unless he gave up his name and, taking another, available one, put his own back into circulation.

A living person's name could be uttered only in exceptional circumstances; and the prohibition became absolute whenever a name, as family property, temporarily had no bearer because of a death, until it was assumed by a collateral relative or given to a descendant. As with the Tiwi, the prohibition could extend to certain common nouns having a phonetic resemblance to the personal name. In this case, a common noun could vanish once and for all from the lexicon, even if the name that had driven it out was taken up again after several years by another person. The procedure was probably not automatic; only high-ranking families could initiate it with any chance of success, for only some common nouns whose exclusion was sanctioned by means of a costly ceremony. Elmendorf has shown, however, that as this custom passed down from generation to generation, it was bound to have a deep impact on the vocabulary. Indeed, the culled examples reveal that most of the nouns coined to replace those eliminated by the prohibition have a descriptive character and lend themselves to grammatical analysis: thus, "red foot" for "mallard duck," "round thing for cooking" for "stone" (not having pottery, the Twana boiled water by dropping hot rocks into it); "trapped by the foot" for "sawbill duck"; "salt water is gone" for "tide"; and so on. The same procedure explains why adult names were meaningless: the common nouns from which they might have been derived had long since been expelled from the vocabulary because of their phonetic resemblance. Finally, since each small group respected only its own prohibitions and was unaware of those in neighboring villages, the custom favored the internal differentiation of dialects belonging to the same linguistic family (1960, pp. 377–96).

The preceding examples are of words that lost their meaning. On the other hand, according to the Witoto in the northwestern Amazon basin, common nouns were originally meaningless and acquired one or more meanings only through usage. Jürg Gasché, who has studied this tribe and graciously allowed me to quote his observations, asked his informants why, in their opinion, clans or individuals bore the names of animals and vegetables. The Indians vigorously denied any such practice. Words, they said, existed first without meaning, and it was only by accident that some words came to be applied, on the one hand, to plants and animals or, on the other, to clans and individuals. It similarly occurs that identical words can designate different things in neighboring dialects.

In such cases as those cited by Saussure, history, language, and religion are closely mingled and influence one another. Yet is the opposition between the two types of deity names as fundamental a trait as the notebook of 1894 maintains? Even if the name Apollo has no satisfactory etymology in Greek, it might have a meaning in the tongue of the Asiatic or Hyperborean people from whom the Greeks seem to have taken this god; in this case, we would still be dealing with a linguistic fact, although one different from the facts that Saussure had in mind. And what about the functional role of Hermes in the pantheon, his affinities with Agni, on which A. M. Hocart has so vigorously insisted (1970, pp. 17-21, 57-59)? Would all this be changed if one attributed or denied to the name of this god a meaning that, in the affirmative, would be very different from that of Agni? (Both theses have had their advocates.) So much the less, it seems, that among the Koryak, each family regarded the stirring stick for making a fire—a stick cut in the shape of a human figure—as a deity, which was called not "Fire" but, through periphrasis, "master of the flock" (a term also applied to Hermes) or even "father" (Jochelson 1908, pp. 32-35). Among the deity names designating something "on earth at the same time," it is necessary also to make a distinction—often difficult to apply consistently— between names corresponding to a concrete reality such as fire or dawn, and those referring to an abstract notion such as wealth or a contract.

Even if a god's name is meaningless, it will insidiously gain one or more meanings if it is contaminated, so to speak, by all the epithets describing a particular god's power and attributes. The god's name might be empty of meaning; but the adjective formed from it *would* have meaning. Conversely, if a god's name originally had a meaning, it would eventually lose it, as happens with personal names taken from things or events with which one would no longer dream of connecting them. Who thinks of a flower or a pearl in regard to a woman named Rose or Marguerite, or of a Moor's blackness, a rebirth, or the number eight in regard to a Maurice, a René,* or an Octave? There is no reason why divine names should be more resistant than human names to this semantic wear, unless we assume the formative process postulated by Saussure to have been demonstrated. For only if we could prove that all the names of deities originally designated real objects, the absence of such a connotation would have to result from a loss or a deprivation. But if such were the case, then our reasoning would be circular.

Finally, to convince ourselves that we are dealing with a type of general explanation, we ought to reveal a more or less constant relationship between the names of deities that have lost all meaning, and names that, in order to designate things, would have replaced them, as is clearly demonstrated, by the Tiwi and the Twana, in the area of common nouns and personal names. For we understand why, in these two languages, the distinctive properties of both have reciprocal functions: the proper names of the Twana are devoid of etymological meaning *for the same reason* that so many of their common nouns do have such a meaning. Saussure, to whom we owe the establishment of the systematic character of language apparent from its synchronic structure, could not make up his mind to extend the same conception to facts observable only in their diachronic development. Of this repugnance, his notes of 1894 offer a new example: a forerunner of structural linguistics, Saussure nevertheless believes that an ensemble of deities can result from an accumulation of flukes and accidents. He does not think that, like language itself (and as the work of Georges Dumézil [1898-], the famous historian of Indo-European ideologies, has amply demonstrated), this set forms a system in which each god (who, in this sense, can never appear "inscrutable" even if his name is) can be understood only in relation to the whole. It appears difficult to interpret divergences and effects of symmetry in the name systems of neighboring groups within the same linguistic family, without regard for the historical context. This helps us understand the systematic character of these divergences, instead of their origin being arbitrary and unmotivated.

According to the testimony of G. Gibbs over a century ago, the Indians of the Puget Sound area named their dogs but not their horses, except for descriptive terms denoting the color of their coat (1877, p. 211). About 120 miles inland, the Thompson Indians generally named their dogs after the markings on or the color of the animal's coat, more rarely after a quadruped or a bird of similar temperament; while horses, though sometimes named in the same manner as dogs, were more often named after people (Teit 1900, p. 292). According to this

*In French, the word *rené* is literally "reborn." (Trans.)

information, it would seem that the system alternates from one group to the next. The documents available on the name system of the various Salish tribes suggest that things were less clear-cut and more complex. Yet, at the same time, they prompt us to take into account historical factors: for instance, the horse was introduced into Thompson culture in the late eighteenth or early nineteenth century and even later at Puget Sound and on the coast, where it was used sporadically (being limited to so-called equestrian groups) and did not have the same importance. On the other hand, several tribes of Puget Sound and the coastal region raised, besides hunting hounds, another breed of dog whose hair they sheared and used in weaving—a practice unknown among the Thompson, who employed only vegetable fibers and the hair of wild goats. These "wool" dogs were never killed, lived in their master's house, and were given special treatment.

Finally, in both groups of tribes—those on Puget Sound and along the coast and those in the interior (Thompson, Lilloet, Okanagon, and so on)—the names of dogs and horses had certain oppositive and correlative relations—although these are not always clear—with the names given to men, reserved for women, or conferred on children of either sex and on slaves. At Puget Sound and along the coast, where the practice of slavery was more developed than in the interior and was integrated into a hierarchical system of three classes (noble, common, and servile), slaves and dogs were often equated: "Even a dog or a slave will do his best if he is well treated." Furthermore, slaves were not allowed to have adult names; they were named or baptized with descriptive sobriquets like those given to little children (Elmendorf 1960, pp. 346-47). In contrast, inland groups like the Lilloet and the Okanagon tended rather to equate dogs and women and put them in closely related categories. An Okanagon myth proposes to explain in a nutshell why there are dogs and women today (Cline et al. 1938, pp. 227-28). In their ritual invocation to the bear, the Lilloet promised: "No woman shall eat your flesh; no dog shall insult you." They tried to prevent women and dogs from urinating near the men's bathhouses, and killed any dog that urinated in the same place as a woman lest it feel a sexual desire for her and other women (Teit 1906, pp. 267, 279, 291). Now, among the Lilloet as among the Thompson and the Okanagon, suffixes sharply differentiated between male and female names. Native evidence from the Okanagon suggests that only male dogs were given names, which were often taken from the ordinary terminology used to designate other animals. The same was true of men's names; but women's names were never formed on this model (Cline 1938, p. 106).

These concordances or their reversals, which have a pervasive effect on name systems, remind me of an amusing criticism of *The Savage Mind*. Several years ago, an unknown British reader sent me a letter, disputing the validity of my interpretation of the names given to human beings, dogs, cattle, and racehorses, and of my attempt to show that these four types of names come from distinct categories forming a system. According to my British correspondent, his compatriots tended to use human names for dogs; and, indeed, neighbors of his, who had lost their young son, even went so far as to buy a dog and name it after the dead boy.

This objection is of methodological interest, not only for anthropology but for all the sciences of man. My critic does not realize that, in our disciplines, facts can never be viewed in isolation but must be seen in relation to other facts of the same category. I had not claimed to establish a universal typology on the basis of the French examples I was citing. I was merely trying to show that, in any society—even if people think they are acting freely—their choice and use of proper names reflects a certain way of slicing up the social and moral universe, of categorizing individuals, and of translating how each culture conceives of the reciprocal relations between human beings and their various domestic animals. It is not that all societies employ the same pattern or are inspired by a single model. Far from invalidating my thesis, the fact that the French and the British use different types of names for their dogs lends further support to my argument. In naming their dogs in a different way from the French, the English betray certain psychological attitudes toward their pets which do not coincide with our own attitudes. We French, too, sometimes give our dogs human names, but in a spirit of mockery of our fellowmen rather than out of consideration for our four-footed friends. And the incident related by my British correspondent would be practically inconceivable in France, where it would inspire universal shock and disapproval.*

---

*"The fact that I have a pet dog called Peter . . . ," Edmund Leach writes as an example (in Goody 1958, p. 124). Pierre is certainly not the first name for a dog that would leap to the mind of a French anthropologist.

Dr. Michael P. Carroll, who has made a specialty of criticizing me without knowing what I have written (see pages 207–8 of this book), tried to refute me with American dogs' names (1980) but did so not knowing that I had already replied to this kind of objection. In *The Savage Mind*, I reasoned in terms of the French system; the fact that dog names are different in the Anglo-Saxon world merely supports my thesis, since the position of dogs in that culture is not the same.

In this case as in others, what matters is that a system exists, not whether it assumes one form or another. In Spanish, the word *mozo* can refer to a cat, a young boy, or a male servant; or, in the Caribbean languages, kinship vocabulary identifies grandchildren with semi-domestic animals (Taylor 1961, pp. 367-70); the Yurok of California similarly equate domestic animals with slaves (Elmendorf 1960, p. 115 n. 89). These are so many valuable indications of the way different cultures slice up or superimpose the human and the animal kingdoms, nature and society. Likewise, the way we categorize proper names—reserving certain preferred ones for human beings, men or women, or for certain animal families to which we sometimes give human names—and the directions in which these practices evolve in the course of history, in correlation with or in contradiction to other transformations of a political, economic, or cultural nature, can provide the historian and the sociologist with data that is all the more useful in that our societies at least have comparatively rich archives covering a long stretch of time. Not long ago, a geographer suggested a method for studies of this type (Zelinsky 1970). Although his work was restricted to personal names, W. Zelinsky demonstrated that the names actually in use have increased considerably, going from several hundred two centuries ago to over three thousand today. These figures prompt us to wonder whether a horizontal diversity among regions that are culturally almost homogeneous might not be gradually yielding to a vertical diversity among subcultures stratified throughout a far vaster territory.

Even if Saussure's thesis about the names of deities cannot be accepted without reservation, it is useful for recalling the importance and the interest of problems connected to the formation and the assignment of proper names, about which anthropology and sociology seem so far not to have sufficiently concerned themselves. Yet this barely cultivated terrain would offer them an opportunity, all too often denied, of working together.

Chapter II

From Mythical Possibility to Social Existence

TO DESCRIBE the diversity of customs, beliefs, and institutions as the result of choice, exercised by each society in an ideal repertoire where all possibilities are set down in advance, seems to some social scientists like an abuse of language, a rhetorical procedure, a series of arbitrary comparisons, irritatingly anthropomorphic and unrelated to any conceivable reality. Societies are not persons. Nothing authorizes us to depict them as customers thumbing through some metaphysical catalogue and obtaining, each for their own use, models different from those other societies would use toward the same ends.

Nevertheless, sometimes this metaphor lends itself to experimental control. Such is the case when a myth suggests several rules of action, and when ethnographic observation verifies the fact that societies stemming from the same overall culture as the myth in question have actually applied one or the other of these rules. From a list of solutions presented simultaneously to the collective imagination, each society would have, according to circumstance, made its choice of practices.

One might object that this is tantamount to turning the problem upside down, and that myths arc actually *a posteriori* attempts to construct a homogeneous system on the basis of disparate rules. This hypothesis would also imply that, sooner or later, mythical thinking conceives of these rules as so many possible answers to a question.

I should like to offer an example from Polynesia. Undoubtedly the myth we are about to consider does not belong to societies whose freedom of choice it seems to restrict to two possibilities; we know, however, that Polynesia was inhabited by navigators of a common origin, who sailed from island to island. The stages of these migrations have been reconstructed; and, notwithstanding differences of dialect, a close linguistic bond confirms the overall cultural unit. It is therefore legitimate to speak of this part of the world as a whole. The experts on it are correct in viewing Polynesian customs, beliefs, and institutions as variations on themes that—from Samoa and Tonga to the Hawaiian Islands, and from the Marquesas to New Zealand—reveal a common heritage.

A patrilineal ideology used to dominate part of the Fiji archipelago. Numerous family lines intermarried freely. But, within each line, a brother and a sister were subject to a very strict taboo: they had to avoid all physical contact and were not even allowed to speak to one another. In Tonga, this taboo prevented any marriage between their respective children, and, in Samoa, even between their distant descendants.

According to the work done by A. M. Hocart (1952) and by B. Quain (1948), other Fiji groups have a distinctly matrilineal orientation. These groups sometimes divide into exogamic moieties and then ignore the sibling taboo. In fact, Quain has shown that in the island of Vanua Levu, wherever exogamic moieties exist, the sibling taboo is absent, and wherever it is present, there are no exogamic moieties. This incompatibility raises a problem, as it is all the more striking in that, except for chiefs, the prohibition of marriage between true cross-cousins was added to the rule of exogamic moieties.

Specialists in Oceania noted long ago that, in Polynesia, the relationship between brother and sister is the opposite of that between husband and wife. The difference is obvious, but not the reason that sometimes one, sometimes another, of these forms is more strongly "marked" in different areas, especially from western to central Polynesia. In Tokelau, a group of atolls some three hundred miles northwest of the Samoan Islands, a brother's and a sister's lives unfold in sharply contrasting domains. Separated by their occupations, they are raised to maintain extreme reserve toward each other and must avoid being in the same place at the same time. On the other hand, husband and wife do not have distinct spheres of activity; nor do love songs attest to any great interest in the relationship between the sexes. Husband and wife participate equally in the life of the household, in accordance with a theory of conception that assigns each spouse an equal and identical role in the formation of a child (Huntsman and Hooper 1975).

Pukapuka, in the northern Cook Islands, has practically the reverse situation. There is no taboo between brother and sister, but the theory of conception assigns a specific role to each sex, and the importance of love songs in the native culture shows that emotional relations between men and women are important here (Hecht 1977).

Now the Pukapuka myth of origin, existing in several versions, juxtaposes the two types of rules and presents them as equivalent solutions to the same problem. It tells us that the island's population originated in the union between an autochthonous male (living in a rock) and a woman from the outside world. This primordial couple had four children, alternately boys and girls. The two eldest children mated and gave birth to the line of chiefs; the two youngest also mated and gave birth to the common people, who subsequently formed two matrilineal moieties that were, in all likelihood, originally exogamic; one was called "of the earth"; the other, "of the sea." The author of a very rich commentary on this myth (Hecht 1977) correctly remarks that, in accordance with local custom, the line of chiefs had to include, from the very start, a brother and a sister having distinct functions: the man exercised the hereditary chieftainry; and his sister became a sacred virgin, dedicated to celibacy and without offspring. Such was the situation in Pukapuka. Thus, the myth suggests two ways of palliating incest, a "bad deed" imputed to the preceding generation: an aristocratic way, which turns the consecrated sister into a forbidden woman; and a common way, which divides the people into two moieties. Despite its remoteness, the Pukapuka myth answers the question posed by the coexistence, at Vanua Levu, of two similarly contrasting customs: the exogamic moieties, which prevent incest, make the brother-sister taboo superfluous. In the absence of moieties, the taboo constitutes an effective barrier. In other words, the same problem can elicit two different answers—one in terms of classes; the other, of relations.

For those who may be disturbed by my citing a myth from southern Polynesia to interpret Fijian customs found in Fiji, some twelve hundred miles away, let me observe that, beside my suggestion about the common origin of all Polynesians, Tonga, which is near Fiji and influenced by it, also had a myth about siblings who are born of a stone and marry each other. On the other hand, Fijian traditions, like those of Pukapuka, describe the local population as descending from an extremely exogamic union between a male outsider and a native woman, thus reversing the Pukapuka situation, but with a correlative switch in the order of precedence: Fijian women being, as a rule, inferior to the men, a sister, says an informant, "regards her brother as a sacred being." Hence, any physical contact and any direct communication between the two are prohibited. On the other hand, in Samoa and Tonga, the female representative of the paternal line (the sister or the father's sister) occupied the privileged position, as in Pukapuka. But then, another difference appears between the two most remote areas: in Samoa and in Tonga, the female representative of the paternal line can curse her nephews and nieces and make them sterile—the same power that the Pukapuka brother wields over his sister when he condemns her to sterility. In Pukapuka, however, it is the wife who curses her husband, the result being that she gives him no children. In Tokelau, there is a different permutation of terms. The sister who, as in Samoa, can curse her nephews and nieces and deprive them of offspring, is called "sacred mother": "sacred," like the Pukapuka sister, she too is struck with sterility; and "mother," like the Pukapuka wife, who, in order to punish her husband, inflicts a similar curse on both him and herself. Yet some nine hundred miles separate Tokelau and Pukapuka. This is a further sign that the social system adopted by a culture is accompanied by a latent awareness of the opposite possibility.

This proximity of different norms (though all are from the same aggregate) raises a problem, to which we will return but which is connected with another that must be mentioned here. Wherever, as in Tonga, a sister's position is superior to her brother's, whom can she marry? In societies of this type, custom requires the husband to have a higher rank than his wife but one lower than his elder sister's, either because more importance is attached to primogeniture than gender, or because, as T. Mabuchi has shown (1952, 1964), women are thought to have a spiritual power in this region of the world and all the way to Taiwan and the Ryukyu archipelago.

It is likely that in Tonga, the king's older sister used to remain unmarried—a solution analogous to the one in Pukapuka. Later, she may have gained the right to marry an outsider, even one of a lower rank. Their union produced the Tamahâ, the woman having the highest rank in the kingdom. Hawaii reversed the problem by allowing and even advocating royal unions between brother and sister. An attenuated form of this solution was also practiced in Tonga, where the nobles would frequently marry their cross-cousins in violation of the brother-sister taboo, which forbade marriage between children of cross-siblings.

The sister's higher position could be interpreted in a different way. In a hypergamic society, where the sister of a great noble ought to marry above her station (a hypothetical demand impossible to meet), one solution would be to postulate that whomever she married would be deemed to be higher in rank. The sister's superiority would thus result from a constraint of the system, which would confer the appearance of reality upon a legal fiction.

In any case, the preceding discussion confirms that a Polynesian myth suggests that there are two conceivable ways of solving a practical problem; and that neighboring groups, situated within the cultural area from which this myth derives, have put either possibility into practice. Thus, they have, in effect, opted between possibilities offered by a way of thinking of which they were unaware, but which was nevertheless representative of it.

The foregoing case is privileged in two fashions. First of all, a single myth incorporates two models of social organization as possible solutions to the same problem. Then, the region that produced this myth includes societies that have simultaneously put these solutions into practice or have chosen one or the other of them. Usually life is not this simple. A myth does not necessarily reveal several theoretical solutions at once. Instead, they appear separately, each illustrated by a variant; and it is only by collating all variants that we can view the overall picture. Finally, we are not often in a position to make philosophical or ethical speculations correspond directly to real choices. Since I listed so many examples of this situation in my Introduction to a Science of Mythology series (1970, 1973, 1979, 1981), it seems superfluous to add to them here.

Nevertheless, I should like to call attention here to an intermediary case, in which a population devotes several versions of one of its myths to examining various possibilities, except for one that would contradict the facts of the problem confronting the group. It therefore leaves a lacuna in the range of possibilities, allowing a neighboring group, which is not faced with the same problem, to take over the myth and fill the gap—but only on the condition of deflecting this myth from its original goal and even of profoundly altering its nature. For, in this case, it is no longer a myth but a "family history," according to Hunt, who collected it, and to Boas, who published it (1921, pp. 1249-55). Or, more precisely, it is a legendary tradition about a noble house, adapted for establishing or enhancing its prestige and situated halfway between speculative thought and political realism—hence, another way of embodying in facts the possible fruits of the mythical imagination.

In twice studying several versions of a myth (called "The Story of Asdiwal") from the Tsimshian Indians of British Columbia (see Lévi-Strauss 1976, 146-97), I tried to show that this myth simultaneously employs several codes—cosmological, climatological, geographic, topographic—to bring out a homology between both natural opposites (empyrean sky/chthonian world, high/low, mountain/sea, upstream/downstream, winter/summer) and sociological or economic opposites (filiation/reliance, endogamy/exogamy, hunting/fishing, abundance/dearth, and so on). It is as if this myth were trying to record the fact that marriage between matrilateral cross-cousins, although preferred by a society made up of rival family lines, fails to overcome their antagonisms. Thus, the function of the myth is to excuse a societal failure by blaming it on the objective absence of mediating terms between poles that nature itself diametrically opposes.

The different versions of this deeply pessimistic myth exhaust all the negative outcomes of a single plot. A hero, incapable of reconciling the successive styles of life that he has experienced, dies a victim of the irrepressible longing he feels for one or the other of them (versions of 1895, 1912-16). Or else, if he manages to avoid being permanently marked by any one way of life, he fails to carry out the mission the myth has assigned to him—namely, to embody their antinomy (version of 1902). The first three versions come from the valley of the Skeena River; the last, from the valley of the Nass River. I shall not review the reasons —bearing on the way of life peculiar to each valley—for the different treatments of the same theme.

The Kwakiutl, who are southern neighbors of the Tsimshian, have borrowed the myth of Asdiwal—that is, not the Kwakiutl in general, but one of their tribes, the Koeksotenok, and within that tribe, a particular noble house, the Naxnaxula, who have made the myth a family tradition. It is worthwhile to investigate how this appropriation of an easily recognizable tale for new ends could have modified both its content and its form.

At first sight, the Kwakiutl version seems like a potpourri of fragments lifted from its models. From the 1895 and the 1912 versions comes the episode where a supernatural spirit, married to a human woman, works magic in order to make his newborn son grow up; from the 1895 version comes the episode where he subordinates his magical help to unspecified prohibitions. But the resemblances begin to multiply with the 1902 Nass River version: the heroines are sisters instead of being mother and daughter as in the Skeena versions; the supernatural protector, who marries one of the two women, commits the initial mistake by making snowshoes for his son; the son is given two magic dogs that can grow bigger or smaller on command. In these two versions only, the protector tests his son's hunting talents by pitting him against a rival, and he hides from his brothers-in-law when the latter return to their sisters. Likewise in these versions, the hero, pursuing a supernatural bear all the way to the top of a mountain, fails to get into its den;

Synopsis of the Kwakiutl Version

Two sisters—one married, the other unmarried—are driven by famine from their respective villages and, walking toward each other's village, meet halfway. On the way, the younger sister has continually called for spiritual help. It now manifests itself in the guise of a handsome man, who gives her food and marries her. She bears a child. Before disappearing, the father makes him a great hunter and endows him with magic powers.

The brothers of the two women set out in search of them and find them. Together, they return to their tribe, and the hero, the son of the supernatural protector, becomes chief of the tribe.

One day he takes off in pursuit of a supernatural bear, which leads him to the top of a mountain; eventually, the hero descends after failing to get into the bear's house. He then goes to another Kwakiutl tribe and marries the chief's daughter.

His brothers-in-law take him hunting at sea. Jealous of his successes, they abandon him on an island, where the inhabitants of the underworld save him and welcome him into their undersea kingdom. There, he cures wounded animals and is paid with magical objects and weapons, thanks to which he avenges himself on his wicked brothers-in-law. He is proclaimed chief of their tribe and henceforth provides the entire population with game from the ocean.

---

and only from outside does he hear the bear sing a song, whose words mean exactly the same despite the different languages.

Both the Kwakiutl and the Tsimshian were great travelers. They traveled by boat to one another in order to wage war, trade, or simply visit. Sometimes friendly, sometimes hostile, the tribes would capture slaves, carry off women, or conclude regular marriages. Thus, there is no reason not to assume that the Kwakiutl heard the versions that Boas collected from the Tsimshian, as well as other versions that we do not know. What remains is the singular fact that the clearest and most numerous resemblances appear between the most remote versions: from the mouth of the Nass, where Boas obtained the 1902 version, to the Koeksotenok territory, the distance as the crow flies is 400 to 500 kilometers (250 to 300 miles), and this area is difficult to cross by land; going by sea, as the Indians usually did, took almost twice as long. There is something odd about this that we ought to consider. We will see that the mystery is explained not by special relations between the Nisqa (people of the Nass) and the Koeksotenok but by formal reasons that—although different in each case—connect the Kwakiutl and the Nass versions while differentiating them from the three Skeena versions.

If we agree for a moment to treat the Tsimshian versions as a whole, we can see how sharply they differ from the Kwakiutl versions. The former take place in river valleys—the Skeena or the Nass—lying roughly on an east-west axis. The Kwakiutl version unfolds far inland on an approximately north-south axis, perpendicular to the flow of the waterways. This version begins in Hâda, at the tip of Bond Sound (Boas 1944: 13.103); then the action shifts southeast, toward Xekweken, at the head of Thompson Sound (15.13). Xekweken occupies an important place in Kwakiutl mythology as the region where the Thunderbird landed on a mountain peak when he came down from the sky (p. 29). It is therefore not surprising that it is from this place—that is, toward the highest mountains—that the hero makes a perilous ascent in pursuit of the supernatural bear. He fails to get into its home (located in the celestial world, according to the Tsimshian versions of 1895 and 1912), because, as the text tells us not very explicitly, "he had transgressed the rules laid down by his father" (Boas 1921, p. 1,253). (Perhaps, contrary to instructions, he neglected to take his magic dogs along on his hunt for the bear.)

The Kwakiutl version explains, from the very beginning, that the younger of the two women has left Hâda in the grip of a famine, in the hope that her married sister, living far away, will be better off; but the latter, a victim of the same fate, has made the same plan, and they meet halfway. While the Tsimshian versions detail the women's journeys, nothing in the Kwakiutl version indicates the starting point of the second sister or the direction taken by the first. It seems unlikely that the older sister came from Xekweken, for the text says that she is married and lives in "a remote village"; and the distance between Hâda and Xekweken seems to have been no more than seven miles as the crow flies or fifteen along the coasts.* The reason for this change is easy to understand. The Kwakiutl version preserves the plot of the Tsimshian myths but treats it differently: the "young virgin," soon to be the mother of the hero, views her search for food as a spiritual quest, whose success will be in proportion to the dangers she voluntarily courts by venturing into a savage country. A known itinerary would ill fit the intentions that urge the heroine on, for she is purified at each stage and hopes that a guardian spirit, a supernatural protector, will reveal himself to her—contrary to the Tsimshian versions, where this protector appears unexpectedly and of his own accord. Only the 1895 version gives the two women a religious attitude: they pray and make offerings, but only after the unexpected appearance of a protective spirit in the form of a bird named Good Luck.

As for the protector in the Kwakiutl version, his name is Q!ômg.ilax-yaô, a compound that Boas did not translate. We may note, however, that it is formed from the root q!ôm ("rich"), thus putting its bearer on the side of the undersea world, ruled by Kōmogwa, the master of riches, whom we shall soon meet. This submarine or chthonian world is diametrically opposed to the heavenly world to which the homologous figure in the Tsimshian myths is connected by his bird nature. Thus, from the start, the Kwakiutl name of the supernatural protector attests to the characteristic orientation of the Kwakiutl version—from high to low—to which we shall return.

Whatever the differences, in all the versions whether Tsimshian or Kwakiutl, the protector takes human form, marries the younger of the two women, fathers a son, provides him with magical objects, and then disappears. According to the Kwakiutl version, when the son grows up he settles down with his mother's family in Xekweken, the southernmost point of his odyssey. There he becomes a great chief but fails, as we have seen, in his endeavor to reach the upper world. He thereupon decides to travel to the Tsawatenok, another Kwakiutl tribe, in

---

*I am grateful to Dr. Peter L. Macnair, curator of ethnology at the British Columbia Provincial Museum, for his help in pinpointing the location of these two places and the distance between them.

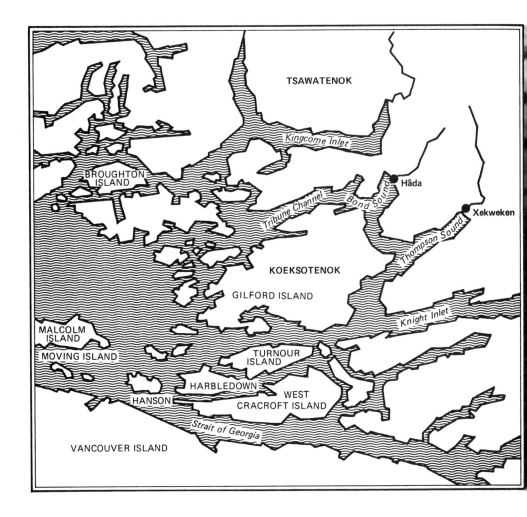

order to marry the daughter of their chief. This will be his only marriage, whereas the Tsimshian versions from 1912 to 1916 attribute four successive unions to the hero and one to his son, with each union illustrating a different form of matrimony.

The Tsawatenok lived in the region of the Kingcome Inlet, north of Hâda; and their country, where the hero finally settles, is the northernmost area he reaches in the course of his travels. Thus, the entire plot unfolds between Thompson Sound in the south and Kingcome Inlet in the north, except for when, after his wedding, the hero and his brothers-in-law go hunting for sea otters on Moving Island, probably the small island of this name located between Hanson and Malcolm islands (Boas 1944, 11.21 and p. 50), where the Strait of Georgia opens into the sea. The hunting expedition has the same consequences as in the Tsimshian versions: abandoned by his jealous brothers-in-law, the hero is taken in by the denizens of the underworld (which, for the Kwakiutl, is also a marine world); there he tends and cures the wounded seals and sea lions, who are the servants of Kōmogwa, the master of the sea and of all bounty. The hero is rewarded with many magical objects: a house that grows and shrinks at his command; a boat, an oar, and a spear that move by themselves; an incendiary cudgel; water that can resurrect the dead; inexhaustible food; and a new name, Chief-of-the-Open-Sea (replacing his former name, Prettiest-Hunter). Returning to his wife's village, he sets fire to it with his magic cudgel and transforms his enemies into rocks. His magic weapons are so powerful that his wife is also turned into a rock, but she is restored with the water of life. In the Tsimshian versions from Skeena, he himself (1912 version) and then his son and the latter's wife (1916 version) are—during foolhardy expeditions to high mountains—changed into stone, this time for good. According to the Kwakiutl version, however, the hero becomes the great chief of his wife's tribe, and his magic equipment allows him to provide his tribesmen with seafood galore.

In regard to the Tsimshian versions, I once noted that "starting with an initial situation characterized by irrepressible movement," they end with "a final situation characterized by perpetual immobility." I added that the Tsimshian myth "expresses in its own way a fundamental aspect of the native philosophy": that is, for it, "the only positive form of existence is a negation of nonexistence" (Lévi-Strauss 1976, p. 175).

These conclusions do not obviously apply to the Kwakiutl version. The latter begins with a quest for a guardian spirit—a voluntary act for which the famine raging in Hâda only furnishes an occasion. At the end, the hero is anything but congealed in a mineral inertia. Endowed with superb mobility by his magic equipment, he moves his house on water without difficulty; his boat moves by itself; his spear, transformed into a serpent, pounces on the seals of its own accord, killing them one by one and then returning to its owner. In sum, the story commences with an initiatory quest and ends with its success: because of his mother's religious fervor, the hero eventually obtains the complete panoply of miraculous objects, in regard to which the supernatural protectors in the Kwakiutl tales are usually more economical.

This finalist construction is also evident in the episode where the hero fails to penetrate the dwelling of the celestial bears. As I have already said, the Kwakiutl version literally reproduces the 1902 Tsimshian version on this point; but the function of this episode is not the same. In the Tsimshian version (collected on the Nass River), the hero's two cosmic voyages are presented as equally meaningless: his visit to the celestial world is unsuccessful; and he has no regrets about leaving the seals. On the other hand, the Kwakiutl version contrasts his unsuccessful visit to the celestial world with his extremely successful visit to the underworld (nowhere else does the hero gain such benefits). But, as a general rule in Kwakiutl mythology, the forebears of noble houses *come from* the heavens more often than they go there; and their descendants, willingly or not, *go to* the underworld, the realm of Kōmogwa, from whom they receive precious gifts.

This orientation is implicit in the framework of the Kwakiutl version and would also be verified if, as I have assumed, the hero's failure with the bears is caused by his forgetting to use his dogs. For the latter are embryonic Dioscuri (Lévi-Strauss 1976, p. 223); and the need to ask for help from the weakest in the series of mediators shows that, from the viewpoint of the narrative, the movement from low to high is less consistent with the order of things than the movement from high to low.

In the light of all this, how do we relate the Kwakiutl version to the Tsimshian versions? The forms of the Skeena versions (that of 1912, and the one of 1916, which follows it, and also the 1895 version) are both extreme and antithetical. In the first, the hero, despite his marriages to coastal women and his sojourn in the underwater world, feels an overpowering homesickness for the mountain where he spent his childhood: he wanders too far on the mountain, loses his way, and is changed into a rock; the 1916 version reserves this fate for his son. In the 1895 version, even though a mountain hunter by vocation, the hero feels homesick for the underwater world; and because his memory of it is so vivid, and he reveals its mysteries, he dies victim of a supernatural punishment.

Halfway between these extreme forms, the Nass version (1902) neutralizes them. After settling on the coast and marrying, the hero feels homesickness neither for the mountain, where he has tested his mettle as a great hunter, nor for the undersea kingdom whose protégé he has become. He puts an end to his wanderings and settles on the coast—that is, between the open sea and the mountain—where he has a peaceful life in retirement. Incapable—according to this version—of embodying the antinomies that form the framework of the myth, and

—according to the Skeena versions—of surmounting them because he identifies completely with one term and dissociates himself completely from the other, Asdiwal is thus, in all cases, an anti-hero whom the Tsimshian versions have no choice but to depict either in an epic or a prosaic genre.

For him to be transformed into a true hero, the glorious ancestor of a noble and esteemed house, it was necessary to point out the gap, in this range of permutations, that the Tsimshian could not fill because of the negative function that they assigned to the myth (to show that it was in the nature of things for there to be an inherent contradiction in their social organization). The "family history" of a Kwakiutl house manages very simply to fill this lacuna: it reverses the framework of the Nass version, which, as we have just seen, is balanced between the Skeena versions, though with a static equilibrium which illustrates, in a different way, the state of inertia in which all the Tsimshian versions end.

Thus, instead of neutralizing the opposing terms, as the Nass version does, the Kwakiutl story synthesizes them: it reconciles them and, far from letting their positive aspects cancel one another out, adds them together. As in the Nass version, a contest organized by his father enables the hero to demonstrate his talents as a mountain hunter; also, as in the Nass version, his care of the seals is rewarded. But only in the Kwakiutl tale does the hero succeed in becoming, on the one hand, chief of his mother's and of his wife's tribes, thus overcoming the antinomy of filiation and alliance; and, on the other hand, in settling into the role of renowned *hunter*, but *on the open sea*, thus overcoming the antinomy between mountain and ocean and attaining a synthesis of these two elements. In fact, this conclusion is foreshadowed by his two successive names: Prettiest-Hunter during the first part of his life; Chief-of-the-Open-Sea, after his visit with the seals.

If we stick to the latter antinomy and agree to differentiate all the versions according to whether each term leaves the hero marked or unmarked, we end with the following table, which sums up our entire argument:

		mountain:	sea:
	1912-1916:	+	−
Tsimshian versions	1895:	−	+
	1902:	−	−
Kwakiutl version:		+	+

THE ENVIRONMENT

Thus, the Kwakiutl story reverses the Nass story (1902) on an axis perpendicular to that on which the Skeena tales (1912-16, 1895) are reversed, thus expressing in spatial terms the conversion of the characteristic east-west axis of these versions to a north-south axis:

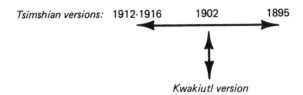

Even one detail, present only in the final Kwakiutl version and seemingly gratuitous, fits in perfectly well with this interpretation. As the guest of the seals in Kōmogwa's undersea kingdom, the hero does not need to communicate verbally with them, for they can read his mind before he even opens his mouth. This hypercommunication, which is characteristic of the netherworld, obviously contrasts with the lack of communication that prevents the hero from entering the home of the celestial bears because he has forgotten or misunderstood his father's instructions. Now, some time ago, I showed that all the Tsimshian versions of the myth of Asdiwal employ diverse forms of communication: indiscretion, as excessive communication with others; misunderstanding, as lack of communication, also with others; forgetfulness, as lack of communication with oneself; and perhaps homesickness, as excessive communication with oneself (Lévi-Strauss 1976, pp. 190-91). The hero of the Kwakiutl tale has no reason to feel homesick, for he knows how to benefit from, and not lose, the experience he acquired as a mountain hunter and as a protegé of the undersea world. Similarly, mind reading, although likewise a hypertrophic mode of communication, has none of the negative connotations attached to indiscretion, misunderstanding, or forgetfulness. Quite the contrary, mind reading enables the hero's benefactors to anticipate his every desire. Consequently, in this case, too, the Kwakiutl story changes otherwise negative values into positive ones.

This operation was forbidden to the Tsimshian for two reasons. They set themselves a problem in terms that made it virtually unsolvable; and they chose to put it in the most general perspective: that of a society, and of a world, conceived in its image, where antagonisms cannot be reconciled. It is a fact that a society made up of rival houses lives in an unstable equilibrium, perpetually challenged; and that the conflicts played out in it have a negative impact on the society as a whole.

On the other hand, this rivalry has a positive value for each house on its own, for it offers a house certain opportunities and enables it to pursue its goals. In order for the initially negative Tsimshian myth to acquire a positive value, two conditions had to be met. First of all, having been borrowed by a group that did not recognize the myth as such, the latter, vulgarized, became a simple canvas on which other motifs could be embroidered. Second, the myth could be taken over not by the whole society but only by one of its segments—and, specifically, by a segment (a noble house) for which rivalry changed from a negative to a positive value. A social and natural philosophy can exclude a certain combination of ideas or maintain them in a potential, unrealized condition. But once it passes into other hands, nothing can prevent this combination from acceding, in a double sense, to actual existence: as a statement in a discourse and as a political instrument.

Two examples—one from Polynesia and one from North America —show, explicitly or by omission, that myths sometimes set up a scheme of possibilities where empirically observable social groups (societies in one case, noble houses in the other) discover formulas for solving their problems of internal organization or enhancing their prestige vis-à-vis rivals. The formulas elaborated by myths can thus be applied practically; and we may say, in this sense, that mythic speculation precedes action. Furthermore, mythic speculation does not have to know either whether the statements it makes on an ideological level are, in fact, solutions for a concrete problem; or whether a choice can be made among the solutions in order to solve a problem. Only the ethnography of a part of the Fiji Islands verifies this situation for the Pukapuka myth. More precisely, if this myth chooses to divide its two formulas between the social classes of a single society (its own), thus validating actual practice, it does not realize that two very distant societies have each adopted one, but not the same, solution. Nor does mythic speculation have to know that (as we have seen in the Tsimshian myth) the formulas, each illustrated by a variant, involve another formula, which can be deduced by a simple logical operation, but whose box will remain empty until neighboring groups take on the task of filling it.

Hence, even in such cases, mythical thinking proves mysteriously prolific. It never seems satisfied with offering one single response to a problem: once formulated, this response enters into a play of transformations in which all other possible responses emerge together or successively. The same concepts, rearranged, exchange, contradict, or invert their values and their functions, until the resources of this new combinatorics are dissipated or simply exhausted.

At first, a kind of intellectual intuition apprehends the world, or a part of the world, in the form of diversely opposed terms. But it does not stop there: this pattern of oppositions widens or shrinks the meshes of its network; it propagates by logical contagion and gains other aspects that are included in the first or that comprise them, because they are all linked by homology. Furthermore, like the light-bulbs on a billboard which go on and off, producing different images —bright ones against a dark background, and dark against bright (a production that is also a creation of the mind), without losing any of their logical coherence the patterns undergo a series of transformations during which certain elements, negative or positive, neutralize one another. The negative elements take on a positive value, and vice versa.* A series of mental catches disposes conceptual fragments in all possible arrangements so long as certain symmetrical relations remain between the parts.

In short, one can willingly believe that intellectual activity exhibits those same characteristics that are more readily discerned in the category of sensation and perception. A bright image on the retina does not disappear with the stimulus that produced it. You close your eyes or turn away, and the burning lightbulb or the red sun sinking on the horizon yields to a round green spot. On a more complex level, we know today that the ganglionic cells that, in a first stage, receive retinal impressions manifest an antagonism between their center and their periphery. Hence it is that a cell constitutionally stimulated by yellow is not insensitive to blue, which, far from leaving it in peace, triggers a negative reaction. A cell stimulated in its center by red responds with active rejection when its periphery is stimulated by green. The entire chromatic code seems to be based on this interplay of antagonistic reactions.

The geometrical representation of a cube or a stairway is seen, within a split second, either from above or below, either from back or

---

*On a different level, think of the formidable orchestral explosion at the end of the dispute in act 2 of *Die Meistersinger*, which, cutting off the tumult of voices, is perceived not as additional noise but as the triumph of re-established silence.

front. If you stare intensely at the photograph of a three-dimensional object, you involuntarily perceive it as either concave or convex from one moment to the next. In Zöllner's illusion, parallel bars, cross-hatched by slanting strokes whose direction is reversed from one bar to the next, themselves appear to be oblique, as if they were slanting in opposite directions. We are also familiar with geometrical or decorative compositions whose figure and background are so well balanced that sometimes the background looks like a figure and the figure like a background. If both depict the same subject, the figure oscillates before our eyes, and we see it alternately as bright on a dark background or even as dark on a bright background. In all these cases, the mind, as if pushed by an inner impetus, goes beyond what it has originally perceived.

These examples point to those more complex forms of activity which are illustrated by the creation of myths. Stimulated by a conceptual relationship, mythic thinking engenders other relationships, which are parallel or antagonistic to the first one. If the top is positive and the bottom negative, then the reverse relationship is immediately induced, as though the permutation of multiple axes of terms belonging to the same network were an autonomous activity of the mind, so that any state of a combination would suffice to get the mind moving and, in one surge after another, produce a cascade of all the other states.

An initial opposition between empyrean sky and chthonian world produces the lesser opposition between atmospheric sky and earth, and then the even lesser opposition between mountaintop and valley. The cascade can also surge from the weakest opposition to stronger ones—for instance, between mountaintop and valley, between land and water, and, finally, between high and low. In spatial terms, these oppositions evoke others by an effect of resonance. Rising or falling, each cascade unleashes other cascades, which are joined to it by harmonic relations even though they are in other registers: temporal instead of spatial, or even economic, sociological, or moral; also, the levels of these cascades are linked transversely.

This type of activity is not unlike what is, in music, called "development": that is, to surround a simple motif with more ample and more complex ones (for instance, the prelude to *Pelléas and Mélisande*), or to work finer and more detailed motifs into the original one (for instance, the prelude to *Das Rheingold*), or even to modulate the original motif in different keys. However, among these modes, a homology must always exist between the original motif and those that encompass it or are encompassed by it, between external and internal enrichment; otherwise, the very notion of development would lose its meaning.

Let us take a final example from the plastic arts. Among other differences is a particularly striking one between the art of the Indians of the northwest coast of North America and that of Western painters (and also, at least in this respect, of Far Eastern painters). When a European painter feels the need to use a large surface, he generally plans to depict a larger number of objects or a vaster landscape than he can treat on a small canvas. Such a choice never occurs to the Indians of the northwest coast, where the subject most often remains the same no matter how large the painting surface, which is usually covered completely. The layout is invariable; with the expansion of surface area, all that changes are the number and the complexity of the accessory motifs that a painter can use to elaborate on the main subject. Of this, the secondary motifs are often replicas; or, at least, they are related to it in their form or content.

As in the case of the Pukapuka myth, cultures that are different from and unaware of one another choose between antithetical types of development that mythic thinking (and doubtless music, too) can implement simultaneously: one develops by contiguity, and another by similitude; and both are within the two axes of metonymy and metaphor. The duality is already apparent in the optical illusions that result sometimes from the presence of contiguous forms that contaminate those in which the illusion is produced; or sometimes from the inherent ability of an image, which may or may not be colored, to transform itself into its chromatic complement or its symmetrical projection.

Traditional psychology ascribed the illusions of perception to excessive sensory or mental activity. From my standpoint, it is a question not of an excess but of the elementary manifestation of an intrinsic power where all activities of the mind originate.* Hence, the essential function of the mind is to create possibilities and arrange them logically, while experience and education later become responsible for thinning out the less desirable ones. Thus, myths concern the psychologist and the philosopher as well as the anthropologist: they constitute an area among others (for we should not forget art) where the mind, relatively free of external constraints, still musters a native activity that we can observe in all its freshness and spontaneity.

---

*This text was already being printed when I read from a specialist's pen: "The perception of form is a process much closer to the cognitive level than has heretofore been recognized. It cannot be explained as a direct outcome of the physiological processing of contours stimulating the retina" (Rock 1981, p. 153).

PART IV

BELIEFS, MYTHS, AND RITES

For example, in The Barrier Gate (Sekinoto) (1784), when "Ki ya bo . . . ," meaning "living," "wild," and "evening," is sung, the actor ignores these meanings and instead mimes "tree" (Ki also means tree in Japanese), "arrow" (ya also means arrow), and "pole" (bo also means pole). . . . It may well be the only dance technique in the whole world based on a pun.

JAMES R. BRANDON

Studies in Kabuki

Chapter 12

Cosmopolitanism and Schizophrenia

A Swedish psychiatrist, Dr. Torsten Herner, has voiced some ideas about the etiology of schizophrenia, which could give anthropologists something to think about. Study of a particular case (1965) suggested to him that this illness originates in an abnormal family configuration characterized by immaturity in the parents, especially in the mother, who either rejects her child or is unable to think of it as separate from herself. If the world is, for the newborn, initially an interdependent one, where child and mother are blended, and then gradually broadens —with the perception and acceptance of their duality—until it becomes the family constellation and, finally, the whole of society, it is conceivable that the persistence of an initial pathological situation may be expressed in schizophrenia as the oscillation between two extreme feelings: the insignificance of one's ego in relation to the world, and the overweening importance of oneself in relation to society. Ultimately, the former feeling can turn into an obsessive sense of worthlessness, and the latter into delusions of grandeur. Thus, the schizophrenic will never achieve the normal experience of living in the world. For him, the part will be equal to the whole. Incapable of establishing a relationship between his self and the world, he will be unable to perceive the limits of either: "The normal person is able to experience his being-in-the-world, whereas the schizophrenic experiences himself *as* 'world'" (Herner 1965, p. 460). The same lack of distinction will prevail in all four stages of one's apprehension of the world: one's own body, one's mother, one's family, the society, all grasped as worlds. And, depending on how far the illness regresses, this same inability of the schizophrenic will manifest itself in different disorders, each having a twofold aspect of only apparently contradictory cleavage or confusion: from echolalia and echopraxis to alternating feelings of being completely controlled by some entity perceived as the world or of being able to exercise over that entity a magical and sovereign power.

When, in the final stage of regression, the world is confused with one's body image, the limits of the body are internalized. They no longer correspond to the boundary between inside and outside, between figure and background: it is the very image of the body that comes apart, creating oppositions of "high" and "low," of "front" and "back," of "right" and "left." In every case, imaginary frontiers divide the body into halves. Hence, the distress felt by some patients who say that their organs are changing places. Furthermore, these halves display independence; the patient perceives them as two individuals, a male and a female, sometimes locked in a ruthless fight, sometimes sexually united. This internal cleavage can go hand in hand with external confusions, establishing different types of connection between the patient and celestial bodies "as if the patient were in familial relationship with the stars, moon, and sun" (Herner 1965, p. 464). Thus, according to our author, the first "world" apprehended by the individual would be equivalent to his image of his body, but this image would be afflicted by an intrinsic dualism which, in normal mental development, is gradually overcome but would betray the split in the family constellation if there were antagonism between the parents or latent antagonism between mother and infant from the latter's birth.

Dr. Herner is aware that comparative mythology offers parallels to his observations, and, without dwelling on any one source, cites at random Bachofen, Frobenius, Robert Hertz, Adolf Jensen, Hermann Baumann, Wilhelm von Humboldt,* as well as the Gnostics and cabalists. Nevertheless, this data is scattered and hard to articulate. No meaning emerges to tie everything together. Furthermore, these

*Johann Jakob Bachofen (1815–87), Swiss jurist and historian, known for his work on the theory of matriarchy; Leo Frobenius (1873–1938), German anthropologist and explorer; Robert Hertz (1882–1915), French sociologist; Adolf Ellegard Jensen (1899–1965), German anthropologist; Hermann Baumann (1902–), German anthropologist; and Wilhelm von Humboldt (1767–1835), German philologist and diplomat.

resemblances in detail between specific belief and specific symptom cannot explain why analogous themes are to be found in individual deliriums in contemporary Western societies and in the collective depictions of traditions in foreign societies. There has never been a better time to recall a comment that Marcel Mauss made for the benefit of psychologists: "While you may grasp only very few of these cases, and often in series of abnormal facts, we constantly grasp very many of them, and in huge series of normal facts" (Mauss 1950, p. 299). When myths so wish, they are perfectly capable of depicting mental disorders. They describe them and diagnose them as such, while relating those incidents in a character's life which triggered the disorder in the first place: repeated social failures, compensated for by inappropriate behavior; or traumatic experiences causing a sometimes fatal manic-depressive psychosis. (I have cited examples elsewhere: Lévi-Strauss 1973, p. 179; 1979, pp. 114-21.)

This reference to lunacy in mythology cannot be compared with the emergence of similar themes in the language of myths and in that of certain madmen. A myth treats madness clinically, while a madman's discourse comes under the clinical heading of one delirium among others. This last confusion has led to countless abuses, which Roger Bastide has always managed to avoid, even though he operates on the borderline between anthropology and psychology. His work demonstrates that it is possible to compare data from different areas without succumbing to the facile solution of filling the gaps in each one with explanations borrowed from the other: "Analogy is not a reduction of a social structure to a different, mental structure; the analogy sheds light on differences as well as on similarities. It is located between the categories of 'same' and 'the other,' but, as Bastide then significantly specifies, "without being taken in by the individual unconscious" (Bastide 1972, pp. 222, 280). Thus, as a tribute to our colleague, I should like here to outline, by way of an example, a method that—without basing anthropological data on psychiatric data or vice versa—can help to account for certain similarities sometimes observed between those two categories, but that, at the same time, respects the specificity that we must recognize in each category, rather than becoming facile and arbitrary.

Now it is true that the motifs listed by Dr. Herner as constituting the etiology of a particular schizophrenic delirium are practically identical with those found in a particular myth of the Chinook Indians. This North American tribe once lived along the lower course and the estuary of the Columbia River, at what is the present-day border between the states of Oregon and Washington, where the river empties into the Pacific Ocean. Recorded and published by the late Melville Jacobs (1959), this myth has already caught my attention in *The Naked Man* (1981; its synopsis appears under the number M598a, pp. 235-37). Here, however, I shall view it from an entirely different standpoint. Let me first go over its essential features. It relates the adventures of a hero whose parents are divorced shortly after his birth, and who is stolen from his cradle when his mother leaves him in the care of five slaves so that, contrary to propriety, she may attend a celebration given by her former husband. Soon, lost in the crowd of spectators and bewitched by the dancing, the young woman forgets about her baby. One after another, each of the five slaves assigned to watch over him hurries to her mistress to tell her that her son is weeping and asking for her; but none of them manages to find her or to return. Only the last one succeeds in finding her mistress and bringing her back after much scolding. They arrive too late: an ogress has carried off the child, to whom she has taken a liking, and she decides to raise him.

The young boy grows up, but the ogress still carries him in a basket on her back whenever she goes out to hunt for the snakes and frogs she feeds him. Covered with reptiles and batrachians, the hero occasionally clings to a branch, and the ogress's elastic neck stretches out, like a thread. Then the hero lets go of the branch, and the neck resumes its normal shape. But one day, on the advice of a supernatural protector, he cuts her stretched-out neck and climbs the tree to which he has been clinging. This ascent leads him to the celestial world, where he meets fleas and lice, then cannibals, whose mischievousness he reduces to everyday proportions. He then meets the mistress of the night and forces her henceforth to alternate with the day. Two hunters, whom he meets at a fork in the road, advise him to take opposite roads. The first road leads him to cannibals, whose taste in food he pretends to share; but instead of eating human flesh, he evacuates it by means of a hollow stem he inserts into his body to bypass his digestive tract. Thereby transformed into a pierced person, he cannot have the girl whom he has been given in marriage because she, in contrast, is stopped up: like her sisters, she has no vagina.

Retracing his steps, the hero then takes the second road and comes to a more hospitable family. This is the family of the sun, one of whose daughters he marries. She soon gives birth to Siamese twin boys. In response to the request of her husband who is homesick, she consents to come back to earth with him and the twins. They find that the hero's family and half the village has become blind, because everyone wept so hard after giving him up for lost. The sun wife restores their eye-sight. A short time later, however, a trickster decides to separate the twins by means of surgery, and the children die instantly. Their deva-stated mother decides to return to the sky, taking along the little corpses, which she says she will change into two stars; these stars will announce death if they are seen flanking the sun (that is, her) when it rises at dawn. As for the villagers, they weep so hard over the deaths of the children that they become blind again.

It is clear that this myth gathers all the etiological factors and the symptoms described by Dr. Herner in a particular case: disagreement between the parents; immaturity of the mother, who is unable to resist going to a party which, since it is being given by her former husband, she cannot with propriety attend. Thus, the infant is abandoned twice by his family: first by his father, then by his mother. With the loss of his family world, all he has left is a social world formed by the five female slaves who watch over him. However, like his kidnapper's neck later, this last bond gradually stretches to the breaking point when the slaves go off one after the other, leaving around his cradle at first only four, then three, then two, then one, then nobody. These experiences of separation are projected on two symbolic levels at the same time—one physical, and one cosmic.

On the physical level, we may first point out oppositions close to the ones Dr. Herner observed in his female patient's delirium. The opposi-tion of high and low: the ogress's neck grows so long that, becoming as thin as a thread, it can be easily cut by the hero. The opposition of right and left sides: the twins are joined by a membrane that likewise becomes thin whenever either of them makes an effort to turn around. Moreover, there are missing or shifting organs: the hero improvises an artificial digestive tract to avoid consuming human flesh; and he finds himself married to a woman without a vagina.

The ogress's family forms a link between the body of the family and the body of the world, since her family consists of all the species of trees, which—in order to avenge her murder—all swoop pell-mell upon the hero. The sole exception is the white spruce, whose branches the escaping hero climbs, but which also has no practical use, provid-ing neither timber nor firewood. This botanical split is echoed by other dichotomies, which affect the universe as a whole. There is the temporal split, between day and night, for which the hero is responsi-ble. And there is the split between the spatial directions, of which he is initially the victim, and which divides supernatural beings into two categories: cannibals with closed bodies; and solar people, who welcome him and provide him with a wife. The latter sequence—a prelude to the split of a heavenly configuration, which announces death when two stars are visible *on either side* of the sun—introduces the motif of family bonds with celestial bodies. This motif, as we have seen, figures in the schizophrenic's delirium.

Each of these motifs can readily be found, isolated or partially grouped, in myths of other peoples. The originality of this myth is that it gathers all the motifs and organizes them around the theme of dichotomy, which is virtually the leitmotif of the plot. This predilection doubtless explains a family configuration—divorced couple, irresponsible mother—of which it would be hard to find other illustrations, especially at the outset of a story, in the myths from this region of the New World. The Chinook myth seems to reconstruct both the etiology and the themes of a schizophrenic delirium.

Can we therefore ascribe a schizoid constitution to these Indians, just as Ruth Benedict attributed a paranoid constitution to the Kwakiutl? Yet (and we will come back to this) the Chinook had a reputation as shrewd businessmen with their feet planted solidly on the ground. Thus, they do not fit this diagnosis any more than (as we know today) the true features of the potlatch of the southern Kwakiutl justify Benedict's diagnosis (Drucker and Heizer 1967, pp. 112-13). Furthermore, just who *is* schizophrenic here? Not the narrator of the myth, who is not its author, and who relates it not because it arouses a morbid state in him, but because he heard it from other storytellers, who themselves drew upon a similarly anonymous tradition. Can we then say that the myth, rather than expressing it subjectively, describes a schizophrenic delirium from the outside? By no means, for the experiences it narrates are not all attributed to the hero; thus, he cannot be likened to a patient. Indeed, even though he has experienced the family ordeals reported at the beginning, he is not himself victim of the anomalies that the myth then relates. The lateralization phenomena affect not his body but the ogress's and then his children. The hero does not suffer a momentary displacement of his digestive tract but ingeniously brings it about in order to escape a danger. It is his wife of one day, and not he, who is not provided with certain organs. Everything takes place thus as if the elements of schizophrenic delirium, subjectively internalized by the patient, were objectively scattered here, by some movement of reversal, among several protagonists and distributed among various aspects of the cosmos. The symbolic materials may be the same, but the myth and the delirium use them in opposite ways.

But the eclectic quality of this myth—in its diversified use of elements that are collected synthetically in an individual's delirium—is also found in the way the Chinook myth can be related to other myths. It was chiefly this last aspect that I investigated in *The Naked Man*, where I emphasized the potpourri quality of the myth or, if you prefer, its recital of North American mythology. As I said (p. 238), this myth constructs its syntagmatic series by borrowing and methodically reversing paradigms from myths of various origins. A reader who is at all familiar with the mythology of these North American regions, will recognize at the start of this myth the cycle called "Loon Woman," as represented further south. The only main difference is that a married sister who feels incestuous urges for her brother is changed here into a divorced mother who neglects her child and who, by approaching her former husband whom propriety forbids her from seeing again, commits a sort of social incest with him.

The episode of the ogress as adoptive mother reproduces and reverses another cycle—that of the "libertine grandmother." Finally, by relations whose ins and outs are too lengthy to trace here, the Chinook myth connects with, but always reverses, the cycles of the "nest robber" and the "star wives." (For a detailed analysis, see Lévi-Strauss, pp. 237-42.)

This eclectic makeup calls for two remarks: one about the myth's form, and one about its content. First of all, the motivation for the initial situation of the parents' divorce and the mother's immaturity does not—and, indeed, should not—depend on a psychic nature specific to the Chinook or on any psychological or social aspects of their culture as determining a basic personality. The initial situation of the narrative and all the subsequent situations can be integrally deduced not from particular traits of the Chinook personality, family, or society, experienced by each member of the group from birth; but from other myths that originate in other populations and are transformed in the borrowing. This relation is particularly clear in the opening situation, which replaces a sister with a wife and sexual movement toward a brother with social movement toward a husband; and which, to justify logically this latter shift, has recourse to divorce as a way of establishing a preliminary distance between the couple. The same reasoning can be applied to the other episodes, and it can be shown that their particular plot construction always results from a logical necessity vis-à-vis other myths. It would be useless and gratuitous to claim that they derive from a psychism (a hypothetical one to boot) that is supposedly the exclusive property of the society from which the myth comes.

BELIEFS, MYTHS, AND RITES

But—and this is the second point—why do the Chinook myths have such a markedly eclectic makeup? Boas has already emphasized that many of their elements exist in the traditions of the Siouan and Algonquin linguistic families and reached the Chinook by way of the Columbia valley (Boas 1895a, pp. 336-63). Our comparative studies of this problem point in other directions as well: south of Oregon and north of California, the State of Washington, and British Columbia. This trend toward syncretism, so plain in Chinook mythology, cannot be explained without reference to sociology. We know, indeed, the Chinook had a very special position on the lower part of the Columbia River and on the Pacific coast. Even the tribes of the estuary, which were relatively far from the site of the great intertribal fairs supervised by their neighbors and congeners, the Wishram and the Wasco, devoted themselves to commercial activities and operated as traders and intermediaries between near and distant tribes. It is, moreover, the reason their language forms the basis of the jargon known as "Chinook," which served as a lingua franca from the coast of California to that of Alaska, even before the arrival of the first white men.

The mythology of the Chinook—who had repeated contacts with tribes having different languages, life styles, and cultures—seems less like an original corpus than an ensemble of secondary elaborations— systematic at first in this sense—to adapt the ones to the others and reconcile, by transforming them, miscellaneous mythical materials. Chinook ideology thus echoes the political, economic, and social experience of a world in a dissociated condition. Through a reverse process from the schizophrenic's—whose experience of a split body produces a split image of the world—here the split experience of the world predisposes the bearers of the mythology to imagine other kinds of split, from the world to the family and from the family to the body. However, even taking this reversal into account, we must not be deceived by the illusion of there being a parallel between the individual unconscious and the collective unconscious. Myth is not in the same category as delirium, nor does it presuppose a manifest or a latent delirium in those who narrate or listen to the myth. Even with all the reservations that we have formulated, the Chinook myth does not illustrate a case of schizophrenia or some morbid state resembling it. It does not translate in its own fashion any mental disorder; it produces, in its own fashion, a theory, and thus places itself on the side of the clinician, not the patient. It would be more precise to say that the cosmopolitanism of the Chinook made them particularly likely to think of the world in the mode of a split and to develop this notion in all domains where it can be applied. Unlike the schizophrenic, who is victim of a split that his inner experience projects outside, Chinook society, because of its specific way of being in the world, uses the notion of a split to create a philosophy.

Chapter 13

Myth and Forgetfulness

TO stimulate his thinking, the eminent specialist in Indo-European languages, Emile Benveniste, did not disdain to investigate the Indian languages of North America. It is thus a way of paying homage to him to reverse the process, for even the student of American anthropology can benefit from a comparison between the Old World and the New. In this brief chapter, I shall try to show, by means of an example, how mythical themes from ancient Greece can help to specify certain hypotheses inspired by the study of Amerindian myths.

In a recent work (1976, pp. 189-91), I outlined an interpretation of the function performed, in North American myths, by the motif of forgetfulness. Far from being a banal device to achieve an easy effect, forgetfulness seems to be a failure to communicate with oneself and, hence, to be one of several modalities of a phenomenon in which we have been inclined to discern a true category of mythical thinking. According to this hypothesis, *forgetfulness* forms a system with *misunderstanding*, defined as a failure to communicate with others, and with *indiscretion*, defined as an excess of communication with others. The proof was supplied by the alternation or accumulation of these motifs in variants of a single myth. I asked Jean-Pierre Vernant, my colleague at the Collège de France and a specialist in Greek religion, about Greek texts of mythological origin in which oblivion plays a part; and he was kind enough to point out one from Plutarch and two from Pindar. After examining them, I felt that they corroborated my interpretation.

In *Greek Problems* (28), Plutarch attempts to explain why flute players were not allowed to enter the temple of Tenes on the Aegean island of Tenedos, and why Achilles' name could not be uttered there. According to Plutarch, a flute player named Molpos perjured himself to back up the second wife of King Cycnus, the father of Tenes, when she—to avenge herself on her stepson for rejecting her advances—falsely accused him of rape. As a result, Tenes was driven from the kingdom. His sister followed him into exile. Now Thetis, the mother of Achilles, told her son never to attack Tenes, who was the son (or grandson) of Apollo. She even gave Achilles a servant to remind him of her warning in case of need. But Achilles saw the sister of Tenes, desired her, and was disrespectful of her. Her brother intervened to protect her, and Achilles, bewildered by his passion, killed his adversary—the servant having forgotten to fulfill the duty with which he had been charged. Pausanias (X,xiv) and Diodorus (V,i) report the same story, though in slightly different terms.

Let us go along with Plutarch's tale. It links two sequences that conclude in parallel ways. At the end of one, the hero is exiled and, thus, socially eliminated; at the end of the other, he is physically eliminated, by death. In both cases, the responsibility for the ending is borne by a subordinate, who is guilty of saying either too much or too little. In bearing false witness, Molpos sins by excess communication with others, an act comparable to indiscretion. In forgetting his duty at the critical moment, Achilles' servant sins by failing to communicate with himself. These are, as in North America, two forms of a pathology of communication which are brought together here.

More complex appears the story told by Pindar in his seventh Olympian ode. Tlepolemus, the son of Heracles, loses his temper and (involuntarily, according to Apollodorus) kills Licymnius, the half-brother of Tlepolemus' great-grandmother, Alcmene. The guilty man goes to consult the oracle of Helios. The god orders him to set sail for Rhodes and to make an offering there, at the altar of Athena. However, "sometimes the cloud of forgetfulness advances and moves the mind from the proper path" (v. 45-48): the people of Rhodes forget to bring the fire when they ascend to the altar; this is the origin of the custom, peculiar to Rhodes, of sacrifice without fire.

Going back to the time when the world was being divided among the gods, Pindar tells us that they forgot Helios. So Helios asks for Rhodes, which has not yet risen from the bottom of the waters. Zeus grants him this island, and Helios falls in love with the goddess of the place.

Three memory lapses follow one another in this story: that of

Tlepolemus who, troubled in mind ("Trouble of the mind leads even the sage astray" [v. 31-32]), and he "forgets himself," as we say, by committing an act of aggression against a relative; that of the people of Rhodes, at the moment of sacrifice; and, finally, that of Zeus, presiding over the gods' drawing of lots for territory.

The fourth Pythian ode closely links this motif with another, and is in a way even more interesting in that it deals with the origin of a territorial sovereignty. Medea tells the Argonauts that a god from the sea will restore to Euphemus, the son of Poseidon, a clod of earth that will assure his descendants sovereignty over Libya. During the voyage, the servants assigned to guard the precious gift forget their orders and dump it into the sea. The taking of Libya is delayed for thirteen generations; and, according to the fifth Pythian ode, Libya is conquered only when the oracle promises Battos, the founder of Cyrene, that he will cure him of his stuttering (his tongue is loosened by fear when he meets a lion, according to Pausanias [X,xv]). Thus, the same event is held up twice—first by a memory lapse, then by a speech impediment: that is, a failure to communicate with oneself, then a failure to communicate with others. Let me note in passing that two neighboring North American tribes, the Tsimshian and the Kwakiutl, use forgetfulness and misunderstanding (which we have defined in the same way) as a dramatic device in a myth known as the "Blind Man and the Diver" (Boas 1916, pp. 246-50; 1910, p. 447).

The Greek examples thus reinforce the hypothesis that forgetfulness occurs in the same semantic field as indiscretion and misunderstanding, although it is the opposite of these two in other respects. May we go even farther and recognize a common character among myths where the motif of forgetfulness intervenes in a particular way? To do so, we must first examine certain North American myths.

The Hidatsa Indians, who lived on the upper Missouri and belonged, with the Mandan and the Arikara, to the so-called village tribes of the Plains, explained their origin by means of two distinct myths. According to the first myth, two demiurges created the earth and had the first human beings emerge from the underworld. After tribes and languages had been diversified, it happened that, in a certain place, a woman offered her young brother-in-law "something to drink" (probably a euphemism). The young man considered the offer improper and refused. Furious at being rejected, the woman accused him of trying to rape her; and pretending to take him to war, her gullible husband abandoned his younger brother on an island. The gods got involved in the issue and took the side of one or the other brother. The younger brother's protectors eventually got the upper hand and destroyed the older brother and almost all the inhabitants of the village in a fire. The survivors were separated. The ones who went north became the Crow-Hidatsa; the ones who went south became the Awaxawi. Later, a deluge forced the latter to migrate to the Missouri, where they subsequently met another Hidatsa group, the Awatixa. As for the Crow-Hidatsa proper, they moved back south, where they split into two tribes, the Crow and the Hidatsa (Bowers 1965, pp. 298-300).

The other myth has the Hidatsa come from the sky, having abandoned it to follow one of their people, Charred-Body, who has descended to earth in search of buffalo that had deserted the upper world. The new arrivals settle in thirteen cabins, each of which is the origin of a clan; and the spirits of the earth fail to destroy the little colony. In a village of the earlier inhabitants of the terrestrial world, there lives a pretty girl. Charred-Body courts her, but she turns him down; enraged, he kills her. The demiurge Coyote, who is related to the ancestors of the Hidatsa, warns Charred-Body that his victim's people will try to avenge the murder; and that, because of his crime (like Tlepolemus, he has "forgotten" himself), his spirit will often go astray. His enemies will take advantage of these moments of inattention to kill him and his people.

And, indeed, so it happens. The village is attacked several times; Charred-Body flies to the battle, but on the way he totally forgets the reasons for his haste. Another time, a weasel crosses his path; and, in pursuing it, he forgets his mission. The village is destroyed, and all the inhabitants die, except for Coyote and the hero's pregnant sister, whom the demiurge has taken care to conceal. The sister is then told to lock the door in order to keep out an ogre, but she forgets. The ogre gets in, attacks her, and she perishes. The twins she was carrying survive; they have all sorts of adventures and nearly die, again because of forgetfulness—a recurrent motif in this second myth (Beckwith 1938, pp. 22-52).

On the other hand, this motif is completely absent from the first myth. Are there other differences between them? Probably, if we notice that the first myth, which gives the Hidatsa a chthonian origin, is almost entirely devoted to migrations, fusions, and separations of groups who have historical reality. Actually, these migrations were caused by the attacks of the woodlands Ojibwa, who were armed by the French colonizers of Canada. As a result, the common ancestors of the Crow and the Hidatsa were forced to take refuge in the plains. Archeology confirms these population movements. The arrival of the

Awatixa on the Missouri and the later breakup of the Crow-Hidatsa into two tribes are likewise historically attested (cf. Lévi-Strauss 1976, pp. 239-55).

But, while the first myth refers to historical events three centuries old, the second myth has an entirely different character. Each of its episodes tries to lay the foundation for a ritual. Despite their parallelism and the obvious way in which their respective episodes reflect or transform one another, the two myths have distinct functions. The first myth provides a structure for a series of historical events; the second myth establishes a basis for a ceremonial calendar—hence, a serial order. Indeed, according to informants, the ceremonies are comparable to knots in a string: "All are independent ceremonies just as each knot is independent of the other knots, but, at the same time, they are connected and related in the same way that knots are related to each other by their order on the string" (Bowers 1965, pp. 294, 303-6).

Under the circumstances, it is remarkable that the motif of forgetfulness is recurrent in the second myth but completely lacking in the first. For, in the Greek myths too, forgetfulness serves to establish ritual interdictions or prescriptions: flutists are not allowed to enter the temple of Tenes, or visitors to utter the name of Achilles; sacrifice is made without fire in Rhodes, and sovereign claims to a territory consecrated to a god are sanctioned by rites.

The myth of the Argonauts completes the interpretation. Seen as a paradigm, it depicts the development of a group of people who are comparable, *mutatis mutandis*, to those that the Americanist calls "transformers": those who put things in order. But why are they not in order at the beginning? The Greek myth indicates two reasons: either excessive fidelity to vows (Laomedon's sacrifice of his daughter Hesione; the unjust punishment of Cleopatra's two sons because their father puts too much trust in the words of a stepmother); or the breaking of a promise (Laomedon's failure to give the promised reward to the gods who built the walls of Troy; his refusal to give to Herakles Hesione and the horses that Herakles had left in his, Laomedon's, care; Jason's forgetting his marriage vows). Thus, in one case, the reverse of a memory lapse (since it would have been better to forget a promise one had, in a fit of passion, made to oneself or to others), and, in the second case, a variant of forgetfulness—this time, voluntary. On the other hand, the Argonauts succeed in their enterprise because they make moderate vows to the gods and observe them meticulously.

Now when we read this story from beginning to end, its syntactical chain seems to be aimed at explaining the origins of place names, which follow in space as the ritual celebrations follow one another through the year. For rites establish the stages of the calendar just as places establish the points of an itinerary. Places are fixed in space; and ritual celebrations, in time.

We can learn two lessons from these brief considerations. First of all, it is a serious mistake to make mythology and ritual seem so much alike as to be one and the same—as suggested by certain British and American anthropologists. The examples we have taken from the Hidatsa show that a variant of a myth, serving to establish the basis for a ritual system, is under different restraints from a neighboring variant that is not directly akin to the first.

Second, if the motif of forgetfulness as it appears in myths signals a failure to communicate with oneself, and if, in very different societies and eras, this motif is used mainly to lay the foundation of ritual practices, then the true function of ritual is, as I have suggested elsewhere (1981, pp. 668-75), to preserve the continuity of experience. For it is this continuity that forgetfulness breaks on a mental level: we recognize this process when we speak of a "memory lapse." And often, in both North America and elsewhere, myths also recognize this when they blame forgetfulness on a *faux pas* ("false step"): the hero loses his memory when he stumbles, catching his foot in a hole, which is a discontinuity of the physical order (Thompson 1966: J2671 and D2004.5). Battos is a stutterer: that is, he stumbles when speaking.

The reader must have noticed that when introducing the motifs of forgetfulness, misunderstanding, and indiscretion, both the Greek and the North American myths resort to the same themes: those of the seductress stepmother or sister-in-law, and the seduced sister. Now I have independently classified the former theme under the heading of the pathology of marriage (1973, p. 302), which is a sociological form of communication. Likewise, any threat to his sister lessens a man's chances of entering into communication with other groups, because the incest taboo and the exogamy rule destine her to be exchanged directly or indirectly. Hence, it is not surprising that these two themes occur in mythological systems in which the good use of communication is challenged by an excess or a failure.

We have also seen, however, that the affinities between the Greek and the North American myths extend to their very metaphors. This would confirm—were confirmation necessary—that even in a case that defies geographic or historical connection, the repertoire from which mythical thinking draws its themes and motifs has limited resources.

Chapter 14

Pythagoras in America

IN this chapter, I shall discuss the particular importance that peoples remote from one another in time and space give to the seeds of certain plants in the ancient family of the Leguminosae (or pea family), of which the Papilionoideae is a subfamily.

In recent works, Marcel Detienne (1970, pp. 141-62; 1972, pp. 96-100, 110-114) takes stock of the controversies generated since antiquity by the Pythagorean traditions, which this author interprets brilliantly. Nevertheless, anthropology must focus on the recurrence of the same beliefs and rites, not only in the ancient world outside the School of Pythagoras, but also, more generally, throughout the Old World and, as I should like to show here, the New. For the comparatist, the Pythagorean attitude toward beans is a specific example of probably earlier ideas and practices, which seem to have been more widely distributed than a limited survey of the ancient world might suggest. Furthermore, even in that world, there were diametrically opposed beliefs about beans.*

In Greece, aside from the Pythagoreans, both the Orphic traditions and the Eleusinian rites proscribed fava beans. According to various sources, the most important of which include Plutarch, this prohibi-

---

*The beans here referred to (*fèves*) are the fava, or broad, beans, native to Europe; they are related to many species of peas and beans (*baricots*) found in the New World. The broad bean is a Eurasian plant, possibly of African origin. Henceforth, unless otherwise specified in this chapter, beans are the *baricots* native to the Americas. (Ed.)

tion normally applied to anyone who wished to lead a pure life. Outside of Greece, the Egyptian priests, according to Herodotus, were not permitted to eat or even to look at fava beans. In Rome, the *Flamen Dialis** could neither eat this legume nor utter its name. But always, in the ancient world, there were also occasions when the use of fava beans was imperiously prescribed. In Attica, boiled beans were consumed during the festival of the Pyanepsia;† and the Romans offered fava beans to various deities as well as to the dead at the festivals of Parentalia, Feralia, and Lemuria. According to Pliny the Elder in the first century A.D. (xviii, xii), the Romans placed these beans as amulets among objects sold at auction.

While the Pythagoreans may have execrated beans, we know of circumstances where the opposite view prevailed. In fact, a commentary by Pliny makes it seem as if this positive view may have been the more frequent one. After recalling the proposition that the Pythagoreans forbade fava beans because they served as a dwelling place for the souls of the dead, Pliny adds that "for this reason, one ordinarily eats fava beans at obsequies or funerals of the dead." Hence it was, he goes on, that "the ancients spoke of fava beans religiously and with great ceremony: for never did they mention grains, only beans, to bring good luck, and thus called them Refrina [*refriva*] because they were frequently mentioned." This etymology may be dubious; but the brief survey preceding it shows that the Pythagorean taboo is but one aspect of how the ancients felt about fava beans. We cannot explain this attitude by focusing only on its negative side. A plausible account would require a single principle explaining why fava beans inspired either horror or respect; why their consumption was sometimes prohibited and sometimes recommended; and why, in short, beans had, in either aspect, a distinctively strong character in the eyes of the ancients.

In North America, we find a virtual echo of these beliefs, in relation to the fava bean's New World cousins (*haricots*). The Pawnee Indians of the upper Missouri have a version of a myth that is widespread throughout North America. Similar to the story of Orpheus and Eurydice, it tells how the hero, after snatching his young wife back from the world of the dead, stops at the home of a supernatural protectress whom he has already visited en route to the underworld. At that time, she gave him red beans, telling him to feed them to the people of his village "so that they would receive power to communi-

*In ancient Rome, a *Flamen Dialis* was a priest devoted to the service of Jupiter. (Ed.)
†The Pyanepsia was a festival of Apollo, at Athens. (Ed.)

cate with the dead spirits." According to one variant, these same beans were used to cast a spell on the living (Dorsey 1906, pp. 413, 537).

These are indeed not common beans but a different species of the same family—*Sophora secundiflora* or *speciosa*—which, in several North American tribes, including the Pawnee, were the object of a cult practiced by brotherhoods, from whose devotees came the preceding myths. One ritually drank an infusion or decoction of seeds having a narcotic or hallucinogenic effect or else wore the seeds as a talisman. Yet, remarkably enough, European folklore also connects more ordinary Papilionoideae with the supernatural world: *Chi manga facili, caga diavoli,* goes an Italian proverb quoted by Chamfort in the eighteenth century (1982, p. 561). This connection was not imposed by the physiological properties of beans *(haricots)* attributed to them by popular wisdom.*

After reading the first version of this chapter, Professor Yoshida Teigo of the University of Tokyo informed me that, in several regions of Japan, people scatter roasted soybeans through their homes to keep out demons, not only, as is well known, during the festival of Setsubun, celebrated before the arrival of spring (Chamberlain 1902, p. 159), but also in late December or early January.† The same custom is practiced in northern Kyushu, where fishermen gather soybeans and hurl them into the ocean to calm the tempest. Elsewhere, they were eaten during a storm to ward off lightning, or thrown about at a crossroads to bar the way to misfortune. Even common beans were the object of beliefs resembling those of the ancient Greeks and Romans in regard to broad beans and of North American Indians in regard to Sophora beans. Red-bean soup with rice, although prohibited at the beginning of the year, was prescribed for certain dates or on certain occasions—childbirth, moving house, burials, or, in old times, as an offering to wolves and to the god of smallpox. In the same parts of Japan people also swallowed or tossed raw red beans as a protection against chills or to keep rabbits away from the fields.

Although the bases may differ here and there, both the Old and the New Worlds seem to have attributed a mystical virtue to various

---

*In his highly informative monograph on Navajo ethnobotany, Francis H. Elmore does not mention the presence or the use of *Sophora secundiflora* but only of *Sophora sericea* (1944, p. 58) which sheep eat. And yet the Navajo use a term, translated into English as "bean shooting," to denote the act of magically lodging particles of coal, precious materials, or bone in an enemy's body in order to make him fall ill or die (Haile 1981, p. 22).

†Personal communication, 10 August and 30 December 1980. I am very grateful to Professor Yoshida Teigo for this valuable information.

representatives of the family of Papilionoideae. Thus, it is not illegitimate to compare the Japanese and the Amerindian rites of throwing these seeds with the Roman rite of the Lemuria. Each father of a family filled his mouth with black beans and then ran through his home, spitting them out behind him. "He believes that the shadow gathers them and, invisible, follows him . . . and he beseeches it to leave his home" (Ovid V, pp. 436f.). In the three cases that I have discussed, the seeds of Papilionoideae play a role in establishing or interrupting communication with the beyond. We can enlarge the paradigm to include the plants of the family of Fumariaceae, genus *Dicentra*, which the Onondaga Indians believed to be the food of the dead; they called it "corn of the spirits" (Beauchamp 1898, p. 199). The fruit of these wild plants, cousins of the Coeur-de-Marie of French gardens (*Dicentra spectabilis*), is an oblong pod filled with seeds. When ripe, the pod opens up in two parts as far as the base and then resembles the beans of the New World.*

Do the American Indian myths help us to understand the role of intermediary between the living and the dead that these Indians assign to seeds that are in the same family as beans or that look like them? In North America, the bean and corn often form a sexual pair, but the sexes attributed to the two plants may be reversed from one tribe to the next. For the Iroquois, corn was male and the bean female. They would plant beans next to corn that was already about six inches high; and the two plants would then grow together, the stiff cornstalk functioning as a stake, and the beanstalk winding around it. On the other hand, a gourd's stem spreads over the ground surface and seems to flee the nearest cornstalk. Thus it is, says the myth, that Corn married Miss Bean instead of her rival (Beauchamp 1898, pp. 1 , 7).

The Siouan-speaking Tutelo transposed the sexes, however, even though (or perhaps because) they lived in contact with the Iroquois: the former made the corn female and the bean male because, as they said, "the men depend upon the women as the beans cling on to corn [stalks] when growing" (Speck 1942, p. 120). The Iroquois symbolism reappears in Mexico and Guatemala, where the Indians often plant corn and beans in the same hole (Pennington 1969, p. 59; Vogt 1969, p. 54). Among the Chorti of Guatemala as well as in Mexico, in the Mitla region, the spirit of corn is male and that of the bean female

*Some people may be surprised that I have not spoken about the allergic reaction called favism. However, the extreme diversity of genuses and species involved in the beliefs about beans makes this phenomenon irrelevant, limited as it is primarily to some Mediterranean regions.

(Wisdom 1940, p. 402; Parsons 1936, pp. 324-29). We cannot be sure whether the American Indians, who see the bean as belonging to the female sex, conceive of the mother earth, as do certain peoples in New Guinea (Berndt 1962, p. 41 n. 8), as a pod producing many seeds. The New World myths about the origins of cultivated plants describe them as being born from different parts of a being that is sometimes female, but also sometimes male. To take just a few examples, corn—according to the Iroquois, the Huron, the Creek, and the Cherokee—came from the breasts, a thigh, the stomach, or the vagina of a woman; and beans from her forelimbs (the fingers, say the Iroquois), her other thigh, or her armpits. In contrast, the Kaingang in southern Brazil speak of a male being: his penis becomes corn; his testicles, beans; and his head, a gourd (Ploetz-Métraux 1930, p. 212).

This latter system of correspondences evokes two others: one that resembles it, and one that appears to contradict it. In the fertility rites of ancient India, a barleycorn symbolized the penis; and two beans, the testicles (Indradeva 1973, p. 37). But, in Japanese mythology, the soybean and other beans came from the genital organs of the goddess Ukemochi (Aston 1896, I, p. 33). Such divergences, of which there are many other examples, could be resolved if we admitted that of a man's sexual organs, the penis—congruent with the rigid stalk of corn or grain—is relatively more "male" than the testicles. The opposition, common in America, between male corn and female beans would thus develop from a relationship of implicit equivalence: in respect to sexuality, the male principle is to the female principle as, in respect to masculinity, the penis is to the testicles:

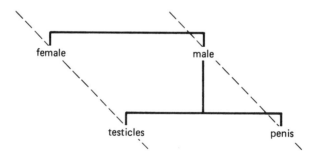

In his correspondence with me, Professor Yoshida Teigo notes that the Japanese word *mame*, which applies to various seeds of Papilionoideae, is also used familiarly for the clitoris. Now this organ, the most "male" part of the female genitals, has a position symmetrical to the one I have proposed for the testicles in the male genital structure.

Yet data that can support this hypothesis comes mainly from New Guinea. Several peoples in this region regard the fruits of the coconut and the areca palm trees as a sexed pair—each element of which, however, is ambivalent, except that a diachronic ambivalence among the Orokaiva (each plant, originally endowed with one sex, eventually acquires the other) appears as synchronic among the Tangu. Despite the geographic distance between the two groups, however, for both of them, coconuts symbolize the female breasts as well as the male testicles (Schwimmer 1973, p. 169; Burridge 1969, p. 390). As for the areca nut —first male and then female, according to the Orokaiva (Schwimmer 1973, pp. 168-70)—they symbolize both testicles and nubile girls for the Tangu (Burridge 1969, pp. 251, 306). Such data clearly suggest that the testicles, the less obvious male part of the male organs, have an ambiguous position between opposite categories as represented in myths in some areas of the world.

These reflections lead us back to Greece and to the debates that have been going on since antiquity about the food prohibitions of the Pythagoreans. Diogenes Laertius (VIII, 34) reports that Aristotle saw the resemblance between fava beans and testicles as one possible explanation among others. Aulus Gellius* goes even farther: "*Kúamous* hoc testiculos significare dicunt" (IV, xi) ["They say that this *kúamous* means 'testicles.' "]; while he denies that the prohibition attributed to Pythagoras and enunciated by Empedocles was alimentary. Gellius cites Aristoxenes to establish that fava beans were one of Pythagoras' favorite dishes (a fine example, incidentally, of the ambivalence of fava beans, concentrated here in the person of their promoter). A contemporary author glosses the Greek name for this legume—"*Kúamoi*, fava beans . . . eggs, receptacle of seeds, of generation"—and links it to the verb *kueîn*, which means "to swell, to be pregnant" (Onians 1954, p. 112)—an astonishing convergence of ancient Greek and Tangu beliefs.

If one dares to assert that, as I have already suggested in regard to America and verified in regard to New Guinea, testicles are generally a mediating term between opposite sexual categories, it appears less strange that, among the foods corresponding to the category of life, fava beans as a symbol of testicles are (unlike grains) relatively closer to the opposite category—that is, death. Indeed, we can observe a clear homology between the two:

*Aulus Gellius was a Latin writer of the second century A.D. who wrote about ancient customs and natural science. (Ed.)

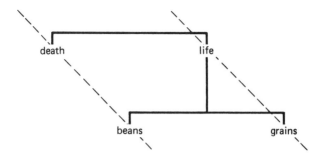

This twofold relation might explain the ambiguous position of fava beans between life and death, on which Marcel Detienne has strongly insisted (1970, p. 153). Also, in the same culture or in different ones, this ambiguous position predisposes them for a positive or a negative connotation (depending on the case), as intermediaries either for opening communication between the two worlds or for interrupting it.

Let me add that the same ambiguity is revealed on the culinary level. Fava beans—which the Romans believed to be the oldest cultivated plant—can be eaten raw when young; otherwise, they have to be boiled in water or even soaked first. Herodotus carefully distinguishes between the two ways of eating, emphasizing that Egyptian priests "do not munch beans and do not eat them boiled" (II, p. 37). On the other hand, the most ancient way of preparing cereals may very well have been by exploding the grains in fire, as we "pop corn" (Braidwood 1953, pp. 515-26). Thus, unlike grains that are edible after a quick roasting, the Leguminosae, shifting between the categories of the raw and the boiled (the latter, as I have shown elsewhere, being also the category of the rotten) are located next to nature and to death.*

Granted that, in the Japanese rite cited earlier, each father of a family tosses roasted soybeans into the air. It has been confirmed *in situ* that such preparation is not part of current Japanese cuisine. It would therefore be tempting to suppose that beans destined for the inhabitants of the beyond (which ancient Japanese mythology describes as a rotten world) are more attractive to them prepared in this, rather than the ordinary, way.

*It may be, moreover, that the preceding remarks have barely scratched the surface of a vast set of symbolic correspondences whose latent, perhaps universal presence is manifested here and there in observable transformations: for example, that of the Pythagorean beliefs into the reverse beliefs of the ancient Taoists, who proscribed grains but had no prejudice against meat.

Pythagoras in America

On the occasion already referred to (p. 194), Professor Yoshida Teigo pointed out the existence, in the Amami Islands (Prefecture of Kagoshima, between Kyushu and Okinawa), of a shamanistic rite, during which roasted soybeans are thrown about inside and outside a house of mourning—at first, in order to evoke the soul of the deceased and then to send it into the other world with no risk of its returning. Just as the roasted seeds cannot sprout, it is said, the soul of the deceased cannot be reborn. The woman shaman then strikes the shoulders of the relatives with a small sheaf of Graminaceae (suzuki, or *Miscanthus sinensis* Anders.) so that their souls may remain solidly attached to their bodies rather than yield to the natural tendency to follow the soul of the deceased.

This information is of twofold interest. In a part of the world unconnected with the Greco-Roman tradition, we find a leguminous plant in the same ambiguous position between life and death, along with its mediating role between these poles. Furthermore, the rite of the Amami Islands illustrates the same opposition between Leguminosae and Graminaceae that entirely different reflections led us to postulate about grains. Yet why suzuki—a non-edible plant—rather than, say, rice? In the rites, suzuki often functions as a signifier of rice (Berthier-Caillet 1981, pp. 215, 331, 337). And perhaps the opposition between Leguminosae and Graminaceae doubles up here with another—that between a cultivated plant and a wild one. For, if the soybean plays multiple parts in Japanese cooking, the suzuki is, above all, a weed (Cobbi 1978, p. 14) and displays prodigious vitality in invading areas that are or have become fallow.

Nevertheless, we should not forget that these reflections were inspired by data from America and must be used only with reservations. Some aspects of this information remain obscure: for instance, the animate nature ascribed to Sophora seeds (holes had to be punched in the leather case in which these seeds were carried as talismans, since they would die if they could not breathe [Howard 1965, p. 123]); or the relationship of Sophora seeds to the animal world, especially to horses. In the same spirit, I was told by Professor Yoshida that, on the Amami Islands, the roasted soybeans scattered through a house and around it outside are supposed to help the soul of the deceased to return because it has no legs. The *Samguk yusa*, a Korean work of the thirteenth century, with many far older elements, relates (Iryon 1972, p. 334) that a magician transforms black and white beans into warriors, so that they can combat and drive away a demon who is tormenting a princess. And the American contribution will remain uncertain so long as we cannot clear up the problem posed by friezes showing running figures—half human, half bean—on some Mochica ceramics (Hissink 1951; Kutscher 1951; Friedberg and Hocquenghem 1977; Hocquenghem 1979). For the time being, and despite the efforts of exegetes, these representations guard their mystery.

Chapter 15

An Anatomical Foreshadowing of Twinship

IN the natural philosophy of the African tribes to which Germaine Dieterlen has devoted her research, the notion of twinship plays a major role. Hence, in order to pay homage to our colleague, I find it appropriate briefly to examine a theme that certain myths, from an entirely different part of the world, link unexpectedly with this notion.

In a work published in 1621, Father Pablo José de Arriaga, a missionary to Peru in the late sixteenth century, relates something curious he observed during a tour (1920, p. 183). When the weather began to freeze in a certain district, they called together all the twins and everyone who had been born feet first or with a harelip (*los que tienen partidos los labios*). The priests accused them of being responsible for the cold weather through having eaten salt and pimientos. They were ordered to do penance by fasting, by being sexually continent, and by confessing their sins.

Almost everywhere in the world, especially in America, the link between twins and meteorological disorders is attested in a positive or a negative way: twins have the power to attract cold or rain or, on the contrary, to drive them away. There is a great deal to say about this connection which I cannot discuss within a short chapter. The association between twins and babies born feet first has been emphasized by N. Belmont, and I shall return to it. It is the third relationship that I should especially like to examine. What reasons could the ancient Peruvians have had to connect twins with harelipped people? To our knowledge, no author has asked this question—not even James G. Frazer, who, however, makes copious use of Arriaga's text (1926-36, I, pp. 266-67). Furthermore, the old mythographers were probably satisfied with a summary answer, simply lumping together harelips and twin births as congenital anomalies. We have become more demanding and expect our interpretations to explain both the content and the form of mythic or ritual themes—no doubt because we have learned that form and content are not really distinct.

As often happens in the New World, the myths of northwestern North America provide the key to a problem raised by data from South America. But, to reassure the reader disturbed by the geographic distance between the sources I am about to compare, let me specify immediately that the myths in question recur throughout the New World: they exist in South America and even in Peru. The North American versions are interesting in that they explicitly mention the harelip theme, which is absent from myths in the Southern Hemisphere but does appear in rituals there.

Both the ancient Tupinamba on the southern coast of Brazil and the Peruvians in the province of Huarochiri (Avila 1966, chap. 2) have a myth about a girl or a woman who is treacherously made pregnant by a wretched and misshapen person. In the most complete version, which was collected in Brazil by André Thevet (1575, pp. 913-20), the woman gives birth to twin sons—one by her husband, the demiurge; and the other by the trickster. Because of their different fathers, the brothers or their doublets have antithetical characters: one is invulnerable, and the other vulnerable. And the story also gives them distinct functions: as protectors of the Indians or of white people; among the Indians, protectors of the Tupinamba or of their enemies, and in charge either of abundance or of want.

The same myth is also found in North America, chiefly in the northwest, where it is distributed densely and continuously, from approximately the Klikitat in Oregon in the south to the Carrier and the Chilcotin in British Columbia in the north. While I have studied the latter group elsewhere (1969b, 1971), I need only point out here that, in respect to the South American versions, the North American have two variations. Sometimes—as among the Kutenai in the Rocky Mountain region (Boas 1918, p. 119)—a single impregnation leads to the birth of twins, who eventually become the sun and the moon. Sometimes—as among the Thompson and the Okanagon, who belong to the Salish of the Colombia plateau—the myth tells of two sisters who are made pregnant by means of tricks played by two distinct personages, Coyote (or Seagull) and Lynx. The sisters each give birth to a boy; it is only through the analogous circumstances of their conception that these children are twins (Teit 1898, pp. 36-40; 1912, pp. 213-17; Hill-Tout 1911, pp. 154-58).

We shall see that these latter versions are the most interesting. They reduce to the extreme the twinship of the heroes, who are here cousins, whose births are only strikingly parallel: both were conceived by means of a subterfuge. It is also notable that the father's ruse is not the same in both cases: it is metonymic for Coyote, who has the girl eat his dried semen (*partie du coït*) in the guise of a meal; and metaphorical for Lynx, who impregnates the other sister with a drop of urine or of saliva (figurative sperm) which he lets fall, either deliberately or accidentally, on her mouth or belly.

By reworking the South American versions, the North American ones nevertheless remain faithful to the same goal. Nowhere are the two heroes real twins, since they have different fathers and even opposite characters, which continue to distinguish their respective descendants. Children who are thought to be twins are, thus, not. Or if they really are twins, as in the Kutenai version I have cited, then their diverging destinies will "untwin" them, as it were. At the outcome of a competition in which all sorts of animals participate, one hero becomes the sun, judged satisfactory for *heating* during the *day*, and the other becomes the moon, judged satisfactory for *illuminating* during the *night*. This cosmological allegory corresponds to others. Although they seem to be twins, the Tupinamba dioscuri, as we have seen, are diametrically opposed in nature and function. The same is true, among the Salish and their neighbors, of Coyote, Lynx, or their sons: one invents the firebreak, the other the heated bathhouse; one is associated with heat, the other with cold; one is the master of the wind, and the other, of the fog. A Nez Percé version of the same myth (Phinney 1934, pp. 465-88) tries to account for ill-matched marriages; that is, why all spouses are not "twins." A myth recorded among the Flathead and the Sanpoil (Hoffman 1884, pp. 34-40; Ray 1933, pp. 142-45), which demonstrably belongs to the same group, relates (in a significant way, in the Flathead version) how the Lynx and the Puma, which belonged to twin species from the beginning of time (*Lynx canadensis* and *Lynx rufus*), developed into different genera—one by losing, the other by gaining, a tail.

As I have pointed out, the Plateau Salish versions attenuate the twinship motif, replacing twins with cousins having analogous origins. In this light, it is instructive that these versions reintroduce the motif indirectly and in a rudimentary form. After leaving her sister, whose misfortune obliges her to marry Coyote, the older sister seeks refuge with her grandmother, Wild Sheep or Mountain Goat. The grandmother hastens her coming and sends Rabbit out to bring her food. Rabbit hides under a tree that has fallen across the trail, and the girl trips over it. Hare catches sight of her private parts and makes fun of their appearance. Infuriated, she hits him with her stick and cleaves his muzzle; and that is how the Leporidae got their harelip. In other words, she begins a cleavage that, if completed, would split the animal's body and turn the animal into twins.

Indeed, how do the inhabitants of this region explain the origin of twins? According to the Havasupai, who live in Arizona (Spier 1928, p. 301), when the pregnant woman who has been lying on her side abruptly turns over, the "fluid" filling her womb is thereby divided into two parts. In an Iroquois myth of the Seneca group, a twin birth is ascribed to the father's power to divide his body down the middle into two parts (Curtin and Hewitt 1918, p. 551). In both South and North America, we find the belief that "a pregnant woman must avoid sleeping on her back; otherwise, the sexual fluids might divide and form twins." This is believed by the Boróro of central Brazil (Crocker, n.d., II, pp. 14-15), and, closer to the area of our myths, by the Twana, a Salish group on Puget Sound (Elmendorf 1960, pp. 421-22). The Twana also prohibit a pregnant woman from eating the flesh of deer because the animals in this family have cloven hoofs. Given the present state of our knowledge, it is harder to interpret the belief of the Lummi (who are related to the Twana) that if a pregnant woman eats trout, her child will have a harelip (Stern 1934, p. 13). In *The Naked Man* (1981), I introduced and discussed a series of myths from the northwestern United States: in these tales, twins are alternately "stuck together" and restored to their original duality, when an arrow shot into the air falls and splits the seemingly single body that they have become after being soldered together by their grandmother. The Bella Coola, an isolated Salish group, believe that a woman who eats spit-roasted salmon will give birth to twins (Gunther 1928, p. 171). Now if twins result from a child, an embryo, or an animal that has split or is about to split, the myths attest that a rabbit and a harelipped human being are themselves the splitters. Nez Percé stories relate how Rabbit manages to keep one of Thunder's wives after abducting her: by splitting the heavy storm cloud with which Thunder threatens him (Boas 1917, pp. 177-78); or, according to another version, by hiding the woman between his thighs, his twin limbs (Spinden 1908, pp. 154-55). For their part, the Kwakiutl (Curtis 1970, X, p. 295) tell the story of a little girl who is despised because of her harelip. Yet when she, along with the children who refuse to play with her, is carried off by an ogress, she is the one who saves them, by using a sharp seashell to split the side of the basket on the ogress's back into which she has stuffed her little victims. Since the girl is at the bottom of the basket, she is the first to escape—and by her feet, just like the rabbit in our myths. Crouching in the middle of the path, he is under the heroine's vagina and looks up at it (between the woman's legs; whereas, in the Nez Percé story, the woman crouches between Rabbit's thighs); hence, in relation to her, the hare is in the same position as if he had come out of her womb feet first.

In a Kutenai version which Reichard (1947, p. 170) compares with those of the Coeur d'Alene Indians who were plateau Salish neighbors of the Thompson and the Okanagon, Rabbit goes to meet the girl and agrees to guide her to her grandmother's home (this time, her grandmother is a frog) only after the girl is willing to call him her husband. This variant supports some interesting reflections of Belmont's (1971, pp. 139-47), who shows why folk beliefs sometimes liken feet-first birth to inverted coitus: the baby leaves the mother's body in the same position in which the penis entered it. A story told by the Micmac, who are eastern Algonquin, establishes a symmetry between the harelip and penetration: Rabbit got his split muzzle by trying to imitate Woodpecker, who pecks at bark in order to get larvae; but instead of his penetrating the tree, it was the tree that penetrated Rabbit's nose (Speck 1915, p. 65). In contrast to twins implicitly thought of as divided, a Polynesian myth offers an "anti-twin," whom it therefore describes as a divider: Semoana, whose name signifies "the ill-born," wants to outstrip his twins and so escapes his mother's body through her head, splitting it in two (Firth 1961, pp. 30-31).

The assumption that a harelip constitutes an embryonic twinship among people afflicted with it, and among the rodents it is sometimes named after, illuminates several problems. First of all, we can understand why the ancient Peruvians placed twins and harelipped people on the same footing. We must add that, according to Arriaga, the natives believed that one twin is the son of lightning (probably because lightning has the power to split). Furthermore, in our time, the Canelo of the Peruvian and Ecuadorian *montaña*, who were visited by R. Karsten (1935, pp. 219 f.), attribute to a demon the paternity of the second-born twin and, for this reason, used to kill the newborn baby. Even today in Mexico, the belief persists that the part of the lip missing from a harelipped person was eaten by an eclipse. In California, twins, who are masters of thunder, are said to be the offspring of a posthumous child, who was raised by a female dog and, at her orders, sliced in half along the median vertical plane (Gayton and Newman 1940, pp. 48-50).

Arriaga relates that, after the Spanish conquest, the natives adopted a custom—fought by the Church—of always giving the name Santiago to the twin who was to be supposed the child of lightning (1920, p. 58). In this respect, we must note that, among the eastern Pueblo, the figure of Santiago appears in a festival at the same time as a figure named Bocaiyanyi or Poshayani, with whom he forms a pair (White 1942, p. 263). In fact, Poshayani is the champion of the Indians against the whites, and his association with a figure taken from Christian hagiography seems to restore the antithetical functions ascribed by the ancient Tupinamba to their serial dioscuri: Sumé and the ancestor of the non-Indians; Tamendoaré, the ancestor of the Tupinamba, and Aricouté, the ancestor of their enemies; finally, the invulnerable son of Mairé Ata and his vulnerable false twin, the son of Sarigoys.

In the second place and above all, the association of the harelip with virtual twinship enables us to solve a problem that has greatly perplexed American mythographers: Why did the Ojibwa and other Algonquin groups make Hare the supreme figure in their pantheon? Any number of explanations have been proposed: the fertility of the species, its food value, its speed, and so on. None of these hypotheses is convincing. In light of the foregoing reflections, it seems more tempting to point to that anatomical peculiarity, common to most of the Leporidae family, that allows them to be seen as potential and even actual twins.

Now the Nanabozho hare is the survivor of twins or sometimes even of quadruplets (Dixon 1909, p. 6; Fisher 1946, pp. 230-32, 238-40). In native thinking, this profusion of babies in a mother's body has a serious consequence: even if there are only two children, they are bound to dispute the honor of being the firstborn; and in order to get out first, one of them, as in the Tikopia myth I have cited, will not hesitate to create a shortcut rather than use the outlet provided by nature. I believe that this feature explains—at least, for America—why feet-first births are likened to twin births. Actually, the prohibition against a pregnant woman's sleeping on her back, according to the Twana of Puget Sound, prevents her from bearing twins and, according to the Yuma in Arizona (see page 204), prevents the baby from being born feet first (Spier 1933, p. 310). In both cases, though for different reasons, these occurrences presage a fatal birth or—looked at in the best way—a heroic one. This ambiguity explains why some tribes killed twins and feet-first babies; while the Peruvian tribes visited by Arriaga held such exceptional children in sacred awe, calling them, respectively, Chuchus and Chacpa and venerating their mummies if they died young (1920, pp. 16, 30, 56-57).

The brother or brothers of Nanabozho are too impatient to be born and so burst their mother's body, causing her to die. This *birth against nature*, which has a central place in Algonquin culture, is transformed on two axes, in the tales of the Salish, into *coitus against culture* with Rabbit killing his grandmother by copulating with her. Between these extreme forms of the same motif, that of Rabbit hiding on the road and peeping up at his "sister's" vulva represents a point of equilibrium: that is, on the one hand, a metaphorical coitus, which, being incestuous, is contrary to culture; and, on the other hand, a birth no less metaphorical, but contrary to nature because the positions of the two characters are the same as if one had been born feet first from the other.

In telling about the mother's death, the Algonquin myths make a point of exculpating Nanabozho. His grandmother welcomes him in the guise of a blood clot that has escaped from the corpse and gradually changes into a hare, an animal in whose split muzzle the essence of twinship is concentrated. In the series of American mediators, which I have outlined elsewhere in an old article (Lévi-Strauss 1963, chap. 11, p. 223), the place of the Great Hare would be halfway between the dioscuri and the trickster. Hence his ambiguous and even contradictory character, which has been thoroughly discussed by other commentators (cf. Fisher 1946, p. 230). Sometimes he is a wise manager of the universe; sometimes, a grotesque figure who passes from one mishap to the next. This duality would be part of his nature if it contained the seed of a homogeneous pair of mediators grafted, so to speak, on a figure of more modest stature whom the accident of birth put on the side of disorder.

Without having read the first version (1978) of this text, Michael P. Carroll accused me of not knowing that Hare is also a personification of the trickster. After reading my text, Carroll declared that he "had nothing to change in my article" because my argument was "completely different" from the one that I had presented in my earlier analysis of trickster figures in North America (Carroll 1981; 1982).

The preceding reflections show that my critic is doubly mistaken. I treated the problem of Hare and, far from employing different arguments, simply took up, and added a point to, the typology of the mediator figure(s) that I had proposed in *Structural Anthropology*, now showing how and why Hare naturally belongs there: between the dioscuri and the trickster proper.

Do these speculations apply only to America? Can they be extended and deepened elsewhere? There is, at least, a parallel in Asia. According to a Gilyak myth, a council, presided over by Hare and Squirrel and made up of the few survivors of the Deluge, decrees that twin births will henceforth be contrary to nature (Black 1973, p. 54). The importance attributed to these two rodents might be explained by the fact that since both have a harelip, each was very nearly born as twins; the two of them, however, do not together form a set of twins. Thus, twinship is doubly challenged: potentially and actually. But we would like especially to know whether the motif of the harelip appears in African mythologies, where the notion of twins plays a major role, and whether it is treated in comparable fashion. And, indeed, such seems to be the case.

First, in Africa as in America, twins are seen as being the product of a division. In Dahomey, one of the signs of geomancy—the eighth —is known as *Aklān-Meji*, "chief of the twins." B. Maupoil, on the basis of data from informants, notes the homophony between this name and the *fon* verb *klã*, "to separate" (1943, p. 493). A proverb containing this verb says in effect: "Conception makes twins and yet they separate [in order to be born]." A legend explains why monkeys have remained half-human (and therefore the twins of mankind): "They all began to shout '*Klã we!*' That is *Klã* [the defective]!" This is the reason twins cannot eat monkey meat, "for the monkey personifies the twins of the forest" (pp. 497, 499).

Likewise in Africa, the harelip can signify the dual nature that impels a class of beings or a single individual toward twinship. According to the Nupe myth of origin, Tsoede, the founder of the kingdom, accidentally cut his lip; as a result, all children born with a harelip are given a name derived from his. Now Tsoede owed his success to his being *half* Nupe, which enabled him "to force unity upon heterogeneous groups and cultures"—an enterprise that "presupposes revolts and quarrels" (Nadel 1971, pp. 127-28, 146) and is bound to remain in an intermediary state (like harelips) between unity and duality.

We know other African dynastic myths in which the sovereign appears "divided," born of parents from different backgrounds or having two mothers, a biological and a social one. Other data, which we cannot go into here, can also support the hypothesis that the African king has a twin essence. In this way may be explained the king of Gonja's privilege, if not obligation, to marry twins. In any case, in light of the facts assembled here, there seems to be no great risk in establishing a link between twins and the harelip that the founder of the Nupe dynasty inflicted on himself.*

*The French edition of this book was already in proof when Professor R. T. Zuidema was kind enough to draw my attention to an article by T. Platt on mirror symmetry, published in 1978, the same year as the first version of this chapter. The author includes a recent observation that directly confirms my interpretation of the link between twins and harelips: "It is also said that if a pregnant woman is frightened by thunder and lightning, the child in her belly divides in two. I was recently told that twins are sometimes born with lips split vertically down the middle: this, too, is attributed to the fear caused by thunder and lightning" (Platt 1978, p. 1,097).

Chapter 16

A Small Mythico-Literary Puzzle

La poésie est le lieu des points équidistants entre le pur sensible et le pur intelligible—dans le champ du langage.

PAUL VALÉRY, *Cahiers*

APOLLINAIRE'S poem *Les Colchiques* ("The Autumn Crocuses") (1965, p. 60) is too well known for me to reproduce the text.* Besides,

*The French poet Guillaume Apollinaire (1880–1918) was a restless technical innovator and an early surrealist. Of his lyrical poems, the most influential books were *Alcools* (1913), in which "Les Colchiques" appears, and *Calligrammes* (1918). Since Apollinaire is not as well known in the United States as in France, the text of "Les Colchiques" follows in its entirety, along with a translation by Theresa Craig. (Ed.)

Les Colchiques

Le pré est vénéneux mais joli en automne
Les vaches y paissant
Lentement s'empoisonnent
Le colchique couleur de cerne et de lilas
Y fleurit tes yeux sont comme cette fleur-là
Violâtres comme leur cerne et comme cet automne
Et ma vie pour tes yeux lentement s'empoisonne

Les enfants de l'école viennent avec fracas
Vêtus de hoquetons et jouant de l'harmonica
Ils cueillent les colchiques qui sont comme des mères
Filles de leurs filles et sont couleur de tes paupières
Qui battent comme les fleurs battent au vent dément

Le gardien du troupeau chante tout doucement
Tandis que lentes et meuglant les vaches abandonnent
Pour toujours ce grand pré mal fleuri par l'automne

A Small Mythico-Literary Puzzle

I intend not to focus on the poem as a whole (of which Jean-Claude Coquet has made a highly penetrating analysis in *Sémiotique littéraire* [1972, chap. 6]) but, rather, to discuss a detail that has remained enigmatic to commentators. Why does the poet equate with autumn crocuses the epithet *mères filles de leurs filles* ("mothers daughters of their daughters" [lines 10-11])?

In his study, Jean-Claude Coquet merely points out that "such phrasing is quite familiar in French." By way of support, he quotes La Fontaine's use of the expression *fils de ses oeuvres* ("son of his works") —a moralizing metaphor that could not have inspired Apollinaire's metaphors; nor do we see why or, especially, how it could have been extended to inanimate beings.

Of course, Coquet's predecessors have come up with some disarming interpretations: "Mothers so outrageously made up that they would be mistaken for the daughters of their daughters," says R. Faurisson (yet the autumn crocus has a discreet and delicate coloring); M.-J. Durry associates the blossomings with the coming of children who "are the flower of humanity." Somewhat closer to a solution, R. Lefèvre discerns "a possible allusion to some botanical peculiarity of autumn crocuses"; but he quickly rejects this idea by adding that "modern botanical works offer no enlightenment." (In regard to these authors, see Coquet 1972, p. 127.) Lefèvre probably did not go to the trouble of consulting older botanical works, which are more attentive than modern ones to the perceptible aspects of things. The *Colchicum* is "a difficult genus, very much confused botanically" (Bailey 1943, I, p. 824). It has at least three characteristics—some, moreover, in common with other plants—that, each in its own way, explain not only Apollinaire's phrase but also his basic reasons for using it in that particular context.

The Autumn Crocuses

The meadow is venomous but beautiful in autumn
The cows grazing there
are slowly being poisoned
There the crocus, the color of a bruise and of lilacs,
flourishes. Your eyes are like that flower,
purplish like its bruise and like this autumn
And for your eyes my life is slowly being poisoned

Children from school come shouting,
dressed in coarse cloth and playing the harmonica
They gather the crocuses which are like mothers
daughters of their daughters and are the color of your eyelids
which flutter like flowers in a demented wind

The guardian of the flock sings very softly
While bellowing the cows slowly abandon
forever this wide meadow shorn by autumn

In French, the autumn crocus is called not only *colchique* but also *veillote* "because it blossoms during the season when the long period of twilight begins" (Larousse 1866-76). The autumn crocus produces long flowers that shoot up rapidly and open in the fall. The blossom has only stamens; the ovary is on the side of the corm, which is buried four to eight inches underground. In fertilization, the pollen descends inside the perianth, which, toward the bottom, continues on as a hollow tube forming a stem five or six times longer than the main part of the leaf; hence, the total distance runs to about twelve inches.

The colchicum has a further peculiarity: "The ovary remains underground, on the side of the corm, until spring. At this time, it appears on the surface of the soil; it then develops and rises above the earth and, upon ripening in June, bears a podlike, three-celled fruit" (Perrot 1947, III, p. 67).

A third characteristic of the autumn crocus is emphasized by the *Dictionnaire des Sciences naturelles . . . par plusieurs professeurs du Jardin du Roi et des principales écoles de Paris* (Levrault, 1816-30,vol. X, entry *Colchique*):

> These flowers appear in September and October, while the leaves do not develop until the following spring. . . . Every year, the corm [*la bulbe*, in the feminine gender according to the usage of older French botanists] that has produced flowers and fruits is exhausted and is destroyed after this period, and replaced by another corm, which has developed right next to it; as a result of this annual renewal of the corms, which always occurs on the same side, the plant moves each year a distance the thickness of its corm.

If the colchicum blossom is, strictly speaking, a hermaphrodite, then its hermaphroditism is quite special, since a maximum distance separates the male and the female organs. The male organ is inside the flower and always at the top; the female organ is several centimeters underground and is an integral part of the generating corm, which is the source of both the present plant and the one that will follow after. Thus, a temporal link is paired with a spatial separation. This distended hermaphroditism might almost suggest two sexes that are separated and united at a distance, in the manner of Adam, who, before the creation of Eve, was a hermaphrodite according to certain Talmudists and had a male and a female body, which were joined in such a way that the male organ had to travel a considerable distance in order to reach the female organ and fecundate the female body.

As we have noted, the flowers of the colchicum appear in autumn, several months before the leaves and the seeds, which come in the springtime of the following year. Yet the seeds seem to play only a circumstantial role in reproduction, which normally occurs as a doubling of the corm. In other words, the autumn crocus belongs to the large family of clones; and we know how difficult, if not impossible, it is to distinguish the mothers and daughters among several individuals. Certain grasses of the Gramineae family form a clone hundreds of meters long and going back more than a thousand years. In the United States, they have found a clone forest of almost fifty thousand aspens covering a total of nearly two hundred acres; another forest of aspen clones has been estimated to be eight thousand years old. In such cases, the distinction between absolutely or relatively adjacent generations loses all meaning.

Hence, among the *Colchicum autumnale*, factors of confusion counter-balance several kinds of shift: a vertical shift characterizes the mode of fertilization; a horizontal shift, the mode of reproduction. To these two spatial shifts is joined a temporal one, since the blossom of a plant appears eight or nine months before its leaves.

This latter trait alone would suffice to explain the epithet "mothers daughters of their daughters."* Botanists once used the term *Filius-ante-patrem*† not only for the colchicum but also for the colt's-foot (*Tussilago*), the butterbur (*Petasites*) [*Encyclopédie Diderot-d'Alembert*, article: "Fils avant le père"], and the epilobium or willow herb. The one term may have been used either because the flowers of all these plants or their stems appear before the leaves, or because their fruit is wholly visible even before their blossoms open. Apollinaire was erudite enough to have encountered and chosen to employ these old terms. And, as I shall show, he had every reason to make them feminine.

The poet probably also knew their remote mystical origin, which made these terms more pungent and eminently suitable for a poetic function. Among their most ancient uses can be cited the pseudo-Augustinian in texts about the Virgin Mary, one from the fifth or sixth century, the other perhaps only from the eighth: "The creator has birthed the creator, the serving-girl has birthed the master, the daugh-

---

*While writing my text, I did not know that this connection had already been made by Michel Deguy (1974, p. 456) and by Maria Vailati in a note accompanying the separate publication of the text by Jean-Claude Coquet (1972). I am grateful to M. Coquet for telling me about this note which, on several points, anticipates my own observations.

†Literally, "Son-before-father." (Trans.)

ter has birthed the father: the daughter, from her divine nature; the mother, from her human nature."* Hence, the later wording in the second text on Mary: "daughter of God, mother of God." This expression is also found in Chrétien de Troyes—"May this be granted by the glorious father who made his daughter his mother!" (1947, p. 195)†—and in Dante.

In a different, though still theological context the figure of speech is ancient: "The Vedic Indians," notes Georges Dumézil, "thought about the ability of fire . . . to renew itself, to engender itself endlessly." Also, they called it Tanūnapāt, "descendent of itself" (1975, p. 66). In the same spirit, the Mabinogion tale of *Kulhwch and Olwen*‡ mentions Nerth son of Kadarn and Llawe son of Erw—that is, respectively, Force son of Strong, and Soil son of Furrow, although, as J. Loth remarks, one would have expected the opposite (1913, introduction).

I have already mentioned Chrétien de Troyes; and indeed, this expression seems to have had a special fortune in Arthurian literature. In the *Parzival* of Wolfram von Eschenbach, Herzeloïde, pregnant by her deceased husband Gahmuret, says: "Younger than he by far, I am both his wife and mother too. I carry here his body and the seed of his life" (§109). At the Castle of Merveille, Arnive holds forth thus to Gawain:

A mother brings a child into the world: and the child then becomes his mother's mother. It is from water that ice comes; but nothing can prevent the ice from leaving water. When I think of my life, I have to recall that my birth was joy and happiness; if I know joy again, we will see the fruit leave the fruit to which it has given birth.

Here we are back to botany again! In a note on this passage, E. Tonnelat cites Symposius, the fourth-century author of a collection of Latin riddles, which, we are told, was often imitated during the Middle Ages (1934, vol. II, p. 194). I have not consulted the Latin source; but, closer to us, Alfred de Vigny says of his ancestors: "If I write their history, they descend from me" (Vigny, 1978, p. 249).§ Finally, to dem-

*Sermo de Virginitate Mariae (*Patrologia latina*, supplement, II, col. 1187); Sermo 195, 3 (ibid., 39, col. 2108). Through the kind intervention of Professor Paul Vignaux, Father Georges Folliet of *Etudes augustiniennes* was kind enough to verify these texts and to furnish their precise reference. I take this opportunity to thank both of them.

†Chrétien de Troyes was a French poet in the last part of the twelfth century and introduced the legend of the Holy Grail in his Arthurian romance *Perceval le Gallois* (see chapter 17 of this book). (Ed.)

‡The *Mabinogion* is a collection of medieval Welsh tales, which contain examples of early Arthurian legends; among these is the tale of *Kulhwch and Olwen*, written before 1100.

§Alfred de Vigny (1797–1863) was a French man of letters and a leader in the romantic school. (Ed.)

onstrate the vitality of this figure of thought in our language, let me quote a recent text by Jean Pouillon: "Tradition marches toward biological heredity but is often presented as modeled after it. Indeed, tradition is a reverse descent: the son produces his father, and that is the reason he can give himself several fathers!" (1975, p. 160). The same kind of semantic latitude, permitted by the reversibility of the terms, may explain how, in Arthurian literature (which may have been known to Apollinaire, who rendered a late version of *Perceval* into modern French), Parzival can be sometimes the heir of Prester John, whose name he takes (in *Titurel* by Albrecht von Scharfenberg), or sometimes his father (in the Dutch *Lancelot*).

We first looked at the anatomy and physiology of the autumn crocus to find an explanation of Apollinaire's epithet "mothers daughters of their daughters." This interpretation was corroborated by the name *Filius-ante-patrem*—identical except for the sex—that old botanists used for the colchicum as well as for other species having the same features. Finally, we tried to restore what might be called the ethnographic context of these figures of thought—that is, the historical and ideological conditions in which they emerged, survived, or were displaced within a given culture. I am speaking of esoteric speculations (of which riddles, as a genre, represent the small change) and of theological mysteries gradually secularized by academic poetry, courtly literature, and the language of the naturalists.

All in all, these considerations help us to understand the *raison d'être* of an epithet that might have been considered incidental. Its purpose seems to be, first, to humanize the flowers or, at least, to turn them into animate beings, the better to situate them at the third corner of a triangle, whose other two corners are already occupied by cows and children. The children as male (*enfant* is masculine in French) will grow up and go away; but for the moment, picking flowers, they are harsh, noisy, and destructive. As Coquet remarked (1972, p. 125), their activity is evoked by the phonetics of lines 8 and 9:

Les enfants de l'école viennent avec fracas
Vêtus de hoquetons et jouant de l'harmonica

In contrast, the cows as female are grazing to the slow beat of the anapest (Coquet 1972, p. 118) and will soon be slaughtered or poisoned. Between these two slopes—the one ascending and the other descending—only the autumn crocuses will remain, on a horizontal level, both literally and figuratively: by being stationary, or almost so, on the surface of the ground (the successive plants being displaced by the thickness of a corm); and by reproducing themselves as identical entities. Thus, the crocuses figure as the stable and permanent element and, as such, give the poem its title.

Moreover, while the interpretation I have just outlined recognizes the symbolic value of three terms—cows, children, crocuses—the symbolism of the first two terms remains vague. Nothing in the text affirms it; it can only be inferred. On the other hand, the symbolic function of the third term is explicitly stated and even provides the initial nucleus of the poem. Through their color, through their swaying in the wind, the autumn crocuses symbolize the eyes and eyelids of the beloved woman, which slowly poison the poet, who lives only for them. Here, consequently, only the autumn crocuses have full and complete value as a sign.

In conclusion, let us listen to the great mathematician René Thom:

> In the interaction of signified and signifier [*Signifié-Signifiant*] it is plain that, swept along by the universal flow, the signified emits, engenders the signifier in an uninterrupted, ramifying wilderness. But the signifier recreates the signified every time we interpret the sign. And, as exemplified by biological forms, the signifier (the offspring) can become the signified (the parent); all it takes is a single generation.
>
> It is through this subtle balancing between two morphologies, through its simultaneous demand for reversibility and irreversibility, that the dynamic of symbolism carries within itself (in a local and concentrated form) all the contradictions of the scientific view of the world; and thus that the dynamic of symbolism is the very image of life. [1974, p. 233]

Seeking to understand a locution that, at first sight, appears bizarre applied to certain plants, we began with botanical observations and, after passing through the history of ideas, wound up with the reflections of a specialist in the most abstract of the sciences: reflections on certain formal characteristics of symbolism, and particularly in regard to the symbolic role of the plants in question. Thus, the concrete peculiarities given them by nature and the semantic function given them by the poet can be united in these flowers, which have become signs. The autumn crocuses are "mothers daughters of their daughters" because of their clone nature and because of the gap both in time between their flowering and the emergence of their leaves as well as of that resulting from the role of signifier that they are called upon to play in regard to the signified. In most plants, leaves appear as precursors of the flowers; but here, we have the contrary case. The formal gap is no less unstable, for, as Thom says, it shifts every time we interpret the sign. This instability emerges in the poem: when Apollinaire describes the crocus as being "the color of a bruise" and then as "the color of your eyelids," he is making the eyelids the signifier of the flowers, which are transformed from being the signifier of the eyelids into the signified.

Thus, in his analysis of the poem, Coquet correctly emphasizes that "the two terms can define one another," and that "we thereby enter a mystical universe . . . the only universe in which it is possible to coordinate two attributes belonging to two contradictory isotopes" (1972, p. 120). Nevertheless, the contradiction that he believes he discerns comes from the choice he makes, in interpreting the text of the categories of active and passive. Yet these categories are not pertinent; the contradiction vanishes when they are replaced with the categories of signifier and signified since, as we have seen, one of the essential properties of the relationship between signifier and signified is endless reversibility.

The brief exercise to which I have invited the reader thus confirms that structural analysis takes place in a continuum where empirical observation of the tiniest details of the natural world is inseparable from a reflection on the formal properties inherent in the mechanics of thinking. Between these extreme poles, there is a whole gamut of intermediary levels. Thus, the "mothers daughters of daughters" function of "The Autumn Crocuses" seems to be refracted by the prism of the analysis, which exert on it the power of discrimination by isolating a structural position in the poem—a semantic ambiguity—from its botanical aspects and its theological and mystical references. A mythical poetic, or more generally artistic, figure moves us because it offers on each level a specific meaning that nevertheless remains parallel to other meanings, and because we mysteriously seem to apprehend them all at the same time.

But when, in order to illuminate the nature of aesthetic feeling, we try to dissociate them, we have no other methods than those of ethnography and history: that is, the ever different ways in which human beings have experienced, and conceived of, and are still experiencing and conceiving of, the world of which they are a part. And if we are to break through the barriers between the intuitive and the intelligible aspects of this world, our only hope of success is to call upon the exact sciences, the natural sciences, and the human sciences.

Chapter 17

From Chrétien de Troyes to Richard Wagner

You see my son,
Here, time turns into space.

*(Du siebst, mein Sobn,
zum Raum wird bier die Zeit.)*

THESE WORDS, spoken by Gurnemanz to the hero in the first act of *Parsifal*, while the scene changes before the eyes of the spectators, are probably the most profound definition that anyone has ever offered for myth. And these verses sound even more apt when applied to the myth of the Grail, about whose historical origin—as well as the places of its birth—all sorts of hypotheses have been and are still being advanced. Some observers, looking to ancient Egypt and Greece, regard the stories of the Grail as containing echoes of very old cults linked to the death and resurrection of a god. Whether that deity is Osiris, Atis, Adonis, or even Demeter, the visit to the Castle of the Grail is supposedly a vestige of a failed initiation into a fertility rite.

Other observers propose a Christian origin, although they conceive of it in differing ways. On a liturgical level, the quest for the Grail could recall the communion of the ill or even such Byzantine rites as the Grand Entrance of the Greek Church, in the course of which a priest symbolically wounds the eucharistic host with a knife called the Holy Lance. It has also been suggested that the story of the Grail symbolizes the passage from the Old to the New Testament: the enchanted castle would stand for the Temple of Solomon; the bountiful cup or stone, for the Tables of the Law and mannah; and the lance, for Aaron's rod. Yet from a Christian viewpoint, it would not be normal for the sacred vessel—chalice or ciborium—to be carried by a woman, as described in the ancient tales. This woman is said to represent the Holy Church allegorically, and the hero's visit to the Castle of the Grail evokes the return to the earthly paradise.

A different exegesis is inspired by Iranian traditions, which speak of a mythical person who resolves to battle with the celestial powers at the head of a troop of demons. Wounded while falling back to the earth, he must wait, disabled, for his grandson to take up the struggle again and win it, restoring him to health in a single stroke. This fable probably stems from a theory developed by the hermetic philosophers of Hellenistic Egypt and transmitted to the West by the Arabs: according to it, divine wisdom will come down to earth, into a huge crater; and one will have only to plunge into it to obtain supreme knowledge —truly a baptism of the intellect. This crater was supposedly confused with the constellation of the same name. Now the old French word *graal* ("grail") derives from the Greek *crater*, perhaps through Latin *cratis* ("hurdle") but, in any case, through Low Latin *gradalis* ("bowl, porringer"). Hence, the etymology allows us to give the Grail a heavenly origin with mystical virtues.

Finally, it would be astonishing if psychoanalysts did not have their say. They see the bleeding lance as a phallic symbol and the Grail itself as a female sexual symbol, and promote this opinion all the more urgently because some versions describe the lance as resting tip down in the Grail.

Today, however, scholars tend to look in a different direction. The stories of the Grail contain numerous elements that seem to come from Celtic mythology, fragments of which are preserved in ancient Welsh and Irish literature. The Grail is supposedly one of those wondrous receptacles (plates, baskets, porringers, drinking horns, cauldrons) that provide the user with inexhaustible food and sometimes even immortality. The Irish and the Welsh traditions gathered in the Mabinogion collection also tell of magical lances that bleed.

The texts depict the king of the Grail as a sovereign whose thighs are wounded. Unable to mount a horse and hunt, he goes fishing for distraction; hence, the name "Fisher King." In Wagner's opera, he appears for the first time on his way to bathe in the water of a lake. These aquatic affinities link Amfortas to a supernatural being: Bran the Blessed of Welsh myth, who corresponds to an Irish god, Nuadu (whose name actually means "fisher"). Both these figures have a wondrous sword and a magic cauldron. In Celtic tradition, the sexual impotence or the moral baseness of the sovereign often leads to the decline of his kingdom and to the sterility of people, cattle, and fields —that is, to misfortunes comparable to those that strike the country of the Grail, as it becomes a wasteland after its king falls ill. The spell can be lifted only if an unknown visitor asks one or several questions —a theme already present in Irish and Welsh tradition.

However, the oldest known version of the Grail story comes not from Britain but from medieval France, from the poet Chrétien de Troyes (a native of Champagne) who composed it between 1180 and 1190. He was working on it when he died in the latter year or the next. Perceval, the young hero, is nicknamed *le Gallois*, or "the Welshman"; and the author explains that he was inspired by a book he received from his patron, Philippe d'Alsace, Count of Flanders, before the latter left on the Third Crusade, in which he perished. At this period, the Norman conquest of England was scarcely a century old; and fifty years before Chrétien began his epic, the princes of the House of Anjou, related by marriage to the Normans, succeeded them as rulers of England and founded the dynasty of the Plantagenets. French, or at least a Norman or a Picard dialect, was spoken on either side of the English Channel; and the court poets traveled back and forth with their lords. Thus, it would not be surprising if the now lost book employed by Chrétien de Troyes dealt with one or more Welsh legends, as is suggested by the nationality he ascribes to his hero and by many other personal and geographic names used by him and by the writers who went on with his work.*

While it would be interesting to trace Chrétien's narrative step by step, it would take too long; a brief synopsis will be enough. After various misfortunes (the loss of her husband, the deaths in combat of her first two sons), a widow takes refuge in a wild forest, where she raises her youngest son without telling him anything about his origins

*For the preceding summary, I followed J. Frappier's fine book *Chrétien de Troyes et le mythe du Graal* (1972).

or about the world surrounding the forest. One day, the naïve boy meets some knights, and so beautiful do they seem to him that he at first mistakes them for supernatural beings. Despite his mother's tears, he decides to follow them; and after diverse misadventures, he arrives at the court of King Arthur, where a maiden who has not laughed for six years breaks out of her muteness and promises him a great future. Perceval, who does not even know his own name, would like to be made a knight; he is mocked for having neither sword nor armor. Dismissed, he goes off and encounters an unknown knight. The boy kills him with a javelin blow, seizes his armor, and then arrives at the home of the sage, Gornemant de Gohort, who takes him in, teaches him the art of jousting, and equips him as a knight. But Perceval is remorseful at having abandoned his mother, and leaves to find her.

On the way, he rescues the lady of a manor who is being besieged, delivers her from her enemies, and forms a tender bond with her. Still, he is obsessed with the thought of his mother. He puts off his marriage plans, takes to the road again, and enters a gorge where he finds a river flowing so swiftly that he does not dare to cross it. Two men in a boat, one of them with a fishing line, tell him how to get to a nearby castle. There, the fisherman welcomes him; he is the king of the country, but he has been crippled when the blow from a lance pierced both his thighs. In the great hall of the castle, Perceval is given a sword by his host. He then watches a mysterious procession which includes, among other participants, a young man holding a lance with a bleeding tip; and two maidens, one of whom carries a grail—that is, a cup, of pure gold decorated with precious stones—and the other, a silver tray. On the tray are slices of meat for the guests; but at each course, the girl with the grail passes through without stopping and enters an adjacent room. Despite his curiosity, Perceval does not dare to ask, "Who is being served?" He remembers that first his mother and then Gornemant have advised him to remain discreet in all circumstances and not to ask questions.

After a sumptuous meal that lasts very late, Perceval is taken to his room. When he wakes up the next morning, the castle is deserted. He knocks vainly at the doors; no one responds to his shouts. He has to don his clothes and his armor without help; and then, in the courtyard, he finds his horse saddled, with his lance and his shield at its side. When he crosses the drawbridge, it rises abruptly and nearly knocks him off.

In the course of new adventures, Perceval learns from a newly discovered cousin that he should have asked the wounded Fisher

King about the bleeding lance and the grail. The boy's question would have cured his host and broken the spell that lay heavy on his kingdom. Perceval's cousin also tells him that his mother died of grief after his departure. This news so stuns Perceval that, in a sort of revelation, he guesses his own name, which until that moment he has not known.

Perceval continues his wandering life and is victor in a combat to avenge a lady's honor. One day, when the ground is covered with snow, a wild goose that has been wounded by a falcon lets three drops of its blood fall upon the snow. This contrast reminds Perceval of the fair complexion and vermilion lips of his beloved. He is lost in a sweet reverie when the knights of King Arthur, whose court is camped not far from there, discover the boy. One of them, Gauvain, who is Arthur's nephew, distracts Perceval from his contemplation and manages to bring him to the king. Arthur has been distressed at not having asked his late visitor's identity. Since then, the king has ceaselessly moved about with his court in the hope of finding the unknown visitor whose great feats have been reported to him.

But now a "hideous damsel" riding a mule appears before the assembled lords and ladies. She insults Perceval and rebukes him for his silence at the Castle of the Grail. He is, she says, responsible for the king's sufferings, which could have been ended by Perceval's questions, and he is responsible also for the ruin and sterility of the country. The hideous damsel then enumerates noble exploits that might tempt knights. Gauvain chooses one such exploit, and his adventures are described in a long narrative.

By the time Gauvain returns to Perceval, five years have passed. Perceval has transcended countless ordeals but has not found the Castle of the Grail. Little by little, he has lost his memory and has even forgotten God. One Good Friday, he rides out fully armed, for which a group of penitents reproach him. On their advice, he goes to the hut of a hermit, there to repent. The hermit reveals that he is Perceval's uncle, brother to his mother and to the unseen person served by the Grail. The latter is an ascetic whose emaciated body has attained so spiritual a nature that a host in the Grail suffices to keep him alive. This personage is also the father of the Fisher King, who is thus Perceval's cousin. Chrétien leaves his hero with the hermit and returns to Gauvain's adventures.

As I have said, death prevented the author from completing his work, and we do not know how he planned to continue with the quest for the Grail.

Thus it is that, from the early years of the thirteenth century, other writers tried to continue the story; some of them may even have been guided by an outline left by Chrétien. There are the Gauvain Continuation and the Perceval Continuation, each named after its protagonist; the Manessier Continuation, named after its presumed author; and the Fourth Continuation, attributed to Gerbert de Montreuil. The Manessier version contains certain Christian themes that probably go back to a large cycle of poems written about 1215 by Robert de Boron, a Franche-Comté nobleman who lived in England. According to him, the Grail is nothing other than the bowl from which Jesus ate the lamb at the Last Supper, and in which, according to the supposedly apocryphal Gospel of Nicodemus, Joseph of Arimathea gathered the blood of the Crucified. Likewise, the bleeding lance was the one used by Longinus to deal the fatal blow to the Savior. Supposedly, Joseph brought the Grail to England, where his descendants always guarded it. The Fisher King is the latest descendant, but since Robert de Boron makes him Perceval's grandfather, the boy is heir to the Throne of the Grail. It is likely that this plot, no trace of which is to be found in Chrétien, was obtained by Robert de Boron from the English abbey of Glastonbury, which was eager to provide glorious forebears for the Plantagenet dynasty (in 1191, it was believed they had discovered the tombs of King Arthur and Queen Guinevere at Glastonbury). The abbey also wanted to supply England with Christian antiquities as venerable as the ones in which the Capetian kings of France gloried for the great ritual of their coronations.

In any case, an enormous contemporary and later literature tried to synthesize all the elements or to reinterpret them according to need: for example, the *Perlesvaus*, composed in England about 1205, in the Franco-Picard dialect; the *Elucidation* and the *Bliocadran*, anonymous prologues to Chrétien's work, written after his death; the Prose *Lancelot*, the *Grand Saint Grail*, and the *Histoire du Saint Grail*. To these must be added the Welsh *Peredur* and, from the fourteenth century, English, Italian, Spanish, Portuguese, and Scandinavian versions.

However, it was in Germany and the German part of Switzerland that Chrétien's work had its greatest effect, as shown by Wolfram von Eschenbach's *Parzival* (dating at least from the start of the thirteenth century) and his unfinished *Titurel*; by the later poem *Diu Crône*, by Heinrich von dem Türlîn, and the poems by Ulrich von Zatzikoven and Wirt von Gravenberg. Wolfram was a familiar figure to Wagner, who made him a character in *Tannhäuser*, found the theme for *Lohengrin* in the last few pages of his *Parzival*, and considered having the hero of the quest for the Grail appear in *Tristan und Isolde*. During the forty years between Wagner's first idea for *Parsifal* and its realization, he was continually haunted by Wolfram's epic.

Wagner himself would, no doubt, have vigorously protested this statement, if we are to believe what Cosima wrote in her *Journal* for Friday, 20 June 1879:

> The lengthy linking of R.'s work to W[olfram]'s *Parzival* he describes as pedantic, saying his text has in fact no connection with it; when he read the epic, he first said to himself that nothing could be done with it, "but a few things stuck in my mind—the Good Friday, the wild appearance of Condrie. That is all it was." [Wagner 1980, p. 327]

Two years later, on Friday, 17 June 1881, Cosima says that "a letter from a man in Duisburg, wanting to link a study of *Parsifal* to a review of Wolfram's *Parzival*, irritates R. He says, I could just as well have been influenced by my nurse's bedtime story" (p. 677).

It would be too easy to ascribe these denials to Wagner's pride. His solution to the problem posed by the mythology of the Grail is powerfully original, as I will try to show; and there is nothing astonishing about the fact that he was aware of his originality. The point that Wagner contested, according to Cosima, however, was that a cause-and-effect relationship existed between Wolfram and him—even though Wagner had intuitively grasped a scheme that he rethought, reorganized, and transformed in the course of time. In other words, an absent or a secondary relationship on the syntactical axis can nonetheless appear on the paradigmatic axis. In this case, the system of differences is the one most appropriate for elucidating the reality and the nature of the relationship between the two paradigms. The question arises first in regard to the subject of Chrétien and Wagner's versions.

There is no doubt that Wolfram was familiar with Chrétien's work, following it step by step and often content simply to translate it (not without making mistakes); Wolfram even admits doing so several times. His poem bristles with French words and names, beginning with the hero's name. Thus, we can rule out the fantastic etymology of *fal* and *parsi*, falsely derived from the Arabic, which Wagner got from Joseph von Görres, a German author of the early nineteenth century. Parzival is Perceval: he who "pierces the mystery of the valley" (French, *val*) where the Castle of the Grail is hidden.

But Wolfram's narrative also diverges in many ways. At the beginning, he dwells at length on the lives of the hero's parents, Gahmuret and Herzeleoyde. He gives Gahmuret a previous marriage to a pagan queen, who has borne him a son with a black-and-white skin (he reappears at the end of the story). Most important of all, after Parzival's sojourn with the hermit (who is named Trevrizent here), Wolfram, like Chrétien, takes up the tale of Gauvain's adventures but then returns to Parzival. The hero arrives at the Castle of the Grail, asks the prescribed question, cures Anfortas, and succeeds him as king of the Grail with, at his side, his wife Condwiramurs and their two sons.

Finally, from Chrétien to Wolfram, the nature of the Grail changes radically. For Chrétien, the word *grail* designates a golden vessel containing a host which is the sole nourishment for an unseen and mysterious person resting in an adjacent room. Wolfram lets us see this person and identifies him as Titurel, father of the dead Frimutel, who is himself the father of Anfortas. As for the Grail, it is no longer a receptacle but a stone, a sacred object that Wolfram enigmatically calls *lapsît exillis;* and every Good Friday, a dove flies down from heaven to leave a host in it and sustain its magic qualities. For the Grail produces all the cooked dishes and drinks that the butler orders when the guests ask for them. Furthermore, the Grail cures the sick and keeps those who contemplate it eternally young. It also bears in fleeting inscriptions the ancestry and name of each person it summons to serve it.

This magic stone, whose name has been interpreted as deriving from that of the philosophers' stone, *lapsis elixir,* was originally in the sky, among the stars. Angels brought it down to earth and placed it in Titurel's keeping. Should we therefore, following an ingenious notion, correct Wolfram's obscure expression to read *lapsit ex illis,* a contraction of *lapis lapsus ex illis,* "stone fallen from them" (the stars)?

Thus, Wolfram knew and utilized other sources than Chrétien. He openly cites one—a Provençal poet named Kyot (the germanification of the French name Guyot, which is not a southern name). There are no traces of this poet, and some scholars feel that Wolfram invented him out of whole cloth. Other, more cautious scholars advance several arguments. On the one hand, Wolfram identifies the knights of the Grail with the Templars, a French order; on the other hand, he makes Gahmuret a prince of Anjou and glorifies the House of Anjou in a very strange manner for a German poet. Finally, Wolfram's epic contains elements not found in his French model: Christian ones as well as many that seem to be non-Christian or, more precisely, Judeo-Arabic in origin. One such element is the reference to a man named Flegetanis, to whom Wolfram attributes this twofold lineage: he is supposedly the author of the first history of the Grail, which the mysterious Kyot would have known; and on the basis of which Kyot composed his own work, which, in turn, Wolfram says he employed to correct mistakes in Chrétien de Troyes. The exegetes who attribute an Oriental origin to the story of the Grail draw their best arguments from Wolfram's narrative.

What did Wagner find in Wolfram? And what did he change in or add to the work of his great forerunner? One only has to read them both together to see that the composer was imbued with the strange half-Christian, half-Oriental atmosphere that I have just mentioned. Wagner, however, accentuated the contrast that was present in Wolfram. Wagner makes Kundry, a simple messenger of the Grail, a reincarnation of Herodias who, because she laughed at the Savior's suffering, is doomed to wander perpetually until His return. Wagner also diverges from Wolfram by going back to the Christian conception of the Grail as found in Robert de Boron:

The hallowed vessel
from which the Savior drank at the Last Supper of love,
into which, from the cross, flowed His divine blood.

(*Daraus er trank beim letzten Liebesmahle,*
das Weihgefäss, die heilig edle Schale,
darein am Kreuz sein göttlich Blut auch floss.)

As Wagner describes them, the ceremonies of the Grail simultaneously reproduce the Last Supper, the liturgy of the Catholic mass, and the miracle of the loaves and fishes. Yet this exemplary Christian sacrifice takes place on the frontier between two worlds, at the borders of Araby, where Kundry seeks a balm to mitigate the sufferings of Amfortas, near the maleficent dwelling of the magician Klingsor: another Venusberg, likewise dedicated to the celebration of pagan mysteries.

The scene of the Good Friday spell in *Parsifal* is closely related to other Wagnerian scenes: the murmuring forest in *Siegfried*, and the quintet in the last act of *Die Meistersinger*. In all three cases, there is a special moment when action is suspended; it is a moment of appeasement and universal reconciliation before the young hero moves forward to receive his consecration. This is a basic pattern in Richard Wagner's thought and work; but, curiously enough, the model can be found in Wolfram, who develops this episode and gives it a far more distinctive poetic coloring than Chrétien did. From Wolfram, Wagner also borrowed the name of the magician, Clinschor (Klingsor in Wagner), which must have been very popular in the thirteenth century, for it has an important place in an epic of that period, *Der Wartburgkrieg*. Actually, Wolfram involves the magician in the adventures of Gawan, not of Parzival. Klingsor is the lord of an enchanted castle, where he imprisons ladies and damsels; in an observatory at the top of the castle, a column polished like a mirror reflects everything that happens within a radius of six leagues. Klingsor is castrated in both Wolfram and Wagner—not by his own doing but by the hand of a betrayed husband seeking vengeance. Wagner also took some other personal names from Wolfram: Gurnemanz (Chrétien's Gornemant), and Kundry, Titurel, Amfortas (Anfortas in Wolfram; derived, no doubt, from the Latin *infirmitas*, "weakness"), all of whom were nameless in Chrétien.

At the same time, Wagner condensed and utterly simplified Wolfram's tale, often switching various aspects. There is the episode of the wounded bird whose three drops of blood on the snow remind Wolfram's hero of his wife's complexion and vermilion lips. Married and the father of two boys, he is not yet the chaste figure that he becomes in later versions, especially when he is confused with Galahad. On this point, Wagner follows the later versions; but rather than omitting the episode of the bird, he turns it into the story of the wounded swan. Likewise, he combines in one person Gurnemanz and the hermit Trevizrent. In both Chrétien and Wolfram, Gurnemanz welcomes the hero after his visit to Arthur's court and trains him to become a knight. Wolfram also makes him the father of a ravishing daughter, Liaze, who is Parzival's first love. Aside from this detail, Wagner's Gurnemanz plays—in the first act—the role assigned by the old authors to his namesake and—in the last—the role of the hermit.

Now let us look at the Flower Maidens. While they do not figure in the old versions of the story of the Grail, the Arthurian romances do take Perceval and Gawain to several enchanted castles inhabited by seductive maidens. Closer to the Wagnerian home, the *Elucidation*, a later prologue to Chrétien's work, explains the origin of the curse inflicted on the Kingdom of the Grail as the result of the rape of some hospitable fairies by a prince and his companions. Nevertheless, Wagner seems to have been inspired more by Buddhist legends, especially one where the Sage, meditating at the foot of a tree, resists the seductive advances of the daughters of the demon of evil, and arrows shot by the demon turn into flowers. About 1856, Wagner sketched a Buddhist drama, *The Victors*, which he abandoned and replaced with *Parsifal*. In the earlier plot, the chaste Ananda, Buddha's favorite disciple, resists a temptress who, guilty of mockery in an earlier life, achieves salvation by renouncing sensual love.

After reading this text in the program at Bayreuth, Jean Mistler, Secrétaire perpétuel de l'Académie française and an eminent Wagnerian, was kind enough to call my attention to the *Roman d'Alexandre*, a French work of the early twelfth century. And, indeed, it seems likely that Wagner took the episode of the Flower Maidens from that source. Among other adventures, Alexander manages to get into a forest whose entrance is guarded by genies. Here, he discovers ravishing damsels, each of whom is installed at the foot of a tree and is lavish with her charms; however, these damsels cannot leave the forest lest they perish. When Alexander asks his guides about this mystery, he learns that these maidens go underground in the winter. With the return of fine weather, they spring up and blossom: "And when the flower opens, the midmost bud becomes the body, and the tiny leaves around it become her garment" (Venice version, §368, v. 6165-6167, in La Du; cf. Paris version, §200, v. 3531-3534, in Armstrong).

Around 1850, when Wagner was beginning to think about *Parsifal*, the *Roman d'Alexandre* was, if I may say so, very much in the news in Germany. The first publication of the French version, by H. V. Michelant, appeared in Stuttgart in 1846. In 1850, H. Weissman brought out the German version adapted by Lamprecht in the twelfth century from the first French text (which had been almost entirely lost ever since). After these two works were published, numerous scholarly studies appeared in the journal *Germania*. Nevertheless, while both the French and the German versions contained the episode of the flower maidens, it is completely absent from the Greek and Latin sources used by the authors of this romance. As other considerations indicate, the very spirit of this motif points to the Orient—a thesis supported by Alexander von Humboldt (Meyer 1886, p. 182).

We recognize the figure of Kundry, who is nameless in Chrétien de Troyes. Wolfram gives her a name but preserves her repulsive looks and her role as messenger of the Grail: "She had a nose like a dog's and two boar's teeth stuck out from her mouth. . . . Cundrie had ears like a bear's . . . and the hands of this charming dear looked like a monkey's skin. Her fingernails ... stuck out like a lion's claws" (Eschenbach 1961, pp. 169-70). Yet at the same time, this maiden is "learned" and is dressed superbly. There is a second Cundrie in Wolfram's epic, and this one is ravishingly beautiful. We may therefore ask whether Wagner, by making Kundry a double creature, was not unconsciously going back to a very ancient tradition, of which only a vestige survives in Wolfram. Celtic literature sometimes describes an old, repulsive hag who offers herself to the hero and then, when he accepts her, turns into a radiant beauty—an image, we are told, of the sovereignty that a pretender to the throne must win.

Furthermore, in order to construct the character of Kundry, Wagner blended into one four heroines of Chrétien and Wolfram: the "hideous damsel" already mentioned; the Maiden-who-never-laughs, except to tell Perceval of his promised destiny; the cousin who tells him that his mother is dead and who, in Wolfram, is the first to call him by his name; and the "wicked maiden," whom Chrétien calls the Orgueilleuse de Logres ("Haughty Woman of Logres"), and Wolfram, following him, Orgeluse. According to Wolfram, this latter figure is indirectly responsible for the treacherous blow that strikes Anfortas down and (through a misreading of Chrétien's text) costs him his virility.

Let us go off on a tangent here. When, in ancient Arthurian literature, a hero (or heroes) manages, after enduring a thousand ordeals, to enter enchanted castles (the Castle of the Grail or the Castle of Wonders, where the magician Clinschor, a descendant of the poet Virgil, reigns over a phantom people), he is actually passing into "another world," perhaps even the abode of the dead. It is thus understandable that the messenger of the Grail, who alone is privileged to circulate between the supernatural and the terrestrial worlds, has a twofold nature and a changing appearance. She is a radiant beauty when she comes from the other world, and a hideous witch when she embodies the temporary curse that weighs upon her.

This opposition explains the motif of the necessary question, which we know to be important in the ancient versions of the Grail story. A spell has disrupted communication between those two worlds, which are distinct—although for the Celtic mind, it is possible to pass from one to the other. Since that break in communication, King Arthur's court, which represents the terrestrial world, has been on the move constantly, waiting for news. In fact, King Arthur never holds court until someone has announced an event to him. Thus, this terrestrial court is in quest of answers to questions that are perpetually posed by its anxious agitation. In symmetrical fashion, the court of the Grail, whose immobility is symbolized by the paralysis of the king's lower limbs, offers, likewise perpetually, an answer to questions that no one asks it.

In this sense, we can say that there exists a model, which may be universal, of "Percevalian" myths. It is the reverse of another, equally universal model—that of the "Oedipal" myths, whose problematic structure is symmetrical though inverted. For the Oedipal myths pose the problem of a communication that is at first exceptionally effective (the solving of the riddle), but then leads to excess in the form of incest —the sexual union of people who ought to be distant from one another —and of plague, which ravages Thebes by accelerating and disrupting the great natural cycles. On the other hand, the Percevalian myths deal with communication interrupted in three ways: the answer offered to an unasked question (which is the opposite of a riddle); the chastity required of one or more heroes (contrary to incestuous behavior); and the wasteland—that is, the halting of the natural cycles that ensure the fertility of plants, animals, and human beings.

As we know, Wagner rejected the motif of the unasked question and replaced it with a motif that somewhat reverses it while performing the same function. Communication is assured or re-established not by an intellectual operation but by an emotional identification. Parsifal does not *understand* the riddle of the Grail and remains unable to solve it until he *relives* the catastrophe at its source. This catastrophe was a rupture; and because the hero feels it in his flesh, the rupture is located no longer only between the natural and the supernatural worlds, but now between the emotions and the intelligence, between suffering humanity and the other forms of life, between earthly and spiritual values. Thus, through Schopenhauer, Wagner joins Jean-Jacques Rousseau, who was the first to see in compassion and identification with others an original mode of communication, predating social life and articulate speech—a mode capable of uniting human beings with one another and with all other forms of life.

But it was Wolfram who had already revealed to Wagner this audacious route, which replaces a sociological and cosmological problem with an ethical and metaphysical one. Not only because of the broad ethical and philosophical scope within which Wolfram sets his hero's adventures (far broader than Chrétien de Troyes), but also for an apparently minor reason: the question that is asked in order to break the spell has to differ in Wolfram and Chrétien, because of their distinctly different conceptions of the Grail. To ask a magic stone—one that dispenses various drinks and cooked food, like the snack machines we see in public places—"whom it serves" would be absurd: it serves everyone who is present. Hence, the nature of the question must change. In Wolfram, the question concerns only Anfortas: once Parsifal has overcome doubt, the corrupter of the soul, and has expiated this supreme sin through humiliation and repentance, he decides to ask, "Good uncle, what is your illness?" In other words, the question takes an ethical turn, assuming a sense of charity and the willingness to participate in someone else's misfortune. One could pay no better tribute to the Minnesinger than by recognizing him as the author of a profound evolution: a story still very close to the myths from which it derived was transformed into a truly ethical reflection.

But Wagner went even farther. In dealing with the old myths latent in the stories of the Grail, he simultaneously surpassed, reshaped, and integrated them. He produced a synthesis that retains their flavor as myths, making his *Parsifal* an original variant, alongside all those fashioned over the centuries on the basis of primal material lost in the mists of time. In Wagner, indeed, there is no King Arthur's court; and hence the issue is not the resurrection of communication between the earthly world—represented by this court—and the beyond. The Wagnerian drama unfolds entirely between the kingdoms of the Grail and of Klingsor: two worlds, of which one was, and will again be, endowed with all virtues; while the other is vile and must be destroyed. There is, hence, no question of restoring or even establishing any mediation between them. By the annihilation of the one and the restoration of the other, the latter alone must endure and establish itself as a world of mediation.

Now in the old traditions (that is, in Chrétien, in his continuators, in Robert de Boron, or in Wolfram), these two worlds are not the opposite realms of here below and the beyond but are two aspects, sometimes distinct and sometimes mingled, of the world beyond. Consequently, in Wagner, alternate images become simultaneous images, which are, however, diametrically opposed.

In what way are they opposites? I supplied the answer in bringing to light the relationship between the Oedipal and the Percevalian myths. These two types, as I said, illustrate the two complementary solutions that human beings have devised for two problems of communication. One problem is excessive communication, too direct, too rapid, and therefore fatally virulent; the other problem is an overly slow, if not interrupted communication, which causes inertia and sterility. Wagner's genius anticipated by a good century the synthesis of universal myths that no one had ever before dreamed of connecting. Klingsor's is an Oedipal world because of the quasi incestuous climate in which the private meeting between Parsifal and Kundry takes place. Kundry hopes to seduce him by identifying herself with his mother:

> With the last kiss of your mother; receive
> the first kiss of love.

> (*Als Muttersegens letzten Gruss—*
> *der Liebe—ersten Kuss.*)

Kundry then even asks Parsifal to embrace her as his father, Gamuret, once embraced Herzeleide:

> Learn thus to know this love
> that once enclosed Gamuret
> when Herzeleide's ardor
> flooded him with flames.

> (*Die Liebe—lerne kennen*
> *die Gamurel umschloss*
> *also Herzeleids Entbrennen*
> *ihn sengend überfloss.*)

Klingsor's world is also one of accelerated communication: magic instruments help him to see across great distances. The Flower Maidens, who combine two natural realms, are living illustrations of lechery and luxuriance, and the chromatics of the music expresses their unhealthy heat and accompanies their excesses. Finally, Kundry—both herself and another, present and past, mother and temptress, under the double aspect of Jocasta and Sphinx—embodies a riddle that only Parsifal can solve.

To this world of debauchery and unbridled communication, that of Amfortas opposes an image of frozen communication; this world is ruled by an impotent monarch, who is incapable of performing his office; here, plants, beasts, and men perish, and an answer is offered in vain to a question that no one thinks of asking. Mediation between these two worlds is nullified because of excess in the one and a lack in the other; and their poles are marked by the *laughter* of Herodias at Christ's sufferings and the *silence* of the Grail visitors at Amfortas's suffering. Thus, the problem, in mythological terms, would be to establish an equilibrium between the two opposite worlds. To do so, one should probably, like Parsifal, go into and come out of the one world and be excluded from and re-enter the other world. Above all, however (and this is Wagner's contribution to universal mythology), one must know and not know. In other words, one must know what one does not know, *Durch Mitleid wissend* ("knowing through compassion")—not through an act of communication but through a surge of pity, which provides mythical thinking with a way out of the dilemma in which its long unrecognized intellectualism has risked imprisoning it.

Chapter 18

A Note on the Tetralogy

IN 1978, Toronto University Press published, under the title of *Myth and Meaning*, a series of five radio talks that I had been reckless or weak enough to give in English as part of the Massey Lectures of the Canadian Broadcasting Corporation. Once again, I was forced to realize how poor my English was, and knew I was incapable of improving the text afterward—disgusted as I am even by my broadcasts in French. I was therefore somewhat distracted when I looked at the transcription. Unfortunately, in regard to Wagner, I made a slip of the tongue (substituting Hagen for Gunther [p. 49]), which destroyed my whole line of reasoning. I am grateful to Professor J. J. Nattiez for subsequently drawing this error to my attention.

The preceding chapter deals essentially with Wagner. It gives me a chance to correct my mistake and, above all, to explain what I meant to say—this time more effectively than before, when I was inhibited by fatigue and by the nervous tension of talking in a foreign language while a tape rolled imperturbably inside a recorder.

I wish to illustrate how Western music, in the eighteenth and nineteenth centuries taking over the functions of myth, resorted to analogous processes in order to achieve the same ends—a phenomenon that, as we know, finds its full expression in Wagner. Needless to say, in order to analyze the transformations of a motif, I shall focus purely on the semantic aspect. Others, more competent than I, can describe and analyze the melodic, tonal, rhythmic, or harmonic transformations that enrich all the supplementary dimensions of the whole.

In Wagner's tetralogy *Der Ring des Nibelungen*, the so-called "love-renunciation" motif appears some twenty times. I will disregard the cases in which the motif says exactly what it means at the moment of an event, or when an event is being recalled, or even in new circumstances that can nevertheless be compared umambiguously to earlier ones (as when, in *Die Walküre*, Wotan renounces his paternal affection for Siegmund and then the filial love with which Brünnhilde has overwhelmed him).

Not all instances are so clear. Sometimes, the recurrence of a motif connects different, not obviously related episodes by pointing out hidden parallels or oppositions that nevertheless underlie the plot. Thus, in *Das Rheingold*, without the first two recurrences of the motif in scene 2, one might overlook that the action is impelled not by one but by two renunciations of love, which are rigorously dependent on each other. Alberich renounces love in order to become the master of the gold; while Wotan renounces (or pretends to renounce—a matter to which I will return) Freia, the goddess in charge of love, in order to obtain Walhalla, a means of power as gold is. For this renuncation Fricka, his wife, reproaches him bitterly. These two acts of renunciation, which are also contracts of exchange, belong to sets of transformations whose invariant structure is signaled by the return of the motif, even though at this stage, each set is illustrated by only one of its several states.

Alberich renounces complete love, which he cannot obtain "by force," but from which he separates physical pleasure, which he can obtain "by trickery." He thus foresees (and he will come back to this in the third scene) that he will seduce Grimhilde with the gold as bait. If complete love forms a whole, Alberich will thus give up only a part of it: his renunciation is synecdochic. In contrast, Wotan renounces not the realities of love (he boasts about his adventures to Fricka) but its metaphorical figure as represented by Freia, who, according to Nordic myth, is the patron of carnal appetite and sensuality—the very aspect of complete love that Alberich does not renounce. And while Alberich reserves this part, the only part he can obtain by trickery, Wotan's renunciation is itself a trick; for despite his promises, he has no intention of handing Freia over to the giants.

Likewise, in *Die Walküre*, act II, scene 2, the return of the musical motif emphasizes that there is both correlation and opposition between the failure of Wotan, who has relied on love to produce a free person, and the success of Alberich, who, by a loveless union, has produced a being subjected to his will. Siegmund and Hagen are thus symmetrical, each the exact reverse of the other. This relationship has a major consequence. Siegmund prefigures Siegfried as a failed attempt; and Hagen has next to him—if not a failed attempt, then at least a pale reflection—the irresolute Gunther, who lets himself be passively led and never completes anything he starts. Altogether, we thus have two sets of three elements: on the one side, Wotan, Siegmund, and Siegfried; and on the other, Alberich, Hagen, and Gunther.

Now, from the beginning of *Siegfried* (act I, scene 2), we know that Wotan as Licht-Alberich corresponds to Alberich as Schwarz-Alberich. We have just seen that the same is true of Siegmund, Wotan's deficient son, and for Hagen, Alberich's effective son. Hence, the two remaining elements, represented by Siegfried and Gunther, must correspond to one another as well—a relationship that will be realized in *Die Götterdämmerung*.

By its recurrence, the motif not only makes perceptible two systems of correspondence but induces us to see them as parallel to one another and to reach a deeper level of meaning from which arise the partial meanings revealed by each system. The problem posed by *Das Rheingold*, and that the three subsequent operas will seek to resolve, is that of the conflict between contradictory demands of the social order which, in any conceivable community, prohibit receiving without giving. The spirit of the laws, as engraved by Wotan on his lance, is that always, even among the gods, and certainly among men, one will get nothing for nothing.

It takes a counterpoint between poem and music to make this formulation explicit. How else can we explain why the renunciation motif accompanies Siegmund when he tears the sword out of the tree and conquers Sieglinde's love? At this extremely dramatic moment, the action seems to belie the message that the musical theme is supposed to express: by means of Wotan's artifice, Siegmund will possess at the same time power and love (as in Wotan's second scenario, which is also doomed to fail, Siegfried will obtain both the power of the ring and Brünnhilde's love). But, justly, the menacing return of the motif contradicts the event as it is unfolding, and reveals the fatal outcome behind the apparent triumph. As though to emphasize this contradiction even more forcefully, antitheses and contrasts come tumbling out of Siegmund's mouth: *Minne / Liebe, Heiligste / Not, sehnende / sehrende, Tat / Tod,* * and so on. These semantic and phonetic oscillations merely attest that even when one believes one has the two things, one cannot

*The literal translation is: "Love/Beloved, most holy/danger, yearning/harming, deed/death." Both *Minne* and *Liebe* mean "love," the former in the courtly, archaic sense, and the latter in the modern use. (Ed.)

hold on to both of them—the unvarying element throughout the plot.

If this interpretation, to which the recurrent musical theme has been a clue, is correct, then there are two consequences. First of all, there is a homologous relationship among several "treasures" that must be wrested from their guardian—creators or holders. These treasures are means to different kinds of power: the gold for forging the ring; Walhalla, where gods marshal an army of warriors to fight for them; the sword; and Brünnhilde herself, who, as she explains in *Die Götterdämmerung* (act II, scene 5), has relinquished her power in favor of Siegfried. Hence, the cycle can end only, in the final scene, with the identification of the first term and the last: the ring and Brünnhilde complete their destiny together.

Secondly, if the central problem of the Tetralogy is that of exchange and its law—a law all the more ineluctable in that it is imposed on the gods even before it is imposed on men—one can expect to find this law formulated in the code of kinship and marriage. This code allows for the connection of nature and culture and gives its rules to society. A brother and a sister, who are also twins—Siegmund and Sieglinde—are united in incest. They thus form a pair of siblings in correlation with and in opposition to another pair: Gunther and Gutrune, likewise brother and sister, but exogamous: their entire problem is to find someone else to marry. It is doubtless no coincidence that the name Gutrune ("good rune," as Siegfried himself remarks) can be freely translated as "good law."

More puzzling, at first sight, is the union of Siegfried and Brünnhilde because of their kinship tie (she is the half-sister of his parents). But the two of them know better: in her very first words, Brünnhilde assumes the position of "supermother" (as we say "superman"). She has, she says, watched over Siegfried even before he was conceived, and protected him since his birth. As for Siegfried, since his discovery of Brünnhilde, he thinks only of his mother and even believes that he can find her in Brünnhilde. Henceforth, there will be nothing but confusion between endogamy and exogamy, between power and love—a confusion illustrated by the bizarre and seemingly incoherent plot of *Die Götterdämmerung*. Aside from mistakes, the renunciation motif, absent from *Siegfried*, recurs only once in *Die Götterdämmerung*: when Brünnhilde, in her dialogue with Waltraute, refuses to exchange the ring for the salvation of Walhalla, which is the opposite of what Wotan did at the opening of the Tetralogy. But then, Wotan saw the ring purely as an instrument of power; while for Brünnhilde, it is merely a token of love. This ring, whose nature is understood only by Hagen, has been circulating among representatives of all cosmic levels: from the Rhine daughters (water) to Alberich (underworld), from Alberich to Wotan (heaven), from Wotan to the giants (earth). But once fallen into Siegfried's hands, it merely turns around (if I may put it thus) between him and Brünnhilde: he gives it to her, takes it back, and she recovers it. Now, departing from endogamy and incest would mean returning the ring to the Rhine (which no one cares to do) and also handing Brünnhilde over to some Gunther or other. By yielding to Brünnhilde's entreaty, Wotan paradoxically makes the same mistake as when yielding to Fricka's demands; the circle of flames in which he encloses the Valkyrie, and which only Siegfried can cross, is also the circle of incest. In the same sense, Gunther and Siegfried represent alternate solutions to the same problem.

This series of confusions, which only get worse as they pile up on one another, can have no other outcome than a cosmic collapse. The treasure wrested from the water returns to the water; the treasure wrested from the fire returns to the fire; the two elements are united on stage. Ultimately, nothing has happened, since the Tetralogy has vainly attempted to achieve impossible reconciliations between terms that a more than human law keeps apart. Once this has been established, human history can truly begin and, replacing the divine saga, will consecrate the success of the supreme exchange of the world of necessity for that of contingency—to which Wotan, unable to ensure the undisputed fruition of either world, is finally resigned.

PART V

CONSTRAINT

AND FREEDOM

Rien ne peut nous consoler, lorsque nous y pensons de près.

PASCAL

Pensées

Chapter 19

A Meditative Painter

IN INSISTING, in the conclusion of a recent book, *The Naked Man* (1981, pp. 625-30), on the passivity and the receptivity of the *author*—whose mind, when at work, is an anonymous place for organizing what can only be called "things" that come from without; so that the self, excluded from the very beginning by that work, seems rather an executor—I had without realizing taken up an idea that Max Ernst had once emphatically expressed. As early as 1934 indeed, he was denouncing what he called the "creative power of the artist." The author, he went on, has only a passive role in the mechanism of poetic creation and can act as spectator to the birth of what others will call his "work." Actually, his work is simply the bringing to light of "lucky finds that have not been falsified," and that emanate from an inexhaustible reserve of images buried in the subconscious.

This convergence has led me to think about the profound reasons that, out of all the modern forms of painting, I am particularly attracted to those of Max Ernst. Does some analogy exist between what I have attempted to do in my books, a long time after him, and the role he always assigned to painting? Like his paintings and collages, my work on mythology has been elaborated by means of samples from without—the myths themselves. I have cut them out like so many pictures in the old books where I found them, and then arranged them on the pages as they arranged themselves in my mind, but in no conscious or deliberate fashion. The structuralist method, as we know, operates by presenting and systematically working out binary oppositions between elements supplied by observation—the phonemes of the linguists or the mythemes of the anthropologist. The method is easily recognized in Max Ernst's definition of 1934, where he extols "the bringing together of two or more elements apparently opposite in nature, on a level whose nature is the opposite of theirs." This is a double play of opposition and correlation, on the one hand, between a complex figure and the background that shows it off or, on the other, between the constituent elements of the figure itself.

It therefore appears significant that Max Ernst chose to illustrate his precept with the famous "chance encounter of a sewing machine and an umbrella on a dissecting table." Who could fail to see that this scene is renowned because it gathers together three objects whose encounter, contrary to what the poet says, is anything but random except in terms of everyday experience? After all, as Ernst makes a point of telling us, their mutual strangeness is a matter of appearance. It would be shocking to find manufactured articles on a dissecting table, instead of the living or dead organisms that it is normally meant to bear, only if this unexpected substitution of cultural works for natural objects did not imply a secret invitation: the simultaneous presence, on this particular kind of table, of these two unexpected objects (which, however, can also "fall ill" and must sometimes be repaired) tends to dissipate the incongruity of their togetherness, precisely by *dissecting* them and by dissecting their relationship to one another.

The association of the two instruments suggests, first of all, that they are named, in parallel fashion, for their inherent purposes: the one "to sew" (*à coudre*, from *machine à coudre*) and the other "for rain" (*à pluie*, from *parapluie*). But this is a false parallel, no doubt, since the second *a* of *parapluie* is not a preposition but an integral part of a morpheme. Nevertheless, it puts us on the trail of a whole system where resemblances and differences correspond: the machine is made *for* sewing, the other device is *against* rain; the machine acts upon material and transforms it, the umbrella offers passive resistance to it. Both articles have a point: the point of the umbrella ensures its protection or, as an ornament, tops off a soft, gently rounded dome, elastic to the touch; the point of the sewing machine is sharp and aggressive and attached to the lower extremity of an angular arm where it bends down. A sewing machine is an orderly arrangement of solid pieces, the hardest of which, the needle, has the function of piercing cloth. The umbrella, in contrast, is covered with a material that cannot be pierced by liquid particles in disorder: rain.

Although there is, at first, no conceivable solution, the equation

$$\frac{sewing\ machine\ +\ umbrella}{dissection\ table} = 1$$

works out when the unexpected juxtaposition of two objects is strongly justified by the fact that they themselves are juxtaposed with a third object. For the latter furnishes the key for analyzing their concept. Totally distinct, the two objects are then transformed into reverse metaphors which, through intuition, give rise to—to pursue Max Ernst's 1934 text—"the joy that one feels at every successful metamorphosis . . . (and which corresponds) to the age-old need of the intellect."

In specifying the nature of this need, Max Ernst anticipated certain ideas of Maurice Merleau-Ponty,* as both view painting as successful when it crosses the boundary between the outer and the inner worlds, providing access to the intermediary zone (the *mundus imaginalis* of ancient Iranian philosophy, as described by Henry Corbin [1972, passim]), where, writes Max Ernst, "the artist evolves freely, boldly, and completely spontaneously." The line of junction thereby turns out to be more real than the physical and the mental parts, which philosophical tradition and ordinary common sense have dedicated it to unite.

However, in Max Ernst, this freedom and spontaneity are states that the artist must first win. In 1933, Ernst (1937) defines the processes he employs—rubbing (*frottage*) and scraping (*grattage*)—as so many "ways of forcing inspiration" and of "helping my meditative faculties" (1934). Patiently he thinks out his paintings and collages, and then works over them for a long time, often taking them out again to smooth away the brushstrokes and render them transparent. His work is rarely the result of a pure lyrical outburst where lines and colors are hurled onto a canvas so rapidly that, with tiny variations, it can be repeated several times in the course of a day. In the art of Max Ernst, painting remains essentially what it was from the late Middle Ages and the Renaissance until the nineteenth century, and that is where it derives all its nobility: a scrupulous labor prepared for by a period of reflection, exercise, and doubt. Rightly or wrongly, one thinks of Ernst as suffering the terrible agony that Ingres endured before starting certain portraits. There is a family resemblance between the hippogriff in *Roger délivrant Angélique* ("Roger Liberating Angelica") and the

*Maurice Merleau-Ponty (1908–61), French philosopher; his major work was *The Phenomenology of Perception* (1945). (Ed.)

raging and stamping creature that Max Ernst conceived in 1937 and ironically named *l'Ange du foyer* ("The Angel of Hearth and Home"). Did not Ingres (whom Ernst did not include in his 1941 list of "favorites") also say that one has to know how to think a long time about a painting before finally being able to execute it "with ardor and at one swoop"? And thus we are brought back to the freedom and spontaneity of which Ernst speaks.

This remote and indirect kinship with Ingres is not, I think, as apparent in the portrait of Dominique de Ménil, or in the strict, controlled draftsmanship of *A l'intérieur de la vue* ("Inside the Vision"), *La Famille est à l'origine de la famille* ("The Family is at the Origin of the Family"), or *La Belle Jardinière* ("The Beautiful Gardener"; this painting, however, made Gaëtan Picon think of the same kinship [1980]), as it is in Ernst's large-scale compositions, several of which were done between 1955 and 1965. Here, the purism of Ingres is transposed into an almost abstract register of infinitely sparkling crystalline and fibrous forms, which are drawn and painted with extreme rigor, their mysterious grace inspiring a metaphysical reverie in the spectator. This is a surprising phase in the evolution of a painter who demonstrates elsewhere a powerful sense of nature through imaginary landscapes revealing distant citadels or forests that seem about to proliferate beyond the canvas, stony piles, and molten minerals alive with eyes, mosses, and insects. The thick paint and the intense style of these paintings suggest affinities with others: with Gustave Moreau, Gustave Doré, and John Martin;* and, farther away in space, with Indian sculptors along the coast of the Pacific northwest; and, further away in time, with Dürer. Between these two extreme manifestations of Ernst's genius, one must place many others. Perhaps at a middle distance belong the paintings with which he decorated Eluard's home:† laconic statements of symbols that seemed lost, like those of the Hopi frescoes at the Awatowi site or of some other civilization as wise and enigmatic as Egypt seen by the later Greeks and, like Egypt, forever vanished. Yet these symbols remain with us, not only because of the graphic composition, but also because each one is clothed in rare, fine, and precious hues, whose choice and relations seem charged with meaning.

---

*Gustave Moreau (1826–98) was a French symbolist painter. Gustave Doré (1833–83) was a French painter with a taste for the fantastic and illustrator of many books, including the Bible, Dante's *Divine Comedy*, and *Don Quixote*. John Martin (1789–1854) was an English landscape and historical painter and creator of large visionary compositions on historical or philosophical themes. (Ed.)

†Paul Eluard (1895–1952) was a French symbolist poet and friend of Ernst's. (Ed.)

If sound and meaning, as Saussure has taught us, are the two indissociable halves of linguistic expression, then the work of Max Ernst speaks countless languages—a discourse always expressed by an unbreakable solidarity between the background chosen and the techniques of execution (which are able to take advantage of every kind of resource); by the arrangement of volumes, lines, values, and colors; by the pictorial texture; by the subject itself; and so on. As Goethe once said of the vegetable world—which has often inspired Max Ernst and which he understands so well (in his own work even more than in that of others)—all aspects in terms of which one can see a painting form a chorus whose singing "guides us toward a hidden law."

Chapter 20

To a Young Painter

A GREAT DEAL of knowledge and a great deal of freshness go into making a painter. The impressionists learned how to paint, but did what they could to forget their training—without much success, thank goodness. They managed, however, to persuade a host of imitators that knowledge is useless, that one has only to give full rein to spontaneity and, according to a formula whose fame was disastrous, "to paint as a bird sings."

Despite the marvelous works that it produced, impressionism led to an impasse, as attested by the brevity of its first phase, as well as by the reform on which Gauguin and Seurat spent themselves. But even if they too, especially Seurat, were great painters, impressionism was still too close, had too much of a grip on them to allow them to do something simple—namely, to seek a solution in returning to be humble servants of the craft. Thus, both painters were aiming far from the target, Seurat short of painting, and Gauguin beyond it. Neither the now obsolete physical theories on which Seurat wanted to base his art, nor the confused mysticism onto which Gauguin tried to hitch his work, could reliably help in reorienting a painting that had lost its way.

Was all this inevitable? We are dumbfounded to read, even today, that the invention of photography supposedly sounded the death knell for naturalistic painting. As da Vinci profoundly understood, the primary role of art is to sift and arrange the profuse information that the outer world is constantly sending out to assail the sensory organs. By omitting some data, by amplifying or reducing other data, by modulating the data that he keeps, the painter introduces into the multitude of information a coherence, which is recognized as style. Can it be said that photographers do the same thing? To do so would be to overlook the fact that the physical and mechanical constraints of the camera, the chemical constraints of the sensitive film, the subjects possible, the angle of view, and the lighting, allow the photographer only a very restricted freedom compared with the artist's practically unlimited freedom of eye and hand, as well as of the mind served by these wonderful instruments.

Impressionism gave up too quickly when it accepted the idea that the sole ambition of painting is to grasp what the theoreticians of the era called the physiognomy of things—that is, their subjective aspect —as opposed to an objectivity that aims to apprehend their nature. An artist considers haystacks subjectively when he tries to render, in a series of paintings, the transitory impressions made by those haystacks on his eye at a particular time of day, in a particular light. Yet, at the same time, he forgoes making the viewer grasp intuitively what a haystack is in and of itself. Earlier painters assumed the same tasks. They never tired of painting arrangements of folds in order to render, from the inside as it were, the countless ways in which a fabric falls depending on whether it is wool or silk, linen or felt, satin or taffeta, or whether it hangs directly on the body or is supported by garments underneath, or whether it is cut along the grain or on the bias, and so on. A painter clung, in one case, to the varied appearances of things that were always the same; and, in the other, to the objective reality of different things. Man's delight in his perception contrasts with an attitude of deference, if not of humility, toward the inexhaustible wealth of the world.

In another area and on another level, the development from impressionism to cubism by way of Cézanne repeats the adventure of Seurat and Gauguin. For it would be as ridiculous to explain cubism by non-Euclidian geometries and the theory of relativity as to explain impressionism by the physics of colors and the invention of photography. Neither art movement can be traced to external causes; on the contrary, they are linked by an internal relationship. Despite his arguments with impressionism, Seurat kept forcing each painting short of nature: between the objects themselves and the way in which they act upon a painter's or a viewer's retina. To escape the impressionist impasse, cubism tried to place itself on the other side of nature; but on the pretext of setting painting back on its feet, cubism knocked it off balance in a different way. And even if it produced a few masterpieces, it was no more durable than impressionism. What impressionism claimed to be in regard to the passing moment, trying to hold it in suspension, cubism claimed to be in regard to ongoing time. Not that (as has been said) a painter took successive views of objects: cubism tried to give a nontemporal view but, in renouncing perspective, gave a view outside of time.

Cubism was trying to do too much. By aiming beyond painting and, like Gauguin (in an entirely different category, needless to say), by assuming inordinate ambitions in both its analytical and its synthetic phase, cubism too "missed the object." Where, originally, and as an effect of shock, a painting seemed to be the instrument of a metaphysical revelation, it has fallen today to the rank of a decorative composition—and thus matters to us chiefly because it illustrates the taste of an era. Ironically enough, this is especially true of Juan Gris, the most philosophical of the cubists; but it is also true of Braque and Picasso. We will not speak about the others.

Where are we today? A crowd of painters persist in repeating the strategy of their elders by gradually aggravating its vices. Rather than laboriously restoring a body of knowledge, they glory in aiming ever further than their predecessors and, like them, shoot in diametrically opposed directions. Some painters wish to go more on this side of nature than impressionism. Having completely dissolved what little remained of representation after Monet, they are devoting themselves to a nonrepresentative dynamic of forms and colors expressing not even the painter's subjective reaction to what he sees, but an alleged lyricism of which the individual alone is the source.

Other painters take the reverse route and go even farther beyond nature than cubism. The latter had already short-circuited nature by turning away from landscape in preference for models from among the works of culture. The newer painters, if one may say so, outdo cubism in their disdain for objects or accessories that still have a touch of poetry; they ask the most sordid products of culture to furnish them with models that have remained so alien to the inspiration of painters that they no longer need even to be interpreted—or so they believe—for painting to be rejuvenated. It is enough to copy them in a manner that aims to be slavish, but that fails because of their lack of craft.

History, said Marx, repeats itself by caricaturing itself. His statement applies perfectly to the history of painting during the past hundred years. Painting has moved from crisis to crisis; and, aside from striking individual successes, it may be said that each stage of painting has reproduced increasingly excessive deviations that can be attributed to the immediately preceding stage.

Baudelaire prophetically saluted Manet as "the first in the decrepitude of his art." What, then, can a young painter do to escape the despair into which he has been pushed by everything that has happened since Manet? At present, the German painter Anita Albus (1942-) strikes me as one of the few who are trying to answer this question. For, in order to rediscover the art of painting, artists had to convince themselves of something that was stated by Alois Riegl in a text no less prophetic than Baudelaire's, even if it did not have the same meaning for its author as later events were to lend it: "The golden age of the plastic arts came to an end at the beginning of modern times; the illusionism of the Renaissance was their final spark as well as their farewell" (Riegl 1966, p. 56).

This is not the first time that, confronted with a situation judged to be critical, artists have decided to go backward and take up the task again at a point when nothing has yet compromised its progress. The example of the pre-Raphaelites comes immediately to mind. In regard to Anita Albus, it is significant that the pre-Raphaelites (as the name they adopted indicates) chose as a point of departure a period in Italian art when it received a great deal more from the painting of Northern Europe than it was to give back through Dürer, as Erwin Panofsky has shown. Furthermore, the origin of the pre-Raphaelite movement reveals a German influence: that of the Nazarenes.* To assure a return to the basic disciplines of painting—an intention expressed in the early nineteenth century by German artists (though we should not forget that, in Rome, the Nazarenes and Ingres admired one another) and, toward mid-century, by English artists—it was the northern tradition, born in Flanders in the early fifteenth century, that proved most effective. For, as Riegl says, this tradition was characterized "by an art aiming at representation and deeply anchored in the mind of the Germanic peoples" (Riegl 1966, p. 118).

Panofsky, in his turn, analyzes the particularizing spirit of the Nordic fifteenth century which

*The Nazarenes were a group of German painters in Rome who, in the early nineteenth century, aimed to restore medieval purity to Christian art. (Ed.)

could operate in two spheres, both outside of Goethe's "natural" or "noble" nature and, for this reason, complementary to each other: the spheres of the *realistic* and the *fantastic*, the domain of intimate portraiture, genre, still life, and landscape, on the one hand, and the domain of the visionary and the phantasmagoric, on the other . . . [the sphere that] lies, as it were, *before* "natural" nature; . . . [the other lying] *beyond* [it]. [Panofsky 1974, pp. 270-71]

What makes Albus's art so fascinating are the almost miraculous rediscoveries of a tradition with two aspects, which probably—and for the reasons I have indicated—only a German painter could revive. The German bestiary has been the richest and most varied since the first century of heraldry. It was in Northern Germany that plants were most often used as the chief device on escutcheons, so there was "an opposition between a Celtic and Germanic-Scandinavian heraldry that is plainly animal and a Latin heraldry that is more linear . . . an opposition that has persisted up to modern times" (Pastoureau 1979, pp. 134, 136, 158). Riegl himself noted that, in Nordic art between the eleventh and the thirteenth centuries, local vegetation gradually replaced Byzantine foliage; and he emphasized that "the basic tendency of all Germanic art is to compete with organic nature" (1966, pp. 50, 108).

How can we fail to think of Anita Albus and the passionate attention that her art pays to all aspects of reality? She gazes tenderly at living creatures—quadrupeds, birds, leaves, and flowers—her scrupulous precision rivaling that of the naturalist. However, like her forerunners of the great era, Albus does not set out simply to copy her models; she deepens our knowledge of them by capturing, with the motion of hand and brush, the surge of natural creation.

Thus, it is not surprising that, beyond the special tradition from which it comes, the art of Anita Albus shows an affinity with undertakings that, although in other climes, had comparable ambitions to her own: to place painting in the service of knowledge and to make the aesthetic emotion an effect of the coalescence—rendered instantaneous by the work—of both the perceptible and the intelligible properties of things. The art of Anita Albus is related not only to the Nordic tradition but also to the work of Utamaro, an outstanding painter of birds, insects, seashells, and flowers.* In the postscript to *Yebon Mushi erabi* ("Selected Insects"), his master Sekiyen said of him:

*Kitagawa Utamaro (1754–1806) was a Japanese painter. Many engravings and color prints were made from his work. (Ed.)

To a Young Painter

To form pictures of living things in the mind and then to transfer them to paper with the brush is the true art of Painting. My pupil Utamaro, in depicting these insects, has produced "pictures from his heart." I remember how [he] in his childhood acquired the habit of observing the most minute details of living creatures; and I used to notice how absorbed he would become when playing with a dragon-fly tied to a string or with a cricket held in the palm of his hand. [Binyon and Sexton 1960, p. 75]

Anita Albus would have her place in this company, which, all things considered, should not seem so exotic. In defining drawing as "intellectual knowledge," Vasari was merely anticipating Seyken. And if our vision of the Japanese print were not contaminated by the misconception of impressionism, we would be more sensitive to the kinship between the art of *Ukiyo-e*, "images of the floating world," and the pursuit—typically Germanic, according to Riegl—of what he calls "the fortuitous" and "the ephemeral." To avoid any misunderstanding, let me note that the fortuitous and the ephemeral here are not accidental, like those that the impressionists wanted to capture, but are natural or intentional in the manner of Jan Van Eyck. This is also true of the Japanese. For if Hokusai (perhaps the most "Chinese" of the Japanese painters of his time) wanted to depict Fujiyama in different lights, he preserved the physical integrity of sky, clouds, and mountain and avoided letting them melt into one another.

While he submits to reality with all his strength, the painter does not make himself its imitator. Borrowing these images from nature, he takes the liberty of placing them in unforeseen arrangements that enrich our knowledge of things by making us perceive new relationships among them. Anita Albus remains faithful to the lessons of the medieval illuminators, who delighted in transmuting forms and in including, in their marginal decorations, "jokes" charged with meaning. Nor does she forget the allegorical inventions of Hiëronymus Bosch, or the divinatory sensitivity with which Georg Hoefnagel, Georg Flegel, Marseus van Schrieck, and Adriaen Coorte re-created reality during the sixteenth and the seventeenth centuries. Closer to us, Albus also remembers the botanical rigor of both a Runge, which he placed in the service of a natural philosophy; and of a Kolbe, who copied very ordinary plants with great precision, enlarging and recomposing their elements in order to construct luxuriant and fantastic forests.*

Meant to be freely interpreted by children, Anita Albus's first book,

---

*Philipp Otto Runge (1777–1810) was a German painter of portraits, historical subjects, and watercolors. Carl Wilhelm Kolbe (1757–1835) was a German landscape painter. (Ed.)

Der Himmel ist mein Hut (The Sky Is My Hat [1973]) echoes mythological themes that are widespread over various areas of the world. There is no certainty, however, that she was acquainted with them; she treats them so personally that one wants to believe she reinvented them. Take the motif of "local spring," illustrated by a gracious dwelling enclosing within its walls a tree whose leaves spill out of the windows, while beyond in the countryside the snow melts. Or, take the motif of the mysterious hole giving access to the other world—a motif represented by the apparatus of the toilet which, more than anything else in our society, plays the role of mediator between culture and man's animal nature. Or, the motif of the animated mountain, evoked by the eye discernible in its rocky folds, an eye gazing all the more absently in that it embraces an idyllic, but deserted landscape. Whether a solitary boat runs aground in the midst of the woods, or a locomotive zooms full steam ahead through an ocean valley where a school of fish materializes in the beams of its lights (while its smoke, imprisoned in an element denser than air, looks like a viscous body)—these images remind the Americanist that the Indians on the Pacific coast of Canada believed that along with "whales of the sea" there existed "whales of the forest." Or, further, constructing a mythology on the basis of verbal clichés and restoring their original expressive force, Anita Albus shows us a peaceful lake—so peaceful that its waters reflect the still-intact image of a house devoured by fire.

The pages of *Der Garten der Lieder* (The Garden of Songs [1976]) keep repeating a frame of horizontal and vertical stripes adorned with flowers, fruits, birds, insects, and seashells. Exquisite in composition and coloring, these motifs draw a singular strength from their precise detail and faithful realism. But it is above all in the medallions placed in the middle of each stripe that Anita Albus gives the measure of her virtuosity and poetic imagination. These medallions, some no more than ten millimeters in diameter, are all drawn to scale. Like miniature windows, they open upon scenes that are sometimes comical, sometimes strange and mysterious, and are always treated with a realism that enchants, for the perfect craftsmanship makes the singularity of the subjects even more intriguing.

In *Eia Popeia* (Hushaby [1978]), Anita Albus takes a different tack. She pays utmost care to the typography, embellishing it with ornamental capitals and borders filling the blank spaces at the end of each paragraph, and also detaches the illustration from the text. Unrelated to the text and apparently unrelated to one another, the plates are like small self-contained easel paintings. So tiny is their format, so refined their execution, and so exquisite their colors that one hesitates to classify these little masterpieces: they are both jewels and paintings. In one, a wild woman with a hairy body and an immense head of kinky hair seems to have sprung from some medieval cosmography; with a child on her lap, she sits dreaming by the edge of a moonlit lake. Another illustration is of a young kingfisher, the jewel of our rivers—and, no doubt, seldom depicted with such fascinating precision. Holding a fish in its beak, it is perched on a small pewter jug, whose oily reflections contrast with the bird's sparkling plumage, which stands out against the black background that is balanced by a piece of white linen with meticulously rendered creases and fringes. As in the dens of old collectors, the shelves of a cabinet reveal many curiosities and conceal others, which are probably even rarer and more surprising, behind a curtain whose folds betray the hand that has only just drawn it.

Furthermore, every painting hides in its own way one or more enigmas, sometimes posed by the subject itself, sometimes by Albus's penchant for pictorial quotations. She uses them intentionally but never reveals her sources—doubtless a desire not so much to play a trick on the viewer as to avoid divulging her encounters with works that have intimately touched her. Thus, the moonlit lake in the background of the cover of *Eia Popeia* reproduces that of Adam Elsheimer's *Flight into Egypt.** And the nipple peeping out from a frilly shirt, glimpsed through a tear in a printed page, pays a doubly secret homage to a female portrait by Palma il Vecchio.†

In this last painting, where Anita Albus has expertly painted the shadows cast by the folds of the leaf—on the corner of which a delicate little insect is advancing—she links what I would venture to call *trompe-mémoire* with *trompe l'oeil*. This latter tradition she revives in other paintings with a brio that one would never have expected possible in a living artist. The *trompe l'oeil* restores the substance and the texture of an old photographic print under a cracked glass; others juxtapose diverse objects in a fashion as apparently arbitrary as the famous encounter (less arbitrary than it appears) between an umbrella and a sewing machine on a dissecting table.

Actually, Anita Albus's art is not imbued only with the archaic. Contemporary influences inspire it—primarily surrealism. Her obvious and scrupulous concern for precision places her at the furthest

---

*Adam Elsheimer (1578–1610), known as Il Tedesco, was a German painter and etcher. He founded modern landscape painting and was a forerunner of Rembrandt. (Ed.)

†Jacopo Palma, or Il Vecchio (1480–1528), was an Italian painter of the Venetian school. (Ed.)

extreme from hyperrealism. Far from artlessly copying the refuse of culture, she depicts the most exquisite creations of nature in all their freshness and intricate complexity. On the other hand, her loyalty to the Nordic tradition, with its urge to unite the real and the fantastic, brings her close to surrealism, even though, to unite those two aspects, she does not always follow in its path.

Surrealism, too, can on occasion be inspired by the past. It was from Leonardo da Vinci that Max Ernst learned to decipher mysterious figures in the cracks in a wall or in the veining of an old, weathered floor. Anita Albus reverses this method: instead of asking the object to be something different from what it is, she assiduously renders with minute precision the weave and drape of a textile or the veins and grain of old wood. We see them as we no longer realized or had forgotten that we could see them. The surprise, the feeling of strangeness, we have from grasping them in their original truth, restored to what W. Worringer would have called their "organic lawfulness" (*Gesetzmässigkeit* [1959, p. 96]).

The history of contemporary painting, as it has developed during the last hundred years, is confronted with a paradox. Painters have come to reject the subject in favor of what is now called, with revealing discretion, their "work"; one would not be so bold as to speak of "craft." On the other hand, only if one continued to see in painting a means of knowledge—that of a whole outside the artist's work— would a craftsmanship inherited from the old masters regain its importance and keep its place as an object of study and reflection.

Made up of recipes, of formulas, of processes as well as of a manual exercise requiring years of theoretical and practical training, this precious lore has vanished today. We may fear that it will go the way of the plant and animal species that man, in his blindness, has been annihilating one after another. But this destruction, while irreversible in the case of living forms which only a divine power could re-create, may not be so in the case of traditional knowledge. The art of Anita Albus demonstrates how painting could be resuscitated—on the condition, however, that painters realize that months of labor are not too much to produce a very small painting (or even a large one: Ingres thought about his for months, sometimes even years), if they are to succeed in fixing a portion of the world's truth after a patient dialogue between the model, the raw materials, physical or chemical laws and properties, and the artist himself. The result will be a work that condenses in a perceptible form the terms of a pact between all these parties.

To a Young Painter

By subjecting her eyes, her hand, and her mind to asceticism, Anita Albus tried to return to the very origins of Western painting and restore the painter's craft in all its rigor. She learned to use vellum as it was used centuries ago, and rediscovered the bright and opaque hues of the illuminators of the Middle Ages and the early Renaissance by applying successive layers of watercolors. Here, too, she remained faithful to her national tradition. For it was Theophilus, a German monk of the eleventh and twelfth centuries, and his treatise *De diversis artibus schedula* that gave us our essential knowledge of the techniques of illumination—preparation of colors, grounds, binders, use of mediums, and so on. Evocative, as a person, of Gothic grace and purity, Anita Albus demonstrates through her art that one does not reinvent the painter's craft without taking things back to their beginnings, without retracing step by step the road followed by the great discoverers, and without restoring bit by bit their secrets and methods and the tricks of their trade.

Painting may have gone in the wrong direction when, after Leonardo da Vinci, one imagined that, by opting for nature over antiquity, one was obliged also to opt for chiaroscuro over outline. There was no connection between these two choices. Nature, which some people have dared to call "small and banal" (Sérusier 1950, p. 39), offers the artist an inexhaustible wealth of motifs; and if he knows how to be attentive to the spectacle of the world, he will have no plausible pretext for giving up the subject. But it is also true that—as was understood by Italian and Flemish painters of the fifteenth century, by Japanese painters up to the nineteenth century, and by Anita Albus today— only by rebelling against the enervating magic of chiaroscuro, and by yielding to the intangible order of things, can painting once again claim the dignity of a craft.

Chapter 21

New York in 1941

DISEMBARKING in New York in May 1941, one felt oneself bathed in tropical moisture—a foreshadowing of one of those humid, stifling summers that forced the writer to wrap his arm in a Turkish towel so that his sweat would not soak the paper. Being able to spend hours walking and exploring the city in light clothing increased one's sense of freedom—a feeling understandable in one who had just managed to reach the United States after a laborious passage that had not been without risk. I strode up and down miles of Manhattan avenues, those deep chasms over which loomed skyscrapers' fantastic cliffs. I wandered randomly into cross streets, whose physiognomy changed drastically from one block to the next: sometimes poverty-stricken, sometimes middle-class or provincial, and most often chaotic. New York was decidedly not the ultra-modern metropolis I had expected, but an immense horizontal and vertical disorder attributable to some spontaneous upheaval of the urban crust rather than to the deliberate plans of builders. Here, mineral strata, ancient or recent, were still intact in spots; while elsewhere peaks emerged from the surrounding magma like witnesses to different eras which followed one another at an accelerated rhythm with, at intervals, the still visible remnants of all those upheavals: vacant lots, incongruous cottages, hovels, red-brick buildings—the latter already empty shells slated for demolition.

Despite the loftiness of the tallest buildings and the way they were piled up and squeezed together on the cramped surface of an island ("This city that awaits you standing up," said Le Corbusier), I discovered that, on the edges of these labyrinths, the web of the urban tissue was astonishingly slack—as has been proved by all that has been wedged in since and that increases my sense of oppression every time I revisit New York. In 1941, however, except in the canyons around Wall Street, this was a city where one could breathe easily. This was so along the avenues flanking Fifth Avenue, which looked increasingly working class the farther east or west one went; even, beyond upper Broadway or Central Park West, around the heights of Columbia University, which were swept by breezes from the Hudson.

Actually, New York was not a city but, on the colossal scale whose measure one can take only by setting foot in the New World, an agglomeration of villages. In each of these an inhabitant could have spent his life without ever leaving except to go to work. Thus were explained, moreover, the profound mysteries of subway express trains. When you got on one—unless you understood the barely visible symbols on the first car—you would be carried along, without the least chance of getting out along the way, either to your destination or to some outlying district a dozen miles away. Taking the same route day after day as they did, most passengers had no need to learn about other routes; familiar signs could remain elliptic.

At the intersections of perfectly straight thoroughfares, which might have appeared to be jumbled up in a single geometric anonymity, the ethnic groups making up New York's population had each found its chosen niche: Harlem and Chinatown, of course, but also the Puerto Rican district (developing at that time around West 23rd Street), Little Italy (south of Washington Square), as well as Greek, Czech, German, Scandinavian, Finnish, and other neighborhoods, with their restaurants and their places of worship and entertainment. One changed countries every few blocks. In this way, New York already anticipated the capitals of Europe after the Second World War, which have been marked by working-class affluence and the concomitant proliferation of diversely exotic boutiques and restaurants. Since 1910 indeed, the proportion of foreign-born inhabitants has not ceased to diminish in the United States, while it has rapidly increased in France and in other European countries. In France alone, the percentage of foreign-born inhabitants is now twice that of the United States.

Other noticeable points of the city revealed more secret affinities. The French surrealists and their friends settled in Greenwich Village, where, just a few subway stops from Times Square, one could still lodge—just as in Paris in Balzac's time—in a small two- or three-story house with a tiny garden in back. A few days after my arrival, when visiting Yves Tanguy, I discovered and immediately rented, on the street where he lived, a studio whose windows faced a neglected garden. You reached it by way of a long basement corridor leading to a private stairway in the rear of a red-brick house. The building belonged to an old Italian, almost an invalid, who expected to be addressed as "doctor," and whose daughter took care of him and the tenants. Anemic and middle-aged, she had remained a spinster either because she was unattractive or in order to tend her father. Just two or three years ago, I learned that Claude Shannon had also lived there, but on an upper story and facing the street. Only a few yards apart, he was creating cybernetics and I was writing *Elementary Structures of Kinship* (1969 [1949]). Actually, we had a mutual friend in the house, a young woman, and I recall that, without mentioning his name, she once spoke to me about one of our neighbors, who, she explained, was busy "inventing an artificial brain." The idea struck me as bizarre, and I thought no more about it. As for our landlord, he was, I gathered, a "godfather" to poor Italian immigrants. He would welcome them, help them get settled, and take charge of their problems. Today I wonder whether the sleazy premises and the down-at-heel daughter were not used as a cover for some shady Mafia business.

North of Greenwich Village, a trade-union and political atmosphere, charged with stale odors from Central Europe, emanated from Union Square and the nearby garment district. Far from here, the middle-class immigrants were concentrated on the Upper West Side between Broadway and Riverside Drive: grim avenues, straight or curving, lined with apartment houses erected at the turn of the century for rich families seeking fifteen- or twenty-room apartments. These once elegant buildings were now dilapidated, and the apartments had been cut up for less affluent tenants. The New York aristocracy resided on the East Side, where town houses, dating often from the nineteenth century, had been *remodelées*, as was said in Franco-American—that is, spruced up like our present-day weekend cottages in France. In its taste for the provincial and the old-fashioned, New York society was ahead of ours. This was the era in which it began to dote on Early American style. A quarter of a century earlier, New York millionaires had spent fortunes importing enormous solid-walnut sixteenth-century furniture from Spain and Italy that their homes might ape the palazzi of Rome. But now, all those items were piling up in the back rooms of second-hand shops on Second and even First Avenue or being auctioned off at Parke-Bernet before an inattentive audience. If I did not have it now before my eyes, it would be hard to believe that I bought one day a sixteenth-century Tuscan sideboard for a few dollars. However, New York (and this is the source of its charm and its peculiar fascination) was then a city where anything seemed possible. Like the urban fabric, the social and cultural fabric was riddled with holes. All you had to do was pick one and slip through if, like Alice, you wanted to get to the other side of the looking glass and find worlds so enchanting that they seemed unreal.

Max Ernst, André Breton,* Georges Duthuit,† and I frequented a small antique shop on Third Avenue which, in response to our demand, became Ali Baba's cave. We quickly solved the mystery of the exquisite stone masks from Teotihuacan and the magnificent wood carvings from the northwest Pacific coast, which, at that time, even specialists regarded merely as ethnographic documents. Similar pieces may sometimes have remained unnoticed in a store on lower Madison Avenue that peddled glass beads and garishly dyed chicken feathers to Boy Scouts who wanted to concoct headdresses in the Indian style. Likewise on Madison Avenue, around Fifty-fifth Street, there was a store that sold South American knickknacks. Once you had gained the owner's trust, he would take you to a nearby street where, in the back of a courtyard, he would open up a shed crammed with Mochica, Nazca, and Chimu vases piled on shelves towering to the ceiling. Not far from there, another shopowner would show us gold boxes encrusted with rubies and emeralds—the flotsam and jetsam of Russians who had fled the October Revolution, as were no doubt the Oriental rugs that a slightly practiced eye could spot among the second-hand articles hawked every week in the neighboring auction houses. It could also happen that you might enter an antique shop to look at a nice Japanese print, and the owner would inform you that, in the building next door, a young man in straitened circumstances had prints to sell. You would then ring the buzzer of his little apartment, and he would unpack whole series of Utamaro prints in contemporary editions. On Sixth Avenue in upper Greenwich Village, a German baron, the purest of his breed, lived in a modest detached house. To his visitors he would discreetly sell the Peruvian antiques that filled his home and his trunks. Sometimes, a full-page Macy's ad in *The New York Times* announced that the next day there would be a sale of a whole shipload of such objects from Peru and Mexico. Between 1946 and 1947, when

*André Breton (1896–1966), a French poet and critic; he was a member of the Dada group and founded the surrealist movement. (Ed.)

†Georges Duthuit, French art critic and historian. He was the son-in-law of Matisse. (Ed.)

I was cultural adviser to the French embassy, I would be visited by intermediaries carrying attaché cases full of pre-Colombian gold jewelry. Or they would show me photographs of gigantic collections of Indian art and offer to trade them for Matisses and Picassos, of which, they felt, the French museums had enough to spare. The French authorities turned a deaf ear to my entreaties, and the Indian collections wound up in American museums.

Thus, New York offered simultaneously the image of a world already finished in Europe and the image of another world that—little as we suspected then—would soon invade Europe. Without our realizing it, a machine capable of both going back and advancing in time took us on an uninterrupted series of pointless exchanges between periods long before the First World War or immediately following the Second. On the one hand, we re-experienced the world of Cousin Pons* where, in the disorder of a changing society, social strata were violently disrupted, sliding over one another and creating huge holes which engulfed styles and bodies of knowledge. Let a generation leave the stage, let a style become passé and another not yet be fashionable —and a piece of human history collapsed, its débris falling into the rubbish. This phenomenon was all the more brutal and poignant because, in the swift evolution of American society, successive waves of immigrants had been invading New York for a century; according to its social level, each new group came bearing rich or meager treasures, which necessity forced it to disperse very quickly. The immense resources which the local plutocracy had to satisfy its whims, made it seem as if examples of the whole of humanity's artistic legacy were present in New York. Shuffled and reshuffled, like flotsam and jetsam, to the capricious rhythm of social ups and downs, some of these examples still decorated drawing rooms or had made their way into museums, while others piled up in unsuspected nooks.

Whoever wanted to go hunting needed only a little culture and flair for doorways to open in the wall of industrial civilization and reveal other worlds and other times. Doubtless nowhere more than in New York at that time were there such facilities for escape. Those possibilities seem almost mythical today when we no longer dare to dream of doors: at best, we may wonder about niches to cower in. But even these have become the stake in a fierce competition among those who are not willing to live in a world without friendly shadows or secret shortcuts known only to a few initiates. Losing its old dimensions one after

*Le Cousin Pons (1847) is a novel by Balzac. (Ed.)

another, this world has pushed us back into the one remaining dimension: one will probe it in vain for secret loopholes.

At the same time and by a singular contrast, New York foreshadowed the recourses of adversity to which—although we did not realize it—we would be reduced in Europe a quarter of a century later. I remember the surprise I felt upon seeing most of the so-called antique stores in New York. Unlike France, which I had just left—where display windows were filled with furniture from the seventeenth or eighteenth centuries, with old pewter and faience—these American stores had old kerosene lamps, outmoded old clothes, late-nineteenth-century industrial bric-à-brac. Today, all these objects are avidly gathered in Parisian shops that likewise proclaim themselves "antiquarian"; and that, twenty-five or thirty years afterward, are copies of the ones that amazed me in New York. (As did those deodorant advertisements, which were so obscene that I was certain we would never see anything like them in France; yet now they pop up everywhere here—but that is another story.) But to return to the alabaster and embossed brass lamps and other objects of the same period, New York taught me that the idea of beauty can take curious shapes. When objects that traditional taste judges beautiful become too rare and expensive for small wallets, then previously scorned items surface and provide the people who acquire them satisfaction of a somewhat different order—not so much aesthetic as mystical and, one might say, religious. As the relics and witnesses of an era that was already industrial certainly, but in which economic pressures and the demands of mass production were not yet urgent and permitted a certain continuity of past forms and the existence of useless ornaments, these articles acquired an almost supernatural quality. They bear witness among us to the still real presence of a lost world. One surrounds oneself with these objects not because they are beautiful, but because, since beauty has become inaccessible to all but the very rich, they offer, in its place, a sacred character—and thus one is, by the way, led to wonder about the ultimate nature of the aesthetic emotion.

The situation was the same when you looked for a place to live in Manhattan. Since really old houses no longer existed, and modern apartments were too expensive, you discovered the charms of the late nineteenth century in brownstones and in once luxurious but now shabby apartment houses. The kitsch fad and the *rétro* craze, now all the rage in France, were being taught and practiced in New York, by the force of circumstance, in the 1940s and probably even earlier. Actually, these trends appeared in two forms. Aristocratic taste leaned toward the naïve, provincial art of Early American paintings and furnishings, which were already being hunted down by the wealthy (but when, as cultural adviser to the French embassy, I sounded out some Americans about mounting an exhibit of Early American painting in Paris, they begged off for fear of presenting abroad an image that they felt could be disadvantageous to their country). However, for Americans who felt emotionally attached to the United States of the late eighteenth and early nineteenth centuries, Early American offered a temporal reference that the inhabitants of a young country could not find further back in time. Other Americans, who had smaller bank accounts or claimed younger family trees—though going back two or three generations—looked to the style of the 1880s, the "Gay Eighties" or "Nineties." And we French, too, have learned to cherish this period, impelled by an evolution in taste that, without the American example, would probably never have been so rapid and dynamic.

I wonder whether even hyperrealism, which moved from America to France, might not have existed embryonically in the dioramas at which I never tired of gazing in the American Museum of Natural History, though some were already of a respectable age. Behind glass panes that were several yards high and wide, one could—and still can —see scrupulous reconstructions of American, African, and Asian fauna in their natural habitat. Each animal, once killed, had been instantly skinned, and a cast made of the carcass, so that the hide would then perfectly match the muscular system. And rocks had been scattered over the ground, and trees had been gathered, as well as imprints of all their leaves, so that the tiniest details of a scene were utterly realistic. The landscape backdrops were painted with stunning mastery. Except, perhaps, for the imitators of John Martin in the nineteenth century, the art of the diorama has never been pushed so far or practiced on such a large scale. We can certainly speak of art here; for contemporary artists, proclaiming aesthetic goals, devote to similar work the same meticulous concern for precision and the same diligence.

In a general way, the European visitor was struck by a paradoxical side of American museums. They had been established much later than ours; but, instead of hurting them, this delay helped them to get ahead of us in many respects. Not being able, or not always, to acquire what old Europe had considered first choice, keeping such objects in its museums sometimes for centuries, America had managed to make a virtue of necessity by discovering first choices in domains that we had neglected. One such was the natural sciences, which Europe had been abandoning since the eighteenth century. America, however, had assiduously created galleries of mineralogy, paleontology, ornithology, as well as aquariums. All these sumptuous places dazzled the European visitor not only because of their treasures from an unspoiled and therefore prodigal continent, but also as they compared with our own rundown galleries of natural history. In Europe, our interest in these collections has reawakened after an eclipse of two centuries—a revival that may well have been sparked, at least in part, by a certain familiarity that Europeans acquired after the Second World War with American museums.

For their part, American museums of fine arts had found shortcuts to make up for their backwardness, and sometimes even outstripped us. Using old stones that we had disdained, they built the Cloisters. Their Egyptian collections were not made up of just a few statues and other major pieces but also included vast arrays of humble, everyday items which afforded a more balanced view of ancient life than such collections of our own. And as for objects from Europe itself, the continent does not have the equivalent of America's sensational collections of weapons and old costumes. While in American museums I learned nothing essentially new concerning the art of Van der Weyden, Raphael, or Rembrandt, it was at the National Gallery in Washington, D.C., that I discovered Magnasco.*

In New York, as we used to say to one another, women do not "dress": they disguise themselves. When we saw them dressed like little sailors, Egyptian dancing girls, or pioneer women of the Far West, we knew that they were "dressed to kill." We found all this very funny. But today you have only to visit any chic boutique in Paris to realize that here, too, New York has founded a school. Furthermore, the art of shopwindows, with its refinement, ingenuity, and audacity, inspired the most extravagant fantasies. Department stores presented their collections on dummies acting out dramatic scenes—rapes, murders, kidnappings—settings, lighting, and colors realized with a consummate skill that would have been the envy of the finest theaters. In everyday life, the sudden changes of clothing I have spoken of expressed the same need for escape that struck us elsewhere: we watched our New York friends switch with almost religious fervor from a luxurious East Side apartment to a wooden shack at the tip of Long Island or even on the narrow dunes of Fire Island, where the only plant life was poison ivy. Or else they went to some rustic house in

*Alessandro Magnasco (1667?–1749) was an Italian painter who specialized in genre scenes. (Ed.)

Connecticut, like the one where André Masson lived,* or, a bit farther away, Alexander Calder's. They indulged in the illusion that they were homesteading in the style of the early settlers. I was very friendly with a famous American sociologist, a somewhat stiff man who, even in conversation, expressed himself with a provincial solemnity. Once I spent the night in his family home, an old farmhouse that had been pushed into an enclave by urban sprawl and now stood on his last bit of acreage in what had become an industrial suburb. It was the most bohemian place imaginable; had the word *hippie* existed back then, it would have been apt. A few surviving trees and a hodgepodge of bushes besieged a frame house all of whose paint was peeling. Inside, the bathroom washbasin had the thickest crust of filth I had ever seen. But for my host and his family, this dilapidation and systematic neglect were finer than a royal castle. By abjuring the rites of ʼgiene and of comfort on which Americans pride themselves—and which these people themselves no doubt scrupulously observed in the city— they felt as if they were preserving a tie with their ancestors who had settled on this soil as homesteaders a few generations earlier. This was outside Chicago; but even in New York, one often noted an ostentatious disdain for what newcomers admired as American efficiency, and the mania peculiar to this country of achieving the utmost perfection of the comforts of civilization.

What, in sum, New York revealed to Frenchmen fresh off the boat was an unbelievably complex image—and one that, had it not been experienced first hand, would seem contradictory—and almost archaic life styles. Refugee colleagues who were folklore experts, and had once combed the most remote countryside of central and eastern Europe looking for the last surviving storytellers, made some astonishing discoveries, right in the middle of New York, among their immigrant compatriots. For fifty years or more, since those families had arrived in the United States, they had preserved customs and stories that had vanished without a trace in the old countries. The same was true of the performances that we watched for hours at the Chinese opera under the first arch of the Brooklyn Bridge, where a company that had come long ago from China had a large following. Every day, from midafternoon until past midnight, it would perpetuate the traditions of classical Chinese opera. I felt myself going back in time no less when I went to work every morning in the American room of the New York Public Library. There, under its neo-classical arcades and between

*André Masson (1896–), French surrealist painter. (Ed.)

walls paneled with old oak, I sat near an Indian in a feather headdress and a beaded buckskin jacket—who was taking notes with a Parker pen.

Naturally, we sensed that all these relics were being assaulted by a mass culture that was about to crush and bury them—a mass culture that, already far advanced in America, would reach Europe a few decades later. This may be the reason so many aspects of life in New York enthralled us: it set before our eyes a list of recipes thanks to which, in a society becoming each day ever more oppressive and inhuman, the people who find it decidedly intolerable can learn the thousand and one tricks offered, for a few brief moments, by the illusion that one has the power to escape.

Chapter 22

A Belated Word about the Creative Child

THE CELEBRATION of L'Ecole Alsacienne centennial in 1974 included a panel discussion at the Théâtre de l'Odéon on "School and the Creative Child." The event was marked by a slow start; there was no common language among participants from very different backgrounds; and the discussion with the audience was kept brief: all these factors explain the dissatisfaction felt on both sides. The speakers did not have sufficient latitude to express their ideas with any subtlety, and the audience went away empty-handed, as it were. Yet the problem raised by the topic is real and deserves to be considered again, even in hindsight.

A question arises at once: What society other than our own has wondered about this subject? Almost none, so far as we can tell. And even here, the encouragement of creativity in the child is of recent vintage: it began no more than a few decades ago. Have we then suddenly discovered the vices of a traditional system of education? Our system in France goes back to the Jesuits and took shape around the seventeenth century. Now there was no want of creative people in that century or in subsequent ones, and the number of people who showed themselves to be clearly precocious was proportionately much higher than now. When secondary education was at its height, during the

A Belated Word about the Creative Child

second half of the nineteenth and the early twentieth centuries, very few students claimed they felt hemmed in or smothered by the training at the *lycée*. Instead, many students showed a maturity and creative talent that would be hard to find in our modern *lycée* students. Men like Jaurès, Bergson, and Proust* felt, so far as we can tell, perfectly at ease in their *lycée*. Seventeen-year-olds even in their first philosophy class were already mature minds, personalities in full possession of their powers. At this moment, there is being performed Montherlant's play *The Exile*, which he wrote at the age of eighteen: he could not have written it had he not for seven or eight years been composing small literary works in notebooks which exist today. This exceptional case is not unique. While I cannot claim that they lived up to all their promise, I knew creative children of my own generation in both primary and secondary school.

Certainly, that was an era in which both public and private secondary education was reserved for a minority. But if we extend—as we should—the concept of the creative beyond scientific and literary activity, then we cannot say that technical or artistic apprenticeship governed by the punctilious rules of the old guilds has sterilized inventive abilities. We need only recall the old masters, who were trained in the hard school of the atelier, or the dazzling flowering of eighteenth-century cabinetmakers, those past masters each of whom made his mark on his art and his time. For centuries, the techniques of the crafts, although handed down by authorities in each generation, were highly conducive to creativity. Even craftsmen whose names were not attached to an invention, a style, or a manner took pleasure in their work and invested it with the taste and the talent with which nature had endowed them. The humblest objects we admire in the Musée des Arts et Traditions Populaires would suffice to convince us, were convincing needed.

Contrary to what the title of the panel discussion seemed to imply, the problem of the creative child does not apparently stem from the imperfection of an old educational system. For a long time, the system that is still theoretically ours solved the problem satisfactorily. If we discover today that a problem exists, then the cause is not that the

*Jean Léon Jaurès (1859–1914), French socialist and politician; Henri Bergson (1859–1941), the French philosopher; and Marcel Proust (1871–1922), the novelist. (Ed.)

system was bad. It was as good as a collective system can be; but it deteriorated and, for reasons beyond its scope, has now collapsed. The problem of the creative child is first and foremost a problem of civilization rather than of education.

At a time when the memory of certain craft techniques was still fresh (I have deliberately selected one that is recent in origin and leaves little room for individual initiative), the old telephone linesmen freely admitted that they were happier when they were using pickaxes to dig rather than mechanical devices that drive the poles into the ground without direct human intervention. The old way took a lot of muscle, but you could vary the work, take a breather after each operation, and chat as you moved along still peaceful roads. Such observations are flimsy; but they take on weight when applied to the assembly line, which has brought about a gap between the worker's personality and the monotonous motions he is forced to carry out.

We thus realize why, despite ever-increasing enrollment, the quality of secondary education has diminished for both teachers and pupils. Not only, moreover, because of larger classes and overloaded programs. The birth and development of what we call mass communication has profoundly altered the transmission of knowledge. It no longer filters down slowly from one generation to the next within a family or a professional milieu but is propagated at disconcerting speed in a horizontal direction and at levels with ruptures between them. Henceforth, each generation will communicate more easily with its members than with the generation that precedes or follows it. Loyal still to the old system, the school is being invaded from all sides and, with the family losing one of its essential functions, can no longer take over that function or expand it. The school is no longer ready to serve as a relay station between past and present in a vertical direction or between family and society in a horizontal direction.

Several panelists rightly emphasized that a reform is needed to adapt the school to this new situation. But we must first agree on its causes. What makes reform timely is not that the traditional methods were bad, but that the social, cultural, and economic context has changed. Here at home, we find ourselves in the same situation as European educators trying to teach children in developing societies. The results are disappointing, and the educators conclude either that these peoples are congenitally less intelligent or that their mental development is impeded by the conditions of their everyday life. Either way, they are inferior. Now we know that this is nonsense. If the schoolchildren in these societies merely learn by rote, quickly forget, and make little progress, they do so because they have not been given the means for organizing and structuring their new knowledge in terms of the intellectual norms of their civilization. As soon as an effort is made in this direction, the resulting improvement is spectacular.

Our educators have, thus, to become amateur anthropologists of a society that is other than the one to which apply the methods they once learned. But even if new methods spark a child's interest in what he does, and help him to understand and enjoy what he is taught rather than memorize it, then the traditional goal of school will remain the same. The child will still have to learn—more effectively and intelligently than before, no doubt, but he will still have to learn to assimilate knowledge and other acquisitions of the past.

Assuming an agreement on the principles, the problem will remain but will become the province of specialists who rely on tested educational methods whose results can be compared. Some of the panelists fit this description. Lacking experience, the others, including myself, could not follow them on unfamiliar terrain. Our training and our preoccupations confined us in theoretical views unrelated to the technical questions that could have furnished material for useful discussion.

But this was not the most serious difficulty. One repeatedly sensed that some of the panelists and certain members of the audience were openly or insidiously intent on challenging the traditional mission of the school. It was as if wanting a child to learn is both a useless wish and an assault on his freedom; and as if a child's native spontaneity and intellectual resources were enough in themselves, excluded any constraint, and left the school with the sole function of not fettering their free development. In support of this thesis, someone even invoked the justly renowned work of Jean Piaget. The master of Geneva would have been very surprised, for he has never claimed that the increasingly complex mental structures that appear, according to him, in the successive stages of a child's development can be arranged and organized in the absence of any external discipline. Furthermore, these structures are of a formal nature and would remain empty and inoperative if they were not grounded on a store of acquired knowledge, whose provision is one of the goals of school.

Today we realize that Piaget's conclusions, whose importance no one would dream of belittling, have to be interpreted in terms of a far different set of problems, rooted in neuropsychology. After the birth of, at least, the higher vertebrates and during the greater part of their childhood, their cerebral structures remain extremely elastic. When newborn rats are isolated either in empty cages or in cages filled with toys (or what is thought to fill this function among rats), a subsequent autopsy of their brains reveals that the nervous projections that connect the neurons have become richer and more complex in the second group than in the first. This experiment certainly cannot be carried out on human subjects; but everything points to the assumption that the same phenomenon takes place in a human child. It would be wrong, however, to conclude that the sole result is enrichment: while some connections are being created, others are being eliminated. These simultaneous processes of construction and destruction go on for a long time. Hence it is that, contrary to what certain psychological experiments have led us to believe, very young children are capable of logical operations that they cannot repeat two or three years later and that they subsequently perform only through other paths.

When we get ecstatic about the creativity of a very young child, we are to some extent victims of an illusion. Such gifts exist but, during this early age, are dependent on many possibilities that are still open and that training and organic maturation will eventually eliminate. If all these possibilities survived, if they entered into competition with one another, if choice did not operate within a genetic program of highly varied origin, if certain neurological pathways did not develop and stabilize their functioning at the expense of others, the brain, and therefore the mind, would never reach maturity. An echo of this research is to be found in *L'Unité de l'homme* (Morin and Piattelli-Palmarini 1974), an engrossing book that came out of a recent colloquium held in Royaumont. This research does not see mental activity as the product of structures that, driven by an internal determinism, gradually build up on top of each other in an increasingly complex order whose development should not be altered or halted. Mental functions result from a selection that suppresses all sorts of latent capacities. So long as they exist, these capacities amaze us, and rightly so; but it would be naïve not to face the ineluctable necessity that all learning, even in school, is accompanied by impoverishment. What happens is that some of the very young child's labile gifts degenerate so that others may be consolidated.

Let us assume that these gifts are preserved in certain privileged cases—for instance, as we are told, in certain poets and artists. Does anyone really think that even these people draw everything from their own resources? As if this preposterous idea could be imputed to Racine, I heard someone cite, in its support, the preface to *Bérénice* during the audience discussion. Invention, says Racine, consists of making something out of nothing—not, in any way, of making something by starting from nothing. Racine himself would never have written *Bérénice* or any of his other works had he not, on a school bench, memorized Sophocles and Euripides, and had long intimacy with the Greek tragedies and with the Roman poets and playwrights not taught him, as he himself emphasizes, to deal with a slight subject by giving it dramatic force. One creates only by starting from something one knows thoroughly—if for no other reason than to oppose and surpass it.

Some educators, however, who find it wonderful to let a child exercise his gifts by struggling with material objects—such as paints, paper, brushes, clay, planks, and blocks—are horrified at the idea of asking a child to react, in a French exercise, to the work of a dead or living author, because, we are told, the child has not thought it up himself! How can anyone fail to see that these are exactly the same situation? In each case, a child is asked to grapple with one or more unfamiliar realities that are either material or spiritual. He is expected to perceive and then assimilate their characteristic properties. Finally, in overcoming their resistance to his attempts at manipulating or understanding them, he is expected to produce an original synthesis of all the elements.

The constraint of school, a favorite butt of criticism, is simply one aspect or expression of the constraint that every reality—and society is one—normally places upon anyone who participates in it. It is considered chic nowadays to deride or stigmatize the resistance of the social milieu to new works. Such critics fail to see that ultimately these new works owe as much to the social milieu as to the creative impulse that turned the traditional rules around and even violated them. Every memorable work is thus made up of rules that impeded its birth—and had to be flouted—and of new rules that, once recognized, it will impose in its turn. On this subject, let us listen to the lesson of a great creator in a work devoted to creativity—Richard Wagner and *Die Meistersinger*:

> Learn the rules of the masters
> So that they help you to preserve
> What was revealed to you in youth
> By the springtime and by love.

And further on:

> Create your own rules, but then follow them.

CONSTRAINT AND FREEDOM

To say that no contest is possible if there is nothing to contest is a truism—but one that has the merit of emphasizing that resistance and the effort to overcome it are equally necessary. The existence of *Les Fleurs du Mal* and *Madame Bovary* required not only Baudelaire and Flaubert but also the exercise of a constraint in the here-and-now which required detours along the pathways of the imagination. Otherwise, these roads might never have been opened; or, had they been, they would not have been the same. Creative work is the result of arbitration and compromise: between the creator's original—and, at this stage, still unformulable—intention and the resistances he must overcome in order to express that intention. Resisting the artist are technique, tools, and material; the writer, vocabulary, grammar, and syntax; and both are resisted by public opinion and the laws. Granted that every work of art is revolutionary, it can be revolutionary only by acting upon what it subverts. Its innovative character (which would disappear if nothing had existed before it) comes from gnawing on the obstacle—but not without giving in to, and modeling itself ever so little upon, it. A masterpiece is, thus, made up both of what it is and of what it denies, the ground it conquers and the resistance it meets. It is the result of fierce antagonisms which it reconciles, yet whose thrusts and counterthrusts create the vibration and the tension that we wonder at.

We see the products of creative freedom that has been neither educated nor curbed, in the houses, villas, and cottages—the ones more hideous than the others—that people have constructed in the countryside. Even intransigent defenders of this freedom seem to agree that the mixing and degrading of styles should be prohibited, and that, in each region, traditional materials should be used and respected. This may be censorship; but even censorship, if exercised by lucid and competent judges, can have its virtues. Having just spoken about the countryside, let us now look at the cities and at what is being done to them today. Is not the reason for this new development the fact that everything that was and is beautiful in the urban scene goes back to the enlightened will of a monarch—to which Paris owes such delights as the Place des Vosges, the Place Vendôme, and the Rue de Rivoli? On the other hand, if a city is constructed haphazardly, yet still remains beautiful, wouldn't the process take a thousand years? Between these two extreme solutions, neither of which is suitable for our time, a certain measure of restraint is called for; and, indeed, it is what everyone prays for.

Anthropologists study societies that do not present the problem of the creative child; nor do these societies have schools. In the societies that I was familiar with, children played seldom or not at all. More precisely, their games consisted of imitating adults. This imitation imperceptibly led the children to participate finally in productive tasks —whether by helping so far as they could to obtain food, or by tending and entertaining their younger siblings, or by manufacturing objects. In most so-called primitive societies, however, this unfocused training is not enough. At a certain point in childhood or adolescence, there must be a traumatic experience varying from a few weeks to several months. Involving very harsh ordeals, this initiation, as the anthropologists say, inscribes the novice's mind with knowledge that his social group considers sacred. And it also provokes what I will call the virtue of powerful emotions—anxiety, fear, and pride—in order to consolidate, in a brutal and definitive way, the diluted teaching that has been going on for years.

Like many others, I was educated in a *lycée* where every class began and ended to the beat of a drum, where the slightest infraction of discipline was severely punished, where compositions were prepared in anguish, and their results solemnly proclaimed by the headmaster and his assistant, leaving us despondent or overjoyed. I do not believe that the great majority of us ever found the system hateful or disgusting. Today, as an adult and as an anthropologist to boot, I find in these customs the reflection—weakened certainly but always recognizable— of universal rites that confer a sacred character on the steps by which each generation prepares itself to share its responsibilities with the one that follows it. To forestall any misunderstanding, let us consider as sacred only those manifestations of collective life wherein the individual feels deeply involved. These manifestations may be ill considered and become dangerous, as happens in various societies, especially ours owing to the early age at which we subject our children to school discipline. So-called primitives generally have more regard for the mental and intellectual frailty of the very young child. But so long as it acts with moderation and adjusts its methods to the present state of morals, no society can ignore or neglect this area.

Finally, it would be wise to distrust the goals that one sets for oneself or for others without first defining their content. What precisely is a creative person? Is the creative person someone who is an absolute innovator or one who delights in creating for himself, even if other people have already done what he does or do it equally well?

The societies studied by anthropologists have little taste for novelty: they justify their customs by how ancient they are believed to be. At least for those societies that have no more than several thousand members, and sometimes not even one hundred, the—of course, impossible —ideal would be to remain as, according to their myths, the gods created them at the dawn of time. Yet, within these non-industrial societies, each member knows how to fashion by himself all the objects he has to use. Let no one speak of instinctive imitation here. The lowliest skills of the so-called primitives require highly complex manual and intellectual operations that must be understood and mastered, and that call for taste, intelligence, and initiative every time they are performed. Not just any tree can supply the wood for a wooden bow, nor just any part of the right tree; the exposure of the trunk, the month and the day for chopping down the tree are also important. The operations of hewing, shaping, and polishing the wood, of preparing the fiber for the binding and the bowstring, and of twisting and fastening these—all require experience, judgment, and flair. A man devotes himself body and soul to these tasks, investing in them his knowledge, his skill, his personality. The same is true of the potter and the weaver. The difference between the work of one craftsman and the next may be minimal, indiscernible to the unpracticed eye. But the artisan notices them, and they inspire in him justifiable pride.

In wishing to make our children creative, do we only want them to be like the savage or the pre-industrial peasant, doing by themselves the same thing that their neighbors are doing, while respecting norms fixed once and for all time? Or are we asking for something more? In this latter case, we would have to confine the term *creation* to a true material or spiritual innovation. Great innovators are, of course, necessary to the life and the evolution of societies: unless such a talent—but we know nothing of it—can be rooted in genetics (rather than being latent in every human being), one must also wonder about the viability of a society that would want all its members to be innovators. It is highly doubtful whether such a society could keep reproducing itself, much less progress, for it would be permanently involved in dissipating anything it acquired.

We may have witnessed such a phenomenon in certain parts of our own culture, especially in the plastic arts. Obsessed by the two major innovations in painting, impressionism and cubism, following one another in rapid succession within a few short years, and remorseful about not having understood them at first, we set up a new ideal: not what fertile innovation can still produce, but innovation for its own sake. Not content with having virtually deified it, we now implore it each day to grant us new signs of its omnipotence. Everyone knows the result: a frenzied cavalcade of styles and mannerisms, even within the work of an individual artist. Ultimately, painting as a genre has not survived the incoherent pressures on it to renew itself endlessly. And other creative areas are suffering the same fate: all contemporary art is hard pressed. The fact that the recent evolution of painting weighs so heavy on the pedagogical methods that are supposed to liberate the child and stimulate his creative gifts, is quite enough to make us distrustful of them.

Let us return to the subjective meaning; but let us also measure the width of the gap in our civilization between the even modest ambition that this meaning implies and our chances of translating this ambition into practice. I recall the excitement of two young American women, during a stay in the French countryside, when they discovered that vanilla is a pod and that one can make mayonnaise for oneself from an egg. For these visitors, these substances and their flavors had previously come from an anonymous repertoire of sachets and boxes whose contents had more or less the same origin. All at once, unsuspected connections were established in their mental universe, and they felt reintegrated into a historical process. By doing a few simple things with their hands, they took part in a creation.

This trivial example pinpoints the drama of our civilization which, long before it resulted in a pedagogical crisis, was at the root of a problem we could only skim over. Our children are born and grow up in a world made by us—a world that anticipates their needs, forestalls their questions, and overwhelms them with solutions. In this respect, I see no difference between the industrial products that inundate us and the "imaginary museums," which—in the shape of paperback books, oversized books of reproductions, and endless temporary exhibitions—enervate and dull the taste, discourage effort, and scramble knowledge. These are vain attempts to satisfy the insatiable appetite of a public flooded with the entire spiritual output of humanity. The fact is that, in this world of ease and waste, school remains the only place where one has to take pains, submit to discipline, suffer frustrations, progress step by step, to live a "hard life" (as they say); and children do not accept this situation because they can no longer understand it. Hence, the demoralization that overwhelms them, as they suffer all kinds of constraints for which neither society nor the family has prepared them, and the sometimes tragic consequences of this removal from their natural sphere.

It remains to decide whether the fault lies with the school or with a society that daily loses more and more of the sense of its own function. By raising the problem of the creative child, we are actually missing the point: for it is we ourselves, the frenzied consumers, who are becoming ever less capable of creating. Tortured by our deficiency, we anxiously await the coming of the creative man. And since we cannot glimpse him anywhere, in despair we turn to our children.

Let us take care nevertheless that, by sacrificing the harsh necessities of training to our self-centered fantasies, we do not end up by throwing the school overboard, with all it represents, and robbing posterity of the few solid and substantial parts of our heritage that we can hand down. If we want to initiate our children into creativity by way of art, then it would be a mistake to employ pedagogical methods inspired by the illusory fruits of our sterility. Let us at least realize that we are seeking consolation: by making the child the standard of the creative human being, we are excusing ourselves for letting art regress to the level of child's play—but without noticing that we are leaving the door open to far more critical confusion between that play and other serious aspects of life. Alas! Not everything in life is play. It is this fundamental lesson, which is owed the young minds whose shaping is our task, that we are asked to suppress for the naïve satisfaction of having children engage in attractive exercises, in the guise of pedagogical reform, to justify what is still called art. In these exercises, too, adults themselves can find a lively pleasure—though nothing more.

Chapter 23

Reflections on Liberty*

A SPECIAL commission of the French National Assembly is now [1976] examining three bills on liberty or liberties. Since it pertains purely to procedure, the bill introduced by the Socialist group is beyond the scope of philosophical reflection. On the other hand, the bills introduced by the majority and by the Communist group get to the heart of the matter. But, while approaching and defining the problem in different ways, these two bills nevertheless overlap in one point: both claim a universal basis for the idea of liberty and for the rights deriving from it. The majority defines liberty as a "distinctive characteristic of human will." The Communist group sees in liberties and their exercise "inalienable rights" possessed by "every human being."

Overlooked are the facts that the idea of freedom as we think of it appeared at a relatively recent date, that the contents of this idea are variable, and that a fraction only of humanity adheres to the first definition and believes that it is enjoying the contents of the second—in a way, moreover, that is often illusory. The great principles of the Declaration of Human Rights in 1789 were inspired by the desire to abolish concrete and historical liberties—privileges of the nobility, immunity of the clergy, bourgeois communes and guilds—whose

*On 19 May 1976, I was invited by President Edgar Faure to speak before the National Assembly's special commission on liberties, and I determined to be brief. The following pages, which are more developed, represent what I would probably have said had I permitted myself to speak longer.

maintenance had prevented the exercise of other equally concrete and historical liberties. In this as in other situations, the forms of practical existence give a meaning to the ideologies that express them. By reiterating the same credo century after century, we may blind ourselves to the fact that the world we move in has changed. The privileged freedoms that the world recognizes, and also the ones we demand, are no longer the same.

This relative nature of the idea of freedom is even more obvious with respect to the so-called underdeveloped countries where, with the International Declaration of Rights of 1948, we peddled, and perhaps even imposed, formulas that were meaningless—given the condition of those countries then and, to a large extent, even now. Were their condition to change, the victims of hunger and other physical and mental miseries would care little whether this change took place within frameworks that we would find unendurable. A regimen of forced labor, food rationing, and thought control might even seem like liberation for a people deprived of everything; for such a regimen would be for them the historical means of obtaining remunerative work, of eating their fill, and of opening their intellectual horizon to problems they would have in common with other people.

Furthermore, the followers of the ideology of a totalitarian state can feel free when they think and act as the law expects them to do. Montesquieu did not foresee that virtue, the incentive of democratic governments, may be inculcated in a people, within a single generation, by training processes that have little to do with virtue. But from the moment when, as in China, virtue reigns, the individual members of the social body, and sometimes the vast majority, turn out to conform to Montesquieu's definition, in *L'Esprit des Lois*, of the right-thinking man: he "who loves the laws of his country, who acts out of love for the laws of his country" (1765, p. *lxxxiv*). Only today, after our many experiences during the past half-century, can we gauge how equivocal the concept of virtue is, and understand that this concept treads a very thin line between spontaneous fanaticism and controlled thought. Nor can we be certain that Montesquieu was not tempted to push his right-thinking man dangerously toward the edge of one or the other of these chasms. For instance when he writes, "Liberty consists not in doing what one wishes, but in being able to do what one ought to wish, and in not being forced to do what one ought not to wish" (p. 255). But how can one know what one ought to wish? Montesquieu knew perfectly well, moreover, that every democratic state is doomed precisely because of the degeneration of virtue.

We must therefore be wary of the apologetic zealot who tries to define freedom as a specious absolute that is actually a product of history. The definition of the right of freedom as being based on the nature of man as an ethical being calls for two criticisms. First of all, this definition can be labeled arbitrary, since the idea of freedom has different terms depending on the time, the place, and the form of government. For centuries, the Old Regime outlawed marriage between minors under twenty-five without parental consent, the rationale being that, since the object of laws is to make all commitments wholly free and voluntary, individuals must be prevented from acting under the sway of their passions.

In the second place, the proposed basis remains fragile because of the necessity of surreptitiously restoring to the notion of freedom its relative nature. All known declarations, including the texts of these bills, formulate each individual right only by subordinating its application to what the laws authorize—a limit that is not precisely defined, and that can be redefined at any time. In other words, the legislator never grants any freedom without reserving the right to curtail it or even, if required by circumstances of which he is the sole judge, to abolish it.

For these reasons, the ideological basis that is taken for granted by these two bills seems quite dangerous; and it would be appropriate to ask their framers to ponder certain judicious remarks made by Jean-Jacques Rousseau in the preface to *Discourse on the Origin of Inequality* (1755):

> People begin by seeking rules, on which they ought to agree for the common good; and then they apply the term *natural law* to the collection of these rules with no other proof than the good they feel would result from their universal practice. This is certainly a very convenient method of setting up definitions and explaining the nature of things by almost arbitrary agreements. [P. 152]

Can we then conceive of a basis for freedoms so self-evident as to impose itself on all human beings without distinction? Only one such basis seems possible, but it implies that man be defined not as a moral but as a living being, since this is his most salient characteristic. But if man possesses rights as a living being, then it follows immediately that these recognized rights of humanity as a species will encounter their natural limits in the rights of other species. Thus, the rights of mankind stop whenever and wherever their exercise imperils the existence of another species.

It is not a matter of being unaware that man, like any animal, derives his subsistence from living creatures. But this natural necessity, which is legitimate so long as it is exercised at the expense of individuals, cannot go so far as to obliterate the species to which those individuals belong. The right to life, and to the free development of the living species still represented on the earth, is the only right that can be called inalienable—for the simple reason that the disappearance of any species leaves us with an irreparable void in the system of creation.

These two bills do not entirely omit such considerations. But, in mistaking the consequences for the premises, they find themselves in the predicament of deciding which specific rights of man can justify the protection of the natural environment. The majority party places this protection under the heading of the right to security and does not dwell on it any further. The Communist group prefers to include it —no less arbitrarily—among the rights to culture and information. The Communists devote two articles to it instead of one but render only more obvious the contradictions inherent in the way the two texts try to resolve the problem. For it is contradictory to proclaim, in one article, the right to "wholly unrestricted" activities ["*en pleine nature*"] and, in the next article, the obligation to improve this same nature "in a rational manner" ["*en valeur rationelle*"]. It is just as contradictory to demand in one and the same sentence "the protection of the flora and fauna, the conservation of the countryside, free access to sites" *and* "the elimination of noise pollution, environmental pollution, and every other degradation of the structure of life." Free access to sites is in itself a form of pollution, and not the most innocuous. In a country more advanced than France in this respect—that is, Canada —I know of a natural park that is insidiously deteriorating, according to those in charge, despite the draconian rules that allow on prescribed itineraries only small groups of five or six nature lovers at a time at intervals of several hours.

As embarrassing as it may be to admit, before we even dream of protecting nature *for* man, we have to protect it *against* him. And when, in a recent statement, the minister of justice stated that "justice cannot remain indifferent to the assaults man endures from pollution," he, too, was turning the facts upside down. Man does not endure pollution: he causes it. The right of the environment, which everyone talks about, is the right of the environment in regard to man, and not the right of man in regard to the environment.

Some people will object that these three bills deal with individual rights, and will ask how individual rights can be derived from rights defined at the level of the species. But this difficulty is only apparent because, when we define man, in the traditional sense, as a moral being, we are actually referring to a special property of social life. As a matter of fact, social life treats each of its individual members as if he or she were a species. By forcing each individual to perform a function, to fulfill one or more roles—in short, to have a personality —the group transforms him into the equivalent of what could be called a "mono-individual" species. To grasp this, we need not even focus on the group as a whole but need only look at the way any given family feels the loss of close relations: it is profoundly affected by the dissolution of an irreplaceable synthesis which, for a time, united in a coherent whole a particular history, physical and mental qualities, an original system of ideas and behavior. It is a little as if the natural order had lost a species, itself a unique synthesis of particular qualities that will never appear again.

When we say that man is a moral being and that this quality creates certain rights for him, we are merely taking cognizance of the fact that life in society elevates the biological individual to another sort of dignity. In recognizing this phenomenon, we are not rejecting the criterion of morality; we are simply integrating it in a more general system. As a result, the respect due to the species as a species—and hence due to all species—comes from the rights that, in our species, every individual glories in as an individual—on the same grounds as any other species, but no further than that.

By itself, the nature of this problem could be assented to by all civilizations. Ours first, for the conception that I have outlined was that of the Roman jurists, who were permeated with Stoic influences, and who defined natural law as the aggregate of general relationships established by nature among all animate beings for their mutual preservation. This concept is also that of the great Eastern civilizations inspired by Hinduism and Buddhism; as well as of the so-called under-developed countries, including the humblest groups among them, the illiterate societies studied by anthropologists. As different as these societies may be from one another, they agree on making man a recipient of creation and not its master. By means of wise customs that we would be wrong to treat as mere superstitions, they limit man's consumption of other living species and impose on him a moral respect for them, in conjunction with very strict rules to assure their preservation.

There can be no doubt that if, in his definition of liberties, the French legislator took the decisive step of basing the rights of man on his existence as a living—rather than a moral—being, then our country would enjoy a new prestige. At a time when the quality of life and the protection of the natural environment are among the foremost needs of man, this reformulation of the principles of political philosophy might even appear, in the eyes of the world, as the beginning of a new declaration of rights. It will be rightly said that social and international circumstances are scarcely ripe for it, but preliminary stages have also prepared others. At the moment, we could expect public opinion to be as aroused as it was following the American Declaration of Independence in 1776 and the French Declarations of Rights in 1789 and 1793, whose principles, we better understand today, chiefly served historical needs. These present projects offer France a unique opportunity to place the rights of man on a foundation that, except for a few centuries in the West, has been explicitly or implicitly accepted in all places and in all times.

It is therefore regrettable that the framers of the texts under discussion chose to repeat ritual formulas and to ignore the confusions and difficulties involved in them. They simultaneously, but tacitly, make use of one philosophy of rights that limits the powers of the state, and of another that increases them. The right of every individual to privacy, the condition and earnest of his freedom, is confused with alleged rights that are no more than various desirable goals of social life. One does not create rights by proclaiming these objectives, for society is not automatically capable of achieving them. A society can ask those who govern it to grant each person a private sphere; no matter how privacy is defined, negative prescriptions are enough. But, as indispensable as the right to work for the exercise of freedom may be, we can have only one of two things: either its affirmation remains verbal and gratuitous, or each person has to accept the work that society is able to provide him. This presupposes either a general good will reflecting overall adherence to the collective values or, for lack of such acceptance, measures of constraint. In the latter hypothesis, the state would deny freedom in the name of the right that derives from freedom; in the former case, everything would be expected of a moral arrangement that freedom, defined negatively, is powerless to create. Montesquieu's "virtue" is not decreed by legislation. If the law can guarantee the exercise of freedoms, then these exist only through specific terms that come not from law but from morals.

Actually, the two bills under discussion contain the same internal contradiction; and from this point of view, the Communist and the majority bills join hands. We cannot adopt a rationalist definition of freedom—thus claiming universality—and simultaneously make a pluralist society the place of its flowering and its exercise. A universalist doctrine evolves ineluctably toward a model equivalent to the one-party state or toward a corrupted and rampant freedom where ideas, left to themselves, will fight one another until they lose all substance. The ultimate choice will be between a liberty that is absent in its presence and a liberty present in its absence; and where—to cite Montesquieu once again—after having been free with laws, one wishes to be free against them.

As a political solution, pluralism cannot be defined in the abstract. It loses all consistency if it is not applied to positive terms that have come from somewhere else and that it is incapable of producing itself: freedoms made up of heritages, habits, and beliefs that existed before the laws, and that the laws are supposed to protect. A constant theme in political thought since the eighteenth century has been the contrast between freedoms designated "English" and "French." Without examining how far these concepts reflect empirical truths (which, in the case of England, seem, at the very least, to be tottering), it would be worthwhile to clarify their philosophical significance.

In the first textbook on ethnography to appear in France (whose bicentennial could be celebrated this year, the first edition having been published in 1776, when its author was twenty-five), Jean-Nicolas Démeunier makes a profound remark.* After noting that the ancients

*In my seminar at the Collège de France this year, my attention was drawn to this footnote by Jean Pouillon in Démeunier's book.

avoided wounding popular beliefs, no matter how absurd they might be, Démeunier goes on:

> One can apply the same reflection to the English. These proud islanders look with pity upon writers who combat religious prejudices; they mock their efforts; and, persuaded that the human species is born to err, they do not go to the trouble of destroying superstitions, which would soon be replaced by others. However, freedom of the press and the constitution of their government allows them to attack the administrators, and they endlessly decry despotism. The first law of a monarchy is to remove the seditious and to abolish the freedom to write: the human spirit, which is indomitable, goes astray and attacks religions. The subjects of absolute rulers are more willing to lend an ear to such speculations; while in England, people are more likely to heed the warnings they are given in order to maintain freedom; and the nation that enjoys, or believes it enjoys, freedom sees and hears nothing except when someone speaks to it about despotism. [1776, vol. II, p. 354 n.]

Almost a century later, in 1871, Ernest Renan made similar comments in *La Réforme Intellectuelle en France:*

> England has achieved the most liberal state that the world has known up to now by developing its institutions from the Middle Ages. . . . Freedom in England . . . comes from its entire history, from its equal respect for the right of the king, the right of the lords, the right of the commons and guilds of every type. France took the opposite road. The king had long ago swept away the right of the lords and of the commons; the nation swept away the rights of the king. The nation proceeded philosophically in an area where one should proceed historically. [P. 239]

On the other side of the Channel, Sir Henry Sumner Maine had already written in 1861, in his famous work *Ancient Law,* that the philosophers of France, in their eagerness to escape from what they deemed a superstition of the priests, flung themselves headlong into a superstition of the lawyers (1963, p. 87).

Of these three parallel judgments, Démeunier's goes farthest in not hesitating to see in superstition the surest antidote to despotism. This idea is relevant today, for despotism is always among us; and if asked where it resides, we will borrow another statement from Renan, one that is even more relevant today than in his time: despotism is located in "the vain impertinence of administration," which burdens every citizen with an unendurable dictatorship (1871). But how, then, can the concept of superstition, which is discredited in modern eyes, oppose despotism? We must understand what Démeunier meant by this term.

He was probably referring, first of all, to all the cultural codes that the Le Chapelier law* would soon eradicate; but also, and more generally, to the multitude of small bonds, of tiny solidarities that prevent the individual from being ground down by the overall society and the latter from being pulverized into anonymous and interchangeable atoms. These links integrate each person into a mode of life, a home ground, a tradition, a form of belief or of unbelief, which not only balance one another like Montesquieu's separate powers, but constitute so many counterforces capable of acting together against the abuses of political power.

By providing freedom with a supposedly rational foundation, one condemns it to eliminating this rich content and to sapping its own strength. For the attachment to freedoms is all the greater in that the rights that freedom is asked to protect have a basis that is in part irrational: they consist of those minute privileges, those possibly ludicrous inequalities that, without infringing upon the general equality, allow individuals to find the nearest anchorage. True liberty is that of long habit, of preferences—in a word, of customs: that is, as France's experience since 1789 has proved, a form of freedom implacably opposed by all the theoretical ideas proclaimed as rational. Indeed, this is their only point of agreement; and when they have reached their goals, there is nothing left but for them to destroy one another. And that is where we are today. On the other hand, only "beliefs" (a term that should not be taken in the sense of religious beliefs, although it does not exclude them) can provide liberty with terms to defend. Liberty is maintained from the inside; it undermines itself when people think they can construct it from without.

The anthropologist has little qualification to speak about these problems, except that his profession leads him to see things with a certain detachment. There is at least one way, however, in which he can make a positive contribution. Some of us devote ourselves to studying very small societies that are on a low technical and economic level and have very simple political institutions. Nothing allows us to see them as the image of the earliest human societies; but, in their simple form, they

*Isaac René Le Chapelier (1754–1794) promoted the so-called Le Chapelier Law (1791) which, in declaring coalitions of workers and/or employers unlawful, gave the guild system a final blow.

reveal—perhaps more clearly than more complex societies—the intimate workings of all social life and what may be regarded as a few of its essential conditions. It has been noticed that, in the areas of the world where these societies still survive, they range between forty and two hundred and fifty members. When the population falls below that minimum, the society vanishes sooner or later, and when the population rises above that maximum, the society divides. It is as if two groups of forty to two hundred and fifty are viable, whereas one group of some four hundred or five hundred members is not. Economic causes explain this phenomenon only imperfectly. One must therefore concede that deeper reasons, both social and moral, keep the number of individuals living together within limits that could be called the optimum population density. Thus, by way of experiment, one would verify the existence of a possibly universal human need to live in small communities—a need, however, that does not prevent them from uniting when one of them is attacked from the outside. Based on the collective possession of a history, a language (despite differences of dialect), and a culture, even a large-scale solidarity like national solidarity results from the congregation of small solidarities within these societies—and doubtless elsewhere as well.

Notwithstanding Rousseau, who wanted to abolish any partial society in the state, a certain restoration of partial societies offers a final chance of providing ailing freedoms with a little health and vigor. Unhappily, it is not up to the legislator to bring Western societies back up the slope down which they have been slipping for several centuries —too often, in history, following our own example. The legislator can at least be attentive to the reversal of this trend, signs of which are discernible here and there; he can encourage it in its unforeseeable manifestations, however incongruous and even shocking they may sometimes seem. In any case, the legislator should do nothing that might nip such reversal in the bud or, once it asserts itself, prevent it from following its course.

References

Abbie, A. A. 1951. The Australian Aborigine. *Oceania* 22(2): 91–100.
———. 1961. Recent Field-Work on the Physical Anthropology of Australian Aborigines. *Australian Journal of Science* 23(7): 210–11.
Albus, Anita. 1973. *Der Himmel ist mein Hut*. Frankfurt/Main: Insel Verlag.
———. 1976. *Der Garten der Lieder*. Frankfurt/Main: Insel Verlag.
———. 1978. *Eia Popeia Etcetera*. Frankfurt/Main: Insel Verlag.
Alexander, R. D. 1974. The Evolution of Social Behavior. *Annual Review of Ecology and Systematics* 5.
Amoore, John E. 1970. *Molecular basis of odor*. Springfield, Ill.: Charles C Thomas.
Apollinaire. 1965. *Alcools*. Paris: Bibliothèque de la Pléiade. Originally published in 1913.
Apollonius of Rhodes. 1882. *L'Expédition des Argonauts à la conquête de la toison d'or*. French translation from the Greek by J. J. A. Caussin. Paris: 1799.
Armstrong, E. C., et al., eds. 1937. *The medieval French roman d'Alexandre*. Vol. 1, edited by Milan S. La Du; vol. 2, edited by E. C. Armstrong, et al. Elliott Monographs in the Romance Languages and Literature, 36–37. Princeton, N. J.: Princeton University Press.
Arriaga, P. J. de. 1920. *La extirpación de la idolatría en el Perú. Colección de libros y documentos referentes a la historia del Perú*. 2nd series, vol. 1. Lima: Sanmartí.
Aston, W. G. 1896. *Nibongi, chronicles of Japan from the earliest times to A.D. 697*. Translated from the Chinese and Japanese by W. G. Aston, C. M. G. Transactions and Proceedings of the Japan Society, London, supp. I. 2 vols. London: Kegan Paul, Trench, Trübner & Co.
Avila, F. de. 1966. *Dioses y hombres de Hyarochiri*. Translated by J. M. Arguedas. Bibliographic study of P. Duviols. Lima: Museo Nacional de Historia y el Instituto de Estudios Pervanos.

Bailey, L. H. 1943. *The standard cyclopedia of horticulture*. New York: Macmillan.
Bastide, Roger. 1972. *Sociologie et psychanalyse*. 2nd ed. Paris: Presses Universitaires de France.
Baudelaire, Charles. 1975. L'Exposition universelle de 1855. *Oeuvres complètes*. Paris: Gallimard.
Beattie, J. H. M. 1958. *Nyoro kinship, marriage and affinity*. International African Institute, memorandum XXVIII.
Beauchamp, W. M. 1898. Indian Corn Stories and Customs. *Journal of American Folk-Lore* 11(42): 195–202.
Beckwith, M. W. 1938. Mandan-Hidatsa Myths and Ceremonies. *Memoirs of the American Folklore Society*, vol. 32. New York: J. J. Augustin.
Belmont, N. 1971. *Les signes de la naissance*. Paris: Plon.

References

Benoist, J. 1966. Du Social au Biologique: Etude de Quelques Interactions. *L'Homme, Revue Française d'Anthropologie* 6(1).

Benveniste, Emile. 1966. Nature du Signe Linguistique. *Acta Linguistica.* Reprinted in *Problèmes de linguistique générale.* 2 vols. Paris: Editions Gallimard. Originally published in 1939 in Copenhagen.

Berlin, Brent; and Kay, Paul. 1969. *Basic color terms: Their universality and evolution.* Berkeley: University of California Press.

Berndt, R. M. 1962. *Excess and restraint.* Chicago: University of Chicago Press.

Berthier-Caillet, L., ed. 1981. *Fêtes et rites des 4 saisons au Japon.* Publications orientalistes de France.

Binyon, L.; and Sexton, J. J. O'Brien. 1960. *Japanese colour prints.* London: Faber & Faber.

Black, L. 1973. The Nivkh (Gilyak) of Sakhalin and the Lower Amur. *Arctic Anthropology* (University of Wisconsin Press) 10(1): 1–106.

Boas, Franz. 1888. On Certain Songs and Dances of the Kwakiutl. *Journal of American Folk-lore* 1(1): 49–64.

———. 1895a. Indianische Sagen von der Nord-Pacifischen Küste Amerikas. In *Sonder-Abdruck aus den Verhandlungen der Berliner Gesellschaft für Anthropologie, Ethnologie und Urgeschichte, 1891–1895.* Berlin: A. Asher.

———. 1895b. The Social Organization and the Secret Societies of the Kwakiutl Indians. In *Report of the United States National Museum.* Washington, D. C.: Government Printing Office, 1897.

———. 1898. The Mythology of the Bella Coola Indians. In *Publications of the Jesup North Pacific Expedition.* Vol. 1, 1898–1900. New York. Memoirs of the American Museum of Natural History. Vol. 2.

———. 1910. *Kwakiutl Tales.* Columbia University contributions to anthropology, vol. 2. New York: Columbia University Press.

———. 1916. Tsimshian Mythology. In *31st annual report of the Bureau of American Ethnology to the secretary of the Smithsonian Institution, 1909–1910.* Washington, D.C.

———, ed. 1917. Folk-Tales of Salishan and Sahaptin Tribes. *Memoirs of the American Folklore Society* 11.

———. 1918. Kutenai Tales. *Bulletin of the Bureau of American Ethnology* 59. Washington, D.C.

———. 1921. Ethnology of the Kwakiutl. In *35th annual report, Bureau of American Ethnology, 1913–1914.* 2 vols. Washington, D.C.

———. 1925. *Contributions to the ethnology of the Kwakiutl.* Columbia University contributions to anthropology, vol. 3. New York: Columbia University Press.

———. 1928. *Bella Bella texts.* Columbia University contributions to anthropology, vol. 5. New York: Columbia University Press.

———. 1932. *Bella Bella tales.* Memoirs of the American Folklore Society, vol. 25. New York: American Folklore Society/G. E. Stechert.

———. 1935a. *Kwakiutl culture as reflected in mythology.* Memoirs of the American Folklore Society, vol. 28. New York: American Folklore Society/G. E. Stechert.

———. 1935b. *Kwakiutl tales, new series.* Columbia University contributions to anthropology, vol. 26. New York: Columbia University Press.

———. 1944. *Geographical names of the Kwakiutl Indians.* Columbia University contributions to anthropology, vol. 20. New York: Columbia University Press.

———. 1966. *Kwakiutl ethnography.* Classics in anthropology. Edited by Helen Codere. Chicago and London: University of Chicago Press.

Boas, Franz; and Hunt, G. 1902–5. Kwakiutl texts. *Publications of the Jesup North Pacific Expedition.* Vol. 3. Memoirs of the American Museum of Natural History, vol. 5. New York: G. E. Stechert.

Bott, E. 1981. Power and Rank in the Kingdom of Tonga. *Journal of the Polynesian Society* 90(1).

References

Bowers, A. W. 1965. Hidatsa Social and Ceremonial Organization. *Bulletin 194, Bureau of American Ethnology.* Washington, D.C.: Smithsonian Institution.

Braidwood, R. J., et al. 1953. Symposium: Did Man Once Live By Beer Alone? *American Anthropologist* 55(4): 515–26.

Brandon, James R., et al. 1978. *Studies in Kabuki: Its acting, musical, and historical context.* Honolulu: University of Hawaii Press.

Burridge, K. 1969. *Tangu traditions.* Oxford, England: Clarendon Press.

Cabiers d'Art. 1937. Special issue on Max Ernst. Paris.

Callet, R. P. 1953–58. *Histoire des rois.* French translation of *Tantaran' ny Andriana* by G. S. Chapus and E. Ratsimba. 3 vols. Tananarive, Malagasy Republic.

Carroll, M. P. 1980. What's in a Name? *American Ethnologist* 7(1): 182–84.

——. 1981. Lévi-Strauss, Freud and the Trickster: A New Perspective upon an Old Problem. *American Ethnologist* 8 (2 [May 1981]): 301–13.

——. 1982. Tricksters and Clam Siphons. *American Ethnologist* 9 (I [February 1982]): 193.

Chamberlain, B. H. 1902. *Things Japanese.* London: John Murray.

Chamfort, Nicolas de. 1982. *Colleccion folio,* no. 8. Originally published in 1803.

Chapus, G. S.; and Mondain, G. 1953. *Rainilaiarivony: Un homme d'état malgache.* Paris: Diloutremer.

Chrétien de Troyes. 1947. *Perceval le Gallois.* Edited by Foulet. Paris: Stock.

Cline, W., et al. 1938. The Sinkaietk or Southern Okanagon of Washington. *General series in anthropology,* vol. 6. Menasha, Wash.

Cobbi, J. 1978. *Le végétal dans la vie japonaise.* Publications Orientalistes de France.

Coquet, Jean-Claude. 1972. *Sémiotique littéraire.* Paris: Mame.

Corbin, Henry. 1972. *En Islam iranien.* 4 vols. Paris: Gallimard.

Crocker, J. Christopher. n.d. The Stench of Death: Structure and Process in Bororo Shamanism. Manuscript, University of Virginia.

Current Directions in Anthropology (Bulletins of the American Anthropological Association) 3 (1970).

Curtin, J.; and Hewitt, J. N. B. 1918. Seneca Fiction, Legends, and Myths. In *32nd annual report of the Bureau of American Ethnology, 1910–1911.* Washington, D.C.

Curtis, Edward S. 1970. *The North American Indian.* 20 vols. Boulder, Col.: Johnson Books. Originally published 1907–30.

Deguy, Michel. 1974. Encore une Lecture des *Colchiques* ou: Un Poème de l'Apophonie. *Poétique* 5(20): 452–57.

Délivré, A. 1974. *L'Histoire des rois d'Imerina. Interprétation d'une tradition orale.* Paris: Klincksieck.

Démeunier, Jean-Nicolas. 1776. *L'Esprit des usages et des coutumes des différens peuples.* 3 vols. London: Chez Pissot.

Detienne, M. 1970. La Cuisine de Pythagore. *Archives de Sociologie des Religions* 15 (29): 141–62.

——. 1972. *Les jardins d'Adonis.* Paris: Gallimard.

Diodorus of Sicily. 1780. *Histoire universelle.* Translated by Terrasson. 6 vols. Amsterdam: D. J. Changuion.

Diogenes Laertius. 1878. *Vitae philosophorum.* Paris: A. Firmin-Didot.

Dixon, R. B. 1909. Mythology of the Central and Eastern Algonkins. *Journal of American Folk-lore* 22(83): 1–9.

Dorsey, G. A. 1906. *The Pawnee.* Mythology (Part I). Washington, D.C.: Carnegie Institution of Washington.

Drucker, Philip; and Heizer, Robert F. 1967. *To make my name good.* Berkeley and Los Angeles: University of California Press.

Dumézil, Georges. 1975. *Fêtes romaines.* Paris: Gallimard.

References

Elkin, A. P. 1938*a*. Kinship in South Australia. *Oceania* 8:419–52.

—. 1938*b*. *The Australian aborigines*. Sydney, London, and Melbourne: Angus & Robertson. (The page references in the text are from the 1964 edition: Garden City, New York: Doubleday.)

Elmendorf, W. W. 1951. Word Taboo and Lexical Change in Coast Salish. *International Journal of American Linguistics* 17 (4): 205–8.

—. 1960. *The structure of Twana culture, with comparative notes of the structure of Yurok culture.* Comparative notes by A. L. Kroeber. Pullman: Washington State University Press.

Elmore, Francis H. 1944. *Ethnobotany of the Navajo.* The University of New Mexico, Bulletin, Monograph Series, no. 7. Albuquerque: University of New Mexico Press.

Ernst, Max. 1934. Qu'est-ce que le surréalisme? *Le Petit Journal des Grandes Expositions.* Paris, 2 April–31 May 1971.

Eschenbach, Wolfram von. 1961. *Parzival.* Translated by Helen M. Mustard and Charles E. Passage. New York: Random House.

Evans-Pritchard, E. E. 1948. *The divine kinship of the Shilluk of the Nilotic Sudan.* Cambridge: Cambridge University Press.

Firth, R. 1961. *History and traditions of Tikopia.* London: Routledge.

Fisher, M. W. 1946. The Mythology of the Northern and Northeastern Algonkians in reference to Algonkian Mythology as a Whole. In "Man in Northeastern North America," *Papers of the R. S. Peabody Foundation for Archaeology,* edited by F. Johnson, vol. 3. Andover, Mass.

Frappier, J. 1972. *Chrétien de Troyes et le mythe du Graal.* Paris: Société d'Edition d'Enseignement Supérieur.

Frazer, J. G. 1926–36. *The golden bough.* 3rd ed. 13 vols. London: Macmillan.

Friedberg, C.; and Hocquenghem, A. M. 1977. Des haricots hallucinogènes? *Journal d'Agriculture Traditionnelle et de Botanique Appliquée* 24 (1).

Gayton, A. H.; and Newman, S. S. 1940. Yokuts and Western Mono Myths. *Anthropological Records* 5(1): 1–110.

Gellius, Aulus. 1549. *Auli Gellii luculentissimi scriptoris, Noctes atticae.* Coloniae Martinus.

Gibbs, G. 1877. Tribes of Western Washington and Northeastern Oregon. *Contributions to North American ethnology,* vol. 1. Washington, D.C.

Giles, E. 1970. Culture and Genetics. *Current Directions in Anthropology* 3 (3).

Gluckman, M. 1950. Kinship and Marriage among the Lozi of Northern Rhodesia and the Zulu of Natal. In A. R. Radcliffe-Brown and Daryll Forde, eds., *African systems of kinship and marriage.* New York, Oxford, and Toronto: Oxford University Press.

Goody, J., ed. 1958. *The developmental cycle in domestic groups.* Cambridge papers in social anthropology, no. 1.

Granet, Marcel. 1939. *Catégories matrimoniales et relations de proximité dans la Chine ancienne.* Paris: F. Alcan.

Groves, M. 1963. The Nature of Fijian Society: A Review. *Journal of the Polynesian Society* 72(3): 272–91.

Gunther, E. 1928. A Further Analysis of the First Salmon Ceremony. *University of Washington publications in anthropology* 2.

Haile, Father Berard. 1981. *Upward moving and emergence way.* American tribal religions, vol. 7. Lincoln, Neb., and London: University of Nebraska Press.

Halpin, M. n.d. Masks as Metaphors of Anti-Structure. Manuscript, University of British Columbia.

Hamilton, W. D. 1964. The Genetical Evolution of Social Behaviour. *Journal of Theoretical Biology* 7 (1): 1–16.

References

Harris, Marvin. 1976. Lévi-Strauss et la palourde. *L'Homme* 16:5–22. Published in the United States in *Cultural materialism: The struggle for a science of culture.* 1979. New York: Random House.

Hecht, J. 1977. The Culture of Gender in Pukapuka: Male, Female and the Mayakitanga "Sacred Maid." *Journal of the Polynesian Society* 86 (2): 183–206.

Héritier, F. 1981. *L'Exercice de la parenté.* Paris: Gallimard-Le Seuil.

Herner, Torsten. 1965. Significance of the Body Image in Schizophrenic Thinking. *American Journal of Psychotherapy* 19 (3): 455–66.

Herodotus. 1946–48. *Histoires.* Text and translation. Paris: Société d'édition "Les Belles Lettres."

Hill-Tout, C. 1911. Report on the Ethnology of the Okanakēn of British Columbia. *Journal of the Royal Anthropological Institute* 41: 130–61.

Hissink, K. 1951. Motive der Mochica-Keramik. *Paideuma. Mitteilungen zur Kulturkunde* 5(3): 115–35. Bamberg: Bamberges Verlagshaus, Meisenbach.

Hocart, A. M. 1952. *The northern states of Fiji.* London: Royal Anthropological Institute Occasional Publications, no. 11.

———. 1970. *Kings and councillors: An essay in the comparative anatomy of human society.* Edited by R. Needham. Chicago: University of Chicago Press.

Hocquenghem, A. M. 1979. Le Jeu et l'Iconographie Mochica. *Baessler-Archiv, Neue Folge,* Band 27.

Hoffman, W. J. 1884. Selish Myths. Salem, Mass.: *Bulletin of the Essex Institute* 15.

Howard, J. A. 1957. The Mescal Bean Cult of the Central and Southern Plains. *American Anthropologist* 59 (1): 75–87.

———. 1965. *The Ponca tribe.* Bureau of American Ethnology, Bulletin 195. Washington, D.C.: Smithsonian Institution.

Hume, David. 1965. *Hume's ethical writings; selections from David Hume.* Edited by Alasdair MacIntyre. Notre Dame, Ind.: University of Notre Dame Press. Originally published in 1748.

Huntsman, J.; and Hooper, A. 1975. Male and Female in Tokelau Culture. *Journal of the Polynesian Society* 84 (4): 415–30.

Indradeva, Shrirama. 1973. La Genèse de la Civilisation Indienne à Travers les Grhya-Sūtra. *Diogene* 84: 28–43. Paris: Gallimard.

Iryon. 1972. *Samguk yusa. Legends and history of the three kingdoms of ancient Corea.* Translated by Ha Tae-Hung; and Mintz, Grafton K. Seoul, South Korea: Yonsei University Press.

Jacobs, Melville. 1959. Clackamas Chinook Texts. *International Journal of American Linguistics* 25 (2, part II): 388–409.

Jakobson, Roman. 1962. *Selected writings.* Vol. 1. S. Gravenhage: Mouton.

———. 1970. La Linguistique. In *Tendences principales de la recherche dans les sciences sociales et humaines.* Paris: UNESCO.

———. 1971a. *Selected writings.* Vol. 2. The Hague and Paris: Mouton.

———. 1971b. The World Response to Whitney's Principles of Linguistic Science. In *Whitney on language.* Edited by M. Silverstein. Cambridge, Mass., and London: MIT Press.

———. 1978. *Six lectures on sound and meaning.* Cambridge, Mass.: MIT Press. Originally published in Paris in 1976.

———. 1979. *The sound and shape of language.* Bloomington: University of Indiana Press.

Jochelson, W. 1908. The Koryak, Religion and Myths. In *Publications of the Jesup North Pacific Expedition.* Vol. 6, part 1. New York: Memoirs of the American Museum of Natural History.

Johnston, F. E. 1970. Genetic Anthropology: Some Considerations. *Current Directions in Anthropology* 3 (3).

References

Karsten, R. 1935. The Head-Hunters of Eastern Amazonas. *Societas Scientiarum Fennica, Commentationes Humanarum Litterarum.* Vol. 7. Helsingfors.

Kilbride, J. E.; Robbins, M. C.; and Kilbride, P. L. 1970. The Comparative Motor Development of Baganda, American White and American Black Infants. *American Anthropologist* 72.

Köhler, Wolfgang. 1910–15. Akustische Untersuchungen. *Zeitschrift für Psychologie.* Leipzig: J. A. Barth.

Krige, E. J. 1975*a*. Asymmetrical Matrilateral Cross-Cousin Marriage—The Lovedu Case. *African Studies* 34 (4): 231–57.

————. 1975*b*. Divine Kinship, Change and Development. In Meyer Fortes and Sheila Patterson, eds., *Studies in African social anthropology.* New York: Academic Press.

Kroeber, Alfred L. 1917. The Superorganic. *American Anthropologist* 17 (2): 163–213. Published later in *The nature of culture.* 1952. Chicago: University of Chicago Press.

Kutscher, C. 1951. Ritual Races among Early Chimu. In *The civilization of ancient America. Selected papers of the XXIXth International Congress of Americanists.* Chicago.

Laguna, F. de. 1972. *Under Mount Saint Elias: The history and culture of the Yakutat Tlingit.* Smithsonian Contributions to Anthropology, vol. 7. Washington, D.C.: Smithsonian Institution Press.

Larousse, Pierre. 1866–76. *Grand dictionnaire universel du XIXe siècle.* Paris.

Leach, Sir E. 1961. *Rethinking anthropology.* London School of Economics Monographs on Social Anthropology, no. 22. London: Athlone Press.

Lévi-Strauss, Claude. 1952. Race et histoire. Paris: UNESCO. Published later in *Structural anthropology,* vol. 2, chap. 18.

————. 1963. *Structural anthropology,* vol. 1. New York and London: Basic Books. Originally published in France in 1958.

————. 1966. *The savage mind.* Chicago: University of Chicago Press. Originally published in Paris in 1962.

————. 1969*a*. *The elementary structures of kinship.* Boston: Beacon Press. Originally published in France in 1967.

————. 1969*b*. *Compte rendu d'enseignement 1968–1969.* Annuaire du Collège de France.

————. 1970. *The raw and the cooked.* Translated by John Weightman and Doreen Weightman. Vol. 1 in Introduction to a Science of Mythology Series. New York: Octagon Books. Originally published in France in 1964 and in the United States in 1969.

————. 1971. Comment meurent les mythes. In *Science et conscience de la société. Mélanges en l'honneur de Raymond Aron.* 2 vols. Paris: Calmann-Lévy. Also published in the United States in *Structural anthropology,* vol. 2, chap. 14.

————. 1973. *From honey to ashes.* Translated by John Weightman and Doreen Weightman. Vol. 2 in Introduction to a Science of Mythology Series. New York: Harper & Row. Originally published in France in 1967.

————. 1976. *Structural anthropology,* vol. 2. New York: Basic Books. Originally published in France in 1973.

————. 1978. *Myth and meaning.* Toronto: University of Toronto Press. New York: Schocken Books (1979).

————. 1979. *The origin of table manners.* Translated by John Weightman and Doreen Weightman. Vol. 3 in Introduction to a Science of Mythology Series. New York: Harper & Row. Originally published in France in 1968.

————. 1981. *The naked man.* Translated by John Weightman and Doreen Weightman. Vol. 4 in Introduction to a Science of Mythology Series. New York: Harper & Row. Originally published in France in 1971.

————. 1982. *The way of the masks.* Translated by Sylvia Modelski. Seattle: University of Washington Press. Originally published in France in 1975.

References

Levrault, F. G. 1816–30. *Dictionnaire des sciences naturelles . . . par plusieurs professeurs du Jardin du Roi et des principales écoles de Paris.* Vol. 10, 1818. Paris: Strasbourg-Le Normant.

Lienhardt, G. 1955. Nilotic Kings and Their Mothers' Kin. *Africa* 25: 29–41.

Livingstone, F. B. 1958. Anthropological Implications of Sickle Cell Gene Distribution in West Africa. *American Anthropologist* 60 (3): 533–62.

Lloyd, P. C. 1960. Sacred Kinship and Government among the Yoruba. *Africa* 30: 221–37.

Loraux, N. 1981. *Les enfants d'Athéna.* Paris: Maspero.

Loth, J. 1913. *Les Mabinogion du livre rouge de Hergest . . .* 2 vols. Paris: Fontemoing et Cie.

Luria, A. R. 1976. *Basic problems of neurolinguistics.* The Hague: Mouton.

Mabuchi, T. 1952. Social Organization of the Central Tribes of Formosa. *International Archives of Ethnography* 46 (2). Leiden: Brill.

———. 1964. Spiritual Predominance of the Sister. In Allan H. Smith, ed., *Studies of Ryukuan culture and society.* Honolulu.

McConnel, U. H. 1940. Social Organization of the Tribes of Cape York Peninsula. *Oceania* 10: 434–55.

McCullough, H. C. 1980. *Okagami, the great mirror. Fujiwara Michinaga and his time.* Princeton: Princeton University Press.

McCullough, W. H. 1967. Japanese Marriage Institutions in the Heian Period. *Harvard Journal of Asiatic Studies* 27: 103–67.

McCullough, W. H.; and McCullough, H. C. 1980. *A tale of flowering fortunes: Annals of Japanese aristocratic life in the Heian Period [Eiga monogatari].* 2 vols. Stanford, Calif.: Stanford University Press.

McIlwraith, T. F. 1948. *The Bella Coola Indians.* 2 vols. Toronto: Toronto University Press.

McKnight, D. 1971. Some Problems Concerning the Wik-mungkan. In *Rethinking kinship and marriage,* 145–80. London and New York: Tavistock.

———. 1973. Sexual Symbolism of Food among the Wik-mungkan. *Man* 8 (2 [June]): 194–209.

Maine, Henry Sumner. 1963. *Ancient law.* Boston: Beacon Press. Originally published in 1861.

Malzac, R. P. 1912. *Histoire du royaume hova.* Tananarive, Madagascar.

Maupoil, B. 1943. *La Géomancie à l'ancienne Côte des Esclaves.* Travaux et Mémoires de l'Institut d'Ethnologie, vol. 42. Paris.

Mauss, Marcel. 1950. *Sociologie et anthropologie.* Paris: Presses Universitaires de France.

Mayne, R. C. 1862. *Four years in British Columbia and Vancouver Island.* London: J. Murray.

Meggitt, M. J. 1962. *Desert people: A study of the Walbiri aborigines of central Australia.* Chicago: University of Chicago Press.

Merleau-Ponty, Maurice. 1945. *The phenomenology of perception.* Translated by Colin Smith. New York: Humanities Press, 1962.

Meyer, P. 1886. *Alexandre le Grand dans la littérature française du moyen âge.* 2 vols. Paris.

Michelant, H. V. 1846. *Li romans d'Alexandre par Lambert li Tors et Alexandre de Bernay, nach Handschriften der königlichen Büchersammlung zu Paris.* Bibliothek des literarischen Vereins in Stuttgart, vol. 3. Stuttgart.

Montesquieu. 1765. *L'Esprit des lois. Oeuvres de Monsieur de Montesquieu.* Vol. 1. Amsterdam and Leipzig.

Morin, Edgar; and Piattelli-Palmarini, Massimo, eds. 1974. *L'Unité de l'homme.* Paris: Editions du Seuil.

Nadel, S. F. 1950. Dual Descent in the Nuba Hills. In A. R. Radcliffe-Brown and Daryll Forde, *African systems of kinship and marriage.* New York: Oxford University Press.

———. 1971. *Byzance noire. Le Royaume des Nupe du Nigeria (A Black Byzantium, 1942).* Paris: Maspero.

References

Nayacakalou, R. R. 1955–57. The Fijian System of Kinship and Marriage. *Journal of the Polynesian Society* 64, 66.

Neel, J. V. 1970. Lessons from a "Primitive" People. *Science* 170: 815–22.

Olson, R. L. 1954. Social Life of the Owikeno Kwakiutl. *Anthropological Records* 14 (3): 213–60.

———. 1955. Notes on the Bella Bella Kwakiutl. *Anthropological Records* 14 (5): 319–48.

Onians, R. B. 1954. *The origins of European thought about the body, the mind, the soul, the world, time, and fate.* New York: Cambridge University Press.

Ovid. 1838. Fastes. In *Oeuvres complètes avec la traduction en français publiées sous la direction de M. Nisard.* Paris: J. J. Dubochet.

Panofsky, Erwin. 1974. *Meaning in the visual arts: Papers in and on art history.* Woodstock, N.Y.: Overlook Press. Originally published in 1955.

Parsons, E. C. 1936. *Mitla: Town of the souls.* Chicago: University of Chicago Press.

Pascal, Blaise. 1877. *Pensées.* Paris: Lemerre.

Pastoureau, M. 1979. *Traité d'héraldique.* Paris: Picard.

Pausanias. 1913. *Description of Greece.* 6 vols. Translated by J. G. Frazer. London: Macmillan.

Pennington, C. W. 1969. *The Tepehuan of Chihuahua: Their material culture.* Salt Lake City: University of Utah Press.

Perrot, E. 1947. *Plantes médicinales de France.* 4 vols. Paris: Presses Universitaires de France.

Phinney, A. 1934. *Nez Percé texts.* Columbia University Contributions to Anthropology, vol. 25. New York: Columbia University Press.

Picon, Gaëtan. 1980. *Jean-Auguste-Dominique Ingres.* Rev. ed. New York: Rizzoli.

Pindar. 1922–23. *Texte établi et traduit par Aimé Puech.* 4 vols. Paris: Les Belles Lettres.

Platt, T. 1978. Symétries en Miroir. Le Concept de Yanatin chez les Macha de Bolivie. *Annales* 33 (5–6 [September–December]): 1081–1107.

Pliny, Gaius (the Elder). 1584. *L'Histoire du monde.* 2 vols. 3rd ed. Translated by Antoine du Pinet. Lyon: Antoine Tardif.

Ploetz, H.; and Métraux, A. 1930. *La civilisation matérielle et la vie religieuse des Indiens Zě du Brésil méridional et oriental.* (Revista del Instituto de Etnología de la Universidad Nacional de Tucumán, vol. I (1), 107–238).

Plutarch. 1584. *La demande des choses romaines.* In Jacques Amyot and Evesque D'Auxerre, trans., *Les oeuvres morales et meslées de Plutarque.* 2 vols. Paris: Guillaume de la Nouë.

Pouillon, Jean. 1975. *Fétiches sans fétichisme.* Paris: Maspero.

Quain, Buell. 1948. *Fijian village.* Ann Arbor, Mich.: Xerox University Microfilms.

Radcliffe-Brown, Alfred R. 1952. *Structure and function in primitive society.* New York: Free Press.

———. 1959. *Method in social anthropology.* Chicago: University of Chicago Press.

Radcliffe-Brown, Alfred R.; and Forde, Daryll. 1950. *African systems of kinship and marriage.* New York: Oxford University Press.

Ray, V. F. 1933. Sanpoil Folk Tales. *Journal of American Folk-lore* 46: 129–88.

Rehfisch, F. 1960. The Dynamic of Multilineality on the Mambila Plateau. *Africa* 30: 246–61.

Reichard, Gladys A. 1947. An Analysis of Coeur d'Alene Indian Myths. *Memoirs of the American Folklore Society,* vol. 41.

———. 1963. *Navaho religion.* New York: Pantheon.

Renan, Ernest. 1871. *La réforme intellectuelle en France.* Paris.

Richards, A. I. 1950. Some Types of Family Structure amongst the Central Bantu. In

References

Alfred R. Radcliffe-Brown and Daryll Forde, *African systems of kinship and marriage*. New York: Oxford University Press.

Riegl, A. 1966. *Historische Grammatik der bildenden Künste*. Cologne: Graz.

Ritzenthaler, R.; and Parsons, L. A. 1966. *Masks of the northwest coast*. Publications in primitive art, vol. 2. Milwaukee: Milwaukee Public Museum.

Rock, I. 1981. Anorthoscopic Perception. *Scientific American* 244(3): 145–54.

Rousseau, Jean-Jacques. 1971. *Discours sur les sciences et les arts. Discours sur l'origine et les fondements de l'inégalité parmi les hommes*. Paris: Garnier-Flammarion. Originally published in 1755.

Sahlins, M. D. 1962. *Moala. Culture and nature on a Fijian island*. Ann Arbor: University of Michigan Press.

Schmidt, Oskar. 1893. Die Niederen Tiere. *Brehms Tierleben*. Leipzig and Vienna.

Schwimmer, E. 1973. *Exchange in the social structure of the Orokaiva*. London: C. Hurst.

Serusier, P. 1950. *ABC de la peinture, suivi d'une correspondance inédite* . . . Paris: Floury.

Shibata, M.; and Shibata, M. 1969. *Kojiki*. Paris: Maisonneuve et Larose.

Shikibu, Murasaki. 1978. *The tale of Genji*. Translated by Seidensticker, E. G. New York: Alfred A. Knopf.

Speck, F. G. 1915. Some Micmac Tales from Cape Breton Island. *Journal of American Folk-lore* 28: 59–69.

———. 1942. *The Tutelo spirit adoption ceremony*. Harrisburg: Pennsylvania Historical Commission.

Spencer, B.; and Gillen, F. J. 1938. *The native tribes of central Australia*. London: Macmillan. Originally published in 1899.

Spier, L. 1928. *Havasupai Ethnography*. Anthropological Papers of the American Museum of Natural History 29 (part 3). New York.

———. 1933. *Yuman tribes of the Gila River*. Chicago: University of Chicago Press.

Spinden, H. 1908. Myths of the Nez Percé Indians. *Journal of American Folk-lore* 21: 13–23.

Stern, B. J. 1934. *The Lummi Indians of western Washington*. Columbia contributions to anthropology, vol. 17. New York: Columbia University Press.

Stumpf, Carl. 1926. *Die Sprachlaute*. Berlin: J. Springer.

Swanton, J. R. 1905. *Haida texts and myths*. Bureau of American Ethnology, Bulletin 29. Washington, D.C.: Smithsonian Institution.

———. 1908. Haida Texts. In *Publications of the Jesup North Pacific Expedition*. Vol. 10, 1905–1908. Memoirs of the American Museum of Natural History, vol. 14. New York.

———. 1909. *Tlingit myths and texts*. Bureau of American Ethnology, Bulletin 39. Washington, D.C.: Smithsonian Institution.

Taylor, D. 1961. Grandchildren versus Other Semidomesticated Animals. *International Journal of American Linguistics* 27 (4): 367–70.

Teit, James A. 1898. Traditions of the Thompson Indians. *Memoirs of the American Folk-lore Society*. Boston and New York: Houghton, Mifflin.

———. 1900. The Thompson Indians of British Columbia. *Memoirs of the American Museum of Natural History*. Vol. 2. New York.

———. 1906. The Lilloet Indians. *Memoirs of the American Museum of Natural History*. Vol. 4. New York.

———. 1909. *The Shuswap*. In *Publications of the Jesup North Pacific Expedition*, no. 2, part 7. Reprint. New York: Memoirs of the American Museum of Natural History.

———. 1912. Mythology of the Thompson Indians. *Memoirs of the American Museum of Natural History*. Vol. 12. New York.

Thevet, A. 1575. *La cosmographie universelle*. Paris: P. L'Huillier.

Thom, R. 1974. *Modèles mathématiques de la morphogénèse*. Paris: Union Générale d'Editions.

References

Thompson, Stith. 1966. *Motif-index of folk literature*. Rev. ed. 6 vols. Bloomington and London: Indiana University Press. Originally published in Copenhagen in 1956.

Thomson, D. F. 1935. The Joking Relationship and Organized Obscenity in North Queensland. *American Anthropologist* 37: 460–90.

———. 1936. Fatherhood in the Wik Monkan Tribe. *American Anthropologist* 38: 374–93.

———. 1955. Two Devices for the Avoidance of First-Cousin Marriage among the Australian aborigines. *Man* 55 (44 [March]): 39–40.

Tonnelat, E. 1934. *Traduction du Parzival*. 2 vols. Paris: Aubier.

Trubetzkoy, N. S. 1969. *Principles of phonology*. Translated by Christiane A. M. Baltaxe. Berkeley and Los Angeles: University of California Press.

Tylor, Edward Burnett. 1889. On a Method of Investigating the Development of Institutions. . . . *Journal of the Royal Anthropological Institute* 18: 267.

Van Wouden, F. A. E. 1935. *Social Structuurtypen in de Groote Oost*. Leiden: Universiteits boekhandel en Antiquariaat J. Ginsberg.

Vernant, J.-P. 1974. *Mythe et société en Grèce ancienne*. Paris: Maspero.

Vigny, Alfred de. 1978. L'Esprit pur. In *Oeuvres poétiques*. Paris: Garnier-Flammarion. Originally published in 1863.

Vinogradoff, Sir Paul. 1920. *Outlines of historical jurisprudence*. New York: Oxford University Press.

Vogt, E. S. 1969. *Zinacantan. A Maya community in the highlands of Chiapas*. Cambridge, Mass.: Harvard University Press.

Wagner, Cosima. 1980. *Diaries*. Vol. 2. Translated by Geoffrey Skelton. New York: Harcourt Brace Jovanovich. Originally published, with vol. 1, in 4 vols. in W. Germany, 1977.

Waterman, T. T. 1973. *Notes on the ethnology of the Indians of Puget Sound*. Indian Notes and Monographs, miscellaneous series, 59. New York: Museum of the American Indian, Heye Foundation.

Weissman, H. 1850. *Alexander, Gedicht des zwölften Jahrhunderts vom Pfaffen Lamprecht*. 2 vols. Frankfurt am Main.

Westermarck, E. 1922. *The history of human marriage*. 3 vols. New York: Allerton.

White, L. A. 1942. *The Pueblo of Santa Ana, New Mexico*. Memoir Series of the American Anthropological Association. Vol. 60. *American Anthropologist* 44 (4 [part 2]).

Wilson, Edward O. 1975. *Sociology: The new synthesis*. Cambridge, Mass.: Harvard University Press.

———. 1978. *On human nature*. Cambridge, Mass.: Harvard University Press.

Wilson, P. J. 1967. Tsimihety Kinship and Descent. *Africa* 37 (2): 133–54.

Wisdom, C. 1940. *The Chorti Indians of Guatemala*. Chicago: University of Chicago Press.

Worringer, W. 1959. *Abstraktion und Einfühlung*. Munich: R. Piper.

Yi Pangja. 1973. *The world is one. Princess Yi Pangja's autobiography*. Seoul and Los Angeles: Taewon Publishing.

Zelinsky, W. 1970. Cultural Variations in Personal Name Patterns in the Eastern United States. *Annals of the Association of American Geographers* 60 (4 [December 1970]).

Zonabend, F. 1980. *La mémoire longue*. Paris: Presses Universitaires de France.

Acknowledgments

Those of the following chapters that first appeared elsewhere are used here by permission.

Chapter 1. "Race and Culture." *Revue internationale des Sciences sociales* 23(4): 647–66. Copyright UNESCO, 1971.

Chapter 2. "The Anthropologist and the Human Condition." Originally published as "The Ethnologist and the Human Condition." *Revue des travaux de l'Académie des Sciences morales et politiques* 132 (4th series, 1979 [2nd semester]:595–614. Reprinted here with some changes.

Chapter 3. "The Family." Revised from *Man, Culture and Society*, edited by Harry L. Shapiro. Copyright © 1956 by Oxford University Press, Inc. Reprinted by permission.

Chapter 4. "An Australian 'Atom of Kinship.'" Translated by the author from the English-language original, written for T. G. H. Strehlow shortly before the latter's death. Unpublished.

Chapter 5. "Cross-Readings." This chapter takes up and develops the material contained in two articles: "Chanson madécasse," in *Orients* (pp. 195–203), Paris-Toulouse: Southeast Asia–1982; and "L'Adieu à la cousine croisée," in *Les Fantaisies du Voyageur, XXXIII variations Schaeffner* (pp. 36–41). Paris: Société Française de Musicologie, 1982.

Chapter 6. "On Marriage between Close Kin." *Mélanges offerts à Louis Dumont.* Paris: Editions de l'Ecole des hautes études en sciences sociales, 1983.

Chapter 7. "Structuralism and Ecology." Translated into French by the author from the English-language original. A previous version of this material appeared in the *Barnard College Alumnae Magazine.* Reprinted with permission.

Chapter 8. "Structuralism and Empiricism." *L'Homme, revue française d'anthropologie* 16 (2–3 [April–September 1976]):23–38.

Chapter 9. "The Lessons of Linguistics." Preface to Roman Jakobson, *Six Leçons sur le son et le sens* (pp. 7–18). Paris: Les Éditions de Minuit, 1976. Previously published in the United States in another English translation.

Chapter 10. "Religion, Language, and History." *Méthodologie de l'Histoire et des Sciences humaines. Mélanges en l'honneur de Fernand Braudel* (II:325–33). 2 vols. Toulouse, privately printed, 1973.

Chapter 11. "From Mythical Possibility to Social Existence." *Le Débat*, no. 19 (February 1982):96–117.

Chapter 12. "Cosmopolitanism amd Schizophrenia." *L'Autre et l'ailleurs. Hommage à Roger Bastide, présenté par Jean Poirier et François Raveau* (pp. 469–74). Paris: Berger-Levrault, 1976.

Chapter 13. "Myth and Forgetfulness." *Langue, discours, société. Pour Emile Benveniste* (pp. 294–300). Paris: Editions du Seuil, 1975.

Chapter 14. "Pythagoras in America." *Fantasy and Symbol. Studies in Anthropological Interpretation*, edited by R. H. Hook (Essays in Honour of George Devereux), pp. 33–41. London, New York, and San Francisco: Academic Press, 1979. This version was modified and developed from the French original.

Acknowledgments

Chapter 15. "An Anatomical Foreshadowing of Twinship." *Systèmes de Signes. Textes réunis en hommage à Germaine Dieterlen* (pp. 369–76). Paris: Hermann, 1978. Republished with several changes and additions.

Chapter 16. "A Small Mythico-Literary Puzzle." *Le Temps de la réflexion* 1 (1980):133–41.

Chapter 17. "From Chrétien de Troyes to Richard Wagner." *Parsifal, Programmhefte der Bayreuther Festspiele* (pp. 1–9, 60–67). 1975. Republished with additions.

Chapter 18. "A Note on the Tetralogy." Originally part of the previous chapter.

Chapter 19. "A Meditative Painter." Written for a collection of essays on Max Ernst which has not yet been published.

Chapter 20. "To a Young Painter." Preface to *Anita Albus. Aquarelle 1970 bis 1980. Katalog zur Ausstellung in der Stuck-Villa München* (pp. 6–28). Frankfurt am Main: Insel Verlag, 1980.

Chapter 21. "New York in 1941." *Paris–New York* (pp. 79–83), Centre National d'Art et de Culture Georges-Pompidou Musée National d'Art Moderne, 1 June–19 September 1977.

Chapter 22. "A Belated Word about the Creative Child." *La Nouvelle Revue des Deux Mondes*, January 1975, pp. 10–19.

Chapter 23. "Reflections on Liberty." *La Nouvelle Revue des Deux Mondes*, November 1976, pp. 332–39.

Index

Index

Benedict, Ruth, 182
Benin, incest prohibition rules among, 90
Bentinck Inlet, 135
Benveniste, Emile, 142, 186
Bergson, Henri, 269
Berlin, Brent, 117
bilateral society, 78
biology, unlinear evolution and, 9–10
Bliocadran, 224
Boas, Franz, 26, 89, 102, 122, 129–35, 141, 162, 164–65, 184
Bonald, Louis de, 26
Boron, Robert de, *see* Robert de Boron
Boróro: bachelor among, 46; conjugal family among, 41; division of labor among, 52
Bosch, Hiëronymus, 253
Bott, E., 94
Braque, Georges, 250
Brehm, Alfred Edmund, 126
Breton, André, 261
British empiricism, 26; positivism and, 26
Buganda, 90–91
Buna, Timor, incest prohibition rules among, 89
burial of the dead, as cultural universal, 34–35
Burke, Edmund, 26
Bushmen, South Africa, family among, 40

Calder, Alexander, 266
Cameroon, 91
Canada, environmental protection in, 282
Caribbean, name giving in the, 156
Carroll, Michael P., 155n, 207–8
Catégories matrimoniales et relations de proximité dans la Chine ancienne (Granet), 139
cerebral activities, structural analysis and, 119–20
Cézanne, Paul, 249
Chagga, conjugal family among, 41
Chamfort, Nicolas de, 34
Chilcotin Indians, 106
Chilcotin myth, 128, 132–35; dentalia shells in, 106–10; mountain-goat horns in, 106–7
children, education of creative, 268–78

China, 73, 280; ancient, 73
Chinook Indians, 179, 182, 184
Chinook jargon, as lingua franca, 184
Chinook myth, 180–85; schizophrenia and, 181–85; syncretism in, 184
Chrétien de Troyes, 221–27, 228–34
Christianity: monogamous family and, 40; sociobiology and, 31
chthonian world, 165, 173
Chukchee, marriage among, 50
civilization, culture and, 26
clam "beard," 126–27
clams, *see* horse clams
clam siphons, 123, 125, 128, 132, 134; as euphemism for "penis," 135–36
cockles, 125n
Coeur d'Alene myth, dentalia shells in, 109
cognates, transformation of, 90
cognation, 94
Colchicum autumnale, 211–13
Colchiques, Les (Apollinaire), structural analysis of, 210–18
colors, phonemes and, 117–18
communication forms, in Tsimshian myth, 170
comparative mythology, schizophrenia and, 178
conjugal family, 44, 49–50; among the Boróro, 41; among the Chagga, 41; in the Emerillon tribe, 49; among the Masai, 41; among the Muria, 41
consonantal system, of French language, 141
constraint: freedom and, 243–88; of school, 273
Coorte, Adriaen, 253
copper, 129–30
Coquet, Jean-Claude, 211, 215, 217
Corbin, Henry, 245
corn and beans: in Guatemalan myth, 195; in Iroquois myth, 195; in Mexican myth, 195
cosmopolitanism, schizophrenia and, 177–85
cousin marriage: in medieval Japan, 73–76; in rural France, 77; *see also* cross-cousin marriage
couvade, 48; among the Nambikwara, 51
creative child, education and, 268–78
creative work, 274
cross-cousin marriage, 56–57; in Fiji Islands, 76–78; in Tsimshian myth, 162

Index

Index

Index

Index

Mabuchi, T., 160
McConnel, U. H., 64–66
McCullough, W. H., 78, 84–85
McKnight, David, 64–65, 67–71
Macnair, Peter L., 165*n*
Madagascar, 80–84
Mae Enga, New Guinea, 90
Magnasco, Alessandro, 265
Maine, Henry Sumner, 286
Malinowski, Bronislaw, 26, 28
Malzac, Father, 80, 84–85
Mambila, Cameroon, 92
mammals, sensory perception in, 116
Manet, Edouard, 251
Manga, New Guinea, 90
marital nomenclature: among the Banyoro, 91; among the Tullishi, 92
marriage, 44–48; as bond between groups, 47–48; between cross-cousins, 56–57; as cultural universal, 34–35; descent rule in, 57–58; exogamous groups and, 58–59; filiation in, 93–94; group, 39, 42; hypergamic, 75; hypogamic, 75; in medieval Japan, 75; monogamous, 44–45; polygamous and monogamous, 45; in primitive societies, 55–58; public authority and, 47
marriage rules: in Africa, 50; among the Andigari, 67; among the Arabana, 65–67; among the Chukchee, 50; for close kin, 88–97, *see also* incest prohibition; among the Gunwinggu, 67; in a hypergamic society, 161; among the Kokata, 67; among the Lovedu, 92; among the Mambila, 92; among the Mohave, 50; phoneme and, 142; in Polynesia, 51; in South America, 51; among the Ungarinyin, 67; among the Wikmunkan, 64–67
Martin, John, 246
Marx, Karl, 250
Marxism, *see* neo-Marxism
Masai, conjugal family among, 41
Masson, André, 266
matrilineal orientation, sibling taboo and, 158; *see also* patrilineal ideology
Maupoil, B., 208
Mauss, Marcel, 34, 179
meaning, sound and, 141–42

medieval Japan, 73, 84–85, 96–97; cousin marriage in, 73; marriage in, 75
Merina dynasty, Madagascar, 81–83, 84–86
Merleau-Ponty, Maurice, 245
meteorological disorders, twins and, 202
Mexican myth, corn and beans in, 195
Michelant, H. V., 229
Mistler, Jean, 229
misunderstanding: forgetfulness and, 186; indiscretion and, 186
Miwuyt, northwestern Australia, 60
Mohave Indians, 50
moieties, exogamic on Vanua Levu Island, 158
Monet, Claude, 250
monogamous family, *see* family
Montesquieu, 280
Montherlant, Henri de, 269
mora, 141
Moreau, Gustave, 246
mountain-goat horns, 128, 134–35; in Chilcotin myth, 106–8, 110; in Bella Bella myth, 107–8
Mundugomor, atom of kinship in, 70
Muria: conjugal family among, 41; legal sexuality among, 51
Murngin, northwestern Australia, 60
music: myth and Western, 235–39; myth compared to, 173
myth: analysis of, 144; environment and, 115; language and, 145; compared to music, 173; social organization and, 157–74; structural analysis of, 122–37; Western music and, 235–39; *see also* North American myth
"mythemes," phoneme and, 144–45
mythology, ritual and, 191
myth transformation, 108; in Salish myth, 114

Naked Man, The (Lévi-Strauss), 180, 183, 243
Nambikwara Indians, 102; *couvade* among, 51; family among, 40
name giving: in the Caribbean, 156; among

307

Index

Index

Index

Twana, North America: name prohibitions among, 151; name system of, 151, 153
twin birth, feet-first birth and, 207
twins: in African myth, 208–9; harelipped people and, 202, 205–6, 208; meteorological disorders and, 202; in myth, 201–9; origin of, 204–5
twin sons: North American myth of, 203–4; South American myth of, 202–3

Ulrich von Zatzikoven, 224
underdeveloped countries, idea of freedom in, 280
underworld, *see* chthonian world
Ungarinyin, marriage rules among, 67
Unité de l'homme, L' (Morin and Piatelli-Palmarini), 272
universals, in culture, 34–35; *see also* cultural universal
Unkel, Curt, 7
Utamaro, 252–53

Vailati, Maria, 213n
Van Eyck, Jan, 253
Vanua Levu Island, 158
Van Wouden, F. A. E., 139
vasu, 82
Vazimba, Madagascar, 81–82
Venda, incest prohibition rules among, 90
Vernant, J.-P., 97, 186
Vico, G., 34–35
Vienna school, in anthropology, 40

Vignaux, Paul, 214n
Vinogradoff, Paul, 94
vision, mechanisms of, 116
visual perception, intellectual activity and, 172–73

Wagner, Cosima, 225
Wagner, Richard, 219–39, 273
Walbiri, atom of kinship in, 71
wedding banquet, in medieval Japan, 96
Weissman, H., 229
Whitney, W. D., 148
wife lending, among the Wunambal, 42
Wikmunkan, marriage rules among, 64–67
Wilson, Edward O., 29–31
Wirt von Gravenberg, 225
Witoto, northwestern Amazon, 151–52
Wolfram von Eschenbach, 224–34
Worringer, W., 256
Wunambal, wife lending among, 42

Yehon Mushi erabi (Sekiyen), 252–53
Yoruba, 90; incest prohibition rules among, 89
Yurok, name giving among, 156

Zatzikoven, *see* Ulrich von Zatzikoven
Zonabend, F., 77
Zuñi, division of labor among, 52